6/21

D0759063

Trust, Computing, and Society

The Internet has altered how people engage with each other in myriad ways, including offering opportunities for people to act distrustfully. This fascinating set of essays explores the question of trust in computing from technical, socio-philosophical, and design perspectives. Why has the identity of the human user been taken for granted in the design of the Internet? What difficulties ensue when it is understood that security systems can never be perfect? What role does trust have in society in general? How is trust to be understood when trying to describe activities as part of a user-requirement program? What questions of trust arise in a time when data analytics are meant to offer new insights into user behavior and when users are confronted with different sorts of digital entities? These questions and their answers are of paramount interest to computer scientists, sociologists, philosophers, and designers who confront the problem of trust.

RICHARD H.R. HARPER is Principal Researcher at Microsoft Research in Cambridge and co-manages the Socio-Digital Systems Group. His tenth book, *Texture: Human Expression in the Age of Communications Overload*, was named Book of the Year (2011) by the Association of Internet Researchers. His earlier books include the IEEE award-winning *The Myth of the Paperless Office*, co-authored with Abi Sellen, and *Inside the IMF: An Ethnography of Documents, Technology and Organisational Action*.

Trust, Computing, and Society

Edited by

RICHARD H.R. HARPER

Microsoft Research Cambridge

CAMBRIDGE
UNIVERSITY PRESS

CAMBRIDGE
UNIVERSITY PRESS

32 Avenue of the Americas, New York, NY 10013-2473, USA

Cambridge University Press is part of the University of Cambridge.

It furthers the University's mission by disseminating knowledge in the pursuit of
education, learning, and research at the highest international levels of excellence.

www.cambridge.org
Information on this title: www.cambridge.org/9781107038479

First published 2014

Printed in the United States of America

A catalog record for this publication is available from the British Library.

Library of Congress Cataloging in Publication data
Trust, computing, and society / Richard H.R. Harper.
pages cm
Includes bibliographical references and index.
ISBN 978-1-107-03847-9 (hardback)
1. Computers – Social aspects. 2. Internet – Social aspects. 3. Trust. 4. Computer
security. 5. Computer networks – Security measures. 6. Computer networks –
Reliability. 7. Information technology – Social aspects. I. Harper, Richard H.R.,
1960–, editor of compilation.
QA76.9.C66T78 2014
005.8–dc23 2013036604

ISBN 978-1-107-03847-9 Hardback

Contents

Author Biographies

Bob Anderson taught in the School of Sociology at Manchester Polytechnic (now Manchester Metropolitan University) from 1974 to 1988 after which he joined Xerox to help set up the social science research group at its newly formed laboratory in Cambridge (Europarc). He became Director of Europarc in 1990, and in 1999 he moved to Sheffield Hallam University as Pro Vice Chancellor for Research and then CEO of University Campus Suffolk. Since then, Bob has held an advisory role at the Horizon Digital Economy Research Project at the University of Nottingham.

Richard Banks is principal interaction designer for Microsoft Research in Cambridge, where he leads a design team that is part of the Computer-Mediated Living group. Richard holds more than twenty patents for design work at Microsoft, is a Fellow of the Royal Society of Arts in the UK and an Honorary Professor of Design at Dundee University, and recently published *The Future of Looking Back*, a book examining issues of digital legacy.

David Clark is a Senior Research Scientist at the MIT Computer Science and Artificial Intelligence Laboratory, where he has worked since receiving his PhD there in 1973. His current research looks at redefining the architectural underpinnings of the Internet and the relation of technology and architecture to economic, societal, and policy considerations. He is past chairman of the Computer Science and Telecommunications Board of the National Academies, a member of the National Academy of Engineering and the American Academy of Arts and Sciences, and co-director of the MIT Communications Futures Program, a project for industry collaboration and coordination along the communications value chain.

Dr. George Danezis recently joined the Computer Science department at University College London. Previously, he was a researcher at Microsoft Research Cambridge, where he worked on anonymous communications, privacy-enhancing technologies (PET), and traffic analysis. He has been a visiting Fellow at KU Leuven (Belgium) and a research associate at the University of Cambridge, where he also completed his doctoral dissertation in 2004. He sits on the PET Symposium board and regularly serves on program committees of leading conferences in the field of privacy and security.

Charles Ess (PhD, Pennsylvania State University, USA) is Associate Professor in Media Studies, Department of Media and Communication, University of Oslo, and emeritus Professor of Philosophy and Religion, Drury University (Springfield, Missouri, USA). He has held several guest professorships in Europe and Scandinavia, including Professor II in the Applied Ethics Programme, University of Trondheim (2005–2008), and, most recently, Professor MSO (med særlige opgaver), Media Studies, Aarhus University, Denmark (2009–2012). His books include *Digital Media Ethics*; *Trust and Virtual Worlds: Contemporary Perspectives* (with May Thorseth); *The Handbook of Internet Studies* (with Mia Consalvo); and *Digital Religion, Social Media and Culture: Perspectives, Practices and Futures* (with Pauline Cheong, Peter Fischer-Nielsen, and Stefan Gelfgren).

Richard Harper is Principal Researcher at Microsoft Research in Cambridge and co-manages the Socio-Digital Systems group. His tenth book, *Texture: Human Expression in the Age of Communications Overload* was named the Association of Internet Researchers' Book of the Year (2011). Among his earlier books was the IEEE award-winning *The Myth of the Paperless Office*, co-authored with Abi Sellen, and I*nside the IMF: An Ethnography of Documents, Technology and Organisational Action*.

Thomas Karagiannis has been a researcher in the Systems and Networking group at Microsoft Research Cambridge, looking mainly at ways to improve the performance and usability of various types of computer networks. He received the ACM SIGCOMM 2011 Honorable Mention Paper Award along with Christo Wilson, Hitesh Ballani, and Ant Rowstron. Prior to joining Microsoft Research, Thomas was with Intel Research Cambridge and the Cooperative Association for Internet Data Analysis (CAIDA), where he introduced novel methodologies for measuring and analyzing Internet traffic with a special focus on peer-to-peer file-sharing applications.

Iacovos Kirlappos is a PhD student in the Security Science Doctoral Research Training Centre and the Department of Computer Science at University College London. His research interests include employee education in organizations, information security policy effectiveness and communication, human behavior in security, and information security management.

Olli Lagerspetz is Senior Lecturer of Philosophy at Åbo Akademi University, Åbo, Finland. His work has focused mainly on moral philosophy, Wittgenstein, and the philosophy of the mind. Lagerspetz is the author of *Trust: The Tacit Demand* and a Swedish book on the concepts of dirt and cleanliness (Smuts: En bok om världen, vårt hem).

William Odom is a PhD candidate in the Human-Computer Interaction Institute at Carnegie Mellon University. With a background spanning design, informatics, and anthropology, William is interested in designing innovative ways for people to engage with their digital possessions in their everyday lives. He was previously a Fulbright Scholar in Australia, and his work has won best paper awards at the Computer-Human Interaction (CHI), Designing Interactive Systems (DIS), and Ubiquitous Computing (Ubicomp) conferences.

M. Angela Sasse is the Professor of Human-Centered Technology in the Department of Computer Science at University College London. A usability researcher by training, Angela started researching human behavior in human-centered security, privacy, identity, and trust in the 1990s, and she now heads the Research Institute for Cyber Security and Information Security Research Group at UCL. She is a member of the British Computer Society and the British Psychological Society.

Wes Sharrock is Professor of Sociology in what is now the Sociology Discipline Area at Manchester University, where he joined the staff in 1966. Over his career, Wes has led the development of ethnomethodology in the UK and is a widely acknowledged interpreter of Wittgenstein's philosophy. His many books include *Brain, Mind and Human Behaviour* (co-authored with J. Coulter); *The Philosophy of Social Research* (with J. Hughes); and *Working for Profit* (with Bob Anderson and John Hughes).

Dr. Thomas W. Simpson is University Lecturer in Philosophy and Public Policy at the Blavatnik School of Government, University of Oxford, and a Senior Research Fellow at Wadham College. He was educated at Cambridge

(BA, MPhil, PhD), where he was also a Research Fellow at Sidney Sussex College. Between earning degrees, he served as an officer with the Royal Marines Commandos. His research is focused on trust, both its theory and practical applications. His work in applied ethics hitherto has been principally on the ethics of information and computing technologies, and of war.

Rod Watson is Professeur de Sociologie in the Department of Sciences Economiques et Sociales at Telecom ParisTech, France. He has published extensively in the sphere of ethnomethodology, conversation analysis, and analytic sociology. His interests include textual analysis, and he published *Analysing Practical and Professional Texts: A Naturalistic Approach* in 2009. He received a sectional Distinguished Publication Award from the American Sociological Association for an earlier article on trust (2009) on which his contribution here draws considerably.

Acknowledgments

All books are completed with forbearance by colleagues and friends. Edited collections are completed with the willing compliance of contributors. In this case, the former, this was true on the part of my colleagues in the Socio-Digital Systems group at Microsoft Cambridge. While this collection was being compiled, my contributions to their activities were diminished. Whether those activities were better because of this is for them to judge. More widely, my role at Microsoft Research Cambridge diminished equally – whether for better or worse is again not for me to say. Because friends and family, meanwhile, seem to treat my distraction as normal, they can hardly be said to show forbearance, but only tolerance. On the subject of compliance, I must thank all the contributors, who, in various ways, had to oblige my cajoling and pestering. A particular achievement has been to get them all to acknowledge the differences in the views of the other contributors, differences that are not so much about evidence as about starting places: "interdisciplinarity" is a modish formula these days, but what has been sought here – and what I chased the contributors for – was not the blurring and merging of their views with half-baked views of other disciplines, but clear, apposite articulations of their own. The result is this book: a collection of dialogues from different points of view.

The motivation for this – quixotic though it might be – derived from explorations outside the usual domain of my research; that is, in the subfield of computer science known as human computer interaction. Current debates across the gamut of social sciences led me to inquire into the current thinking on the nature of ideas-in-action in philosophy because here, I imagined, I would find some root and stock examination of central ideas in many of these debates. PhDs were funded and collaborations with various philosophy departments initiated. One such work led to a workshop titled "Trust and Cloud Computing" at Corpus Christi College in Cambridge. This was wonderfully organized by Tom Simpson. What came out of that event was the discovery that many philosophers are more or less out of touch with the changing landscape of computer-mediated living. This is not to diminish the excellent work of a handful of philosophers who cannot be so accused. One can think of the books and collections of Floridi, for instance, and of works by Charles Ess and his collaborators, too. There are others of course. This book derives in part from an attempt both to focus the attention of other philosophers who have not followed in the wake of these mentioned and to direct attention to how the world actually is as a lived phenomenon – that is, massively connected in and through the Internet and its supporting infrastructures, among other things. As it does this, so it also brings together others, from different disciplines – sociologists, designers, anthropologists, and others – to support and engage in this attempt at learning; to inform not just the all too often laggardly world of philosophy but to foster dialogues across disciplines and across other divides that don't so easily scale onto academic divides. The resulting chapters display, I think, a remarkable diversity as well as a compendium of points of view on trust, computing, and society that cannot be found anywhere else.

On a more logistical level, I would like to thank the Cambridge University Press New York office for encouragement and tolerance in the preparation of the collection – particularly Ada Brunstein and Lauren Cowles and an anonymous but hugely supportive copy editor. Specific acknowledgments are in the footnotes for the chapters.

Dialogues

Trust, Computing, and Society:
Introduction

1

Introduction and Overview

Richard Harper

Preamble

Any glance at the contemporary intellectual landscape would make it clear that trust, society, and computing are often discussed together. And any glance would also make it clear that when this happens, the questions that are produced often seem, at first glance, straightforward. Yet, on closer examination, these questions unravel into a quagmire of concerns. What starts out as, say, a question of whether computers can be relied on to do a particular job often turns into something more than doubts about a division of labor. As Douglas Rushkoff argues in his brief and provocative book, *Program or be Programmed* (2010), when people rely on computers to do some job, it is not like Miss Daisy trusting her chauffeur to take her car to the right destination. But it is not what computers are told to do that is the issue. At issue is what computers tell *us*, the humans, as they get on with whatever task is at hand. And this in turn implies things about who and what we are because of these dialogues we have with computers. I use the word dialogues purposefully here because it is suggestive of how interaction between person and machine somehow alters the sense a person has of themselves and of the machine they are interacting with, and how this in turn alters the relationship the two have – that is, the machine and the "user." According to Rushkoff, it is not possible to know what the purpose of an interaction between a person and a machine might be; it is certainly not as simple as a question of a command and its response. In his metaphor about driving, what come into doubt are rarely questions about whether the computer has correctly heard and identified the destination the human wants – the place to which they have instructed the machine to navigate them. The interaction we have with computers lead us to doubt why a particular destination is chosen. This in turn leads to doubts about whether such choices should be in the hands of the human or the computer. The computer seems to "know" more; why should it not decide? Thus, my use of the term "dialogue." Our interactions with computers are like those we have with people, they alter the sense we have of ourselves. Or, rather, the dialogue alters what we think we are and what we think the other is; in this case not merely a machine that acts on our command, but something greater, something in which we might come to trust.

In *From Gutenberg to Zuckerberg* (2012), John Naughton raises similarly large issues and again illustrates with destinations; but, for Naughton, we need to ask whether we can trust computing (and the Internet in particular) to lead us to dystopia or to heaven. Although the contrast he presents is not entirely without irony, heaven is represented in the duplicitous appeal of Huxley's *Brave New World* (1933), and dystopia is represented in the self-evidently bleak form of Orwell's *Nineteen Eighty Four* (1949). Meanwhile, in his *Filter Bubble* (2011), Eli Pariser complains that we cannot trust the dialogue we have with search engines. Today, in the age of "the Cloud" and massive aggregation systems, search engine providers can hide things from us in ways in which we cannot guess. When we ask search engines something, we cannot know what the answer will be, because search engine technology is now deciding what we need or want and even what is good for us to know. That this is so is at once sinister and capitalistic, Pariser argues: sinister because it disempowers humans, and capitalistic because it places the market above the public good. Search engines take you to what companies want to sell, not to what you want to know. A onetime capitalist himself, William Davidow is likewise agitated, although it is not salesmanship that worries him. We are now "overconnected," he argues in his book *Overconnected: What the Digital Economy Says about Us* (2011); we cannot trust ourselves to reason properly.

The sheer volume and scale of this discourse leads one to doubt whether any single, unified view on trust will arise from it, even if many of the authors in question want to offer one. With his highly readable *Liars and Outliers, Enabling the Trust that Society Needs to Thrive* (2012), Bruce Schneier comes to mind, as he expounds precisely such a hope. Furthermore, in addition to this list of well-known texts in the public domain, there are equally many in the more scholarly worlds of philosophy, social sciences, and, of course, computer science. In philosophy, there are an immense number of books, including Charles Ess and May Thorseth's *Trust and Virtual Worlds* (2011) or the extensive works of Luciano Floridi (e.g., 2010 and forthcoming). There are also many in sociology, including Diego Gambetta's edited collection of 1988 (which includes some philosophers, such as Bernard Williams) and, more substantively, Barbara Mitzal's *Trust in Modern Societies* (1996). Since then, there has been Piotr Sztompka's *Trust: a Sociological Theory* (2003) and Guido Möllering's *Trust: Reason, Routine, Reflexivity* (2006), and others also, too numerous to mention. In economics especially, there has been a flowering of interest through the deployment of new experimental techniques – behavioral economics. Ernst Fehr comes to mind, with his work on the "biology of trust" (2009; see also Joseph Henrich et al.'s *In Search of Homo Economicus*, 2013). There are also a great many papers and books in computer science and human computer interaction (HCI), some of which seek to bind sociological treatments of trust to computer science terms – that is to say, to formulate sociological trust "computationally." Clark Thomborson's *Axiomatic and Behavioural Trust* paper (2010) comes to mind, as does Virgil Gligor and Jeannette Wing's *Towards a Theory of Trust* (2011). Others within the world of computer science have tried the reverse – that is, to make computational tools that are designed essentially on sociological premises, as represented in Karen Clarke et al.'s collection, *Trust in Technology* (2006). Some researchers have been even bolder, seeking to create not just summaries of computer science and sociology, but also a host of other disciplines, such as psychology and philosophy. Piotr Cofta certainly attempts this in *The Trustworthy and Trusted Web* (2011).

So what is one to make of all this? There are, I feel, five points to be discussed. First, these arguments and debates reflect and announce a historical moment, at the center of which is the concern that computer scientists have raised in the past decade or so. As Craig Mundie et al. noted in *Trustworthy Computing* (2002), the move in the late 1990s toward a computer-enabled "ecosystem" was being resisted by a public that was becoming increasingly doubtful of the trust it could invest in that ecology. Mundie and his colleagues sought to encourage a program of activities that would make the engineering of that ecosystem more robust and safe. They urged procedural and regulatory improvements that would guarantee the trust that users would need to place in computer-mediated interaction if the new ecosystem was to flourish. Before we say anything about whether those hopes have materialized, it may be worth noting that Mundie and his colleagues were not concerned with trust that users had in freestanding computers. They were interested in the connections that could be made between or through computers – in the human and business networks, in other words. As it happens, ergonomists and human factors' engineers had, in the years before, examined things such as whether the speed with which a system responded to a user command was critical to inducing or undermining trust by the user in the device itself (it is, by the way). Mundie and his colleagues were, however, interested in matters beyond the keyboard or the intricacies of "input" and "output." Their concerns resonate with the doubts that are raised by the likes of Rushkoff and Naughton. It is not the computer interfaces that matter; what matters is what computers and people do together at large. The dates of Rushkoff and Naughton's books (2010 and 2012, respectively) would suggest that the hopes of Mundie and his colleagues have not yet been met. Nearly a decade after the publication of *Trustworthy Computing*, computer scientists are still arguing that this trust has not yet been delivered. As it happens, the solution sought by those within computer science has evolved with, for example, Gligor and Wing (2011) proposing that a formal theory that can guarantee trust in the general needs to be devised. Gligor and Wing are much more assertive about the role of computational theory in solving general doubts about trust than Mundie and his colleagues were. Be that as it may, computer scientists still think that there are big questions to do with trust, computing, and society.

It is not only computer scientists who think this; it also is not a response to their urgings that the interest of the social sciences has been piqued. Social science turned toward the topic of trust somewhat before the likes of Mundie and his colleagues. At the cusp of the twentieth century, the great French sociologist Emile Durkheim investigated the breaking down of trusted relations in books such as *On Suicide* (1897) and the *Division of Labour* (first translated in 1933); a century later, on the cusp of the twenty-first century, Barbara Mitzal argued in *Trust and Modern Societies* (1996) that the topic had come to be neglected and a renewed focus was necessary. Without such attention, the malaise about which Durkheim worried – or a form similar to it – might resurface. Concurrent with Mitzal, many economists were seeking ways of explaining apparently irrational behavior, with the question of why people trust in some situations and not in others being especially perplexing to them. This question was certainly not explicable from the utility maximization models that economists had preferred to use up to that time. The emergence of so-called institutional and behavioral economics reflected attempts to account for these ineffables. In this view, the constraints on human reasoning are sourced in such things as an aversion to rejection. This can be a determinant of choices about who and what to trust. This was the rub of Fehr's work (for example, see Fehr, 2009; see also de Quervain et al., 2004).

In philosophy, there was a similar turn toward trust and a claim that the concept had been neglected for too long. In the late 1980s, Annette Baier produced a number of influential papers arguing just that. These papers eventually appeared in her commonly cited book *Moral Prejudices* (1994) in which she suggested that trust has an affective dimension, insofar as the trusting of one person in another turns around the fact that the trusting person would, in their trust, be seeking some kind of action on the part of the trusted person. Their trust would be seeking to affect them. Onora O'Neill developed this theme in her "Reith Lectures" of 2002. Since then, a whole raft of philosophical work has emerged: the work of Ess and Thorseth (mentioned earlier) comes to mind. The same too has occurred in political science in the work of, for example,

Russell Hardin, (*Trust and Trustworthiness*, 2002) and more recently, Helen Nissenbaum (*Privacy in Context*, 2010).

One could go on. The scale of the interest in trust across the social sciences has been considerable in the past fifteen years or so, just as it has been within the world of computer science. However, no end would be served by trying to list and taxonomize all these efforts at this point in our concerns. But what is important to note, and this is the second of my five points, is that this combination of interests not only asserts the connection between computing, trust, and society, but it can result in a blurring of the differences in these concerns. When we try to navigate to issues of trust, it is often not clear what we are looking for. Are we looking for trust in some general sense or in some particular way, related specifically to computers? Or is it trust in some bigger sense, in relation to the regulatory frameworks in which we use computers? Or, for a third possibility, is the concern related to some very particular disciplinary focus? Computer scientists have a strong interest in cryptography, for example, which is not the same as the philosopher's interest in conceptual clarity, even if both concerns seek to deliver trust – trust in a system in the first case, trust in understanding in the second. It is often quite difficult, however, to identify issues when a confluence of disciplinary interests conflates topics and agendas. Just as it might be true to say that issues of trust, computing, and society are multidimensional, it is also true to say that the dimensions in question are all too easily confused when the various perspectives of different disciplines are thrown in.

This leads to the third point. If it is the case that various disciplines turned to issues of trust at a similar time, it needs to be recognized also that the differences have led to diverse treatments. Thus, although various disciplines might announce a concern with trust, one must not be tempted to think that their approaches, considerations, and insights will all fit together. They might fit together in some respects, but care is required; often they do not. Additionally, part of the value that might be found here has to do with these very differences, which might be lost through integration and merging. Differences can produce a wealth of reasoning – greater coinage for the mind, if you like. Melting that coinage does not necessarily increase the volume or the value. It can, in fact, result in less. It can debase the coinage. The situation is not helped by the rhetoric of many of the disciplines involved, a rhetoric that can resonate with rather gross claims – such as the science in question "uncovering the truth" and "getting to the reality." There can be no doubt that disciplines (often) get to views that accord with these claims, but this needs to be understood within the frame of the inquiries in question. One needs to be sensitive to the significance of perspective, methods, and topics between disciplines. One needs to be open to the possibility that when, say, sociologists look at trust, the phenomenon of interest to them may not easily fit into the concerns of, let us say, an economist. It is similar with the earlier example about philosophy and computer science, illustrated with their respective concerns for cryptography and conceptual analysis. These concerns are of two very different kinds, yet both disciplines are seeking assurances of one kind or another. The important point is that, although both consider trust, they do not do so in equivalent ways.

This leads to my fourth point, which questions whether trust is something that can be treated with the "scientific method" as is implied in some of the debates and misunderstandings alluded to previously. Trust is, after all, an idea – a state of mind, if you like – and not a physical phenomenon. It is hardly surprising then – despite all the debates, the papers, and the calls for action – that trust has a vitality in everyday life that makes the concept robust; how the concept is used in the traffic of living remains pretty much how one would expect it to. People don't find their understanding of trust altering in light of these debates; only the applicability of the concept shifts. What was once trusted may now not be, for example. How to use the concept remains the same regardless; its use is common sense, if you like, a skill constitutive of competent language use. As Peter Winch noted long ago in his *The Idea of a Social Science* (1958), concepts like trust are best thought of as philosophic in nature. Inquiries into their nature are akin to studies into linguistic practice and use; the purpose of such inquiries is to offer perspicuity and clarity when that is required – as it is today in regard to trust, when technology and trust are paired in ways that can be confusing as well as enlightening. Here I must pay heed to my own intellectual roots, not so much in Winch as in the philosophical investigations of Ludwig Wittgenstein and Gilbert Ryle (in such works as the *Philosophical Investigations* (1953) and *The Concept of Mind* (1949)).

It is also hardly surprising that when one looks at the immense literature on trust, computing, and society, one sees a raft of inquiries that rely on the concept so as to ask focused questions. It does not matter that in some instances these questions are large and worrying, as we saw with Pariser and Naughton. These authors are not asking what trust means in any perplexingly radical ways. They do not need to suggest redefinitions of how trust is to be understood or used. All they are trying to say is that questions of trust apply more than we might think in our everyday interactions with computers. Pariser and Naughton are making judgments about scale, if you like, about how much trust there is (or isn't), or where trust is absent when one would expect it to be present. They are not seeking to alter how the concept of trust is to be used, only where and when; theirs is a concern with empirical matters, not conceptual. In these and other cases, one does not find that the concept of trust is altered. Its meaning remains taken for granted. As Wittgenstein and Ryle showed so clearly, and, in their wake, as Peter Winch also, any attempt to explore concepts used in everyday life must depend in the first place on vernacular competence with those concepts. Therefore, what the various inquiries into the topic of trust achieve has not been, in my mind, redefinitions of trust; instead, the outputs of these inquiries relate to questions of particular interest given the meaning of trust as it is already known to be. When I read claims by various authors that they are offering definitions of trust, I am often skeptical; I am suspicious that they hide the fact that they are using the term in everyday ways even as they claim to do otherwise. One might allow this dissembling if it leads to a useful nuance and focus for some inquiry, but one ought to balk at such claims, especially if these arguments end with directives about how the concept "ought to be used." This distracts from the value that can be found in their studies, their conceptual vanities notwithstanding.

Key to judging any and all inquiries on the topic of trust, computing, and society is, it seems to me, to evaluate findings in terms of the proper use of perspectival and methodological constraint. These constraints should not confound sensible use of the concept. An analogy might be helpful here. It seems to me that, in its use, the concept of trust has similarities with the concept of truth. When one uses the concept of truth, one does not ask what the concept means (one does not ask "what is truth?"), for if one asked that, one would not be able to deploy the concept. Instead, one asks what is true in some particular context. One asks what is true "here" or "here." This allows us to look at evidence, at what is relevant, and at what is a reasonable judgment in some situation. And I think the same holds for trust. Trust is a concept that allows us to make judgments, to call attention to issues, and to account for choices of various kinds. But this use only succeeds if it starts with (or from) competent understanding of how to use the concept in the normal traffic of living.

My fifth point follows directly from the fourth. In one important respect, the concept of trust is not like the concept of truth, because truth suggests an orientation of neutrality – a calmness, if you like. But a property of the way the concept of trust gets used is to cause agitation. Leaving aside what might be addressed when the term is used – questions of scale and connection mentioned earlier, for example – the use of the term can also cause (and lead to) worry. In many cases, of course, such worry is needed and indeed rightly sought. Part of Nissenbaum's book *Privacy in Context* (mentioned previously) is utilized precisely to make people more concerned than they are. She uses the term "trust" as a method to negate complacency. In this respect, the concept can be a lightning rod, which can come at a price. It is not always sensible to use the term "trust" in this way. Often, this use results in trust pushing other ways of thinking about an issue out of the mind; it can somehow come to dominate explanation. In my view, use of the term "trust" can sometimes undermine more sensitive and careful deliberations in which other concepts are more applicable.

Some of this edging out of other concepts is quite subtle. When one looks at the literature of trust, one becomes very aware of how little attention is given to something that would be ironically central to these concerns: that is to say, what happens when trust does occur. The literature is really about *mistrust*. The use of the term "trust" does not lead to examinations of trust, then; on the contrary, much greater attention is given to those situations when trust is *absent*. Richard Holton's (1994) response to Baier's (1994) analysis of the affective in trust comes to mind; neither Holton's nor Baier's study is really interested in normal affairs, in activities in which trust is taken for granted. Their focuses are instead on those situations in which trust is *not* present; they seek to reconstruct what normal affairs might be in that light. This seems a peculiar way of doing business, the kudos Holton's work currently receives notwithstanding.

In other words, the concept of trust can both point to – lead the eye to see – one set of issues and make other issues disappear from view. Given what I have already said about the conflation of disciplinary perspectives, this is, I think, a real concern. One needs to be wary when the term "trust" is used: wary of what we are not seeing as much as what we are being led to see.

Overview of the Book

It is in light of these considerations that the following collection has been brought together. The arguments have been selected to provide a balanced set of perspectives. Each articulates a different purpose, or proposes a different emphasis given its disciplinary starting point. The overall goal of the collection is to provide the reader with a sense of – and perhaps a sensibility for – the overall topic that these views represent: the topography of arguments about and issues related to the general question of trust, computing, and society. Part of this sense will consist of the ability to historicize the arguments in question, to see where they come from, what they are trying to do, and where they are trying to go. And part of gaining this sensibility has to do with appreciating the difference between analytical and theoretical discussions about trust and society and arguments and considerations that are primarily pragmatic, as when design and engineering are at hand. As will be seen, when principal turns into practical choices, it does not mean that principal disappears or that the theoretically deduced concerns are lost. They remain but often in different forms, often with more nuances. Sometimes questions of trust lead to an adjustment of what is seen as topical (for example, much of the debate about trust in computer science is about trust between persons when mediated or enabled by computers as when people contact each other via the Internet), but design highlights the fact that users have to trust in themselves before they can act with others. The problem of trust and design are more subtle when this is seen, when this principle becomes clear through practical considerations – in this case, design considerations.

Be that as it may, the overall hope of this edited collection is to offer the reader a sense of the kinds of dialogues that can be made across and between varying disciplinary points of view, such that readers will be better able to determine when to deploy disciplinary perspectives for their own ends or when they might want to move beyond these perspectives toward their own post-disciplinary points of view. It is not possible to know where this move from the particular to the general might occur; nor is it certain beforehand where disciplinary perspectives are key to leveraging open problems and their solutions. I am convinced, however, that providing readers with a sensibility for the approaches at hand will put them in good stead for sorting out when to make these choices and how to adroitly address the topic of trust, computing, and society.

More particularly, the book consists of thirteen chapters divided into three sections. After this introductory essay, the first section, "The Topography of Trust and Computing," defines the empirical context of the debates, explaining the features of computing that are causing concern. It also provides an intellectual history that shows how there has been a merging of social and philosophical concerns about trust that seem driven by a general social malaise, a doubt about modernity, with concerns about trust that are closely associated with the technology of the Internet (and later, the Cloud). Having set the scene, the second section, "Conceptual Points of View," describes both the evolution of thinking about trust and the different points of view enabled by various treatments of the topic over the past ten or twenty years. It is important to note that these treatments are not just from the starting point of the Internet, even though the landscape of the Internet – or that which is enabled by the Internet – is a world in which the Internet is central. Irrespective of their starting points, however, these various treatments have consequences for how we think about the topic of computers and trust. At times, these treatments seem to be at a very high level, although careful examination will show how they pertain. If these and prior chapters provide a sense of the different views one can have on the idea of trust – on trust as a sort of conceptual tool and as a demonstrable feature of all social action – then the third section, "Trust in Design," engages with trust as a matter of practical engagement with the socio-digital material facticities of the world. To say that use of the Internet entails the deployment of trust in various forms elides the fact that this engagement is through experienced entities: icons, devices, and, of course, the symbolic universes these represent. The chapters here look at how to design interfaces to convey the fact that some systems stand *between* persons and processes in ways that (somehow) require the demonstration of trustability – both in the technology and the parties using it. At the same time, designing interfaces is not simply a matter of labels that show trust; when designers approach the "problem space" of the Cloud, for example, they have to consider the ontological "sense" that their designs provide. Do users come to trust in their relations to their digital "stuff"? Does that trust resonate with how those people get on with their lives, lives that are suffused with digital materials but that are, also, essentially about material properties that stand as part and parcel of their human endeavors? These are anthropological concerns, as much as they are technological and design questions; they are as much cognitive as they social.

The book is commenced and concluded with chapters that try to frame these sections. The chapter by David Clark, co-inventor of TCP-IP, the key communication protocol of the Web, sets up the call from computer science that issues of trust are not simply computational; they have to do with a range of practices in society that, in various ways, turn on trust. Because more and more of society's actions are mediated by computers, by the Internet, and more recently by the Cloud, Clark makes it clear that computer engineers like himself cannot be held accountable for delivering that trust; other disciplines need to be brought to account, too. Society at large (if one can put it that way) needs to take on the burden of thinking about these issues; this is not merely an academic or scientific concern. The final chapter, written by the editor, looks at this and the many other issues surveyed in the book and offers a comprehensive summary. In addition, the final chapter seeks to combine the academic nature of some of the concerns presented in the book – many being methodological and conceptual rather than pragmatic and grounded – with the concerns that are often raised outside of academe – ones to do with whether one can trust the brands that are creating verticals in the commercial space of consumption, for example, or whether new regulatory frameworks need to be developed when computing powers are let loose on the data circulating around the Web. 'Big Data' is a term regularly used by computer scientists to label the large volumes of data held on cloud farms, the outcomes of analysis of that data, and some kind of mysterious value that derives from that analysis. Big Data is then something of a catch-all phrase, labeling hopes as much as anything real. Even the most ardent advocates like Viktor Mayer-Schönberger and Kenneth Cukier (2013) admit there is some exaggeration in claims made about Big Data – although they insist that a revolution will be created by it. Given this, it seems a tall order to expect legislators to come up with tractable ways of taming infelicitous and unethical use of that data if what it is and what it generates is unclear. Key to how Big Data can be made to be tractable are questions of how to link data trails to plausible human actions. How cookie trails provide manifest data residues of human action on the Web provide a case in point. Although these trails remain largely hidden from view at the current time, current research in HCI is looking at how to make them visible to users in ways that will allow those users – and their representatives in the form of government legislators – to more effectively grasp what those trails say about user behavior. Thus, the concluding chapter returns us to the beginning, to the question of what dialogues are possible when the landscape of human affairs is mediated by and rendered through computing.

Part One

The Topography of Trust
and Computing

2

The Role of Trust in Cyberspace

David Clark

Introduction

One view of cyberspace is that it is made up of technology: personal computers, the routers that support the Internet, huge data centers, and the like. Another view is that cyberspace is made up of people: people who interact over the Internet; people who run the Internet and the data centers; people who regulate, invest, set standards, and do all the other actions that make up the experience of cyberspace. The latter view is probably the more relevant; technology is only the foundation.

If cyberspace were only technology, we might properly ignore issues of *trust*. We might ask whether we have *confidence* that the technology will function as intended, and our everyday experience tells us when that confidence might be misplaced. But to the extent that cyberspace is made up of people, we should ask whether issues of trust are important in the proper functioning of cyberspace. I argue that trust is central in many ways.

Trust, as I use the term, is a relationship between trustor and trustee in which the trustor is willing to assume that the trustee will act in the best interest of the trustor. This does not mean that the trustor can predict exactly what the behavior of the trustee will be, but that the trustee will use judgment and intelligence to restrict the range of actions undertaken. One who is not trustworthy may be malicious or simply inattentive, incompetent, or in an unsuited role: trust is usually accepted with respect to a particular role. We, as humans, use a mix of means to assess how trustworthy a party is: past experience, explicit information, the nature of the relationship ("blood is thicker than water," etc.), the role in which the party is to be trusted, and so on. Among humans, trust is a matter of judgment and emotional reaction for all the parties. But what does this have to do with the online experience?

Communication across the Internet is a shared experience defined by the goals and wishes of the various participants. Whether sending and receiving email, looking at Web pages, or reading reviews of restaurants or products for sale online, we are interacting with other people using technology as the medium. All of these experiences can be mapped along a spectrum of trust. At one end we have a set of parties that fully trust each other. At the other end of the spectrum there are people who want nothing to do with each other and want barriers to keep the others away. But most activity is in the middle, where we accept that we are going to communicate with some other party that we do not fully trust. This situation maps well to the real world in which we deal daily with people we have no reason to trust fully. But if this context is familiar in the off-line world, it is less well studied and framed in cyberspace.

If people in cyberspace were able to make trust determinations – if they were able to assign different levels of trust to different people – how might this modulate what happens in cyberspace? Email provides a good case study. A wide variety of attachments can be sent with email today – images, text files, executable code, formatted documents, and so on. Some of these are benign, some can cause harm to the machine that receives them. Some email contains pointers to Web pages, which may be legitimate or may be fake pages attempting to masquerade as legitimate. If our email-receiving software knew that we trusted some senders but not others, it might block attachments from untrustworthy senders, strip out or deactivate Web links in that email, and so on. It might open attachments in a "safe mode" in which the attachment is isolated so that it cannot do any harm. But for senders we trust, the software would do its best to facilitate efficient, unregulated interaction. Software today cannot do anything like this; our systems lack any way to make and record trust decisions about those we communicate with, and we have no robust way to verify with whom we are communicating. Without a foundation of identity, discussion of trust is useless.

Trust and Constraint

When we are in a situation in which we lack trust, we use tools and methods to impose constraints on the interactions. We do not meet strangers in a dark alley, we use third parties to verify and assure major financial transactions, we go with a friend to a club, and so on. The same is true online. When we communicate with someone we do not fully trust, we invoke mechanisms to constrain the communication. We want checking, validation, witnesses (trusted third parties), and so on. We want viruses removed from incoming email, we want spam stripped out, and so on. But constraint on behavior is not a basis for trust. Constraint is in some sense the opposite of trust. Because one person trusts another, the trustee is expected to "do the right thing," even though he/she is not externally constrained to. A police state may greatly constrain what its citizens do, and this may provide certain sorts of predictability and assurance of behavior, but it does not induce trust. For real trust to develop, there must be freedom for that trust to be tested; there must be the potential for that trust to be violated. It is this risk, and the freedom that accompanies it, that is the essence of human trust. Society gives us the tools to constrain interaction as well as the means to bypass them. The nature of the original Internet, which has been called "open" or "transparent," is the constraint-free context in which trusting parties interact. And it is among trusting parties, where the overhead of interaction is lowest, that we most easily find innovation, novelty, and originality.

As we come to grips with the painful fact that not everyone on the Internet is trustworthy, we see two trends. One trend is the adding of constraints and restrictions on patterns of communication to try to prevent bad things from happening. For example, we now have programs that try to delete emails the software identifies as spam. One side effect of this, of course, is that these tools sometimes delete a valid message by mistake. Blocking spam has made email less reliable. The other trend is a gradual drawing back from the optimistic position that anyone should be able to communicate with us at will. Email is like the telephone in that anyone can pick up a phone and call someone if they know their number. For both the phone (with unlisted numbers and Do Not Call lists) and email, we now see tools to restrict this behavior. For other sorts of tools, such as online chat and instant message tools, participants use "buddy lists" to specify from whom they will receive messages: many users have fallen back to a sort of Victorian model in which they will not talk to someone unless they have been introduced first. This limits intrusions by unwelcome messages, but also eliminates the open character that we associate with the Internet and its early applications, such as email.

I believe that the fundamental challenge as we "secure" the Internet is to preserve the freedom we associate with the open Internet, while giving assurance to parties that do not fully trust each other that there are enough constraints available so that an interaction can be made safe enough to be undertaken.

Can Technology Substitute for Trust?

One of the most persistent concerns about the Internet is its bewildering range of security problems, from nuisances such as spam to much more serious problems such as identity theft and network-based attacks. The Internet's designers have known for more than twenty years that it has security problems, and there have been numerous studies that document the poor state of security (both on the Internet specifically and in the computing world more broadly). Indeed, over the past decade there have been many improvements in the technology and practice of security. Many threats that concerned us ten years ago have been contained. But as the level of attack rises, there is a sense that our overall level of protection has not improved, and indeed may have gotten worse, even as we depend more and more on the Internet and the computers it connects.

This observation naturally begs the question of whether better mechanisms for security are the key to a "better" Internet. In this respect, I make a perhaps over-broad claim: better technical security mechanisms cannot make a secure Internet. They can improve certain aspects of security and provide reasonable protection against some classes of attack, but in general, technical mechanisms by themselves do not give assurance of correct operation. Only when security is combined with trust do we get a network in which we can hope for secure, reliable, robust operation.

In general, security mechanisms detect various sorts of failures, attacks, and the like and turn those events into "clean failures." Imagine a user connected to the Internet at a WiFi "hot-spot" where the user fears the provider of connectivity may spy on or attack his/her connection. When the mechanisms of IPsec (Internet Protocol Security), which provides packet-level encryption and can prevent spying, detect attempts to modify the sequence of packets, IPsec responds by closing the connection.[1] Attacks lead to "clean failure": the attack fails, but so does the intended communication.

The Domain Name System (DNS) provides another example. To retrieve a Web page, the information in the URL (the name of the Web page – the Uniform Resource Locator) must be extracted and used to obtain the Internet address of the server. The normal mechanism to do this is the DNS, which takes a *domain name* as an input (e.g., www.example.com) and returns an address. The DNS has been subject to a number of attacks that cause it to return the wrong address for a given domain name. In fact, some providers of DNS services sometimes return the wrong address on purpose, to allow subsequent manipulation of the eventual data transmission. To prevent this sort of attack, a secure form of DNS has been proposed, called Secure DNS or DNSSEC. Using encryption

---

[1] The term "packet" is used to describe the units of data into which a message is broken before being forwarded across the Internet from sender to receiver. Each packet carries a destination address on the front, somewhat analogously to a letter in its envelope, and is forwarded across the network by a series of specialized computers called "routers" until it reaches the destination and is reassembled there with the other packets to form the complete message.

techniques, DNSSEC provides a digital signature that allows the recipient to detect if he/she has been given an invalid answer. However, DNSSEC cannot assure that the correct answer is always delivered, only that the recipient will be told if an incorrect answer is delivered. Again, this should lead to a "clean failure" in which the download of the invalid Web page is prevented, but the user does not get the page he/she desired.

If security mechanisms can only stop the operation when something goes wrong, what can we do to ensure that the operation actually succeeds? In general, the answer is that the design of the system must give the users enough control – enough choice over providers of critical services – that the user can avoid the untrustworthy providers and pick providers that operate in the expected way. Technical mechanism cannot always force them to operate properly; it has to be some other constraint.

Often, the reason that service providers in fact behave properly and deliver the expected service is that they would suffer greatly from loss of reputation if they did not. Internet Service Providers (ISPs) that deliver poor service lose customers. But the counterexample is also true. In cases in which the loss of reputation may be of little consequence, service providers often do not behave as we might like. Most people will not walk out of a hotel because the Internet access is poor or insecure. Knowing that, hotels, hot-spot operators, and the like often do things we would consider untrustworthy.

In this respect, what disciplines an actor to behave in a trustworthy manner is little different from what we see in the off-line world. People are concerned with reputation, being an accepted member of a social context, not being shunned. And we often decide to trust them not because their character is free of flaws, but because they are disciplined by the context in which they find themselves, such that they have the incentive to behave in a trustworthy way. It is this discipline – not just the imposition of technical constraints – that makes cyberspace work.

Four Questions about Trust, Constraint, and Security

I have just described a spectrum of trust. These four questions, to some extent, explore that spectrum.

1. At one end of the spectrum are the parties that are prepared to trust each other. To support this case, how do we develop trust? What tools are needed to support the shared basis of trust and the resulting modes of communication?
2. The common case today is "in the middle" of the spectrum: parties that are prepared to communicate but need protection if the opposite party is not trustworthy. What tools are needed to make this case as safe as possible?

This is the space of attack and defense, the classic space of network and computer security. How can we prevent people from carrying out misdeeds and attacks and hold others accountable for misbehavior? What tools are needed for this task?

3. At the other end of the spectrum, one party does not trust the other at all and has no desire to communicate. How do the issues of trust inform this case?

4. Finally, and perhaps orthogonal to this spectrum, is the question of policing misdeeds of cooperating parties. To what extent should the system allow for the observation of and intervention in the ongoing communication among trusting parties, without their agreement, to carry out tasks of policing and enforcement?

I suggest that if we could answer these questions, we would have a basis to discuss the security and safety of the shared experience in the Internet. And I suggest that, in fact, we know a lot about these questions and how we solve them. Finally, I note that this framework does not render irrelevant the traditional security objectives of disclosure control, preservation of integrity, and availability; instead, these objectives will take on different forms along this spectrum.

Question 1: Developing Trust as a Basis for Action

One building block of trust is identity. If I cannot know for sure with whom I am communicating, then it is very hard to make any trust assumptions. The identity need not be that of a specific person – it can be a known role, or an institution as a whole. I may be talking to a policeman or to my bank. But if I cannot be sure that the policeman is really a policeman, or that the bank is actually my bank, there is no basis for any sort of confidence in anything, and no basis for any sort of trust.

How do we come to develop a sense of trust? This is not a technical problem, but a social one. Part of it is a process of "getting to know one another," which depends on an important aspect of identity, namely continuity. The necessary building block of this process is not a certification of attributes or absolute identity, but the assurance that the person today is the same as the person yesterday. The richness of the characterization can be built over time, but only on the basis of continuity. Out of continuity can be built reputation, and reputation is central to the creation of trust.

Another source of trust is the embedding of an experience in a larger context. I trust a policeman if I know the reputation of the police force of which he is a part. I trust a bank because I have a sense of the trustworthy nature of banks in my culture. There might be parts of the world in which I would not choose to trust a policeman or a bank, and people moving from one culture to another – from one context to another – may make the wrong starting assumptions about trust. There are cities in which one can walk alone at midnight with no fear of being mugged, and cities in which this action would be total folly. We as individuals, therefore, depend on our social context to help us make efficient, sufficient decisions about the degree of trust we assign to specific situations. We mutually depend on others to build up a shared framework of trust assumptions.

In some cases, this requires the ability to share cues for trust, such as identity, with others. It is much harder to develop a robust assessment of trust in isolation. In early applications built for the Internet, there were few tools to create that ability to share. Reputation management systems and collaborative filtering systems are examples of explicit efforts to build communities for the purpose of assessing (and enhancing) trust in useful ways. Taking a cue from society, we should expect to move away from a model in which every user acts in isolation and toward a model in which decisions about identity and trust are made in a more collective way.

A specific and formalized aspect of collective trust is the use of credentials and other sorts of third-party players to vouch for an actor. The use of a government identification when you fly, a passport when you enter a country, and so on are examples of formalized credentials, and we have online examples of third-party credentials, in the form of so-called merchant certificates, which are used as part of secure Web communications. In fact, most users never see these (although it is possible to do so); the Web browser performs the task of checking them. It is interesting that most users do not even know what is happening here, how much decision making and trust management they have delegated to this software running on their behalf. To a very considerable extent, the ultimate control over trust in the Internet today is in the hands of the creators of the browsers: these include Microsoft, Apple, Google, Mozilla (the creators of the Firefox browser), and Opera.

One specific question about identity is to what extent, and under what circumstances, users should be able to take on different identities. Tools for managing Internet identity first emerged within specific applications, and users had to manage many different and distinct identifiers and passwords: email names, eBay identities, Instant Message (IM) identities, and so on. There is no reason to believe that the application (email, IM, or the like) is the natural partitioning if a user has multiple personas; a person might want one identity to use at work, another to use among friends, and yet another for interaction with strangers, but in each case the user might want to use multiple applications. This situation is now being supplanted by the next phase in application-level identity management in which popular applications such as Facebook let people use their Facebook credentials to identify themselves to other applications. This sort of linking may be convenient, but it offers its own risk: if every action one takes on the Internet is associated with the same signal of identity, it may reveal a lot about them to someone who can observe and aggregate their actions.

Here are some specific questions about trust and identity:

- Should the Internet include a service (or multiple services) for creation and use of identities that function across applications?
- How can we move to a more collective basis for assessment of trustworthiness?
- What are the right tools to help a user manage multiple identities and use them in the intended contexts? How can this situation be made tractable?

Question 2: Making Communication Safe in the Absence of Trust

As discussed previously, when the parties to a communication are not prepared to declare each other trustworthy, but still wish to communicate, they turn to constraints on the communication to prevent undesirable consequences. One of the consequences of communication with untrusted or unknown parties is that they may actually be malicious and launch an attack. The goal of constraints is to mitigate the consequences of such an attack. Whether the "attack" is just a nuisance (such as spam email) or more dangerous (such as the attempt to install malware on the target computer), the inability to mitigate the attack will reduce people's willingness to engage in any communication with parties they do not accept as trustworthy. Such an outcome would greatly diminish the vitality of the Internet as a sphere of global communication. On the other hand, inspection of actions to prove them harmless is quite hard in general (consider airport screening), and this point on the spectrum is perhaps the cause of the most obvious security problems in the Internet.

One important form of constraint is the inspection of network traffic to detect undesirable or unwelcome content. For example, much email today is inspected in transit to remove spam and viruses. This can be seen as just another role for a trusted third party, but it is important to note that if this inspection is truly "in the middle" of the communication path, then this third party has to be able to see, and in some cases to modify, the content being sent. This objective is the direct opposite of the traditional goals of disclosure control and preservation of integrity, if integrity is defined simply as making sure that what the receiver gets is exactly what the sender sent.

When two parties want to interact but do not sufficiently trust each other for the task at hand, they often turn to outside agents to help them: trusted third parties and intermediates, brokers, registries, and so on. These can be from the private sector (credit card companies) or public sector (registries of deeds) and are often quite nuanced in terms of the service they provide and the protection they offer. The simple, two-party model of Internet communication does not directly capture this richness, but in fact, third-party agency can be built in, and many applications have this sort of structure. The most obvious example is e-commerce on the Internet, which works because of credit card companies that track the identity of both the buyer and the seller (and take on the role of insurance company as they shoulder the risk of fraud). eBay (and its escrow service) plays a similar role. (eBay also importantly provides a reputation management service to allow a communal development of trust among the players.)

These sorts of schemes also depend on identity. A buyer and a seller on the Internet may not know much about each other, but will transact because they can trust that the credit card company knows a lot about each of them.

Another mechanism to deal with low assurance of trust is to pick randomly the person with whom you will interact. One bit of advice given to a child is that if you get lost, find someone in uniform and ask that person for help. In fact, it is very good odds that if a child asks *anyone* at random, the person will be caring and helpful, and very low odds that the person will turn out to be a sexual predator. The odds change greatly if the adult initiates the contact. It is often safe to depend on the kindness of strangers, if *you* pick the stranger

We see examples of "picking at random" in the Internet in mechanisms such as onion routing,[2] in which a message is sent sequentially through a random sequence of anonymizers, any one of which may not be trustworthy, with the expectation that the sequence of actions will be sufficient in total for anonymity.

In fact, choice, which is often seen primarily as an economic tool to impose the discipline of competition, is also a part of trust because it prevents someone in power from forcing a user to make use of a component they do not wish to trust.

A final means to deal with lack of trust is to require that two or more unrelated actors must agree so that some important action can occur. In business, where there is concern about dishonest employees, there is a well-understood principle called *separation of duties*, in which two separate people must concur for a check to be cut, for example. We have not incorporated this technique into many technical systems outside of business support systems, even though it has an interesting implication: it must not be possible for one person to play both roles by taking on two identities; it imposes an interesting constraint on the design of the identity scheme that supports it.

---

[2] See https://www.torproject.org/ for a discussion of onion routing.

Some design questions are important:

- What aspects of constraint and trust-modulated transparency can be implemented in the core mechanisms of the Internet itself, as opposed to the applications running on top of these mechanisms?
- Are there approaches to providing protection that recur across applications? Are there "application design patterns" that we should provide to application designers to ease the task of modulating communication among untrusting parties?

Question 3: Preventing Unwelcome Communication

The first two questions describe circumstances in which people were mutually prepared to communicate with each other but had varying degrees of trust about the other parties. The total refusal to communicate can be seen as the end point in the spectrum of trust – parties that do not know and do not sufficiently trust each other simply do not communicate. One manifestation of this approach is the creation of closed networks with restricted communities of users, as we have today with corporate intranets. Total rejection of the outsider is relatively easy to implement, but creates gated communities.

Today, the Internet contains crude tools to try to protect users from unwelcome communication. Most obvious is the firewall. Firewalls impose constraints based only crudely on identity (e.g., the firewall separates the world into "inside" and "outside," a "semi-closed" regime that cannot deal with the insider attack or the trusted person at a distance). Firewalls (and many other forms of constraint) control behavior based on what the users are doing (what application they are running), not who they are. Firewalls have no way to make fine distinctions that cleanly divide good behavior from bad, which is why I am arguing that constraints and protections need to be modulated by knowledge of who is communicating and the degree of trust between the parties.

For parties connected to the open Internet, because anyone can send a packet, a user can be attacked by anyone who chooses to do so. This is the space of classic "network security," and its mitigation might seem to have less to do with trust (or its absence) than the redesign of protocols to make it harder for a sender to send to an unwilling receiver. But, in fact, identity and trust (and its assessment) must be central to any such scheme. The protection decision, whether to block or allow, must be based on a decision about the identity of the opposite party. If the network protocols are going to block (or not) communication at the packet level when communication is initiated, then cues about identity (and thus trust) must be in the first packet where they can be checked based on contextual information from the receiver. This approach is tricky and not at all the way the Internet works today. What we see today is decisions about blocking or constraint being made at the application level.

- Should the network level protocols of the Internet provide the option for some sort of identity credential in the first packet of an exchange? If so, how standardized should this credential be, and which network elements should be able to understand and act on it?

Question 4: Policing the Conspiracy

In the first question, we consider the case of fully trusting communicants and how to facilitate their interaction. The classic framing of the "network security problem" is how to protect this communication from other attackers. However, there is another form of the story in the first question: the conspirators and the police. In this version of the story, there are fully willing (and perhaps fully trusting) communicants who want to carry out some action that another party wants to prevent. The other party might be a private sector actor (the recording industry trying to control music sharing), or a public sector actor (the police) trying to prevent distribution of child pornography or detect terrorist plotting. In this case, it can be assumed that the conspirators will take every possible step to avoid observation, including encryption of their communication, and the problem of interdiction becomes most challenging, if not impossible.

Law enforcement agents will acknowledge, if only privately, that if two willing parties want to have a private exchange on the Internet, they can probably figure out how to do it, and we should not imagine that we can build in mechanisms that prevent this. The more interesting case is when one of the actors needs to take on a more public role as a part of the activity. Music sharing servers have to advertise themselves, however discretely, to be of use to potential recipients, which may open them up to detection. This raises images of "gentlemen's clubs" and other such groups that form by mutual consent, scrutinize their membership, and try to carry out marginal activities within a closed group.

The relevance of this question to our spectrum of trust is that this objective may impose a limit on the freedoms that we allow to those parties that choose to trust each other.

The Landscape of Identity

As we have mapped the spectrum of trust, we have in passing started to lay out the range of requirements for identity as well.

Between parties that have somehow come to trust each other, there is a strong requirement to be able to verify who the others are, but this can be done in ways that are private among them. There is no reason that the identities used among trusting parties be revealed to outside parties.

Users, however, may want to have communication from both trusted and untrusted parties distinguished in the network so that it can be subjected to different levels of constraint before it reaches the intended recipient. This means that there has to be some indication of identity that can be understood by trusted third parties in the network. Two points are worth making. First, this visible signal of identity need not be the same as the one used by the end points, although in many cases it may be convenient to share the indication. Second, this externally visible indication of identity does not have to be meaningful "everywhere" in the network. From the perspective of a receiver, it is only useful if the signal is meaningful to agents that the recipient trusts, because there seems little use in invoking an "untrusted third party" to impose constraints. One way to characterize this sort of limited scope of identity is that an end node can "out-source" into the network (or into a server in the network) some aspects of checking and constraint, and because the end points can (in general) pick the agents to which the functions are out-sourced, this pattern can still be seen as an "edge-driven" mode of managing identity and trust.

When we are attacked in the real world, we fall back on accountability and deterrence. We call the police, we bring lawsuits, and so on; and here the nature of identity changes. Here we need to prove the identity of a party that does not want to be identified – that is, identity that will hold up in a court of law, identity that cannot be abandoned at will, and so on. This might be called adversarial identity, in contrast to the willing (if partial) construction of identity that supports questions one and two. Adversarial identity is much harder to arrange, and given the easy and undistinguished border-crossing communication of the Internet, accountability and deterrence seem somewhat uncertain, unpredictable, and not very reassuring. It is in this area in which both users and designers of the Internet struggle the most.

One question is whether there is an online analog of the security camera in the convenience store? What should an observer be able to capture about an exchange of packets that can be used to deter an attack or hold the attacker accountable? One answer is that we might design a system by which any packet (or any packet that is the first in an exchange) might be required to carry some globally meaningful indication of identity. But this begs the question of jurisdiction, as well as validity of the identity in a court of law. Furthermore, I believe that it would have very negative social consequences; it would uniformly turn the Internet into a panopticon where everything a user does can be observed and logged.[3]

If all communication had to be associated with a strong form of adversarial identity, there would be no opportunity for anonymous communication or action in which the identity is private to the communicating end nodes. To allow for private and anonymous communication in cases for which it is desired, the network and applications must provide strong enough constraints and other mechanisms so that the risk of attack can be mitigated to the point at which accountability after the fact is not a necessity. These mechanisms, as discussed earlier, can include actual inspection of the message contents and the tools by which trust can be developed and maintained over time so that users are willing to accept the absence of external accountability in their communication.

At a minimum, a receiver might try to facilitate accountability and deterrence by refusing to receive an encrypted message from an unknown sender. Having an encrypted conversation with a stranger is like meeting them in a dark alley – whatever happens, there are no witnesses. Witnesses, just like security cameras, are useful in deterrence, and only providers of certain particular sorts of services may wish to offer the option of encrypted conversation with strangers.

When we consider deterrence and accountability, we must consider how this can be implemented. The most basic deterrence is shunning. Shunning does not require the intervention of a police element – it is (to use imagery from the Internet) an end-to-end form of deterrence. The problem with shunning is that it does not work if the offender can simply abandon his identity, create a new one, and return in this new guise. Credit bureaus implement the possibility of shunning in the real world, because they maintain not only a record of your credit but a strong idea of who you are, linked to where you live and where you work, and other attributes that are hard to escape. But the Internet today has few such attributes that are "hard to escape." Perhaps the most persistent form of identity (the one that we will least want to walk away from casually) is the identity we construct in a social network such as Facebook. We see Facebook identities being used today in various applications as a persistent identity for trust and accountability.

When we go beyond shunning, the issue of jurisdiction and boundaries arises. In what jurisdiction can you be held accountable, prosecuted, sued, and

[3] There is a significant difference between the security camera "in the convenience store" and one "on the street." The security camera in the store is installed and used by the owner of the store and is set up knowing the goals of the store owner. The security camera on the street, perhaps installed by the police, is in a much more public place and looks for a much more general range of activities. Different agencies may be trusted in different ways.

so on? As private sector actors, credit card companies are transnational, but they can only shun, not arrest. Part of the problem with spam, phishing, and the like is that it seems to originate in foreign countries in which, even if treaties of various sorts exist, it will be difficult to instigate an investigation. So it seems as if the victim has little recourse. There is the additional issue that each such action by an attacker may seem de minimis, while the sum of the actions may be quite material. The Internet may allow the possibility of a million dollar fraud, one penny at a time.

If we wanted to add some manifestation of jurisdictional boundaries to the Internet, we can see a range of ways to do it. One would be to add that knowledge "into" the Net, so that it is possible to tell, based on some signal such as packet address or route, whether the various parties are in the same jurisdiction. The original designers went to great pains to avoid this capability, arguing that it would bring more harm than good. The alternative would be to add the capability for end nodes to obtain robust (hard to forge) certificates of home jurisdiction that they can exchange as demanded by the other parties. These, again, would probably work only if they were connected to a base identity that is hard or impossible to abandon, but they might preserve anonymity unless a third party (e.g., a court of the jurisdiction) found that there was cause to reveal the identity. This scheme is one in which the responsibility for correct operation would be shared among technical and social institutions.

A design question:

- Could we invent a form of identity that would permit shunning while still allowing the option of anonymous communication – an "end to end" form of deterrence?

Trust and the Design of Applications

In several places, I referred to the "user" of the Internet. It is important to distinguish between two classes of user. One is the human at the computer, who is engaged in the overall experience of using the Internet. The other is the "user" of the Internet communication service, the application designer. Earlier, I wrote a sentence that might have triggered some doubt: "the design of the system must give the users enough control – enough choice over providers of critical services – that the user can avoid the untrustworthy providers and pick providers that operate in the expected way." While users can perhaps make high-level trust decisions, we cannot expect ordinary users of the Internet – the humans at the computers – to be making complex technical decisions about selection of trustworthy components. It must be software running on behalf of the user that is making these choices. That software is the application. The designer of the application must identify the critical components of the system, must design the application so that there can be diversity in these components, and must provide some way for high-level trust assertions to be translated into choices among these components.

In some cases, the high-level trust assertions will come from the actual users. In the case of email, a user may tag certain other users with a "trusted/untrusted" indicator. In other cases, the trust assertions may be embedded in the application itself. In the design of the secure Web (Web sites identified by a URL that begins "https" rather than "http"), there are a set of actors called Certificate Authorities that provide attestation that a Web server is authentic. But how should a user know which Certificate Authorities to trust? As described previously, today's Web browsers contain a list of Certificate Authorities that are trusted by default. In effect, the browser is telling the user what to trust, unless the user manually edits this list. Few users do.

I observed previously that, in the real world, establishment of trust is a collective, human activity. People live in a society with friends and colleagues, not in isolation. But in the online context, the collective and collaborative development of trust can only happen if the application gives the users tools to do this. The simple applications from the early Internet did not provide many means to do this, but more applications are doing this today. For example, the review site Yelp allows users to rate each other, as well as the services being rated. Yelp reviewers develop a profile over time, and users can see each other's profiles – how many reviews they have written, the range of review scores, how others have rated the reviews, and so on. eBay, the online auction site, allows buyers and seller to rate each other, and prospective participants can see the ratings of the other parties. Today, the mechanisms that are used for these purposes are application-specific. A question for the future is whether these mechanisms (and the trust assumptions embedded in them) could or should be extracted from the applications and made a part of a "trust management subsystem."

In still other cases, the human user may choose to download a "trust profile" from a third party. This is a form of delegation of responsibility to an agent with more technical skills and perhaps a broader perspective. Enterprises may mandate that their users (e.g., employees) use a specified trust profile. These examples beg the question of which actors really control the choices about which components to trust, and how an application should be configured so that it meets the needs of its users.

There is another important role for the application once we develop a landscape of trust – applications must be designed to modulate their behavior based on the relevant signals of trust. As I discussed earlier, the behavior of email might change depending on whether the receiver trusts the sender, for example removing potentially dangerous attachments from untrusted senders. Email does not work this way today. We are now seeing the emergence of "trust-aware" applications. For example, Yelp, the rating site mentioned previously, not only lets users rate each other, but develops an internal model of how trustworthy different reviewers are, and may "filter" certain reviews it deems unreliable. In this case, of course, it is Yelp and not the individual users that develops the model of trust.[4]

Why Do We Trust the Applications?

The software that intermediates among users is the application code: email, instant messaging, eBay, Yelp, and so on. Our ability to communication with the desired protections depends on the software functioning as expected. Why do we trust that software?

I earlier made a distinction between *trusting a person* and deciding that technology is *reliable*, yet here I asked about *trusting* the software. I would say that both words are relevant, and describe different issues. Software is *unreliable* if it crashes or is otherwise technically flawed. But software is designed and operated by people, who – like any other people – may have interests that are more or less aligned with the interests of the user and may be more or less constrained to behave in trustworthy ways. If a user gives personal information to an application and the operators of that application sell that information to a third party without permission, that is not an unreliable system (it may have been designed technically to very high standards) but an untrustworthy system. So a careful way of asking our question might have been: "Why do we trust the designers and operators of an application?"

The answers to that question are in fact very similar to the answers I gave about trusting other users. We may trust the creator or operator of an application because they are known to us personally (e.g., a local system administrator), or because the provider is constrained by laws and regulations (with real penalties for misbehavior) or because the providers fear loss of reputation (and business) if they are seen as untrustworthy. The discipline of competition can motivate operators and service providers to operate in a trustworthy way, if the consumer has the option of choosing among competing providers. Therefore, choice – and the ability to use the option of choice as a discipline on the provider – is

---

[4] For those who are not familiar with Yelp, the Yelp Frequently Asked Questions (FAQ) page gives a good introduction to the operation of the system. At the time of publication, this could be found at www.yelp.com/faq.

a tool that allows the user both to pick trustworthy providers of service and to discipline providers of service found to be untrustworthy. But this process only works if the user actually has choice.

Who Controls the Choices?

An actor that controls choice is an actor with power. Power is a concept well studied by political scientists and sociologists. It should not be a surprise that power is an important issue in the design and operation of the Internet, but it has not been well studied and categorized. As a practical matter, issues of power come up every day as we worry about the market power of broadband providers of consumer Internet access or we worry about the balance of power in rights of privacy. But there has been no methodical discussion that attempts to catalog the tools of power in the Internet or the stakeholders in the power struggles.

Contested Control: The End User and the ISP

A much-quoted design principle of the Internet is the "end-to-end argument," which states a preference for placement of function outside the communications substrate and in the end node (Saltzer et al. 1984: 277–288). This design approach can be contrasted with that of the telephone system in which the intelligence is in the switches, and the telephone equipment (the "end node") has very little function. This distinction has been summarized as the "smart network" (the phone system) and the "stupid network" (the Internet).

One of the benefits of the Internet's design is that the user can run the code of his choice on his end node without requiring permission or modification of the network itself (the switches or routers). When a new application is invented, such as the Web, instant messaging, or a multi-player game, users can simply download new code and start running it. This feature has contributed to the explosion of innovation that has occurred on the Internet, the (perhaps over-) investment and experimentation in new applications, and the rapid creation of new value for the consumer.

It can be argued that all Internet stakeholders benefit from this innovation and the creation of new value, but the nominal power in this version of the story lies with the end user and the application designer who provides the software, not with the ISP or the regulator. The ISP just carries packets and, although it may (or may not) benefit financially as the amount of traffic goes up, does not control which traffic is sent or have many opportunities to set prices based on value. Needless to say, the real story is more complex than this.

There is a myth about the Internet that, because there is no such thing as a "call" or "call setup" and the traffic just flows as it is directed dynamically by the underlying routing and forwarding protocols, it is impossible to watch or manipulate what the sender is sending in any reliable way. In the "center" of the Net, that is true. But it is not true at the edges, where the consumer attaches to the network, or at "constriction points," where traffic is funneled into a restricted path (such as where a corporation connects to the rest of the Internet over a small number of paths). For residential users, who usually connect over a single broadband circuit, all of their traffic flows over a path that is highly predictable and stable. This gives the owner of this path, the access ISP or broadband provider, the power to observe all of the user's traffic and to exercise whatever sorts of controls or discrimination that can be devised from what can be seen in the traffic.

Corporations often use their points of connection to the public Internet to observe and police what their employees do, looking for forbidden activities such as downloading pornography or online gambling. These points can also be used to log activity, such as capture and retention of email and instant messaging. Whereas security folks use these points to filter what comes *in* (using devices such as firewalls), it is also common to control what goes *out*.

These constriction points also make a useful target for third parties (such as the government) who want to observe and control. These points, therefore, become favored options for wiretap exercises.

An Example of Contenting over Choice: Email

An example may help clarify how these factors play out as the user contends with others to make choices about trustworthy components. When a user sends an email, it normally does not go directly from the sender's computer to the recipient's computer. Instead, the email is normally sent from the sender's computer to the sender's mail server and from there to the receiver's server, where finally the receiver retrieves it using one of two mail retrieval protocols: POP or IMAP. The original reason for this design was to permit users (and their computers) to exchange email even if their computers were connected to the network only occasionally. This structure is of considerable value today, with the prevalence of laptops and mobile devices that are intermittently off the Net. This feature also allows a user to read his email (using IMAP, for example), from one of several end nodes, and have actions taken at that end node (e.g., deleting a message) visible to the same user from any other of the end nodes.

The question about power and choice is very simple. Can the user select the server that he uses to send and/or receive email, or does some other actor constrain that choice and impose the answer on the user? In the original conception of email, this question was not an obvious one to ask, because the designers were not thinking about actors with adverse interests and assumed that the user would pick a service provider based on convenience and reliability. The design of the email protocols does not constrain the ability of the user to choose, and most email software allows the user to configure it with the choice of servers for sending and receiving. So it would seem that the user has the power to choose.

However, some access ISPs, by virtue of their control over topology (discussed previously), have imposed traffic blocking and rerouting that attempts to constrain that choice. There are several reasons why an ISP might want to do this. One is to create customer "stickiness." When a user picks an email server to use, he picks his email address. If a user obtains email service from the "xyz.com" company, then his email address will be something like user@xyz.com. Once the user has given this address to all of his friends, he is not likely to change it casually. To avoid this "capture," some users take advantage of third-party providers (such as Google) that offer services that give users an email address independent of their ISP. Many universities will give their alumni an address (for free, to make connections to their alumni community), and many professional societies will provide email addresses to their members. This removes the element of customer stickiness that an ISP would like to create. One response by ISPs was to try to block the use of such addresses. This behavior could be observed in prior times, but has essentially vanished as an ISP strategy because of consumer protest.

For another class of users, corporate users working from home, the motivation may shift from stickiness to additional revenue. For such users, by blocking their ability to use their corporate email address from home, it might be possible to shift them to a higher-priced access service. This strategy, as well, has failed because of consumer protest.

Where users have complained about these restrictions, the ISPs have in some cases relented from this blocking, and justified them in other cases with some arguments (if not compelling justification) about preventing spam. Corporate users respond by creating encrypted Virtual Private Network (VPN) connections back to their corporate network, and then sending and receiving email over that connection, so that the access ISP cannot see or block their activities. In some parts of the world, ISPs have responded by blocking encrypted VPN connections. Users respond with intense complaint, and some balance is struck. Most ISPs today do not attempt to block VPNs, so for savvy users that can master the mechanics of making encrypted connections, the ISPs have little ability to inspect or block. Again, choice is available, but only to the sophisticated user.

The details of contestation over choice will differ for different applications. Centralized applications such as Facebook or Twitter give the user essentially no choice as to which provider to use. For many users, Facebook is such an important application that they decide to use it even though they may not be certain how trustworthy the provider is. In this case, the only tools available to the user are collective protest, perhaps to the provider and perhaps to some regulator that can assert pressure on the provider.

Final Thoughts

At the beginning of this chapter, I claimed that while technology was the foundation of cyberspace, its essence was connecting people through the medium of the computer. This point was not well understood when shared computers and networks first emerged. When computer networking was first conceived, the presumed purpose was to give programmers access to computers. In other words, the relationship was between man and machine. In 1962, Doug Engelbart[5] of SRI wrote a long report for the Air Force Office of Scientific Research titled "Augmenting Human Intellect: A Conceptual Framework." This report directly builds on the earlier paper of Vannevar Bush (Bush 1945) and presents a rich discussion of cognitive processing enhanced by computing, but only near the end of the 132-page report is there a mention of collaboration. On page 105 of the report, a section titled "Team Cooperation" begins with the following suggestive text: "Let me mention another bonus feature that wasn't easily foreseen. We have experimented with having several people work together from working stations that can provide intercommunication via their computer or computers.... This proves to be a really phenomenal boost in group effectiveness over any previous form of cooperation we have experienced."[6]

The idea that the actual purpose of networks was to connect people together mediated by a computer emerged early in the network era, with email as the first example. However, research in the human factors that allow people to interact without a presumption of total shared trust has lagged behind practice. Now that we understand that the experience of using the Internet is just

---

[5] Engelbart, an early leader in man-machine interaction, is known, among other things, for the invention of the computer mouse.

[6] It should be noted that the concept of time-sharing had emerged while Engelbart was writing. Time-sharing is a scheme that allowed a number of users at terminals to interact simultaneously within a single computer, so that it was possible to perform experiments in which several users interact and collaborate without having to envision the possibility of computer networks.

a technology-created reflection of much of what can happen in the off-line world, we should turn our careful attention to the methods and principles that will allow effective and constructive communication and collaboration among people, with variation in trust among the participants determining the patterns of constraint and freedom provided by the application.

3

The New Face of the Internet

Thomas Karagiannis

Introduction

In reality, the Internet, as a networking person would define it, has not changed much since it was commercialized in the 1990s. The main Internet concept is still there, and so are its core technologies and applications; for example, the protocols that are responsible for transferring bits between two computers have been virtually unchanged since the inception of the Internet. However, many things have evolved and have tremendously impacted the way we communicate, perform computation, and conduct business online.

This chapter highlights recent trends and technology evolutions that appear to be shaping perhaps not the Internet itself (as seen in the strict definition of a networking person), but everything around traditional approaches to computing and communication. In my opinion, there are three main such transforming trends: the Cloud and the promise it brings for computing; the new Web with its intertwined services and applications; and Big Data computing, which opens up new horizons and opportunities with fast processing of diverse, dynamic, and massive-scale datasets. Each of these trends is not disconnected from the others, but interlinked, which – as I discuss – is the case with every aspect of the Internet today. This maze of interconnected services, applications, users, and devices is one of the two main themes that are omnipresent in the Internet today. The other is an implicit notion of shared trust, a trust that appears to transfer – irrespective of user intentions – through the links of this maze, reforms our online experiences, and also bears tough challenges for user privacy.

The Cloud

{Θε.} [τί φής;] νεφέλης ἄρ᾽ ἄλλως εἴχομεν πόνους πέρι;

{Servant}: [What do you mean?] Do you mean we struggled in vain for just a cloud?
EURIPIDES, HELEN, 706-7

A cloud was the source of big misfortunes for Greeks and Trojans according to Euripides's ancient tragedy *Helen* (412 BC), leading to the famous ten-year Trojan War. The war was the result of Helen, the wife of the Mycenaean king Menelaus, running away with Paris, the son of the king of Troy. According to the Euripides's tragedy, however, Helen was never at Troy during the war. Instead, a mad Hera, after Paris selected Aphrodite as the most beautiful of the goddesses, had Helen replaced with a "cloud," a fake phantom-Helen who followed Paris to Troy. The real Helen remained trapped in Egypt, faithful to Menelaus, who discovered the truth only after the end of the war. Today, more than two millennia later, another cloud aims at revolutionizing computing. Is this cloud a mirage too, another fake Helen, or can it actually fulfill the promise of reducing the struggles in the Information Technology (IT) industry?

Cloud computing is ubiquitous. Accessing the Internet today is synonymous to using some form of "the Cloud" either directly or indirectly. From simple apps on our mobile devices, to the large-scale complex systems that compute the results of a search query, populate our Facebook wall, or update our Twitter feeds in a few hundreds of milliseconds; from Cloud-based storage applications such as DropBox or SkyDrive, to Internet-based video-calling through Skype or entertainment through Netflix video streaming; cloud computing is the reference point. From a users' perspective, it may not be an exaggeration to argue that today, the line between the Internet and the Cloud is quite thin, if not invisible. This is perhaps why the term "cloud" is said to originate from the Internet – in the computer networking and systems communities, clouds are often used to graphically symbolize networks connecting end users or systems.

The easiest way to define the Cloud is by referring to the usage of computing resources on-demand, as a utility. Such resources can be compute power, storage, or even software that are remotely hosted by a third-party, and are thus accessed as a service through a network which in most-cases is the Internet. Hence, as with traditional utility services (such as electricity or natural gas) that are offered to the consumers as a service by a provider and consumers pay based on their usage, Cloud providers (such as Amazon EC2 or Microsoft Azure) offer users the possibility of renting computing resources on-demand and charge them based on the time they use these resources. The most common interface to the Cloud is simply a Web-browser.

Defining the Cloud as a utility service is, of course, a simplification. Contrary to existing utility services, for example, the Cloud is not regulated by any government or other agency, nor does it constitute critical public infrastructure (although many would argue otherwise regarding its criticality); similarly, switching from one cloud provider to another is not as straightforward as with traditional utility services. In my opinion, however, the notion of delivering computing resources as a utility best conveys the aspirations of the Cloud.

Interestingly, cloud computing is not a new concept. The overarching vision of the Advanced Research Projects Agency Network (ARPANET), the network created in the late 1960s and which later evolved into today's Internet, was interconnecting computers with the goal of time-sharing remote computing resources. Likewise, the core applications delivered through cloud computing are not novel; editing documents was possible before Office365 and Google Docs, file hosting and sharing solutions obviously preceded DropBox, and email existed before Gmail – in fact, the underlying technology of email is virtually unchanged over the past decades. So, where is the big fuss about the Cloud coming from?

Cloud computing essentially democratizes computing. To a large extent, computational resources that were once the privilege of large companies are now available for everyone, typically at an acceptable budget. Access to data aside, nothing prevents – for example – a small company to run PageRank, the algorithm that powers Google's search engine, at large scale through the Cloud. Hence, cloud computing is not about new technologies per se, but instead revolutionizes the way computing resources are delivered; resources are available, can be rented, accessed through the Internet, and scaled on-demand, in real-time as is necessary to meet business needs.

To better understand this, let us first take a look at the factors that made cloud computing feasible and see what the cloud model brings for the three main parties involved in cloud computing – namely, the cloud providers, the cloud tenants or service providers, and the end users. In the following sections, I discuss both the benefits and the risks provided by the Cloud, focusing mainly on trust issues.

What Made the Cloud Possible?

In my opinion, three main factors contributed to the current explosion of cloud-provided services – virtualization, high-speed networks, and the on-demand charging model.

The advancement in virtualization technologies allows computer resources to be virtualized and efficiently shared across multiple instances of an operating system. This means that multiple operating systems can run simultaneously in one physical server, each of which is provided with the illusion of its own resources, such as a Central Processing Unit (CPU), access to storage/memory, and so on. Virtualization is critical in cloud environments because it facilitates renting one physical server to multiple users, providing the same user experience as when users were running their applications in separate, isolated computers. The main benefit of virtualization is cost reduction; less hardware is required to support multiple cloud users, which also implies reduction of complexity and IT costs (less physical resources to manage), and energy efficiency. Additionally, virtualization enables user and application state to be maintained by quickly suspending and resuming a virtual machine; essentially the whole state of a virtual machine can be thought of as a file, which contains all the configurations, preferences, and data of its user and which can be saved for later usage. Hence, virtualization allows for the whole user state to migrate from one physical server to another (because it is just a file) in case of hardware failure, for example. This is equivalent to "hibernating" your computer and then starting another computer with the same hibernated state of the first one.

Cloud computing would be infeasible without high-capacity networks. Because cloud computing refers to services delivered through the network, the network infrastructure is critical to the cloud model. Imagine a user running a word processing application on a virtual machine hosted remotely; in such an application, a performant, high-speed network is critical for the responsiveness of the application. Network evolution was important both in Local Access Networks (LANs) (such as the ones found within enterprises or data centers), but also in broadband and wireless. In LANs, high capacity networks are essential to enable large-scale distributed applications, to quickly transfer huge volumes of data, and to unlock the benefits of virtualization (e.g., fast migration of virtual machines). From the availability of 100Mbps in the mid-1990s, 10Gbps enterprise networks are now becoming commonplace, and high-end data centers are already moving to 40Gbps technologies, with 100Gbps coming within the next few years. On the other hand, broadband networks were crucial in delivering cloud applications to the end user (e.g., to the home or small enterprises) and have advanced from access speeds of a few hundreds of Kbps ten years ago to broadband speeds of tens of Mbps that are now typical. Similarly, wireless access technologies (such as WiFi, 3G, or 4G) further extend the cloud paradigm to mobile devices (such as laptops, tablets and mobile phones), thus allowing for a holistic user experience across technologies and devices.

Whereas virtualization and high-speed networks were the technological advancements that made cloud applications feasible, the pay-as-you-go charging model introduced an alternative and attractive business model for managing IT resources. The model provides two main benefits. First, it eliminates upfront infrastructure costs; start-up businesses can focus directly on building their desirable service instead of figuring out what infrastructure (e.g., server, switches, management software) they can afford and should buy, and how to configure it. Second, companies can scale IT resources up or down dynamically by tracking user demand and expect to pay based on resource usage without having to worry about provisioning or management.

Of course, on-demand charging preceded the Cloud. Renting managed or unmanaged servers in data centers typically of large Internet Service Providers (ISPs) – such as AT&T – was feasible before cloud data centers. Such hosting meant that actual servers were provisioned for customers by the provider, who also was responsible in maintaining the hardware and other software components (such as the operating system) if the service was managed. However, the whole process was quite cumbersome and time-consuming, taking days to deploy, with customers having to actually talk to operators over the phone to decide server specs; and charging was done on a monthly basis. Similarly, Web hosting companies, that traditionally hosted Web services and served Web content since the 1990s, have been charging on a monthly basis, and pricing depended on Web site popularity, which was typically reflected in network bandwidth usage. ISPs have also been pricing their services based on bandwidth usage per month, and customers could buy more or less capacity based on business needs. However, it is its dynamicity that truly makes the cloud charging model unique and has allowed it to become mainstream. Charging occurs at a very fine granularity, tracking resource usage per hour (or lately, per minute!) instead of per month and for resources beyond network capacity, for example, by extending the pay-as-you-go model to computation or usage of other services (e.g., cloud storage). Firing up a virtual machine in the Cloud can be completed in a few minutes through a Web interface and with a credit card, with the whole process being lightweight and transparent – you are charged for the resources you use. Virtualization technology was key to enable this, but so was the realization about transparency and ease of use.

Benefits and Risks of the Cloud

There are three entities involved in cloud applications: (1) cloud providers own the infrastructure – such as large-scale data centers – where cloud applications run; (2) tenants or service providers that develop cloud applications by typically renting the infrastructure of the cloud providers; and (3) the end-users of cloud applications.

Cloud providers develop and manage the infrastructure that makes cloud computing possible. This infrastructure is typically in the form of large data centers comprising hundreds of thousands of servers. Because of the investment needed to build data centers, these usually belong to large companies such as Google, Microsoft, Amazon, Facebook, and others. To get a feel for the size of modern data center facilities and their associated investment, Apple's data center in Maiden, North Carolina, is a 500,000-square-foot facility with a reported cost of $1 billion and power consumption of roughly 100 megawatts (Miller, 2010; Hamilton, 2012). Comparable numbers are reported for Microsoft's Chicago data center (700,000 square feet, $500 million [Miller 2010]).

The computation or storage resources of these massive data center facilities are typically rented through virtualization to customers, referred to as *tenants* in data center jargon. Because tenants can be internal or external, data centers can be characterized as private or public. In public data centers, the provider rents data center resources to external customers. In comparison, private data centers serve only the needs of the data center owner and host applications from one or more of its business departments (i.e., internal tenants). One example is Facebook, whose data centers are only used to provide the functionality necessary to Facebook's internal operations (for example, to maintain, compute, and store friendship relationships, or to identify and store the content needed to populate one's wall). There are also hybrid clouds in which applications use both public and private resources, choosing to keep only parts of their operations or data on-premises. For tenants, hybrid clouds provide the scaling benefits of the public cloud, but also allow for tight control of critical operations or confidential data that are hosted locally.

Amazon was the first to envision that renting spare computing or storage capacity from its data centers was a promising opportunity. Building Web services requires provisioning for peak load, which in most cases in the Internet world is significantly higher (orders of magnitude) than the average load of a service. What does this mean in practice? Think of a retail Web company (i.e., CoolWeb.com) trying to provision the resources needed to meet customer demand. Before the Cloud, CoolWeb.com would need to provision and deploy resources for peak load, for example, to ensure that customer demand during the Christmas sales season can be satisfied. This implies that for the rest of the year, when demand is significantly lower, a large fraction of these expensive computing, network, or storage resources are underutilized. In essence, CoolWeb.com had to buy and deploy resources that would only be fully utilized for a small fraction of time.

Amazon, being a retail company and itself suffering the peak-to-average resource provisioning, realized that by renting out some of its unused large-scale infrastructure, it would not only help companies avoid the cost of deploying and managing similar infrastructure, but it could also make some money along the way. Hence, with the launch of their cloud services, S3 storage, and EC2 computing services in 2006, Amazon became the market leader in cloud computing.

Today, there are three main cloud service models: Infrastructure as a Service (IaaS), Platform as a Service (PaaS), and Software as a Service (SaaS). The common theme in each of the models is the "as a Service" paradigm which precisely conveys the notion of each of the offerings (Infrastructure, Platform, or Software) as a utility. The IaaS model specifies that the cloud provider provisions and manages the infrastructure resources (the network, the physical servers, and the storage). Customers can then run their preferred operating system and applications on top of this provided infrastructure. Typical examples for this model are Amazon EC2 and Microsoft Azure. With PaaS, in addition to the basic infrastructure, the cloud operator also provides and manages the operating system running on top of the physical servers, as well as a set of libraries and other software tools that customers can use to build their own applications. Google App Engine is a prominent example of a PaaS model. Finally, SaaS models move yet another level up on what is often referred to as the technology "stack" (hardware, operating system, applications) by providing specific applications as a service; for example, small enterprises can rent access to database software instead of installing and managing their own local database. Salesforce.com is one of the prominent examples of the SaaS model.

From where do cloud provider benefits come? Mostly, their benefits come from economies of scale. Building a large data center may require a substantial investment, but it also brings significant bargaining power in terms of prices. For example, buying hundreds of thousands of servers can lead to a significantly reduced cost per server, and evidence has shown that – compared to the average enterprise – large-scale data center providers can expect their costs for servers, networking, and administration to be reduced five to seven times (Hamilton 2010). Additionally, hardware vendors are more willing to work with large-scale providers when it comes to specific server designs or features, possibilities that are naturally nonexistent for average enterprises. Therefore, cloud providers can operate custom-designed hardware that allows for automation of processes and cost reduction. Overall, economies of scale allow for a sustainable business model, even when virtual machines are offered at very low prices. For example, at the time of writing, a small Amazon virtual machine costs just $0.060 per hour.

Cloud pricing opens up further possibilities that extend on-demand charging. Providers can even auction off unused capacity, with prices determined by data center utilization and tenants bidding for resources based on their desired prices. This model, which resembles a stock-market exchange for resources, is quite favorable to both parties. Cloud providers can profit by mopping-up any unused capacity, and tenants can achieve even lower prices for their noncritical tasks. If a tenant is outbid, however, he/she loses her resources and any unsaved computation results.

Economies of scale and pricing aside, providers also benefit from the ability to "lock" tenants to their infrastructure by providing technologies and services that are custom-designed. For example, cloud providers can optimize their infrastructure to work with a specific set of programming tools or languages potentially offered at a discounted price; but when a tenant builds their service on top of such tools, it would be hard (both costly and time-consuming) to migrate to other cloud providers.

On the flipside, low profit margins and trust are the two main risks faced by cloud providers. Regarding low profit margins, competition among the big players has resulted in pricing being a race to the bottom, with providers lowering their already quite low prices every few months to attract new customers and gain market share. Profit margins become lower with time, and sustaining a profitable business may become quite challenging. Currently, cloud providers try to offset this lowering of profits by constant innovation and adding features or services on top of the main cloud infrastructure, which are then provided to tenants for an extra charge. Such added services can also offer some provider differentiation and a potential competitive advantage, although it is questionable to what extent this will be possible in the future because customer-facing features can be copied. Cloud providers will need to differentiate through fine-grained Service Level Agreements (SLAs) offered to customers (for example, guaranteeing different properties when storing "hot" or "cold" tenant data), pricing incentives (for example, waiving network transfer charges when uploading data to the Cloud), or reduced operating costs through software and hardware innovation. The overall trend is still set by the market leader: Amazon – being a retail company – is accustomed to low operating margins. Therefore, the risk for cloud providers' offerings is becoming a commodity as Nicholas Carr describes in *The Big Switch* (2009), with providers maintaining critical but commodity infrastructure where the margin for profit and differentiation is slim.

Trust is the other pillar that, if breached, can bring down the entire cloud model. Quoting from a blog post by James Hamilton, "in the cloud there is nothing more important than customer trust" (Hamilton 2013). Trust in the Cloud is present in many forms and across several dimensions, which I further discuss in the following paragraphs that describe data center tenants and users of cloud services. To provide a few examples here, when tenants move their IT infrastructure (data and computation) to the Cloud, they implicitly trust the provider to offer an experience that is similar to the one, the traditional in-house IT infrastructure offered over the previous years. Trust in the Cloud can thus refer to a tenant's expectations about application performance and user experience. Additionally, tenants need to trust the cloud environment from a privacy perspective. Because the Cloud is a shared environment, the cloud provider needs to ensure that customer data and computation are isolated across tenants, even if they are placed in the same hardware devices; trust here implies the expectation of a secure, "vaulted" environment. From a technology perspective, such customer expectations may not always be straightforward. This is why achieving isolation among cloud customers – for their computation, data, or network transfers within the data center – is currently one of the big bets for cloud providers. Tenant isolation is a hot area for innovation and development not only in industry, but in academia as well (see Eno Thereska et al. 2013; Hitesh Ballani et al. 2011; David Shue et al. 2012; Alan Shieh et al. 2011). In his blog post, James Hamilton offers yet another, more subtle, dimension of trust; namely, offering an alternative service once an existing service is retired.

Tenants or cloud service providers build their services or applications on top of the offerings of cloud providers. Depending on the underlying cloud model, cloud services can range from applications such as cloud-based email or storage (Gmail, Hotmail, DropBox, and others) to full-blown software solutions to manage IT departments or customer relationships (such as the ones from Salesforce.com).

The benefits of the Cloud for service providers are multiple. In the absence of the Cloud, service providers would have to deploy, maintain, and manage the infrastructure needed to develop their applications (and this is not a negligible investment). The Cloud presents a unique opportunity to eliminate such costs. Generally, this is referred to as converting capital expenditure (CAPEX) to operating expenditure (OPEX). CAPEX reflects costs related to buying servers and infrastructure; OPEX describes costs related to day-to-day operations. For small or average enterprises, converting CAPEX to OPEX is considered beneficial because enterprises focus on their daily operations without caring about deploying and managing infrastructure.

What is more important, however, is the flexibility and agility offered to service providers in terms of resource provisioning – resources can be scaled up or down dynamically to match demand, and costs reflect the actual usage of these resources. The Cloud is ideal when dealing with the peak-to-average provisioning problem referred to earlier, which is present in most Internet services. Similarly, for start-up companies, resorting to the Cloud is a "no-brainer." The Cloud facilitates fast and cost-effective deployment of new services; it eliminates up-front infrastructure costs (for example, buying and maintaining servers) and allows for fast scaling if the start-up suddenly becomes popular. Additionally, the cost of failure is not as high. To put it simply, the Cloud can reduce the time for a start-up service to go live from several months to only weeks, if not days.

Trust, however, is often cited as one of the key hindrances to cloud adoption. Trust issues manifest across several dimensions in the cloud paradigm. With the responsibility of running the fundamental infrastructure (which is shifted from the tenant to the provider), tenants "outsource" part of their control over the deployed application to the provider. Depending on the level of expertise and application requirements, enterprises might be comfortable with such control transfer – after all, it might be better to trust an expert to maintain critical infrastructure. But this is not necessarily always the case, and some enterprises have to compromise by placing part of their trust in the cloud provider.

Besides the obvious concern that companies or application developers trust cloud providers with proprietary code and sensitive data, trust underlies the relationship of the two entities, providers and tenants, across a variety of forms:

- Application performance – the cloud provider needs to ensure that cloud-based applications perform well and predictably, as if they were hosted locally on end-user machines or in a dedicated server farm.
- Availability – outages or other failures in the provider's own infrastructure should not impact tenant services or applications. Cases of major provider outages that result in application unavailability are not uncommon; for example, popular applications such as FourSquare or Reddit were unavailable because of an Amazon outage in October 2012 for several hours (similar incidents took place within the same year for Google that affected a number of its services, including Gmail and Microsoft Azure). Availability incidents might lead to significant revenue loss for cloud services.
- Security – includes simple protection from malware as well as prevention of abuse and denial of service attacks. In addition to normal application disruption by wasting resources, attacks might lead to increased tenant costs because tenants are charged based on the usage of these resources. Attacks on cloud services can be either external – that is, originating from the public Internet – or, increasingly, internal – that is, sourced from other tenants that are co-located on the providers' infrastructure. Because the Cloud offers an infrastructure in which tenants can run any type of application and scale it dynamically, nothing prevents malicious code from running within data centers, which can unfortunately become an attractive vector for launching attacks. Such was a recent attack on U.S.-based financial institutions which was sourced from compromised data center servers (Rashid 2012).
- Charging – tenants trust that charging by providers is fair. One might ask when a price is ever fair, but fairness here refers to two unique aspects of today's cloud. First, metering might not be standard (as it is for example

in common utility services), with tenants having only limited visibility on how charges are calculated. In some cases, charging might be straightforward, calculated – for example – by counting the number of virtual machines rented per hour; in other cases, it requires complex bookkeeping in which providers need to track CPU cycles or storage operations used by an application. Second, because clouds are shared infrastructure, placement of a tenant's virtual resources in the data center might directly influence its cost. For example, co-placement of a tenant's virtual machines on the same physical servers with other network-aggressive tenants has been shown to affect the performance and the cost of the tenant's applications. Several academic papers addressing this concern have been published in recent years (Ballani et al. 2011; Popa et al. 2012).

Interestingly, the Cloud implies a shared accountability model for the first three of these concerns. Depending on the model (IaaS, Paas, or SaaS), cloud providers and tenants are accountable for different parts of the application performance, availability, or security. In IaaS, for example, the provider ensures that the infrastructure is secure, performant, and available, and the tenant is responsible for the same properties at the service/application level. Despite the fact that relationships between providers and tenants are business relationships, and contracts and complex Service Level Agreements (SLAs) specify the extent of such accountabilities (for example, providers commonly offer availability SLAs of 99.9 percent), it is mainly the trust between the two parties that powers the cloud model.

Beyond these points, service providers face other, more subtle risks with cloud computing, such as provider lock-in – service providers might depend so much on the technology and the infrastructure of a specific cloud offering that they become "locked" in it. Simply, moving to a different cloud provider might be prohibitive in terms of the cost and time of redeploying the service. Additionally, nothing prevents service providers becoming intermediate cloud providers themselves – that is, a tenant can rent virtual machines from a cloud provider on top of which he/she can provide services that the cloud provider also provides. This creates interesting conflict-of-interest relationships between the cloud provider and the service provider, as the cloud provider would actually be competing with one of his/her customers (Leinwand 2013)! From a service provider perspective, the risks of competing with one's cloud provider as well as the risks described above such as resiliency against failures have increasingly led tenants to replicate their services across multiple cloud providers. Although this is beneficial, it does not come without the overhead costs of supporting a service across multiple, most likely different, infrastructures.

Along with cloud providers and their tenants, there is the end user. Today, connectivity is the norm and being off-line is the exception. Users are constantly online through a number of different devices in every aspect of their everyday lives. Desktop computers, laptops, tablets, smartphones, and game and entertainment consoles provide the user with a constant interface to the online world. Coupling this constant connectedness with the Cloud provides the opportunity to offer a seamless experience to end users, as their data, configuration settings, and preferences are now stored in the Cloud and transparently move with the user across devices or environments. This model is true not only for data, but extends to applications as well. Similar to the web-based email with which one can access email irrespective of location or, lately, device, the Cloud now extends this experience across most of the popular applications.

The flexibility of the Cloud, however, comes at the cost of trust and control. Trust is implicit in the cloud model. An application automatically replicating user preferences across devices implies that these preferences are visible to the cloud service provider; editing documents stored in the Cloud similarly implies that such documents are stored on and managed by the provider's infrastructure. Essentially, reaping the benefits of a ubiquitous cloud service implies that users need to increasingly trust cloud service providers with their personal data, and control shifts from the user to the Cloud. The cloud service now has complete visibility to data that in the pre-Cloud era were only accessible by the user's own programs or devices. As it was with the relationship between tenants and cloud providers, this model has both pros and cons. Users do not need to care about data backups or failing hard disks because cloud storage services become responsible for the maintenance and availability of their precious data. On the other hand, users place considerable trust with the Cloud, believing that the cloud service will keep their data private, that data will not be lost or tampered with, and that data will be constantly available and accessible. For example, what happens to all the user data once a cloud service stops or a cloud provider goes out of business?

Similarly, when data is deleted or when an account for a cloud service is cancelled, users have the expectation that the cloud service will remove all data associated with the account, including potential data backups that were taken to prevent data loss. This is, however, hardly true with the Internet today. The rule of thumb for informed users is that once data goes online, it will be there forever in some form or another. Data retention policies can be quite complex; retention times may depend on the type of data, and data is typically coupled with metadata and other information that is used to manage it. The scale of the Cloud further magnifies this problem as data may be geo-replicated across several data centers.

Whereas the general concept of trust spans both the provider-to-tenant and tenant-to-user relationships, however, requirements and expectations are significantly different. For example, the concepts of performance, security, and availability have most likely quite different meanings to a user than to a tenant. Additionally, the relationship between tenants and cloud providers is clearly defined through SLAs, which one could consider as a type of trust safeguards (Columbus 2013). In contrast, there are no contracts between users and service providers. There are, of course, terms and conditions when using a cloud service, but in most cases these are ignored by users. Therefore, trust in the Cloud can take a variety of forms and span different types of interactions between users, tenants, and providers.

One might think that this shift of trust and control from the user to the Cloud is conscious and clearly visible to the user and ultimately reflects a users' choice (when, for example, a mobile application asking for permission to access one's location to provide location services). However, trust relationships can be quite complex, and – especially in the connected world of today's cloud services – user trust may "transfer" to services or applications without the user's explicit knowledge or consent. Users trust the cloud service. The cloud service then trusts the cloud provider that maintains the infrastructure on which the service runs and user data is stored, typically without informing the user. Although this trust composite brings multiple benefits enabling the cloud model, frameworks for managing and seamlessly exposing such trust relationships are missing.

David Clark mentions that "communication in the Internet is a shared experience." This shared experience extends to the Cloud, where multiple entities – providers, tenants, users – interact through implicit or explicit trust relationships. As is discuss later, this paradigm of *shared trust*, this *web of trust* between providers, services, and applications, is omnipresent in every facet of our online experience today.

The Evolution of Computing and Communications

How did we reach the Cloud as the mainstream computing model? Let us take a short detour, quickly looking at some of the computing models and architectures over the previous years.

Computation in the 1950s involved large mainframe computers. To get a feel for the size and cost of computers roughly half a century ago, one of the first – developed by IBM in 1943 known as the Harvard Mark 1 computer – had dimensions of fifty-one feet in length and eight feet in height, weighed roughly five tons, and reached a project cost of $200,000. This was the first automatic digital calculator which was essentially born out of a need to solve a set of nonlinear equations. The computer was able to roughly perform three additions/subtractions per second, but it took six seconds for a multiplication operation.

Of course, computers were not interconnected back then. Interconnection started to materialize several years later with the Advanced Research Projects Agency Network (ARPANET) in 1969, which was a project with the initial aim of interconnecting the Department of Defense's computers in the United States. This led to a research project within the Advanced Research Projects Agency (ARPA) to create a network of computers. As there were only a few powerful computers available, typically located in universities, there was a need to create a network so that a large number of scientists and researchers could access them. In essence, resource sharing was the driving need. In December 1969, the ARPANET comprised four nodes located in the University of California in Los Angeles and Santa Barbara, in Stanford University, and in the University of Utah. In addition to ARPANET, other networks started to develop around the same time in Europe and elsewhere, although they did not follow the same ARPANET technologies.

The Internet's goal was to interconnect all the separate networks that started to appear in the 1970s. This happened with the adoption of TCP/IP in 1983. TCP/IP, developed as part of the ARPANET, was the protocol (actually TCP/IP refers to two protocols almost always used together, TCP – Transmission Control Protocol, and IP – the Internet Protocol) designed to specify how data between two computers are transferred even if they belong to networks of different design or architecture. Eventually, the term Internet was coined to describe all the networks that started to interconnect. The fact that the Internet comprised numerous interconnected networks resulted in one of its key properties – namely, its distributed nature. The Internet is essentially a community of networks without centralized control, a governing body, or a single failure point. Agencies or regimes trying to restrict access in the Internet have undoubtedly experienced the difficulty and frustration in achieving such a goal.

The design of the Internet followed the belief that the underlying network should only be responsible for carrying data and all intelligence and application logic should reside at the end systems. This is known as the *end-to-end principle*, which leads to a dumb network with smart end points. The Internet is also known as a *best-effort network* in which no guarantees are provided about communications by the network. As David Clark also discusses in Chapter 2, these two principles allowed the Internet to thrive because novel applications could be developed at the edge of the network without the need to change the entire Internet infrastructure for them to be deployed. The first Internet applications were, as one might imagine, file transfers, remote processing, and email. The Web as an Internet application had to wait until the 1990s.

In one form or another, these initial Internet applications have survived even in today's complex Internet ecosystem. However, even though the main Internet principles and TCP/IP are still present, the overall character of the network has evolved considerably. Compared to the initial ARPANET goal of interconnecting computers so that users can connect to a specific mainframe or server, users are today interested in connecting to a service, an entity providing a service or a piece of content, irrespective of the computer that is responsible for hosting the content or running the service. From a trust perspective, this implies that, instead of trusting a specific end machine, user trust has shifted toward a higher layer. One needs to trust the actual service and not necessarily the individual machines (or virtual machines) running the service. This will become clearer as we later look at current application trends and, specifically, the Web.

In its beginning, the Internet was an academic network and commercial use was forbidden. However, as the network was growing and the first ISPs started to appear in the 1980s, the pressure to connect with commercial networks increased. This eventually happened in 1995 when the Internet was commercialized. This is less than twenty years ago.

The Internet's growth, along with its openness and distributed nature, meant that its initial trust model and network structure was not viable. As in the real world, trusting a few people you know is quite different from extending your trust to millions of strangers. As David Clark describes, when the Internet grew from a few hundred university nodes to billions of connected machines, constraints on communication started to appear – devices and software solutions such as firewalls and intrusion prevention systems have become an important piece of the Internet puzzle. Such systems effectively prevent connections to and from arbitrary end points, restrictions for which the initial Internet architecture did not account. Similarly, the vast majority of home networks today connect to the internet through NAT-enabled (Network Address Translator) devices, which – among other things – restrict visibility of a home network to the public Internet. In short, in the name of trust and security, the transparency of the initial Internet design has to a large extent perished (Handley 2006).

Computing models have also evolved with the Internet. Traditionally, the most common approach was the *client-server model*, which is still present in most applications today. As the name suggests, a computer server provides a service, which might translate to running an application, hosting content or a Web page, or sharing resources such as CPU or storage. Today, most Internet-connected devices are instead clients, which – through the network – contact server computers. Every time a Web page is requested through a browser, the device running the browser is a client connecting to a Web server. In effect, one can think of a server being time-shared across several clients, which (as discussed) was the original motivation of ARPANET.

Nothing prevents a computer from being a client and a server at the same time for different applications. For example, a computer can run an email client connecting to an email server, while at the same time also running Web server software to serve web content for other computers. However, being a client and a server simultaneously for the same application, essentially sharing one's resources as part of this application, describes the *peer-to-peer* model. In 1999, peer-to-peer applications became famous with the launch of Napster, which was a peer-to-peer file-sharing application for sharing music and mp3 files. Napster allowed computers to connect to one another, without the need for any centralized server, hence its "peer-to-peer" nature. All computers were acting as both clients and servers and facilitated the discovery and easy sharing of music files. Napster quickly became very popular, leading to several other similar applications, such as the KaZaA, Gnutella, eDonkey or BitTorrent peer-to-peer networks, which extended file-sharing to video, software programs, and other files. Eventually, Napster had to shut down in 2001 because of legal and copyright issues brought forward by the Recording Industry Association of America (RIAA). However, several of the other peer-to-peer networks are still active and popular today.

Peer-to-peer applications are not limited to file-sharing. Skype is one of the most prominent peer-to-peer applications. Because one's Internet calls could be served by other peers in the Skype network, the Skype application acted as both a client initiating calls and as a server forwarding calls of other Skype users. Interestingly, the creators of Skype were also the initial developers of the KaZaA peer-to-peer file-sharing application.

From a trust and privacy perspective, the peer-to-peer model most resembles the architecture of the initial Internet. Peer-to-peer networks comprise nodes that implicitly trust one another, without the existence of a central reference point such as a trusted server that mediates peer communications. Trust here pertains to the user expectation that all peers participating in the peer-to-peer application share a common goal – for example, sharing of files and that these files are indeed what their name suggests. In reality, however, this nominal goal might not hold for all participants! What peer-to-peer file-sharing applications exposed in my opinion, is the willingness of users to "sacrifice" a bit of their trust by connecting to several unknown and, most likely in other circumstances, untrusted computers. Participating in peer-to-peer file-sharing networks requires the bypassing of firewalls to prevent connections from arbitrary machines. Because no central trusted component in the system exists, participants can easily inject malicious code or fake content into shared files – a risk which is more or less well-known to participants. But taking these security risks (not to mention the risks of lawsuits from RIAA) was deemed acceptable as the incentive of acquiring favorite songs or movies was of a higher value to users. We see a similar trend with today's online social network services in which some users might give up a bit of their privacy for a better application experience.

Peer-to-peer networks have no single point of failure, which makes them robust to attacks or malfunction of equipment. This is why RIAA has been unable to stop file sharing despite all its legal battles and lawsuits for the past ten years. Napster was an easy target. Because its creators and those maintaining the software and the service were easily identifiable, lawsuits against the company were enough to bring the Napster network down. Most subsequent peer-to-peer file-sharing networks, however, are run by several individual user groups that develop and maintain the service in a distributed, peer-to-peer fashion. This is similar to the open-source software initiatives through which multiple user groups all over the Internet (but unknown to each other) are contributing code for the same computer program.

Their distributed nature and lack of a central point make peer-to-peer networks ideal for providing anonymity. The most prominent anonymity-oriented peer-to-peer network is Freenet, which users can use to publish and retrieve content anonymously; participating users cannot track who is transferring data from whom or decipher what the data is besides the user requesting the data. Such a network is ideal for avoiding censorship or tracking. Instead, in the Internet, when connecting to a Web server, the entity operating the server can determine what data were requested from the server and more or less track where the client is located physically.

Lately, the advancements in the Cloud coupled with the evolution of the Web, as discussed next, have to some extent reduced the popularity of peer-to-peer applications. However, peer-to-peer networks have several desirable properties that render them attractive as the communication or computing model of choice. This is also true outside computing where proposals suggest that even societies should organize based on a peer-to-peer model inspired from the Internet's design (Johnson 2012). On the flipside, trust is a peer-to-peer network's Achilles' heel, as peers need to implicitly trust one another. Yet, as the popularity of file-sharing applications has shown, people are willing to lower their trust bars once presented with the right incentives.

Figure 1. The Internet's Hourglass.

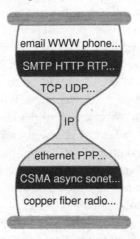

The Web: Evolution and Trends

It is common in the networking community to symbolize the Internet's protocol stack and layered architecture through an hourglass. A multitude of physical layer protocols toward the bottom of the stack that provide ways of sending signals across different hardware technologies are connected to higher-level applications (such as email, the Web, or BitTorrent) through a narrow waist in the middle. This narrow waist abstracts away the idiosyncrasies of lower level protocols exposing a common interface to the applications and protocols above it. Traditionally, the waist mainly comprises the well-known IP and TCP protocols (as previously discussed, commonly referred to together as TCP/IP) that specify how data can be transferred between two computers. Hence, higher-layer applications or protocols that need to transfer data in the Internet need to comply with the specifications of TCP/IP. Although several changes and innovations have occurred at the two ends of the hourglass, where numerous new physical-layer technologies, protocols, and application have appeared over the years, the waist has remained virtually unchanged since the specification of TCP/IP that was standardized in 1982. Today, more than 95 percent of Internet traffic is carried through TCP/IP.

However, recent trends signify that another protocol, an application protocol instead of a transport protocol, appears to be evolving into the Internet's new application waist. The Hypertext Transfer Protocol (HTTP) that powers the World Wide Web (WWW) is informally becoming the new standard on top of which most applications build their communication channel. Indeed, recent reports show that at least half of the Internet's traffic today is HTTP (Labovitz et al. 2010), whereas its share was significantly lower a few years ago when peer-to-peer (file-sharing) applications were dominating (Karagiannis et al. 2004);

this trend is so strong, that one can speculate with reasonable confidence that perhaps in a few years the new Internet's waist of the hourglass will be HTTP/TCP/IP. Academic studies suggest that HTTP could even by itself be the narrow waist of the future Internet (Popa et al. 2010).

What changed and what is so important about HTTP? HTTP is the Web protocol. It specifies how WWW data will be formatted and transferred so that any browser is able to render a Web page. When browsing a Web page, data is transferred from the Web server to the client through HTTP as the application layer protocol (which of course uses TCP/IP as the lower-layer networking protocol; essentially, HTTP is what the browser understands, and TCP/IP is what the network interfaces and devices understand). Obviously then, the rise of HTTP traffic must signify an increasing popularity of Web-based applications. And this is indeed true.

Traditionally, from Tim Berners-Lee's first proposal for the Web in 1989 until just a few years back, Web applications were more or less synonymous to Web-page browsing. Services or applications – such as email, online gaming, online chatting, media streaming, and file transferring and sharing – used to run through their own custom software programs, typically transferring data through distinct, most of the times proprietary, application protocols. Today, however, this is no longer the case. Web browsers are the de facto interface to the most popular applications and services, from online chatting and social networking to video streaming and file sharing. Effectively, the Web browser is the new user Desktop (Google's laptop Chromebook takes this to the extreme by only supporting Web-based applications). The paradigm of "everything on top of the web (HTTP)" is also well aligned with the Cloud; computation, applications, and data reside remotely and are accessed through an interface, which – of course – is the Web-browser.

The ability to offer multiple applications and experiences through the Web and the advent of "Web 2.0" (which is discussed later) led to increasingly complex Web pages. Compared to the early days of the Web in which a Web page mostly consisted of static content comprising text and images, a typical Web page today is a complex, dynamic amalgam of different components, such as audio and video media content, interactive animations, connectors to Social Networking Sites (SNSs), user comments, news tickers, search bars, banners, advertisements, and more. Although this diversity and dynamicity is attractive from a users' perspective, from a system's perspective, rendering a Web page involves a set of mechanisms to collect and display all these components. For example, typing and requesting a URL through a browser leads to a series of data transfers corresponding to all the objects comprising a Web page. Web objects could be as simple as text and images, and as complex as actual code the browser will run on user actions. Some of these objects are visible to the user, whereas some are never to be seen and are hidden from the user (e.g., the code). According to measurement studies today, the number of objects per Web page ranges from a few tens to several hundreds (Butkiewicz et al. 2011).

The notion of shared trust, as discussed for the Cloud, then further applies to this modern Web – trusting a Web page implies trusting all of its individual components. Trust here might refer to the user expectation that components of a Web page will, for example, not be installing malware in the users' computer or attempt identity theft through phishing. And trust relationships might have been straightforward if all components of a Web page belonged to the same entity, but as one might expect, displaying a modern Web page means downloading data from multiple entities. Typical Web sites today employ several third-party components, such as advertising services, analytics that track user activity, and Content Distribution Networks (CDNs) to deliver media content, to name a few. For example, when connecting to facebook.com or cnn.com, not all content of the Web page originates from or belongs to Facebook or CNN. Hence, when constructing a Web page, a browser needs to transfer data and connect to a number of different servers, several of which belong to a variety of entities; and although the user might trust the original owner of a page (i.e., cnn.com), clicking on cnn.com implicitly creates trust relationships between the user and all components of the cnn.com Web page. Note that nothing prevents third-party components of a page from further requesting and embedding objects from yet other parties. Studies have shown that to render typical Web pages, the browser contacts dozens of different third-party servers; for a significant fraction of these pages, most content and Web objects originate from external sources (Butkiewicz et al. 2011).

Hence, as in the cloud model, where trust might transfer from a user to the service provider and then to the cloud provider without explicit user feedback, user trust in the Web is shared across a number of entities the user might or might not otherwise trust. And as in the cloud model where the user is typically ignorant as to whom the cloud provider is, it is similarly quite hard even for expert users to untangle all the hidden actions that occur (and the relationships that these actions imply) after requesting a URL.

Web 2.0 and the Reign of Content – Trends of the New Web

In 1996, one of Bill Gates's articles targeted at Microsoft employees focused on content. Titled by the now well-known quote "Content is King," the article stressed Bill Gates's belief of the importance content will bear in the future and predicted that "content is where I expect much of the real money will be made in the internet." Whereas content as a definition can be used quite broadly in the context of the Internet, Bill Gates focused on "supplying information and entertainment."

Since Bill Gates's article, the Web has changed dramatically, with content being one of the most important drivers of its transformation. This is easily confirmed by looking at simple statistics of popular services. For media content for example, YouTube today serves more than 800 million unique viewers per month who watch an aggregate of more than 4 billion hours of video monthly, whereas Netflix claims 25.1 million subscribers in the United States. Even as early as 2006, traditional media sources like BBC have started noticing a drop in TV viewing times in favor of online media sources,[1] an observation that perhaps led to the BBC iPlayer two years later, offering a free streaming service for BBC programs. Content is also critical in affecting a Web site's popularity and discoverability, because – among other things – search engine results and relative Web site ranking depend significantly on content. The higher the rank for a Web site, the more referrals it will receive from popular search engines. This is why strategies for content Search Engine Optimization (SEO), one of the most important jargon keywords for Web sites today, are decisive on affecting a Web site's visibility.

Perhaps what Bill Gates underestimated in his article was the importance and rise of User Generated Content (UGC). UGC refers to content that is created by the user of a Web site or application instead of the Web site owner. Blogging, forums, user uploaded videos and photographs, wikis, comments, and reviews are characteristic examples of user generated content. User participation and interactivity is now the standard for any Web site, and this was made possible with what is referred to as the "Web 2.0" paradigm. Web 2.0 does not signify a new Web specification, but a conceptual evolution – there was never a Web 1.0 document specifying what the Web is. Web 2.0 abstractly describes Web pages that offer dynamic content and facilitate user participation and interactivity. Web 2.0 encompasses a number of technologies, the most prominent of which was Ajax, which stands for Asynchronous JavaScript and XML (Extensible Markup Language). As the name suggests, Ajax allows for asynchronous transfer of data from the client (browser) to the Web server in the background and vice versa, without the need to refresh all the content of a Web page, hence providing the mechanisms to offer dynamic and interactive user interfaces.

The rise of online social networking sites around 2006 – such as Twitter, LinkedIn, Facebook, and its predecessors, MySpace and Friendster – introduced

---

[1] BBC, "Online video 'eroding TV viewing'", 2006, "http://news.bbc.co.uk/2/hi/entertainment/6168950.stm.

a new type of UGC, which some refer to as the micro-UGC. Status updates, tweets, likes, FourSquare checkins, quick reviews, and star ratings all fall within the micro-UGC concept in which short and quick user engagement provides application content. Although short, this type of content is actually quite powerful as it provides the context within which the content or user action was generated – visibility that applications never had before. Additionally, it provides a fast and unobtrusive mechanism of getting user feedback and data, which when aggregated can prove quite valuable within the realm of Big Data analytics. We talk about Big Data later, but it is UGC and micro-UGC that offer a unique opportunity for applications to understand users, their choices, and the context in which these choices were made. This allows, for example, Amazon to provide accurate customer recommendations based on similar customer preferences or Google/Bing to interactively suggest search keywords and results as one types his/her search query. Some claim that if Content was the King, then Context is the new King.

Obviously, owning and offering popular content as a Web site is not only desirable but can prove quite profitable as well. A significant fraction of today's Web site monetization results from advertisement displays and clicks in the Internet – this is how Google makes money, after all. Therefore, controlling the popular content attracts users who, by clicking or viewing advertisements, generate revenue for the Web site. It is thus not surprising that over the past few years, the Internet has experienced a consolidation of content sources.

This means that content is increasingly concentrated to a small number of players that contribute the majority of the Internet traffic. Large-scale research studies have unveiled an impressive trend (Labovitz et al. 2010). Whereas in 2007, 50 percent of Internet traffic was contributed by thousands of distinct organizations, only two years later in 2009, a mere 150 organizations contributed half of all Internet traffic! According to the researchers, this consolidation has its roots in the rapid rise of content contributors, such as Google, Microsoft, Facebook, or Baidu (the most popular Chinese search engine). In July 2009, Google alone accounted for 6 percent of all Internet traffic. Another 10 percent of traffic is attributed to Content Distribution Networks (Akamai and Limelight being the two most prominent examples) that typically distribute media content. A second trend unveiled in the study is that content providers increasingly try to directly interconnect with the consumer, bypassing intermediaries that, in the Internet context, are companies that provide transit connectivity. In addition to cost savings, getting closer to the user both provides content providers visibility into the user preferences and allows them to more tightly control the user experience (for example, to ensure good application performance by reducing service latency).

Content consolidation bears two main implications for end users. First, as big content providers get bigger and the number of content sources reduces, one might argue that trust may be simplified – it is easier to trust a few known and reputable big players than it is to trust thousands of unknown sources. On the other hand, user privacy is harder to ensure as the big players now have a more comprehensive view of users' online activities. This view is crucial as the offered content is gradually becoming a personalized experience, tailored to the preferences of individual users – search results today can be different across different users depending on their online profile as formed by search engine providers such as Google, Microsoft, or Yahoo!. The Big Data framework that facilitates running complex algorithms in large-scale data centers across thousands of servers makes this feasible today. Second, it is unclear how this consolidation will affect the diversity and wealth of content in the Internet in the future. It is this pluralism that has been one of the key drivers behind the Internet's evolution over the years.

Mobile Computing and Apps

Mobile Internet traffic is exploding, and this is no surprise. From a minimal fraction of 1 percent of the total Internet traffic at the end of 2009, it now accounts for more than 10 percent of the total traffic (according to KCKB 2012). Cisco predicts a 78 percent annual growth from 2011 to 2016, with mobile traffic expected to grow to 10.8 Exabytes per month (Cisco 2012). As one would suspect, media content and the increasing number of connected mobile devices are the two main contributors toward this trend. The report projects that by the end of 2016, the number of connected mobile devices will be more than 10 billion, exceeding the world's population. Besides smart phones, laptops, and tablets, this estimate accounts for all connected devices such as sensors, meters, or other appliances connected typically to cellular and usually referred to as M2M (Machine-to-Machine) technologies. As the name suggests, M2M refers to communication between devices only without human intervention. Examples of such applications include asset tracking, industrial and home automation, and telehealth.

The particularities of mobile devices, such as the small screen, limited battery life, and nonstandard input methods (i.e., no mouse or keyboard) led to the introduction of apps as the main interface to the Internet. The term "app" is simply an abbreviation of "application" and is effectively a program that provides custom-designed access to Web services that take into account the limitations but also advantages of mobile devices. Apps provide an interface both to simple Web sites and to complex Web-based cloud applications.

Mobile apps provide unique opportunities to services or application developers. Mobile devices feature a variety of sensors – such as GPS, accelerometer, compass, proximity, gyroscope, and so on – whose data is readily accessible by apps. In addition to sensor information, mobile devices also contain a wealth of personal information, such as contact lists or call and text histories. Therefore, in addition to user actions relevant to the application itself, apps can obtain context information about these user actions, by, for example, knowing the location of the user or whether the user is stationary or moving. This provides value to the users as well – apps can provide personalized information, customized to fit user intention based on context information. For example, users expect that search results for a dinner venue should be customized to their location and include preferences based on their profile and previous search history.

The availability of this sensor data creates interesting challenges regarding user privacy. Typically, apps request user approval before using extra information. It is unclear, however, how consciously user consent is provided. This is similar to accepting terms and conditions when first using traditional programs or Web sites, to which users most always consent without reading. What is more worrying, however, is the frequent coupling of mobile apps with advertisements and third-party tracking software. Studies have uncovered that user information is commonly passed to such third-party software (Han et al. 2012). Whereas in traditional personal computers users can, for example, block or delete cookies to stop tracking, this is not as straightforward in mobile devices. Researchers have found that even identifiers such as device IDs, which in effect allow user action tracking across apps for the same device, are passed to advertising agencies. In some cases, it is not even clear that such information is required for normal application operation – the researchers note an example of a game with no location requirements that uncovered multiple instances of geo-coordinates of a user to a third-party advertising service.

This is another instance of shared trust in the new online world. Shared trust across services or applications may indeed provide value to the user through personalized, context-aware services. However, there appears to be a lack of effective mechanisms that would truly express user privacy needs and preferences, and at the same time would be transparently enforced by apps – the user should not be asked to consent to pages of agreement terms for every action.

Online Social Networks – The Community is the New King!

According to Boyd and Ellison (2007), the first Online Social Network (OSN) appeared in 1997. SixDegrees.com (named after the famous Milgram experiment[2] that led to the well-known six degrees of separation result) was the first to introduce the notion of a Web site with online profiles and lists of friends, but quickly failed as a service as it could not engage users – there was nothing to do besides accepting friend requests. Although SixDegrees.com closed in 2000, it was after 2001 when the most OSNs started to launch. The most famous of those, similar to today's Facebook, were Friendster and MySpace (launched in 2002 and 2003, respectively). Other well-known services, such as LinkedIn and Last.fm, also launched in 2003.

Both Friendster and MySpace failed to be premier OSNs, although they were first in the space because of different reasons. Friendster was a victim of its own success, having several technical difficulties with scale – supporting millions of users within months of launch is not straightforward! Additionally, fake accounts diluted Friendster's community structure (Boyd & Ellison 2007). MySpace capitalized on Friendster's problems to attract users and it was the first to introduce profile personalization. But it was Facebook that dominated the OSN space for two main reasons. First, it introduced the notion of applications by providing programmatic access through Application Programing Interfaces (APIs) to its infrastructure, thereby incentivizing developers to create different types of experiences such as games or community visualizations to its users. Second, Facebook chose to grow slowly, by creating a strong community structure between its existing users before expanding – it was first available to Harvard students only, to other student and high-school networks later, and then to corporate networks before being available to everyone in the end. This allowed Facebook to gradually build a strong user base with users that were more engaging – its community ties were stronger because it was only about Harvard in the beginning.

Today, it is hard to imagine Web services not employing some form of OSN or community features. These may range from simple features that are visible, such as social connectors that expose other users that have "liked" or commented on a specific Web page, to more complex recommendation systems that implicitly use community knowledge to power a service. This is, for example, how YouTube.com and Last.fm recommend videos or music, respectively, or how online gaming services match opponents so that games are balanced. Other applications are explicitly built on top of communities with crowdsourcing

---

[2] Milgram studied the length of the acquaintance chain between two arbitrary target persons in the United States. The experiment involved asking people to forward a letter to an acquaintance of theirs, with the goal of the letter finally reaching a target recipient. By examining the chains that were completed (letters were actually delivered to the target), Milgram found that the average chain length was approximately six – hence the "six degrees of separation"; although Milgram has not used this actual phrase.

being a prominent example – shared effort toward a common goal. OSN features essentially provide collective and interactive user experiences in which users are no longer browsing the Web in isolation, but with participation of friends and family that is constant and engaging. Sharing experiences, data, and effort with others has become a key concept in the modern Web.

In addition to engagement and enhanced user experience, OSN concepts provide significant insights. Web services can quickly discover new trends or community interests or gauge public opinion by having easy access to data that would otherwise be hard to obtain (for example by measuring likes of a page, a product, or a news article). Additionally, they can employ methodologies to more effectively attract users or even influence them (for example, through targeted marketing campaigns in social media). The community in modern services is so powerful that, in addition to content and context, community is also one of the kings for the modern Web!

The notion of shared trust is embedded in OSNs, and the simple connectedness through a community structure can lead to tough questions regarding trust relationships and privacy. For example, are trust relationships transitive? Accepting a friend request provides access to one's content – status updates, pictures, opinions, and so on; but should a friend-of-a-friend be able to access this content? In the face of modern interconnected Web services, answers to such questions can be even more challenging. Tweets and comments to news article or sites can automatically be uploaded to one's Facebook wall, which can be further accessible by third-party apps. In mobile devices, such information can be coupled with location or other sensor and personal data – a location check-in through a FourSquare mobile app, connected to Twitter and Facebook, forwarded by friends or followers, and accessed by third-party apps or advertising services. Indeed, the reach and power of a simple status update is currently an open problem in sociology and computer science and for network scientists in general. And, of course, this may provide an impressive user experience, but it is unclear both whether this interconnected app experience is desirable at all times and how we can further scope application operations to match user intention.

What Does all this Mean? Big Data has the Answer

Data Analytics

The amount of data generated online is unimaginable. Either generated by users or by sensors and meters through the M2M technologies, IBM estimates that more than 2.5 quintillion bytes of data are created every day, with 90 percent of the data in the world today being created over the past two years alone! Irrespective of whether such estimates are hyperboles or not, a simple look at the most popular services today confirms the overall trend – Google answers more than 1 billion queries per day, more than 72 hours of video is uploaded to YouTube every minute, Twitter handles half a billion tweets per day, Facebook's 1 billion users have produced more than 1 trillion likes and 219 billion uploaded photos.

Big Data as a computing term refers exactly to making sense of such massive volumes of diverse data that are generated at unprecedented rates. Although the term "Big" dominates in the definition, the IT industry typically refers to the three "Vs" of Big Data – velocity, variety, and volume – to best express the Big Data concept. Big Data sums up all aspects of such massive datasets – from mechanisms to capture, format, and store the data, to technologies to manage and efficiently process it; from tools to analyze massive datasets, to complex machine-learning algorithms to distill useful information out of them to improve business practices. Big Data typically refers to data processing across several servers; at the extreme, this could reflect data processing at the data center scale where hundreds of thousands of servers could be involved in analyzing a single dataset – for example, analyzing the Web graph to create a search index that is used to produce results for online search queries.

The importance of Big Data stems from the belief that optimizing business strategies through data analytics can lead to competitive advantages, and hence increased profits and returns. McKinsey estimates that retailers, by understanding Big Data, can increase their operating margin by more than 60 percent and refer to Big Data as the next frontier for innovation, competition, and productivity (McKinsey 2011). With Big Data still in its infancy, it is unclear whether such estimates will prove realistic or not. However, examples of data analytics are already present across diverse types of businesses. Examples include Walmart's use of pricing, economic, demographic, and weather data analytics to adapt sales (Lohr 2012); niche applications like sport analytics through the usage of slow-motion video cameras, heart monitors, and shoes sensors in athletics; food analytics to fuel innovation in restaurants; and even Twitter mood predictions to predict the stock market and measure the impact of marketing campaigns.

Factors and Frameworks

Three main factors contributed to the craze for data analytics and the boom of Big Data. First, there is the wealth of generated data previously discussed. Second, lower computing costs compared to the past, and the advancements in cloud and distributed computing technologies made it feasible and cost-effective for organizations to collect, store, and quickly process data. Put simply, large-scale, real-time analysis of data was not feasible in the past. Third, the realization that machine-generated data can provide valuable business insights and possible competitive advantages. This data does not necessarily refer to newly developed data sources, such as the lately introduced Internet-connected sensors, but also to previously unexplored and ignored pieces of information such as machine logs or records that were generated as part of normal business operations.

The 3Vs of Big Data summarize its technological challenges – data is produced at high frequency, massive scale, and huge varieties and formats. As such, organizing this data through traditional storage and analysis tools – such as relational databases – is practically infeasible. Relational databases are well-suited for storing and managing well-organized data that can be described based on a priori decided schema – imagine well-structured data stored in tables of formally defined rows and columns. Instead, Big Data refers to unstructured data, typically stored in simple text files not strictly tied to any predefined schemas, where any character can be a text-delimiter for separating a text line into columns, and in general arbitrary transformation of data is allowed – imagine processing data representing a users' Facebook wall and Twitter feeds or server logs with raw event information. Although such data sources might seem unrelated, Big Data aspires to combining such seemingly unrelated data sources to potentially increase system efficiency and lower costs for large distributed applications. As an example, this is what Big Data graph partitioning algorithms aim to achieve by producing an efficient mapping of user data to storage servers; that is, identifying closely related users at the community level allows for storing their data in servers in the same rack in the data center to minimize cross-rack communications, thus reducing service latency and communication costs. Identifying such relationships could be achieved by simply examining friends lists, but also the strength of a relationship could be better inferred by analyzing one's tweets or comments; the latter type of analysis hints toward the complications of processing unstructured data as they represent free-form, human-generated text.

MapReduce is the framework most commonly associated with Big Data processing. Originally developed by Google, MapReduce specifies a programming model to parallelize large-scale processing of data across several servers, typically referred to as a MapReduce cluster. As the name suggests, MapReduce essentially comprises two main operations: (1) a Map function specifies how pieces of data are transformed and processed in parallel across the cluster servers, and (2) a Reduce phase collects the output of the map processing and specifies an aggregation function to form the final output. Imagine, for example, a simple word-count application for a huge text corpus. Several map processes running across multiple servers process a small piece of the whole data corpus by performing an initial counting of words. Each reducer is then responsible for the final counting for part of the corpus. For example, a reducer that is responsible for counting all words starting with A, will receive the relevant input from all mappers that have processed words starting with A, and will aggregate their intermediate results. The most well-known instantiation of MapReduce is the java-based implementation Apache Hadoop, which is offered as open-source software. Cloud-based offerings of MapReduce are currently available in most of the main cloud providers, such as Amazon EC2 or Microsoft Azure.

Conclusions

Understanding and predicting user and customer behavior is the Holy Grail, and for enterprises and online services, Big Data promises deep and timely insights. Through analyzing and correlating data from a variety of sources reflecting both user activities across platforms, devices, and applications, as well as internal business processes, organizations have the ability to improve the quality of operations and decision making, quickly discover new trends and spot opportunities that can ultimately increase margins and revenue.

However, getting lost in data can be easy. Processes to store, manage, secure, analyze, summarize, and visualize data in a scalable way become crucial when dealing with voluminous data, and more so if data is produced in real time. Challenges posed by Big Data are deemed so important that reports have started to caution about the lack of Big Data talent (McKinsey 2011) and regard the Data Scientist "as The Sexiest Job of the 21st Century" (Davenport & Patil 2012)! Asking the right questions is key, as is respecting customer privacy and sensitive data by ensuring that information does not leak. From a business perspective, Big Data essentially pushes organizations to be flexible and adaptive to trends and customer needs; this implies that corresponding processes to achieve the required flexibility need to be in place to capitalize on the insights the data offer.

From the user perspective, Big Data promises applications and services that are truly personalized to user needs and preferences. Interconnected devices, applications, and experiences allow the collection of user data in a holistic way, which allows for accurate user profiling. Personalized services imply better recommendation services, such as targeted discount coupons or shopping offers to match user interests, user interfaces that are automatically customized to user preferences, and filtering engines that offer information that is scoped to user interests. As David Clark suggested in Chapter 2, online identity will play a critical role here, because users will be tied to their identity, and it would be these online personas for which such services will be provided and tailored. Even today, two people asking the same question to an online search service will most likely receive different sets of answers based on their online profiles. Similarly, displayed advertisements and prices are customized to user profiles as seen across different Web sites (Mikians et al. 2012). Big Data and the Cloud can easily extend such practices to account for the device used, the present location, the weather, user mood as derived from Twitter, and so on; news aggregator algorithms can display different sets of news articles for different users depending on user previous browsing patterns or "likes"; online radio stations or streaming services can offer distinct content across users.

Aggregation of user data creates further challenges for user privacy. It should be acceptable, even desirable, for Big Data to offer insights to organizations at an aggregate level. However, Big Data also facilitates zooming into individual people's lives, potentially uncovering private information by combining diverse data sources. This can be a grey area as to what is and what is not acceptable from a user's perspective. Especially, as younger people grow up in a constantly connected online environment, developing the awareness of whether a piece of information is or should be in the private versus the public domain is a continuing challenge.

The extent of such content personalization has spurred numerous debates as to where this new online world is leading us. Does this new face of the Internet enable an increasingly diverse online community and collective intelligence extending the Wikipedia model (see Chris Anderson's *The Long Tail* [2006] or Don Tapscott's and Anthony Williams's [2006] arguments), or is it making us more stupid as Nicholas Carr (2010) would argue? Machine-learning algorithms understanding human intention and facilitating personalization may be fascinating, but how easy will it be for users to discover new information, outside of their customized content silos once they have been assigned a specific online persona? News article are customized to our political and religious beliefs, and our Twitter feeds follow people with potentially similar experiences or opinions. Ironically, as the diversity and pluralism of the information available in the Internet might increase, it might also be harder for users to discover or even be aware of it. As in most cases, the truth lies probably somewhere in the middle.

4

Trust as a Methodological Tool in Security Engineering

George Danezis

Introduction

Ken Thompson was the 1984 recipient of the Turing Award, the equivalent of the Nobel Prize in Computer Science. His recognized contributions include the design, while at Bell Labs, of the UNIX operating system, that later led to the free software flagship Linux, and today Android, which has the largest share of the smartphone market. Yet, in his acceptance address, Thompson did not choose to talk about operating system design, but instead about computer security, and specifically "trust." His thoughts were later collected in an essay entitled "Reflections on Trusting Trust" (Thompson, 1984), which has become a classic in the computer security literature. In this work, Thompson examines to what extent one can trust – in an intuitive sense, but as we will see, also a technical sense – a computer system. He recounts how computer systems are built on layers of hardware, but also by layers of software – computer code that provide instructions for how they should perform high-level operations, such as writing a document or loading a Web page. How could anyone foresee what these devices could do under different circumstances? First, they would have to examine what the hardware would do under all conditions. Although this is expensive, it is possible, as hardware is composed of fixed arrangements of wires, silicon, and plastic. Naively, one could assume that software could also be examined in a similar fashion: by reading the source code of the software to understand how it would behave.

Thompson argues that this is not sufficient. Source code is a high-level representation of the instructions that are processed by the computer hardware. Another program, the compiler, translates those high-level instructions into machine code. A malicious compiler writer could therefore introduce into this translation a deliberate error – or "backdoor" – making the system behave in a way that is observable neither though examining the hardware nor the high-level source code of the software. Surely then, the compiler itself should be examined for such faults or malice. Yet, the compiler is also written in a high-level language that is compiled to build the compiler. It is often the case that a compiler compiles itself. Therefore, one would have to go a long way back in the engineering history of the compiler, starting from the first fragments of hand-written machine code, and trace forward every change to the compiler, to make sure that no backdoor was ever introduced leading to unpredictable behavior in the final system under examination.

It turns out this task is nearly impossible. Computer systems and compilers – particularly in the UNIX world – have evolved from each other since the original design of the system in the 1970s. One would have to examine pretty much every piece of software from the beginning of this era to become conclusively satisfied that no such back door is present in a system today.

This conclusion is as bleak to computer security professionals, as it is puzzling to non-experts. Why would anyone seriously consider such an unlikely event? Who would plant such a backdoor in the hope that it might lead to some unexpected or malicious behavior in the future? Furthermore, why consider that trust is about an absolute certainty about the behavior of a system under all circumstances? A more casual notion of "trust" may seem more relevant to most users; namely being able to foresee what a system would do under reasonable conditions, and mostly from past experiences.

To fully appreciate Thompson's argument, and its impact on the computer security community, we must look at the special role "trust" plays in the process of security engineering. In that context, intuitive notions of trust are mixed with technical definitions, as well as methodologies relying on establishing whether specific pieces of equipment, software, people, processes and even abstract mathematics are in fact to be "trusted."

Secure Systems and the Trusted Computing Base

Secure systems operate within a context of adversity. Central to the notion of a secure system is the security policy that describes what the correct operation of the system is, what should happen under different conditions, and – conversely – what should not happen. What differentiates secure systems from safety-critical systems is the assumption that a motivated and strategic adversary exists that will try to make the system deviate from its security policy. Whereas safety-critical systems can be modeled according to the probability of the natural occurrence of "acts of god," security critical systems cannot.

For example, it might be perfectly adequate to avoid a button being accidentally pressed to cover it with a lid, as the probability of accidentally lifting the lid and pressing the button is seriously reduced. On the other hand, to avoid deliberate misuse of a button might require the lid being secured by a key only available to authorized parties. A well-crafted security policy contains a specialized discussion describing the capabilities of the adversary against which the policy must hold. This section is often called the "threat model." Interestingly, the threat model does not describe the intentions or motivations of the adversary, but only their capabilities. It is implied that the intention is to violate any aspect of the security policy. The threat model also does not enumerate the ways in which the adversary may deploy their capabilities to violate the policy: it is assumed that they will strategically deploy such capabilities to best violate the policy – and the secure system must withstand any strategy within the means of the adversary in the threat model.

We should take a step back and ask ourselves: "Why not consider either the motivations of the adversary?" Intuitively this may lead to better security systems. Defining a security policy relates as much to business concerns, overall risk management, insurance, and liability as to the technological basis that an organization uses to function. For this reason, a security policy is drafted by a security manager that takes into account both the likely motivations of the adversary and repercussions for an organization of different threats. It is not traditionally the role of security engineers to perform this risk management task. Their role is to build components and systems that can operate as prescribed within the policy, despite the best efforts of an adversary with defined capabilities to detail them.

This separation between the security manager and the security engineer is near absolute when an off-the-shelf system is purchased, because the security manager has little influence on its development. At the same time, off-the-shelf systems will only be configurable to a point, and may only support a restricted set of security policies. On the other hand, interactions between security managers and security engineers are more intense when custom solutions are built to support an organization. In those cases, the security policy – as set by the security manager – and its cost-effective technical feasibility – as determined by security engineers – influence each other quite intimately.

Once a security policy and a threat model are set, how can one go about showing that a system is secure? This is probably the most difficult task and is the core competency of security architects and engineers. It was recognized early on (Brooks 1987) that arguing that a large and complex computer system has any property at all – let alone in the face of a motivated adversary – is hard.[1] Therefore, a security argument is often made by designing a system in such a way that only a small subsystem's correct operation guarantees that the security policy is not violated. The hopefully small core of the system on which the security policy relies is called the Trusted Computing Base (TCB). Conversely, one could say that the TCB actually includes anything that can violate the security policy. If the adversary has the capability to tamper, read, or somehow interact in an unauthorized way with part of the TCB, then they can violate the security policy.

We will use as an example a well-known policy for protecting the confidentiality of documents, the Bell-LaPadula Policy (BLP) (Bell 1996), often found in government or the military systems. In BLP, all documents are tagged with a level of sensitivity, or their classification, which ranges from "public," to "restricted," to "confidential," to "secret," and to "top secret," in ascending order of sensitivity. Users of the system are also each assigned a clearance status from the same categories. The policy states that during normal operation, information must not flow down the level of classification. So for example, a user with secret clearance can read documents with public to secret classification, but not top secret documents. Similarly (and rather strangely), a user with secret clearance can write documents with secret or top secret classification, but cannot write a document at the restricted level. Writing information down is a special operation called declassification that can only be performed by specific authorized parties.

The threat model in the BLP may have deep repercussions on how such a system is implemented. For example, if the adversary is considered to be external to the organization, and not an insider, BLP can be implemented simply by providing each employee a computer at each level along with guidelines for not writing information down from, say, a secret terminal to the public terminal. On the other hand, if the threat model stipulates that some of the personnel may be controlled by the adversary, a system might have to place the secret computer systems in a different room, with armed guards searching any personnel exiting the room for media that could be used to leak information down to a public terminal.

In both cases, the technical TCB can be minimized by not allowing the separate computer systems to communicate with each other, except through well-defined and monitored networks. One such device was the "NRL Pump,"

---

[1] In fact, even properties that one may consider trivial – such as whether a running program will eventually terminate or whether a process in a distributed system will make any progress toward a set goal – are generally very hard to demonstrate for larger systems, unless they are built in a very formalized and restricted manner.

a one-way network device that allowed information from lower confidentiality levels to be copied to higher confidentiality levels, but not the other way around. In that case the computer systems at each level of confidentiality can behave in arbitrary manners: the technical TCB is composed of both the Pump and the physical separations of the system from any other device; both of which are hopefully easier to verify than arbitrary large computer systems.

For a security engineer's perspective, the personnel reading and writing documents in the first case is within the TCB – that is, users could violate the security policy if they were to be corrupt, but they are "trusted" not to be at the level of the security policy. In the second case, users are explicitly not "trusted" to assist in implementing the security policy and cannot be relied on for the correct functioning of the TCB. It is the role of the security system to prevent the security policy being violated despite their hostile actions and to ensure they can only transfer information down at a very low rate. On the other hand, the armed guards searching personnel are in the TCB of the second system, in that their failure to search for removable media may lead to policy violations.

It is obvious from these simple, but quite real, examples that the TCB in fact contains much more than computers and software, but also people, processes, training, and so on. This brings traditional notions of "trust," as in how one can trust people, to the heart of the computer security problems. Yet, those are often resolved at the level of the security policy, and are not a concern of the security engineer. For example, vetting personnel and assigning a clearance to users is performed outside the computer system, and is simply a given for the computer. In addition to being a simple illustrative example, it turns out the BLP multilevel security policy, is of particular historical importance. In 1983, the year before Thompson was awarded the Turing Prize, the U.S. Department of Defense issued Trusted Computer System Evaluation Criteria (TCSEC) guidelines, also known as the "Orange Book."[2] Those guidelines were used to assess the security of systems processing classified information, on the basis of slightly more general BLP multilevel security policy than the one previously discussed. At high levels of assurance, the Orange Book stipulates that a Trusted Computer System, must minimize its TCB, and even verify it using formal methods.

It is against the backdrop of the Orange Book design principles that Ken Thompson builds his argument, that to trust a computer system, even a minimal TCB, you have to trust the compiler, the complier and the tools that built the compiler, and so on. Thus, the minimal TCB is in fact an unattainable myth: by the time all components that can violate the policy are taken into

[2] National Security Institute – 5200.28-STD Trusted Computer System Evaluation Criteria.

account, the TCB is large and pretty much impossible to verify. Furthermore, any verification effort could only lead to assurances about the software or hardware components – not the people and procedures on which a security system relies. Thus, the Orange Book approach is, in spirit at least, unfeasible to establish whether or not a computer system is to be trusted (or whatever it is that the Orange Book means by "trusted").

Who Trusts Whom, and for What?

The Orange Book was hugely influential in terms of thinking about trusted systems, but the frame of mind it evoked has not been overall positive. The government and ministry of defense was mainly concerned about a very narrow set of properties – namely, confidentiality through the application of a BLP multilevel security policy. A system designed by an external company was deemed trusted by the government if it reliably and securely implemented such a policy. In that setting, there was a clear government organization that purchased or commissioned a system, with a clear security policy that benefitted them.

On the other hand, a number of commercial computer applications, services, or infrastructure do not have a single client, and their security policies need to reflect the needs of a multitude of users. This opens the question of who sets the security policy. Who verifies that the system securely implements the security policy? And what does it even mean that one "trusts" the system?

An example technology that was developed and widely deployed in the early 1980s is first-generation cellular phones. In terms of security policy and quality of protection, the cellular system was terrible on two fronts. On one hand, it was easy for crooks to clone phones, and use the account of unsuspecting users to make expensive long distance calls. On the other hand, privacy was poorly protected as the calls transmitted over the air interfaces were available for anyone to intercept and listen to. Interestingly, the first issue was hurting the telecommunication companies as disputed bills were a huge liability. The second issue was a sore point for customers, but they had no recourse to the telecommunication operator when their privacy was possibly violated.

The second generation GSM mobile phone system partly improved the security of mobile telephony in truly interesting and telling ways. First, the policy and implementation mechanism to prevent cloning was strengthened. The now-familiar subscriber identity module (SIM) card was introduced, which the handset uses it to authenticate itself to the network. In that respect, the SIM card is the TCB that implements the "no cloning" policy for GSM at quite a high management and manufacturing cost at the time. On the surface, GSM technologies also strengthened privacy. At a very high level, security policy stated that the communications were to be encrypted to prevent eavesdropping. The catch was to be found in the underlying threat model.

First, GSM communications were only encrypted between the handset and the telecommunication operator base station – namely, just over the air interface. After that, the voice and data were decoded and traveled over the remaining network, but were susceptible to eavesdropping. This is in sharp contrast with an alternative possible approach that might allow for calls to be encrypted end-to-end between handsets, making interception at any point of the network difficult.

Secondly, the mandated encryption algorithm, A5/2, was purposefully crippled to satisfy export control regulations around cryptography. This meant that an adversary with moderate computational power would be able to break through the encryption and read the data. Later, it was discovered that all variants of the A5/1 cipher had serious cryptographic weaknesses that allow us today to break through the encryption in real time.

Finally, the network does not authenticate itself to the handheld device. This means that, although it is not possible to make calls pretending to be another phone (cloning), the handset has no way of ensuring it is talking to a genuine, let alone trusted, network. This created a market in active interception equipment: medium-range base stations that pretended to be a home network to a target device. Once the handheld device is fooled into pairing with the rogue network, interception can occur at will. Law enforcement and intelligence services have used this technique as a means of spying on calls for some time, and now the equipment necessary is within the reach of individuals.[3]

What is the tale that GSM is telling us about trusting computerized systems? It is clear that the mobile network needs to jointly satisfy needs of both end-customers and operators. They are both security properties in that both cloning prevention and privacy protection need to stand against strategically motivated adversaries. Yet, cloning prevention disappeared overnight, whereas privacy continues to be a problem today. Is GSM a trusted system, from a security engineering perspective? Surely, it is from the point of view of the operator. From the point of view of the privacy-concerned customer, however, it is less clear: if the threat model is amateur eavesdropping on the air channel it might be satisfactory. If, on the other hand, the threat model includes entities

---

[3] Sean Hollister, "Hacker Intercepts Phone Calls with Homebuilt $1,500 IMSI Catcher, Claims GSM is beyond Repair." Posted on July 31, 2010 at www.engadget.com. See also Chris Ziegler, "Meganet's Dominator I Snoops on Four GSM Convos at Once, Fits in Your Overnight Bag." Posted on May 10, 2010 at www.engadget.com.

with significant computational power, such as the telecommunication operator itself, the government that can compel them to eavesdrop on a call – or an adversary with the sophistication (and budget) to acquire an active rogue base station the system – cannot be trusted to provide privacy to communications.

The outcomes of engineering GSM security is a warning sign: a system can be perfectly adequate from the perspective of one party, and totally trusted, while not fulfilling the need of a whole other class of users. The question "is the system trusted?" is under-defined from a security engineering perspective in many ways: By whom? For what property? Against what adversary?

In 2006, Ross Anderson and Tyler Moore introduced the field of *Security Economics* (Anderson & Moore 2006). They observed that security problems tend to occur in large systems when the actors that have the power to secure the system are simply not incentivized to do so. In the GSM example, this manifests itself in two forms. The GSM system was financed by Telco operators and the International Telecommunication Union (ITU), which was composed of government representatives. The operators were both in a position to influence the design of GSM and fully incentivized to protect their revenue by securing billing against cloning. On the other hand, they had no specific interest in privacy, beyond safeguarding the credibility of the system. Governments and law enforcement agencies, on the other hand, have full incentives to maintain wiretapping and eavesdropping capabilities and have the ability to mandate technologies that allow for those through conditions on the licensing spectrum. The end users who might be keen on privacy simply never had any ability to influence the standards. In fact, the details of the technical privacy protections in GSM, namely the A5 algorithms, were kept secret from their inception in 1986 to 1996. As soon as they were reverse engineered, they were found to be cryptographically weak (Golić 1997).

A cynic may say that whoever commissions the system – that is, whoever funds the system or deploys the system – simply states its security policy. This policy will reflect their concerns and aims, no matter what needs other users of the system may have. Furthermore, even when other concerns are taken into account, the subtleties of the threat model are important.

Trusted Computing, Trusted Hardware, TPM, and DRM

The GSM security model and implementation is a classic case of a system with many stakeholders with different security objectives. In some cases, not only do the security properties required by different parties diverge, but they are actually opposed. A hint of this is present in the need to prevent cloning in the

GSM system. Cloning is bad for business both because it lowers the reliability of billing, but also because it seriously limits the tariff structure the operator can implement. For example, an operator may choose to allow a user to call certain numbers for a flat fee per handset. A user cloning their mobile phone allows others to call those numbers at no cost to them, and no additional cost to the user. Thus, a user may actively wish to clone their phone. The SIM is not only there to prevent third parties from stealing credit from an unsuspecting user, but also to prevent the user from cloning their own device.

Protecting the SIM from the user requires special tamper-resistant hardware. The SIM is designed to resist low-cost attempts to clone the secret information inside it, even if someone has physical access to it. The SIM is just one of a class of trusted hardware devices that are meant to offer a form of authentication or integrity. As we will see, these devices have an ambivalent track record in terms of the security policy goals they serve.

In general, authentication is the process by which a user establishes some form of their identity within a computer system. This "identity" may be very limited. For example, many online news services offer the ability to register and then log in to leave comments. In that case, authentication ensures that the person registered is the same person that comments on the article. Yet, any other information provided at registration time is usually voluntary, in the sense that the news service cannot readily check its validity (and it would be imprudent to rely on it).

A robust authentication is a mechanism that can be used to support security policies that benefit the user. For example, a user may store their files online and wish to be the only one able to retrieve them. Authentication needs to withstand an adversary that tries to impersonate the user to access the stored files. On the other hand, authentication may be in place to support a security policy that benefits another entity, or even that is not in the strict interest of the user. In our example, a news service – a subscription system – may be implemented by only allow paying users to access the full content of the news service. In that case, the user is authenticating to prove to the service they have paid the subscription – a property that the news service cares about, but the user does not have any stake in. In fact, the user may wish to share their subscription information with family and friends. This is in their interest, but not in the interest of the news service. Suddenly, the threat model of the system should include the capabilities of users who wish to bypass authentication, clone their credentials, or access content without paying the subscription. More often than not, authentication plays a dual role. On the one hand, it protects assets of the users and confers privileges. On the other hand, it provides a log of activity to the service provider, linking actions in the system with specific users, with the aim to detect any deviation from policy, and eventually ascribing blame, shifting liability, and taking punitive actions.

Another example of the latter uses of authentication is the introduction of Chip & PIN technology in UK banking. Unlike previous technologies that based bank cards on magnetic strip technology that was easy to clone, Chip & PIN cards are based on a smart card that is difficult to clone. SIM cards and Chip & PIN cards use the same underlying technologies in that respect. Because authentication using a Chip & PIN card is considered unclonable, more liability has been shifted to customers. Whereas a disputed transactions was previously considered routine and canceled upon customer request, a logged Chip & PIN transaction with the card present and PIN-verified is difficult to contest as not having been authorized by the right customer.

The conflict between security policies and user expectations has been greatest around Digital Rights Management (DRM) and "Content Protection" technologies. Information goods – such as recorded music, movies, e-books, software, and computer games – lack characteristics of other private goods: they are naturally non-excludable and non-rivalrous, as they can be copied and shared without depriving the original owner from the good and without loss of quality. Controversially, the aim of many multimedia security technologies is to prevent such items from becoming public goods by enforcing a security policy that artificially imposes scarcity, by preventing copying and specifically online copying. This is a policy that primarily supported the interests of the content-producing industries, including industries that gained a certain market position through the control of traditional distribution channels.

In fact, once the object of a security policy is to support a business model that may not even exist without it, the potential for business innovation is boundless. For example, DVD videos were encrypted with keys that only certified devices had access to (Bloom et al. 1999). This not only created a market in DVD videos that was free of copying, but also a market in DVD equipment that was difficult to disrupt. The certified DVD players were tested to ensure that they enforce the policy prohibiting copying, but they also went further. Each DVD was region coded, and a certified player was to not play a movie if it was from a different region. Not only did the security policy transformed a public good into a private good, but it created restrictions on the conventional property rights of the users as to where they could see or resell the media. More modern DRM systems are even stricter. Although it is easy to at least lend a DVD to a friend, the same is not true for a lot of content available from online services – for e-books or music, for example. In such services, the policy often does not allow lending (even exclusionary lending) or reselling. Content is in fact licensed to users; it is not even owned as a traditional private good.

It is clear from the examples of DVD players, e-book readers, and dedicated games consoles that implementing a security policy around DRM requires tight control over the hardware of the devices that can process them. Where does that leave general-purpose computing? Could you ever trust a PC to play media without copying it? This was in part the aim of including a trusted platform module (TPM) component in most personal computers. The TPM monitors what software is running on the PC, and can remotely attest what the configuration is (Coker et al. 2011). This, in turn, could be used to load only specific decoding keys or transfer content if the configuration was trusted. In practice, no real-world system has used this feature, because of the familiar problem of the size of the TCB.

Attesting that a computer runs a specific operating system does not provide very strong security guarantees, because it is impossible to ensure that every component works correctly, in the sense that no combination of malicious actions could lead to copying of content. As such, content industries have been traditionally reluctant to support content delivery on personal computers. On the other hand, the users of services with a primary purpose of copying and sharing music (often of doubtful legality) have blossomed: for example, BitTorrent traffic accounts for 30 to more than 50 percent of Internet traffic, depending on the region (Schulze & Mochalski 2009).

What does it mean in that context to "trust" a DRM system? To some extent it means it will enforce the security properties of its designer, irrespective and often in conflict, with the wishes of others, including its owner! Sometimes this may be for the overall public good – because there is no public funding of creative works like books or films, it might be the case that the market would collapse without protections. On the other hand, it might just mean that the market would transform into a different business model of experienced goods, support, or interactive entertainment. But, one can be sure that the DRM systems were never designed to serve a public purpose that did not directly benefit those who commissioned them. That is, families that wanted to share them, libraries that wanted to lend them, public archives that required their long-term preservation, or blind people who need specialized technologies to access them were simply never represented in their design. The idea of trusting such technologies may seem paradoxical to these constituencies.

Trusting Numbers

As we have seen, and in many cases, arguing that a system is secure comes down to ensuring that the physical security of the system is guaranteed, through traditional security measures (doors, locks, concrete, guards, dogs, and so on) or trusted hardware (such as SIMs), as well the software ensuring logical operations functions correctly. The last one is difficult, hence the need to keep the software TCB as small as possible. Thompson argues that even then absolute certainty about its behavior is quasi-impossible.

This was very much the dominant architecture of mainframes popular in the 1970s. For example, a university service would run a mainframe in a secure room that was accessed only by authorized personnel. Students or researchers would access the mainframe through thin terminals in another room. The key aspect of the software TCB that had to function correctly was the authentication mechanism: upon approaching a terminal, a user would be prompted for their username and password that would then be checked on the mainframe to grant specific privileges to the session.

This raises a key question that seems a bit pedantic at first. Is the communication wire that connects the terminals to the mainframe part of the TCB? In the 1970s university setting, the answer could be "yes, but who cares?" If an adversary can see the traffic on the wires, they can intercept the username and passwords of legitimate users and impersonate them. Yet, the threat model may well exclude physical attacks on the wire, which are on university premises and in buildings. A risk assessment may conclude that students and researchers may not be willing to commit property damage, vandalism, and burglary to interfere with a computer system. Because the wire part of the TCB security is not within the threat model, the wire part of the authentication system can be deemed secure.

Now, let's fast forward ten years and consider this same system being used in the mid-1980s, as users want to use this mainframe from their own homes using modems over the telephone network or even the Internet, which is rising in popularity. Suddenly, the wire is no more protected by the university's physical security, but instead relies on the confidentiality of the telephone network or the Internet service provider network. If we fast forward another ten years, to the 1990s, the home Internet connection has now become wireless. Anyone can eavesdrop on it with a radio. The security of the authentication protocol now relies on the adversary not having a $10 device and being in radio range with anyone using the mainframe remotely.

What is the point of all this? First, the changing technological environment changes the nature of the threats. Underlying technologies (such as communications) evolve, but legacy systems are slow to change. As a result, cracks appear between the assumptions made when drafting policies and hypothesizing threat models and the reality of the system as used and implemented at any specific future time.

Secondly, assumptions of physical security are brittle, and should be subject to the same minimization principle as software TCBs. Although it is possible to secure a room, or even wires running to the room next door, it is impossible to physically secure the wires of a whole campus, city, or continent. Furthermore, some technologies (such as wireless transmissions) are irresistibly convenient, but simply cannot be secured physically. A different mechanism, traditional cryptography, has to be used to argue they are secure.

Cryptography has been used for centuries to secure military, diplomatic, and commercial communications that may fall into the hands of enemies and competitors (Kahn 1996). Traditional cryptography concerns itself with a simple problem: Alice wants to send a message to Bob over some communication channel that may be observed by Eve, but without Eve being able to read the content of the message. To do this, Alice and Bob share a short key, say a passphrase or a poem. Alice then uses this key to scramble (or encrypt) the message, using a cipher, and sends the message to Bob. Bob is able to use the shared key to invert the scrambling (or "decrypt") and recover the message. The hope is that Eve, without the knowledge of the key, will not be able to unscramble the message, thus preserving its confidentiality.

It is important to note that in this traditional setting we have not removed the need for a secure channel. The shared key needs to be exchanged securely, because its compromise would allow Eve to read messages. Yet, the hope is that the key is much shorter than the messages subsequently exchanged, and thus easier to transport securely once (by memorizing it or by better physical security). What about the cipher? Should the method by which the key and the message are combined not be kept secret? In "La Cryptographie Militaire" in 1883, Auguste Kerckhoffs stated a number of principles, including that only the key should be considered secret, not the cipher method itself (Kerckhoffs 1883). Both the reliance on a small key and the fact that other aspects of the system are public is an application of the minimization principle we have already seen in secure system engineering. It is by minimizing what has to be trusted for the security policy to hold that one can build and verify secure systems – in the context of traditional cryptography, in principle, this is just a short key.

Kerckhoffs argues that only the key, not the secrecy of the cipher is in the trusted computing base. But a key property of the cipher is relied on: Eve must not be able to use an encrypted message and knowledge of the cipher to recover the message without access to the secret key. This is very different from previous security assumptions or components of the TCB. It is not about the physical restrictions on Eve, and it is not about the logical operations of the computer software and hardware that could be verified by carful inspection. It comes down to an assumption that Eve cannot solve a somehow difficult mathematical problem. Thus, how can you trust a cipher? How can you trust that the adversary cannot solve a mathematical problem?

To speak the truth, this was not a major concern until relatively recently, compared with the long history of cryptography. Before computers, encoding and decoding had to be performed by hand or using electromechanical machines. Concerns such as usability, speed, cost of the equipment, and lack of decoding errors were the main concerns in choosing a cipher. When it comes to security, it was assumed that if a "clever person" proposes a cipher, then it would take someone much cleverer than them to decode it. It was even sometimes assumed that ciphers were of such complexity that there was "no way" to decode messages without the key. The assumption that other nations may not have a supply of "clever" people may have to do with a colonial ideology of nineteenth and early twentieth centuries. Events leading to the 1950s clearly contradict this: ciphers used by major military powers were often broken by their opponents.

In 1949, Claude Shannon set out to define what a perfect cipher would be. He wanted it to be "impossible" to solve the mathematical problem underlying the cipher (Shannon 1949). The results of this seminal work are mixed. On the positive side, there is a perfect cipher that, no matter how clever an adversary is, cannot be solved – the one-time pad. On the down side, the key of the cipher is as long as the message, must be absolutely random, and can only be used once. Therefore the advantage of short keys, in terms of minimizing their exposure, is lost and the cost of generating keys is high (avoiding bias in generating random keys is harder than expected). Furthermore, Shannon proves that any cipher with smaller keys cannot be perfectly secure. Because the one-time pad is not practical in many cases, how can one trust a cipher with short keys, knowing that its security depends on the complexity of finding a solution? For about thirty years, the United States and the UK followed a very pragmatic approach to this: they kept the cryptological advances of World War II under wraps; they limited the export of cryptographic equipment and know-how through export regulations; and their signal intelligence agencies – the NSA and GCHQ, respectively – became the largest worldwide employers of mathematicians and the largest customers of supercomputers. Additionally, in their roles in eavesdropping on their enemies' communications, they evaluated the security of the systems used to protect government communications. The assurance in cryptography came at the cost of being the largest organizations that know about cryptography in the world.

The problem with this arrangement is that it relies on a monopoly of knowledge around cryptology. Yet, as we have seen with the advent of commercial telecommunications, cryptography becomes important for nongovernment uses. Even the simplest secure remote authentication mechanism requires some cryptography if it is to be used over insecure channels. Therefore, keeping cryptography under wraps is not an option: in 1977, the NSA approved the IBM design for a public cipher, the Data Encryption Standard (DES), for public use. It was standardized in 1979 by the US National Institute for Standards and Technology (NIST).[4]

The publication of DES launched a wide interest in cryptography in the public academic community. Many people wanted to understand how it works and why it is secure. Yet, the fact that the NSA tweaked its design, for undisclosed reasons, created widespread suspicion in the cipher. The fear was that a subtle flaw was introduced to make decryption easy for intelligence agencies. It is fair to say that many academic cryptographers did not trust DES!

Another important innovation in 1976 was presented by Whitfield Diffie and Martin Hellman in their work "New Directions in Cryptography" (Diffie & Hellman 1976). They show that it is possible to preserve the confidentiality of a conversation over a public channel, without sharing a secret key! This is today known as "Public Key Cryptography," because it relies on Alice knowing a public key for Bob, shared with anyone in the world, and using it to encrypt a message. Bob has the corresponding private part of the key, and is the only one that can decode messages used with the public key. In 1977, Ron Rivest, Adi Shamir, and Leonard Adleman proposed a further system, the RSA, that also allowed for the equivalent of "digital signatures" (Rivest et al. 1978).

What is different in terms of trusting public key cryptography versus traditional ciphers? Both the Diffie-Hellman system and the RSA system base their security on number theoretic problems. For example, RSA relies on the difficulty of factoring integers with two very large factors (hundreds of digits). Unlike traditional ciphers – such as DES – that rely on many layers of complex problems, public key algorithms base their security on a handful of elegant number theoretic problems.

Number theory, a discipline that G.H. Hardy argued at the beginning of the twentieth century was very pure in terms of its lack of any practical application (Hardy & Snow 1967), quickly became the deciding factor on whether one can trust the most significant innovation in the history of cryptology! As a result, a lot of interest and funding directed academic mathematicians to study whether the mathematical problems underpinning public key cryptography were in fact difficult and how difficult the problems were.

---

[4] FIPS PUB 46–3: Federal Information Processing Standards, U.S. Department of Commerce/ National Institute of Standards and Technology Data Encryption Standard (DES).

Interestingly, public key cryptography does not eliminate the need to totally trust the keys. Unlike traditional cryptography, there is no need for Bob to share a secret key with Alice to receive confidential communications. Instead, Bob needs to keep the private key secret and not share it with anyone else. Maintaining the confidentiality of private keys is simpler than sharing secret keys safely, but it is far from trivial given their long-term nature. What needs to be shared is Bob's public key. Furthermore, Alice need to be sure she is using the public key associated with the Bob's private key; if Eve convinces Alice to use an arbitrary public key to encrypt a message to Bob, then Eve could decrypt all messages.

The need to securely associate public keys with entities has been recognized early on. Diffie and Hellman proposed to publish a book, a bit like the phone register, associating public keys with people. In practice, a public key infrastructure is used to do this: trusted authorities, like Verisign, issue digital certificates to attest that a particular key corresponds to a particular Internet address. These authorities are in charge of ensuring that the identity, the keys, and their association are correct. The digital certificates are "signed" using the signature key of the authorities that anyone can verify.

The use of certificate authorities is not a natural architecture in many cases. If Alice and Bob know each other, they can presumably use another way to ensure Alice knows the correct public key for Bob. Similarly, if a software vendor wants to sign updates for their own software, they can presumably embed the correct public key into it, instead of relying on public key authorities to link their own key with their own identity.

The use of public key infrastructures (PKI) is necessary in case Alice wants to communicate with Bob without them having any previous relationship. In that case Alice, given only a valid name for Bob, can establish a private channel to Bob (as long as it trusts the PKI). This is often confused: the PKI ensures that Alice talks to Bob, but not that Bob is "trustworthy" in any other way. For example, a Web browser can establish a secure channel to a Web service that is compromised or simply belong to the mafia. The secrecy provided by the channel does not, in that case, provide any guarantees as to the operation of the Web service. Recently, PKI services and browsers have tried to augment their services by only issuing certificates to entities that are verified as somehow legitimate.

Deferring the link between identities and public keys to trusted third parties places this third party in a system's TCB. Can certification authorities be trusted to support your security policy? In some ways, no. As implemented in current browsers, any certification authority (CA) can sign a digital certificate for any site on the Internet (Ellison & Schneier 2000). This means that a rogue national

CA (say, from Turkey) can sign certificates for the U.S. State Department, that browsers will believe. In 2011, the Dutch certificate authority Diginotar was hacked, and their secret signature key was stolen (Fox-IT 2012). As a result, fake certificates were issued for a number of sensitive sites. Do CAs have incentives to protect their key? Do they have enough incentives to check the identity of the people or entities behind the certificates they sign?

Cryptographic primitives like ciphers and digital signatures have been combined in a variety of protocols. One of the most famous is the Secure Socket Layer SSL or TLS, which provides encryption to access encrypted Web sites on the Internet (all sites following the https://protocol). Interestingly, once secure primitives are combined into larger protocols, their composition is not guaranteed to be secure. For example a number of problems have been identified against SSL and TLS that are not related to the weaknesses of the basic ciphers used (Vaudenay 2002).

The observation that cryptographic schemes are brittle and could be insecure even if they rely on secure primitives (as did many deployed protocols) led to a crisis within cryptologic research circles. The school of "provable security" proposes that rigorous proofs of security should accompany any cryptographic protocol to ensure it is secure. In fact "provable security" is a bit of a misnomer: the basic building blocks of cryptography, namely public key schemes and ciphers cannot be proved secure, as Shannon argued. So a security proof is merely a reduction proof: it shows that any weakness in the complex cryptographic scheme can be reduced to a weakness in one of the primitives, or a well-recognized cryptographic hardness assumption. It effectively proves that a complex cryptographic scheme reduces to the security of a small set of cryptographic components, not unlike arguments about a small Trusted Computing Base. Yet, even those proofs of security often work at a certain level of abstraction and often do not include all details of the protocol. Furthermore, not all properties can be described in the logic used to perform the proofs. As a result, even provably secure protocols have been found to have weaknesses (Pfitzmann & Waidner 1992).

So, the question of "How much can you trust cryptography?" has in part itself been reduced to "How much can you trust the correctness of a mathematical proof on a model of the world?" and "How much can one trust that a correct proof in a model applies to the real world?" These are deep epistemological questions, and it is somehow ironic that national, corporate, and personal security depends on them. In addition to these, one may have to trust certificate authorities and assumptions on the hardness of deep mathematical problems. Therefore, it is fair to say that trust in cryptographic mechanisms is an extremely complex social process.

Trusting the Kindness of Strangers

As we have seen in the previous section, for a cryptosystem to deliver any functionality, one must at the very least ensure the security of its key. In the case of shared key systems, the key has to be kept secret while in transit between Alice and Bob, while Bob is using the system, and often for a long time afterward. In the case of public key cryptosystems, public keys and identities must be associated securely. Private keys must be kept secret to their owner and are very high value because they are used by all other parties to encrypt or verify messages.

The banking industry was an early adopter of cryptography to protect communications within networks of branches and Automatic Teller Machines (ATMs). Banking is also an industry accustomed to dealing with insider fraud. Mechanisms, such as double-entry bookkeeping, have evolved to deter and detect fraud. The prospect of having one key protecting communications is appealing, but also very dangerous if that key falls into the wrong hands. All the benefits of cryptographic keys being short, easy to store, easy to copy, and painless to transport also make them ideal targets for theft and abuse. Along with cryptography, the banking sector made early use of secure coprocessors also known as Hardware Security Modules (HSMs). These are specialized computers that have as a primary aim to protect cryptographic keys stored inside them. HSMs are expensive versions of the consumer end smartcards, designed to protect and destroy cryptographic key material in case there is an attempt to physically extract it. A series of logical operations are allowed for using the key and with appropriate safeguards. In brief, it is a system designed to enforce a security policy on its direct user; and the key aspect of that policy is that they should not be able to get to the key. But how does one seed a cryptographic key into the secure coprocessor or even an ATM? If a single person was to transport the key from branch to branch, they might be tempted to copy and misuse it.

To solve the problem of key initialization and transport, the idea of dual controls were adapted to the new realm of cryptographic keys. A key is simply split in shares, and these shares are given (by the module) to different key operators. The operators can then take their shares to another module and import them one by one to recreate the key. At the end of this process, each operator cannot reconstruct the key, even though the modules at both ends know all shares and can now communicate securely.

Is this secure? The key security assumption is social: colluding to perform an unauthorized action is considered less likely (or more risky) than deviating from a policy on your own. Intuitively, the more distinct people involved, the less likely a conspiracy is to materialize. In practice, however, this may not be true. As the number of shares increases, each key operator's compromise may have less effect on the security of the key. While this is good in principle, the operators are aware of it and may therefore become sloppier with the procedures and security precautions necessary. With a dilution of risk, comes a dilution or responsibility that may make operators more susceptible to have, for example, their keys stolen. This is a crucial aspect of security and applied psychology that has been understudied. Involving more people in a protocol may prevent key loss or compromise, but – as a side effect – the system becomes less responsive and available. A single person (i.e., a share) that is missing prevents the key from being constructed and used.

A similar issue had emerged as part of an attempt in the 1960s to secure nuclear warheads against unauthorized launch and detonation. The order to unlock the weapons was checked by two people – no more, no less. One person alone could have abused the system, but more than two people may have slowed down a strike or counterstrike. Increase that number, and the likelihood of at least one officer purposefully refusing to initiate Armageddon might be dangerously high. The lesson here is clear: if you are not in a position to trust a single person, you can use cryptography (like secure secret sharing), to ensure that many people would need to collude to violate your security policy. This can prevent insider fraud and makes coercion less fruitful, but may also slow down the operation of the system (which in itself might be security critical).

An important class of systems that are entirely based on this principle are anonymous communication systems. Imagine a policy that requires some actions to be anonymous. Secure voting is a good example: there is a need for cast ballots to be unlinkable to the individuals that cast them. A simple mechanism to implement this policy involves a proxy that relays all communications, and anonymizes them. In that setting, Alice would send a message to the proxy, asking it to relay a message to Bob. The proxy would relay the message to Bob without any mention of Alice. Single relays suffer the problems of single persons: they could be corrupt and may come under pressure to reveal who the real senders of messages were. This is far from being a merely theoretical concern: one of the first such proxies, anon.penet.fi, was under multiple occasions forced to reveal senders under legal threat, most notably by the Church of Scientology. In 1981, David Chaum published a seminal work on how to implement such systems securely, making use of the newly available public key cryptosystem RSA. He proposed chaining multiple relays together so that all would have to be compromised to trace the originator of messages. In effect, this applies the technique of splitting "trust" among multiple parties.

Much later, the onion routing system took this principle much further by allowing volunteers to relay traffic to provide anonymous communications, mostly for Web browsing. At the same time, a number of other proposals were put forward to use peer-to-peer network architectures to relay traffic. The logic of those systems is an extreme form of dual-control: the more people involved in a protocol, the less likely they are to all be colluding and corrupt; the less likely it is that they are all coerced.

It is important to note the radical break made by these systems: banks or nuclear weapons operators split functions between a number of people that are known and usually vetted. At the very least, one can argue that these people are distinct and randomly assigned to the security task. Peer-to-peer systems, on the other hand, are usually open for anyone to participate – that is, there is no vetting involved – and it is even hard to ascertain whether two entities in the network are distinct or controlled by one party. In Chapter 2, David Clark is right to say that "[i]t is often safe to depend on the kindness of strangers, if you pick the stranger." As we will see, picking a random stranger in a peer-to-peer system is in itself a challenge. The doctrine that "more people must lead to better security" again comes under question: the more people that are involved in a protocol, the less each of them can be placed under scrutiny to establish their motives or their likely actions. In other words, the bigger the crowd, the less each person in the crowd needs to be known or "trusted." The lack of a foundation for trust in peer-to-peer systems takes extreme forms: it is even difficult to know whether two entities are in fact independent and distinct and it is hard to even cap the number of entities that a single adversary can simulate as distinct. This is known as the Sybil attack, and solutions to it have been the subject of considerable study. This has profound implications: for example, a popularity contest mechanism, say by voting, will always be meaningless. The adversary will simply simulate enough distinct entities to elect whomever they wish (or multiple adversaries will fight it out). The result will never be the will of the majority of genuine distinct users. In fact, it is hard to imagine any collective decision system that would not become dysfunctional under a Sybil attack.

A number of strategies have been devised to deal with Sybil attacks: at their core they all attempt to impose some penalty on the adversaries' ability to simulate multiple entities. Some require them to link to a single established entity outside the system, others require them to expend resources, and the most interesting one assumes that social network links are expensive to form and act in effect as decentralized "trust" judgments. Even these mechanisms are brittle: some adversaries are in fact better resourced than genuine nodes, and if the only foundation to distinct identities is resources, then they will still be able to rig any collective process.

The issue of Sybil attacks is fascinating, not only because it is hard to solve online, but because it is should also be hard to solve off-line. Imagine one organizes a poll in a local (online) newspaper about which is the most beautiful country. If for some reason the Chinese government decides this is a poll on which china should come out on top, they can mobilize all their civil servants to vote in it. The naive solution of requiring residence in the area may offer partial protection, but it is still easy enough for a large entity to buy a lot of real estate if the stakes are high enough. So the questions become: How do we constitute off-line groups within which collective decisions are taken? How is it that we do not see the prevalence of Sybil attacks and sock puppetry that we observe online? How is it the case that powerful entities do not seem to mobilize their resources to take over any collective process they wish? Or are they? In fact, a new technique in marketing and advocacy is an off-line form of Sybil attack, namely "astroturfing." This is the practice of setting up artificial grassroots lobby groups on specific issues, backed by private funders with a vested interest in the matter. These are designed to give the illusion of a mass movement of distinct persons, whereas a single entity fully controls the agenda. We have seen that splitting trust among multiple parties allows one to trust each less and sometimes the whole system more. Yet, this scales worse than thought: once many entities are involved, each may lose motivation to perform their task well and any failing reduces availability. As the idea of distributing trust scales up, we end up in a situation where no one knows anything about anyone else to the point of not being sure they are distinct entities. From there, it is hard to guarantee any security properties at all, and even collective action and decision making system designed to prevent a minority of cheaters are ineffective. How one can start from the latter state of confusion and recover into a state in which someone can at least believe that some entities are distinct, is probably one of the most interesting technical and philosophical problems in security engineering today.

Conclusion: Securing the Mundane

The technical depth of security engineering, and the associated cryptology field, is astounding. This is particularly striking when one considers the relative youth of security as a field of open research and outside the confines of government and military agencies. Yet despite this technical depth, and the strict methodological use security engineers around "trust" (in terms of defining what components are part of the TCB, and on which of their properties a secure system relies), security engineering has not in any noticeable manner solved the general problem of "trust on the Internet" as understood by end users. A number of people within the security engineering field have reflected on this. In his essay "Computer

Security in the Real World" (2004), Butler Lampson notes that traditional security engineering strives to achieve some sort of "perfect" security, or at least extremely robust security.[5] This is, as we have already discussed in relation to Thompson's essay, extremely difficult to achieve. Lampson argues that, as a result, security systems are difficult to configure and use, and thus – even when available – they are never deployed because they are an impediment to the day-to-day function of a computer system. There is plenty of evidence to suggest that security systems are poorly designed and rather unusable. Alma Whitten and J. Doug Tygar has published one of the first works on this subject, entitled "Why Jonny Can't Encrypt" (Whitten & Tygar 1999), effectively launching the field of research in usable security. They looked at the mature PGP 5.0 email encryption systems and, through user studies, demonstrated that a large fraction of users would not be able to use it in a secure manner because of confusion and frustration. Although the lack of useable security is a demonstrated problem, it only partly explains the failure of security engineering in providing what users would define as trust. For example, it does not explain why security engineering does not play a more prominent role in the technical hearts of the systems that are only used by computer experts; why ciphers that are deployed are weak; or how, after ten years of development in the field of useable security, this line of work does not have a better record at fielding more "secure" systems than previous attempts.

David Clark, one of the pioneers of the Internet, provides an alternative explanation in Chapter 2 in which he describes the evolution of the Internet protocols, from tools used in the shielded environment of research labs to the infrastructure that is today ubiquitous and used by everyone and for any purpose. He reports that issues of authentication or privacy were not initially considered vital, and the focus was instead on building an "open" network of networks that would provide any functionality at all. Security, for good reasons, was an afterthought, and the Internet today has inherited a number of security problems as a result. In fact, early attempts at securing the Internet could have challenged its "openness" by imposing a security policy that serves some but not others. Thus, one must resist reading his essay as a call to "build security in from the start," an idea that is gaining popularity. We must realize that, at the time of engineering, an infrastructure it is impossible to predict the "tussles" (Clark et al. 2002) that different parties may engage in through it. Even when conflict points are apparent early on, it is unclear that technologies

---

[5] It is interesting to note that the proposed solution for security in the real world, namely better authentication and authorization logics, has also not taken off in the ten years since the publication of this excellent essay.

are available to mediate them. Thus, waiting for a perfectly secure design may jeopardize a deployment, as Lampson points out. Clark goes as far as stating that technological mechanisms can never provide the assurance necessary for trusting an open infrastructure like the Internet. This is a controversial claim, and because so many sources of end user pain have technical solutions (that are not deployed), it remains to be seen whether or not it is true.

An even more challenging opinion about the overall insecurity of end user machines and the poor state of security on the Internet has emerged from the field of security economics. In his critique, Lampson urges security engineers to move their focus away from prevention of security breaches and toward detection followed by traditional and imperfect crime-fighting to detect and punish those responsible. Such a policy challenges preconceptions of security engineering inherited from military and government applications, where even a single breach may have catastrophic consequences. In fact, Cormac Herley argues that most users may in fact find such an approach quite sufficient for their needs (Herley 2013). He notes that the majority of home users concerned about security privacy and trust on the Internet are very unlikely to be threatened by sophisticated, targeted computer attacks, such as those we have seen against government targets (Chen & Abu-Nimeh 2011). On the other hand, home users could be threatened by bulk Internet crime, such as attempts to steal financial credentials or passwords on a large scale. Preventing those can be more effectively achieved through a mixture of technical computer security measures, detection at large financial and Internet providers, and organizational measures making it harder to monetize those attacks at scale.

This is a point of departure from the traditional security engineering goal in which attacks have to be prevented against adversaries within a threat model and toward a view of security and trust on the Internet as a social good. Under that view, it is fine if some users succumb to online fraud and technical attacks, as long as their overall number and overall impact is kept to a minimum or at least a socially optimum level.

One may conclude, as Richard Harper notes in the conclusion to this book, that the trust concerns of home users seem to be rather mundane compared with the concerns of governments and companies. They are about spam, cold calling, their friends seeing something they posted on a social network, or their computer slowing down because of malware, rather than state secrets. It is, therefore, not clear that the same security engineering thinking – with its need for security policies, adversary models, and TCBs – applies when it comes to addressing their worries about trust. This conclusion probably reflects "the average user," and their needs. On the other hand, totally embracing this conclusion erases very important classes of users with specific needs when it comes to trusting the technology they use. As we have seen from the case study of mobile telephony, once an infrastructure is established, it is used by everyone for everything. The Internet today is no exception, and amid torrents of YouTube cat videos, idle chat exchanges between teenagers, and boring international orders of produce, are also buried messages relating to political organizing, plans to start up businesses, records of electronic votes, and affairs of key public figures. Whereas the sensitive information may be low in volume, and may even affect only a minority of users for a minority of their time, not providing support for such sensitive activities is key to eroding trust on the Internet. Thus making a caricature of Herley's and Lampson's arguments,[6] and arguing that the typical home user should not worry about targeted attacks, implicitly assumes that they will never be party to a serious conflict, be it personal, business, or political. This is a slippery slope to treating ordinary users with contempt and denying their agency in society. It is both historically inaccurate and a poor starting point to do better security engineering for a broad market.

---

[6] We note that Herley is very careful to limit the scope of his claim to financial concerns and does not extend his argument beyond this.

Part Two

Conceptual Points of View

5

Computing and the Search for Trust

Thomas W. Simpson

Introduction

Trust – and its lack – is a hot issue. This is especially true of public discussion of one of the defining features of contemporary life – namely, computers and the varied technologies that are built on them. We want trust but doubt whether it is well-grounded. Nor is it clear how it could be so grounded. Where is rational trust to be found? Call this *the search for trust*. Meanwhile, computers become a more pervasive part of our lives. Uncertainty and risk increase. The search is urgent.

There is an obvious way to resolve the search for trust. To build trust in a technological world, we need to know what trust is. Philosophers answer questions of the form "what is f?" They do so paradigmatically through conceptual analysis. Therefore, philosophers should analyze trust, thereby answering the question "what is trust?" Such an analysis will explain when trust is grounded and when it is not. It will then be possible to identify how trust can be grounded in the specific context of the new modes of living that computing technologies have created. The response concludes: let's get started.

I think that there is both something wrong and something right about this proposed resolution of the search for trust. The "something wrong" is the idea that trust can be analyzed. I disagree; there are strong grounds for supposing that it cannot. Whereas philosophers *can* answer the "what is trust?" question, the method for doing so is not that of conceptual analysis. Nor does the answer yield a road map to the grounding of trust. Instead, it explains why jeremiads about the need for and lack of trust are apposite in contexts of risk and in times of fast-moving change. The "something right" is the conclusion that, nonetheless, philosophers can contribute to the project of identifying how trust can be grounded. The task of this chapter is to defend both of these claims in application to the contemporary technological context.

I first explain what conceptual analysis is and the traditional vision for why one would undertake it. I then show how this has been applied to trust and argue that these attempts fail. Instead of analyzing trust, I propose that the notion ought to be elucidated via genealogy. A genealogical account explains why trust has such value by identifying the function performed by the concept. I illustrate some implications of the account by examining why "trust" is apposite in discussions of cloud computing and in the discipline of security software engineering. I conclude by arguing, nonetheless, that there are ways in which philosophers can help identify how to ground trust in technology.[1]

Conceptual Analysis

What is conceptual analysis? Analysis is the practice of breaking something down to its constituent parts. To analyze water, for instance, is to identify it as constituted by two hydrogen atoms and one oxygen atom joined by covalent bonds. Take any water you choose; it is made up of two hydrogen atoms and one oxygen atom joined by covalent bonds. That is, something is water only if it is made up of two hydrogen atoms and one oxygen atom joined by covalent bonds. That atomic constitution is a necessary condition for being water.

Conceptual analysis is the practice of analysis applied to concepts and at its most general involves breaking concepts down to their constituent parts. This is trivial in some cases. For example, what does it mean to be a "bachelor"? To be a bachelor one must be unmarried. That is a necessary condition of bachelorhood; one is a bachelor only if one is unmarried. But that is not a sufficient condition. It is not the case that if you are unmarried, then you are a bachelor. That is, although some women are unmarried, they are not bachelors. It is also necessary that one must be a man. But nothing else is required to be a bachelor. So you are a bachelor if and only if you are an unmarried man. This is an analysis of the concept of bachelor.

Although trivial, the example illustrates two important points. First, I can determine what it is to be a bachelor a priori. I did not need to do any empirical research to determine what is required to be a bachelor, such as going out and taking photos of lots of bachelors to determine what they have in common or conducting a questionnaire and seeing what the majority of people believe.

---

[1] Some sections are abbreviated versions of an argument I have developed at greater length in my article, "What is Trust?" (2012a), and §9 summarizes the argument of my article, "Evaluating Google as an Epistemic Tool" (2012b). I am grateful to publishers at Wiley-Blackwell for permission to use this material.

Philosophy, traditionally, has been a discipline conducted "from the armchair." So it is no surprise that conceptual analysis has been one of the kinds of inquiry in which philosophers have traditionally engaged. Second, the process of analysis frequently relies on counterexamples. The existence of unmarried women is a counterexample to the analysis of bachelor as someone unmarried. Pointing out that some women are unmarried but that they are not bachelors is enough to force a revision of the analysis. This would be so even if no unmarried women actually existed (imagine we lived in a society in which there were so many more men than women that all women were married at birth). The possibility that unmarried women could exist, and our refusal to count them as bachelors, would still force the revision.

More significant notions may also be the subject of conceptual analysis. A classic subject is knowledge, the analysis of which started with Plato. In the *Theaetetus*, Socrates asks the eponymous interlocutor "what is knowledge?" Theaetetus proposes an initial answer: "Knowledge is nothing other than perception" (151d7-e3). Among Socrates's counterarguments to this proposal is the point that we can know something by remembering it (163d-164b). So it is not true that knowledge is necessarily nothing other than perception. Theaetetus tries again: "Knowledge is true belief" (187b). Socrates points out that it is possible for a skillful lawyer to lead a jury to believe something true, but they may believe that it is true because of the lawyer's rhetoric and not because of the evidence. Therefore, whereas they may have a true belief, it is only accidentally true and thus not knowledge. True belief, then, is not sufficient for knowledge (201b-c). The attempt to analyze knowledge continues in contemporary philosophy. For some time, a popular view was the following analysis of knowledge: for any p, a person knows p if and only if p is true, they believe that p, and they are justified in believing p. ("p" is an abbreviation for a proposition; the outlines of the account are also from the *Theaetetus*, 201d-210a.) Edmund Gettier (1963) gave counterexamples to this analysis, often termed the 'JTB' analysis after its constituent parts. Imagine Smith has strong evidence for the proposition "Jones owns a Ford." From this, he validly infers the disjunction, "either Jones owns a Ford, or Jones is in Boston." Boston is chosen by Smith at random. Now suppose that, unknown to Smith, Jones sold his Ford yesterday and is currently driving a rental car. Nonetheless, also unknown to Smith, Jones is in Boston at a conference. The disjunction "either Jones owns a Ford, or Jones is in Boston" is true; Smith believes it; and it is justified for him. Yet he does not know it, for it was only through luck that Jones was in Boston, and it was that fact that made the disjunction true, not Jones's Ford-ownership status. Attempts to analyze knowledge have proliferated in response to Gettier; Robert Shope charts the first two decades in *The Analysis of Knowing. A Decade of Research* (1983).

Trust is a candidate for analysis. There are a number of philosophical questions that arise in relation to the concept of trust, both because of the intrinsic interest of the topic, and also because it is so fertile a perspective from which to approach different topics related to the way we live together. A reason for analyzing trust is the hope that an analysis will answer some of these questions. One inquiry, for instance, concerns the moral status of trust, whether it is permissible, obligatory, or praiseworthy. Relatedly, another inquiry concerns the reasons that determine when trust is permitted, obligated, or praiseworthy. Karen Jones calls this "the justification conditions of trust" (1996: 4). Another concern is whether trust is voluntary or involuntary, with the corollary of whether one could be held responsible for trusting or distrusting another. A further inquiry addresses whether there is a justified presumption of trust or whether we require evidence before trusting rationally. Conceptual analysis, on this view, is both possible and valuable.

Yet is it? There is a grand view, a modest view, and a skeptical view on the value of analysis. The grand view derives from Plato and Aristotle. On this, things have essences. Essences are the "what it is to be" of a certain thing; equivalently, they are what being a certain kind of thing consists. Plato famously named the essence of a thing its "Form." The view still has adherents, most recently Colin McGinn. According to McGinn, conceptual analysis is a way of understanding reality. "We discover the essential structure of reality – what the world is like in itself – by analyzing our 'concepts.' . . . Concepts are not the *object* of our interest – things are – but our method is to view things conceptually, that is, as we conceive them" (2012: 5).

The modest view demurs. According to it, we learn the supervenience relations that one set of vocabulary has in relation to another through conceptual analysis. (Supervenience is the relation that holds between a set of A properties and a set of B properties, when no A properties can differ without a difference in the B properties.) Analysis is important because philosophers are interested in the kinds of notions that have supervenience relations (for example, "Do brain states supervene on the mind?"). Frank Jackson defends the view: "Conceptual analysis is not being given a role in determining the fundamental nature of our world; it is, rather, being given a central role in determining what to say in less fundamental terms given an account of the world stated in more fundamental terms" (1998: 44). Conceptual analysis thus has a tidying function: it makes clear to what our folk concepts are committed. Where their commitments are inconsistent, it reveals those contradictions, preparatory to the concept's refurbishment for philosophical use.

The skeptical view says "don't bother." It alleges that conceptual analysis misconstrues the way language works. Ludwig Wittgenstein is the preeminent exponent. In addressing attempts to analyze language, he declares: "These phenomena have no one thing in common which makes us use the same word for all – but that they are *related* to one another in many different ways.... Don't think, but look!... And the result of this examination is: we see a complicated network of similarities overlapping and criss-crossing" (1953: §§65–66). Another source of skepticism about conceptual analysis is the view that some of our most philosophically important notions are themselves basic and therefore un-analyzable. G. E. Moore took this position with regard to goodness; Timothy Williamson does so with knowledge (Moore, 1903; Williamson, 2000; for a mitigated and more general variant of this view, see P. F. Strawson, 1992).

At issue between these positions is the nature and role of language. Does language carve nature at its joints? If so, analyzing concepts yields knowledge and understanding of the world (the grand view). If not, conceptual analysis can tell us only about language (the modest view) – if indeed language is amenable to analysis (the skeptical view). My own view is a compromise between the modest and the skeptical views. Conceptual analysis is sometimes possible, as when a folk concept is relatively tidy. At other times it is not, for our folk concepts are sometimes too variegated and diffuse. Trust, I argue, is in the latter category.

Analyses of Trust and e-Trust

Why should trust not be amenable to conceptual analysis? The dominant philosophical treatments of trust have presumed that it is. I do not have an argument to show that trust *must* be too heterogeneous to be defined, so I have no conclusive reply to the question. But even if no conclusive reasons are available, I suggest that some forceful ones can be given for not persevering with attempts to analyze trust and for trying a different way.

An inductive reason is the ease with which counterexamples can be produced to existing definitions. Three major ways of thinking about trust have emerged in the literature. The first significant philosophical treatment was Annette Baier, who endorses a broadly affective approach. She claims: "When I trust another, I depend on her goodwill toward me" (Baier 1994: 99). Instances of trust abound, however, where goodwill does not seem to have much to do with it. Against Baier, Onora O'Neill makes the point nicely that a patient may trust a doctor to exercise proper professional judgment in their case, while knowing full well that the doctor finds him/her particularly irritating and bears him/her no goodwill (O'Neill 2002b: 14). Not only is goodwill not necessary for trust, it is also not sufficient. Richard Holton points out that a conman may rely on his victim's goodwill, while not trusting him (Holton 1994: 65).

Although Karen Jones concurs with Baier that trust has a distinctively affective dimension, she adds a role for affect to the trustor as well as the trusted. Trust "is an attitude of optimism that the goodwill and competence of another will extend to cover the domain of our interaction with her, together with the expectation that the one trusted will be directly and favourably moved by the thought that we are counting on her" (Jones 1996: 4). In addition to O'Neill's objection, this is vulnerable to additional counterexamples in which trust seems to be a matter of cold calculation on the part of both parties. Think of a group of oligarchs arranging a price-fix. There is no love lost between the ruthless competitors. But they may still successfully manage to collude on raising prices over a staggered period of time – to avoid the suspicion of coordinated action – with at least the initiating party having to trust that the others will follow his/her lead and not take advantage of the price differential to increase market share. The initiating oligarch does so only because she has good reasons to believe that the others will follow; optimism does not come into it. Trust is not always an affective matter.

Richard Holton's treatment of trust is equally influential. Rather than a primarily affective relation, his account sees trust as characterized more by normatively laden attitudes. "When you trust someone to do something, you rely on them to do it, and you regard that reliance in a certain way: you have a readiness to feel betrayal should it be disappointed, and gratitude should it be upheld" (1994: 67). This range of reactive sentiments is a result of adopting "the participant stance" (the idea is adopted from Strawson [1974]). Again, it is not hard to find cases of trust that do not fit this description. A mother certainly could be relied on by her son while he adopts the participant stance toward her. But it is odd to suppose that the participant stance is doing any distinctive work here. The son trusts his mother because he knows she loves him. He need not even have the concepts required to adopt attitudes such as those mandated by the participant stance. Philip Nickel's closely related account declares trust always to involve the ascription of an obligation to another (Nickel 2007). It falls foul to the same kind of counterexample.

A different way of thinking about trust sees it fundamentally as a matter of rationality, understood with the economists as forward-looking, interest-maximizing action. The baldest, most austere version is James Coleman's. He asserts that "the elements confronting the potential trustor are nothing more or less than the considerations a rational actor applies in deciding whether to place a bet" (1990: 99). One "places trust" if one acts in a way that relies on another person, and which thereby exposes the trustor to risk. But defining trust as an action, which one places or not, fails to describe situations in which trust is latent. Out of kindness to the child she never had, a rich aunt promises her nephew that if he ever fell on tough times, she will bail him out. As it happens, the nephew does well and wants for nothing. Yet he still trusts that she would have fulfilled that promise if things had not gone so well. So the nephew trusts, but never acts in a way that relies on another.

Russell Hardin's encapsulated interest account of trust is similarly inspired by rational choice models of action. He defines trust simply as a belief about another's trustworthiness. "The declarations 'I believe you are trustworthy' and 'I trust you' are equivalent" (2002: 10). But belief that the other is trustworthy is hardly necessary for trust. A father may give his daughter some money and a list of shopping to get from the local store, despite her known predilection for cola bottles. He may do so as a form of moral training, despite having no fixed belief that she will be trustworthy, or even despite believing that she will succumb to the temptation. There is surely a permissible sense in which he trusts her.

The problem of vulnerability to counterexample reiterates in regard to attempted analyses of e-trust. Take e-trust to be that trust which is mediated by information and computing technologies. Previous philosophical elucidations of technologically mediated trust show the same desire for analysis as conventionally practiced. The most significant such enterprise is a series of articles by Mariarosaria Taddeo (2009, 2010, 2011) in which she claims to have given "the right definition" of trust and e-trust (2010: 255). In reply, I show her definition also to be inadequate.

Taddeo starts by giving an analysis of trust between artificial agents (AAs), or hardware or software based computer systems (2009: 30). Her next steps are controversial. Taddeo proposes that trust between AAs constitutes a "streamlined and fully-controlled scenario, which turns out to be useful for identifying the fundamental features of e-trust." This applies to trust between either artificial agents or human agents (HAs; 2011: 76–77), giving the following possible paired relations between trusting and trusted parties: AA-AA, AA-HA, HA-AA, and HA-HA. Her (2010) definition of e-trust between artificial agents is then modified to include HAs.

Definition: Assume a set of first order relations functional to the achievement of a goal and that at least two agents (AAs or HAs) are involved in the relations, such that one of them (the trustor) has to achieve the given goal and the other (the trustee) is able to perform some actions in order to achieve that goal. If the trustor chooses to achieve its goal by the action performed by the trustee, and if the trustor considers the trustee a trustworthy agent, then the relation has the property of being advantageous for the trustor. Such a property is a second-order property that affects the first-order relations taking place between AAs, and is called trust.

(2011: 85)

In including both humans and artificial agents, Taddeo defines trust generally, and does not focus solely on e-trust.

The problems with this are numerous. I make four criticisms for Taddeo's account, in ascending order of seriousness. First, it is false that my choosing to achieve a goal through your action, and my considering you to be trustworthy, is sufficient for that relation to have the property of being advantageous for me, as my consideration may be mistaken. If you turn out to be untrustworthy, that is disadvantageous for me. This criticism is not decisive, for it can be met by refining the definition such that I must "consider the relation to have the property of being advantageous."

Second, trust is sometimes not "functional to the achievement of a goal," because there is no separate goal aimed at by trusting the other. If I am concerned simply that you know of my affection and regard for you, there is no action you have to perform for me to achieve my goal. Your knowledge of my trust in you is sufficient alone to achieve that.

Third, in stating that it is necessary for trust that the trustor "achieve its goal by the action performed by the trustee," the definition excludes instances of latent trust. Latent trust is clearly an instance of trust; so a definition must be rejected that fails to account for it.

Fourth, both in the definition and in surrounding text, it is unstated how the second-order property of "being advantageous" affects the first-order relations. The first-order relation seems to be shaped by the trustor's decision to achieve his/her goal through the trustee's action, and this decision is based on the trustor's considering the trustee to be trustworthy. But if it is not stated how the second-order property affects the first-order relation, then Taddeo's definition is not substantially different from James Coleman's functional definition of trust. That is, trust is the decision to rely on another, based on an assessment of the likelihood of trustworthiness, the possible costs and gains of trustworthiness and untrustworthiness respectively, and a calculation that I will probably gain rather than lose in the transaction (Coleman 1990: 99). It is noteworthy that Coleman's definition also falls foul to counterexamples based on latent trust, consistent with this diagnosis.

Not only is the relation between the second-order property and the first-order relation unstated, the definition gives rise to a paradoxical result. If the second-order property affects the first-order relations such that the trustor no longer chooses to achieve its goal by the action performed by the trustee, or no longer considers the trustee a trustworthy agent, then the property disappears. If the second-order property does not affect the first-order relations in either of these ways, then it is merely epiphenomenal. There is a dilemma: defining trust as a second-order property either undercuts itself or is epiphenomenal. Not only is it unclear what is gained by specifying trust to be a second-order property, it is unclear that there could be anything to be gained.

As reasons of space prohibit surveying all claims of the form "trust is *this*," I can do no more here than report that counterexamples can be similarly easily generated to all those I have found. I suggest the reader will find the same. As the authors mentioned represent the major ways of thinking about trust and e-trust in the literature, this is inductive reason to think that other such attempts will be similarly vulnerable to counterexample. Yet trust has received relatively little attention from philosophers, especially when compared to endeavors like the analysis of the concept of knowledge. So a defender of the possibility of an analysis of trust might reply that the vulnerability of existing definitions to counterexample does not show that trust is not amenable to such a treatment. Perhaps no one has given it a really decent try yet.

I am dubious. The ways in which the word "trust" is used are simply too various to be regimented into one definition. Sometimes "trust" is naturally understood as referring to a sort of affective attitude ("I will trust my husband, I will not be jealous"); at other times to a conative one ("Come what may, I will trust you to the end"); and at yet others to cognitive ones ("I know you are an honorable woman, so I trust you"). Sometimes it is not a mental state but an action that is described as trust ("The patrol followed the scout, trusting him to spot any ambush"). Similarly, it is used in situations in which the motivation to trustworthiness is dramatically varied: love, or mutual gain, or moral considerations may all count as reasons not to betray someone's trust. These all support the inductive argument against the plausibility of analyzing of trust. Counterexamples can be given so easily *because* there are so many ways the word may permissibly be used, and so it would be foolish to seek a single definition.

This observation is not yet decisive. For a defender of the possibility of conceptual analysis may propose a disjunctive analysis: "You trust someone if and only if *either* you rely on their goodwill *or* you adopt the participant reactive stance towards them *or* you believe it is in their interests to be trustworthy *or* . . . " The advantage of the strategy is that any plausible view about trust can be accommodated, and so the analysis can be made immune to counterexample. The disadvantage of the strategy is that any plausible view about trust can be accommodated. It can be made immune to counterexample not because it is true but because it is ad hoc.

On Frank Jackson's modest view of conceptual analysis, is the method applicable in the case of trust? He points out that, for most of the concepts philosophers in which are interested, there are supervenience relations with other concepts; pretty much everyone agrees that knowledge supervenes on truth and belief, for instance. But if so, he asks, how can knowledge be sui generis? I accept the point. Yet parallel claims apply to trust, for we make judgments about whether someone trusts another in virtue of more basic features of that relation, such as whether they are relying on them and the reasons for their reliance. So as trust supervenes on other more basic concepts, I do not claim that it is sui generis and unanalyzable. But if trust is not unanalyzable, why not analyze it? Jackson himself provides the answer. Granted that most philosophically interesting concepts are not sui generis, he still needs to explain why conceptual analysis is so difficult. Part of his explanation is a recognition that different people can use the same word to represent the world in subtly different ways, with representation for Jackson a matter of referring to patterns in the world. Jackson concludes that "smart philosophers' recherché examples . . . reveal that there are a number of candidate patterns [referred to by the same word]. What the counter-example refutes is the view that there is a single, fixed concept which we all, or nearly all, use the word 'knowledge' for" (2005: 135). The vulnerability to counterexample of putative analyses of trust warrants the same conclusion. There is no single, fixed concept which we all, or nearly all, use for the word "trust." Your disagreement with my analysis simply reveals that we represent the world differently with that word. There may be no fact of the matter about which is right.

In addition to the inductive case for the unsuitability of trust for conceptual analysis mentioned earlier, there is further reason for trying a different approach. Even if a successful analysis was given, there are some interesting itches that such a result would fail to scratch. In particular, why should trust seem so important a concept in our practical lives? Simply establishing that a concept answers to a particular set of conditions holds little prospect of answering that. I turn now to elucidate an alternative way of answering the question, "what is trust?"

Genealogy

This alternative takes the value of trust as first importance. A genealogical approach addresses the concept obliquely, by asking why we might have the concept that we have, given some broad facts about how we live and the projects we pursue. A full defense of this method is beyond my scope here. I am indebted for it to the fertile treatments of knowledge by Edward Craig and truthfulness by Bernard Williams, and must refer the unconvinced to their longer defenses of the strategy, from which the following brief remarks are drawn (see Craig, 1990: section I; and Williams, 2002: chapter 2).

The genealogist proposes that if we can give a "role description" for an important concept that looks and feels very similar to a notion that we actually operate, explaining what is needed of a concept to do a particular job, then that sheds light on the content of it. Rather than trial by thought-experiment, it instead accommodates the vagueness and conflicting intuitions that surround difficult and abstract notions. There is no doubt that all the advocates of the "trust is *this*" claims I critiqued earlier have replies to my counterexamples. But the sorts of replies on offer tend to consist of arguments over the cases and ultimately a discovery that we use the word "trust" to describe different things on different occasions, which illustrates Jackson's point. What would be genuinely revealing is an explanation of *why* the term permits this variability.

In addition to yielding a clearer grasp on the content of the concept, such an approach also makes it entirely perspicuous where its value comes from. Two results for the price of one inquiry is no bad thing in these straitened times.

Finally, the genealogical method is broadly naturalistic in that, with Williams, it "helps to explain a concept or value or institution by showing ways in which it could have come about in a simplified environment containing certain kinds of human interests or capacities" (2002: 21).

Although an analysis of trust cannot be ruled out, the burden of proof remains squarely on those who espouse its possibility, and alternative approaches should be seriously entertained. As to the possibility and fertility of a genealogical account – to which I now turn to develop – let the proof be in the pudding.

The Generative Conditions

Although it is a platitude that man is a social animal, it is an important platitude; and it is the starting point for reflection on the concept of trust. The isolated life, when there is no possibility for sociable contact, has a quality of the nightmare about it. Robinson Crusoe *endures* his isolation until Man Friday arrives, questioning what God intends by providentially requiring this ordeal of him, and so illustrating quite how deeply abnormal it is to live alone (Defoe 1719: 107). Yet even Crusoe had a father and mother whom he was aware of hurting when he ran off to be a sailor, and the idea that a significant population of *Homo sapiens* might each live in conditions of thorough-going isolation, except for the bare necessities of mating and parenting, is so outré as to forbid that population being described as human. Social contact constitutes a very great share of the well-lived life in which we laugh, are musical, gossip, adorn the houses we share, and otherwise enjoy passing the time together. In describing ways of living and acting that are possible only if humans live socially, I do not suggest that it is somehow a voluntary decision to undertake them.

Yet the nature of the projects that are possible only if humans live together is significant. Perhaps the kinds of project that are most obviously made possible are those that require the joint action of several individuals toward the same end. Crusoe was able to fell a tree and carve a dugout canoe from it by himself, but he only discovered later, and to his cost, that the craft was too heavy for him to push to the sea, so he had to abandon it in the forest (1719: 137). It takes little imagination to multiply other examples of joint action from evolutionary, just-so scenarios of groups of humans being able to hunt down prey or defend themselves against predators that would easily evade or overcome a lone individual.

These examples of hunting and protecting are reassuringly simple instances of joint action, for they portray a situation in which you and I must cooperate together for this same period of time, and then – if successful – we both enjoy the same benefit at the same time, whether it is relief from danger or being fed. But the Crusoe example opens up the possibility of more complex forms. It need not be the case that you and I both work on the dugout at exactly the same time if we are to make a canoe and both benefit by it. Individual action can be separated over time and still successfully be joint. Separating participation by time is more complex because it demands that both parties are able to take account of the other, not only in their presence, but also in their absence, which demands a degree of socialization.

In addition to joint actions, however, there can be social forms of action with individuals acting in a coordinated way, but nonetheless toward different ends, ends which would not be achievable, or at least not so readily, by one person acting alone. I may be particularly good at making pots and you particularly good at making ploughs. I give you a pot in return for one of your ploughs, and we both benefit. Joint actions and exchanges are both instances of mutualism in which both of us benefit in ways that would not be possible without cooperation. Like joint actions, exchanges can also be separated by time. I might offer you some fish I have caught now, in return for your giving me some wheat later this autumn. But exchanges separated by time have an additional complication, in that for one party at least there is a more beneficial option; having got the fish, you now might decline to give me the wheat. Some joint actions are subject to the same temptation; letting others go and man the barricades means that I do not run the risk of death. These situations are more socially demanding, because they require people to recognize the collective benefit of not doing what is in their maximal individual interest.

A further form of coordinated action is also necessary for social life. The examples so far discussed are well characterized as "positive" projects, with people trying to make things better for themselves and others. Equally essential are "negative" projects in which people must not make things worse for others. Bringing rapine, violence, and other antisocial behavior to a sufficiently low level for those who live in a community is a basic precondition of the well-lived human life; life is still possible in an environment of constant threat, but almost everyone finds it very unpleasant. It is not necessary that everyone without exception abstains from such acts. All that is necessary is that enough people act cooperatively to secure a relatively threat-free social environment.

I suggest that these various forms of shared existence – the domestic life of child-rearing and shared company, of exchange and of joint, positive, and negative collective action – constitute the basic forms of social life. I also suggest that these provide the generative conditions in which the root notion of trust arises. Call this simple root *Ur-trust*. Three features are salient.

First, these social forms of action are all occasions in which people rely on others. Although the notion of reliance is commonsensical, it has an important implication worth highlighting. Reliance permits in degrees. You are *very* reliant on me if the consequences of my unreliability are very serious for you. You can also be reliant on me to a greater or lesser degree in achieving a particular goal. These two dimensions of variation are separable: I may be essential to your achieving some trivial goal, or I may be tangentially involved in securing a very important goal. Because you rely, you are exposed to risk of loss.

The second feature of these social forms of action is that they require people to behave cooperatively. The notion of cooperative behavior can again be left largely intuitive; even though I take it that it should not be reduced to rule-observance, but is instead best stated in terms of motives to action. To behave cooperatively means that you take account of others' good in how you act. At the least, this means ensuring that your action is not directly detrimental to others. It may also mean acting for their good when appropriate.

How costly is cooperative behavior? Sometimes, it is not very costly at all. Negative collective action merely requires abstaining from possible gain, which can often only be won through some act of violence with its concomitant risks. But even here, gain foregone through being negatively cooperative may nonetheless be significant. Other forms of cooperative action may be more costly. Keeping a promise, sometimes, can be a demanding thing to do, if things have turned out differently than the way you expected when you made it, or you made the promise rashly, without considering its implications. Yet breaking promises is a very uncooperative thing to do. Other instances of collective action can also be personally costly; sometimes being cooperative involves refusing the temptation to free-ride and paying your share of the bill, even though you could get away with not doing so. Cooperative behavior is most valuable and in most jeopardy precisely when it requires overcoming the temptation to personal gain, either foregoing gain that would have been at others' expense or contributing your part toward the shared project.

A third feature of these forms of social action is that, as well as a risk of loss, there is uncertainty as to whether those I interact with will be cooperative. This is for the simple reason that the workings of others' agency are not under my control – people are free to decide what they do. (No metaphysical commitments are made here.) I can influence others' decisions, to be sure. But if I were able to control what someone else did, it would no longer be him/her who was acting, and so it would not be *his/her* cooperation about which I was concerned.

In a social world, then, where we raise families and enjoy living alongside each other, where others let us get on with what we are doing when it does not affect them, and where we can achieve things together that we could not do alone, I am routinely reliant on others' free and cooperative action. This, I propose, constitutes the Ur-trust notion: I trust someone when I rely on their freely cooperative behavior. This reliance is a property of my action, in the first instance. The importance of reliance on others' cooperative behaviors to the continued existence of a community makes it highly desirable that they possess a word in their language to describe that property of action. The term "trust" enables English speakers to refer to their reliance on others' cooperative behavior (mutatis mutandis for other languages); this is what the term is for. On this notion of Ur-trust, it is not that action that is reliant on others' cooperative behavior is *evidence* of a preceding or contemporaneous mental state that provides part of the practically rational basis for that action, and which we call "trust." Instead, that action *is* trust. An implication of this is that Ur-trust is possible for those who act without conscious deliberation, but in a way that is reliant on others' cooperative behavior, such as infants or the mentally impaired. This seems correct, or we would not take infants' thorough-going dependence on their parents as a paradigm kind of trust.

The root notion says nothing about why people act cooperatively. All that matters for Ur-trust to arise is that people do rely on others to act cooperatively often enough to need to talk about it. For this reliance to be a stable pattern of behavior, people must actually be cooperative relatively frequently. But there need be no particular reason why they are cooperative.

The Ur-notion provides a clear explanation of why trust comes in degrees. The variability in the cost of unreliability is one source of the variability in degree of trust. If another person were to act uncooperatively in a way that resulted in very serious harm for me or my interests, then my reliance is correspondingly greater. The degree to which I rely on another person in pursuing my projects constitutes another source of variability. And there is a third source of variability, the degree of uncertainty about whether another person will prove cooperative. If cooperative behavior does not cost much, for instance, then there is less chance of failure, and thus less trust is required. But if cooperative behavior would be more costly, then the likelihood of failure is higher, and thus more trust is exhibited if the trustor chooses to rely. Soldiering represents the limits of this, as all three variables are pushed to or toward the maximum: your life is at stake; you are nearly wholly dependent on others playing their part for you to stay alive; and because the cost to others of taking account of you may well be their own life (leading to great temptation not to be cooperative), there is considerable uncertainty. In these respects, soldiering is a feat of trust. (As rock climbing also pushes the first two variables to their limit, it too is a feat of trust.) So the notion of Ur-trust, of reliance on freely cooperative behavior, comes in degrees.

The type of action referred to by the root notion also explains why trust should be so valuable. As social existence would not be possible without reliance on cooperative action, so threats to Ur-trust constitute threats to the continued existence of society. The analogies here become superlative: trust is like the air we breathe (Baier 1994: 98), or the cement that holds society together (Acton 1974: 14). The genealogical account explains why such analogies should be pertinent.

The Rhetoric of Trust

The Ur-notion of reliance on cooperative behavior does not exhaust the complexity of the concept of trust. I suggest that certain contexts of use of this root create added resonances, which amplify and subtly alter the concept itself, toward the richer notion that we actually apply. It is this which accounts both for the invisibility of trust and for its rhetorical force when it becomes the subject of conversation.

As a starting observation, it is a basic datum of the psychology of action that a very great proportion of what we do is not the outcome of a formal process of deliberative, conscious reasoning. (This implies nothing about the rationality of that action in any but a trivial sense of that protean term.) This is no less true for cooperative action than it is for individual action. Habit, not ratiocination, is the standard mode in which we conduct ourselves, although we switch to the latter in times of stress or uncertainty.

This observation, however, has a striking consequence for the concept of trust. Because reliance on others to act cooperatively is such a routine part of life, we very often trust without talking about it. Most of the time, it just happens. The actuality of trust may be very present; but it does not need to be talked about unless there is some problem, and so trust is invisible. So it is precisely non-routine contexts which generate the need to start talking about trust. "Non-routine" is too bland a description, however. It is contexts which are new and unfamiliar, or in which things have gone wrong, or where there is some particular reason to worry that things might go wrong – perhaps where the stakes are particularly high so that I am very reliant on others – that there is pressing need to draw attention to my reliance on someone else to act cooperatively. It is in the breach that the term "trust" is particularly apposite. As such, it acquires a resonance of crisis. Talk about trust functions as an alarm bell; when it goes off, it acts as a signal that, for some reason, the habitual assumption of cooperative behavior no longer applies. The notion of Ur-trust as simple reliance on cooperative behavior thus acquires a rhetorical resonance, as a warning signal to stop and think about what you are assuming of others. The very fact that someone has asked the question "Should I trust?" implies that there is a problem in the offing. Paradoxically, talk of trust can be a potent indication of suspicion. That talk of trust can be an indicator of suspicion has a further corollary: that it is only when we *stop* talking about trust that the kind of trust sought as the precondition of social living can be presumed.

"The breach" is a metaphor. This should not be allowed to obscure the severity of situations in which the assumption of cooperative behavior no longer applies. Widespread anomie and social breakdown are recurring features of dystopian visions of the future or of warning stories from the past. Deep and irreversible conflict has very significant imaginative potency. The seriousness of anomie explains why trust – in invoking its specter – tends to trump other values in conversation.

"Trust," then, comes to acquire other resonances. One is of hope for the possibility of the broad sunlit uplands that beckon if people could live together harmoniously, being kind and considerate to one another. Another resonance is of the threat of interpersonal conflict: screw me around and I'll make you pay, and hopefully the community will too. Think what it is to be asked, "Can I trust you?" It is impossible to answer "No" without near ending a cooperative relationship, while answering "Yes" is a tacit acceptance of the questioner's ill-will and possible revenge should you not come up with the goods. It is not a kind question to be asked at all.

Forms of Trust

Contexts in which the notion of Ur-trust is apposite, then, result in the term "trust" being used in such a way that it acquires additional, richer resonances of meaning: of hope and of threat. Yet we are inventive language users, and happily appropriate terms for use in contexts analogically related to their original conditions. This is equally the case for trust, such that we must recognize plural, analogically related variants of the concept.

Recall that the notion of Ur-trust is generated by the need to refer to individuals *acting* in a way reliant on others' cooperative behaviors. In simple creatures, action may be a hardwired response to stimulus in the environment. But with more complex cognitive abilities, a person's action is preceded by practical deliberation and decision. Once the cognitive ability to support deliberation and decision is in place, it is a small step to describe as trust those mental states that are important constituents of the process leading to actual reliance on another's freely cooperative action. Furthermore, these same mental states may be present in cases in which I do not actually rely on another, but in which I would be disposed to do so under different circumstances, as in the rich aunt case. So the term "trust" may be felicitously used to describe mental states that result in dispositions to rely on cooperative behavior, as well as actual instances of reliance. The sorts of mental states that may lead people to have a disposition to rely on others includes beliefs about what will lead the other party to be trustworthy. But there is no reason to suppose that it is restricted to beliefs. Loving someone may prompt a disposition to trust, and a very robust one at that, often surviving despite evidence of untrustworthiness. And this is what we observe. The different uses of the word canvassed in Section 2 show "trust" used in ways that refer to cognitive, conative, and affective mental states. All of these may be significant in issuing in a disposition to trust; therefore all of these are felicitously described as trust. Call beliefs that lead to a disposition to trust, *cognitive trust*. Call judgments, decisions, intentions, and resolutions that lead to a disposition to trust, *conative trust*. Call emotional states that lead to a disposition to trust, *affective trust*.

There is a second noteworthy way in which repeated analogical use of the term extends its meaning further. Trust arises in interpersonal contexts. Because it is never certain that a person will act cooperatively, however, it is a de facto feature of trust that it always occurs in situations in which, from the subjective standpoint of the putative trustor, it is possible that they will be let down. Sometimes, however, we rely not on other people, but on things. Although things are clearly not capable of cooperative action, it may nonetheless be opaque to us whether they will prove reliable, and their unreliability may affect us. When I lay the branch of a tree out over the ravine to bridge it, I may not know whether it will take my weight. The consequence of its unreliability is significant and costly to me. These allow the analogical extension of the term "trust" to describe my walking out on the branch. In this way, I can trust things, not just people. It is an ameliorated sense of "trust," to be sure, but it is indubitable that we sometimes use the term in this context, with connotations of exposure to risk and uncertainty of outcome. Call this *predictive trust*, because trust here involves nothing more than a prediction of reliability and specifically no expectation that the trusted may take account of me in their action.[2]

For clarity, I have represented the differences between "trust" as it arises in its generative conditions and these discrete notions of cognitive trust, affective trust, conative trust, and predictive trust by labeling them distinctly. The fact that – in each of these situations – we naturally apply the term "trust" without adjectival qualification, however, illustrates my point. Because the analogies are so close, and the use of the term "trust" so apt to describe them, repeated use has hardened these into discrete notions. We can talk about plural forms of trust, and "trust" may refer to different forms in different contexts. There is no reason to suppose that I have identified all the forms of trust; those that I have noted are merely the most obvious forms.

Cloud Computing and Security Engineering

What are the implications of the foregoing for the present enquiry? There are three implications I wish to highlight: an explanatory implication; an hortatory implication; and, finally, a practical implication. (I discuss two in this section and reserve the third for Section 9.)

The first implication is this: the genealogical account explains why "trust" is an apposite term for contemporary discourse which concerns computing technology. Consider how such contexts exemplify the three features of the generative conditions for Ur-trust. When current users of technology go online, go mobile, or use any computer-based technology, they do so with a variety of goods at stake. Privacy is a very obvious one. So is the security of one's money. So is the continued retention of one's documents, files, and other data. Success in communication is another. Failure of a system to perform its function is another. As an example, take the Internet-enabled systems that control major public infrastructure, such as power supply or traffic networks. In interacting with computing systems and other end users, we rely on them to take into account these goods that we value. That we rely is shown by the risk involved if these goods fail to be respected: we face shame or financial loss or wasted work or the frustration of our practical projects. Certainly, the agency involved in relying on a computer system is – at least at present – at most an "as if" kind. (Computers do not currently have the same kind of agency that people do; at minimum, the quantitative difference is so severe as to constitute a qualitative one, and the difference seems to me to be one of a kind.) The sense of trust

---

[2] I take the labels from Hollis (1998: 10).

involved there is merely predictive. Nonetheless, the term "trust" neatly refers both to attitudes that take systems and other people as objects.

It is a truism that computing technology moves fast. The context is thus one where, for the great majority of those who do not work in that world, new ways of navigating the hybrid digital/off-line world are continually encountered. And even where there is a degree of experience, these ways of navigating the world retain an unfamiliar "alienness" for a time. Along with the risk involved if our goods are not valued, there is also uncertainty about whether they will be. The workings of computers' "as if" agencies are inscrutable to most users (indeed, to most technicians too; debugging is a time-consuming and complex business). And the workings of other peoples' agency remain as inscrutable as they were in the pre-online world. In the face of this uncertainty and risk, articulating the need for trust in technological contexts to be grounded thus functions as an alarm bell. It warns your interlocutors that the practical environment cannot be taken for granted. Contemporary fears – as Clark points out in Chapter 2 – generate contemporary anxieties over trust.

To make these general points specific, consider the public discourse around cloud computing. Cloud computing has been a buzz-concept at the center of discussions in the world of information and computing technology. The underlying technology is prosaic: it is a change in the geography of computing. Instead of the bit of hardware on your lap or desk doing the computing, data storage and processing are done by hardware held in a different and likely unknown location, accessed remotely, with users simply making use of the results from wherever they happen to be, with their own devices often needing to run only a browser. Facebook, Windows Live (Hotmail) and Gmail, DropBox and Flickr are all well-known examples of computing in the Cloud (see Hayes 2008 for a summary). The prospective benefits of cloud computing are principally practical and commercial: large remote data centers provide all the hardware and software individuals or companies could need. Users pay for only what they need and the economies of scale make the management and protection of data considerably cheaper. Pervasive connectivity gives reliable access to these data centers, whereas the proliferation of devices makes it increasingly preferable to host data elsewhere for accessing when needed, rather than on the devices themselves.

The obstacle to take up cloud computing is the lack of trust. In relying on another company to supply their hardware and software needs, users make themselves vulnerable to problems arising from that company's incompetence or venality. The issue is not merely theoretical. In April 2011, Amazon's Elastic Compute Cloud service crashed during a system upgrade, knocking customers' Web sites off-line for anywhere from several hours to several days. That same month, hackers broke into the Sony PlayStation Network, exposing the personal information of 77 million people around the world. In June 2011, a software glitch at DropBox temporarily allowed visitors to log in to any of its 25 million customers' accounts using any password. A company blog reported: "This should never have happened."[3] Given these possible problems, it is natural to ask whether cloud computing can be trusted. Ross MacDonald asks exactly that, justifying the enquiry with the remark that: "There is much fear, uncertainty and doubt out there when it comes to security on the internet and with it an undermining of trust" (2012). Laments among the technorati about a lack of trust signify that a new technology has arrived and that it may go wrong in ways that we cannot fully predict. Of course there may actually also be an underlying problem; but that is not the primary function of the speech-act.[4]

But it is not clear that this situation will endure. Humans are adaptable and learn to live in new environments. We can compare the way that languages are appropriated between populations. When two populations come into close contact but speaking different languages, a pidgin dialect usually arises – a reduced language which incorporates vocabulary from both substrate languages, influenced by the meaning, form, and grammar of the others. A pidgin is no one's native language. But as people are born and grow into the linguistic community where a pidgin is spoken, the language stabilizes and formalizes, regaining features characteristic of language that were previously absent. It becomes a language in its own right – a creole (Holm 1988).[5] A parallel process of indigenization occurs with technology. For one generation, some new technology that affects how they live constitutes an intervention and is perceived as problematic. For the next generation, it is merely part of the background of their lives. John Palfrey and Urs Gasser refer to these latter as "digital natives" (Palfrey and Gasser 2008). My contention is that trust will cease to be an issue for digital natives in the way it currently is for nonnatives. Specific trust issues will no doubt continue to arise – ought I to trust *this* person, *this* website? – but the question will not be asked about the technology generally. Asking "ought we trust cloud computing?" will one day make as much sense as the question "ought we trust telephones?" does now.

Another area in which the same observation applies is the discipline of security software engineering. "Trust" has become a term of art within this community. If a system, component, or person is trusted, then their failure would break the security policy; if they are trustworthy, they will not break the security

---

[3] These examples are from Cachin and Schunter (2011).

[4] Olli Lagerspetz (see Chapter 6) likewise emphasizes the performative dimensions of the term "trust."

[5] I owe this analogy to David Good.

policy (Anderson 2009: 13). This usage has significant influence beyond the security engineering specialism, however, and is arguably dominant among those who write the code. Thus Microsoft Word includes a "Trust Center": "The Trust Center contains security and privacy settings. These settings help keep your computer secure."[6] At the time of writing, Microsoft has a "Trustworthy Computing team," headed by a corporate vice president, which has the same concerns. A similar emphasis on the integrity of the underlying technology derives from those who wish to promote e-commerce (e.g., Salam et al. 2005; Corritore et al. 2005). The origin of this usage is historic. As computers began to be used by the U.S. military establishment, the question of how to ensure the security and integrity of information had to be considered. Their Orange Book (U.S. Department of Defense 1983) introduced the concept of the Trusted Computing Base, the set of all hardware and software, a failure in one part of which jeopardizes the security of the whole. Good security engineering thus requires minimizing the Trusted Computing Base. In this context, trust is an undesirable but unavoidable necessity. Using the term "trust" to include security concerns is certainly permissible. After all, the technology has let you down if there is a security breach.

This distinctive usage illustrates the hortatory implication of the genealogical account. The implication is this: beware ambiguity. Part of the reason for the richness of the term "trust" is that it has many possible referents. The notion of trust that is in play in technological contexts is importantly different from the richer conception at use in interpersonal contexts. Security enables (mere) predictive trust, better described as reliance. Philip Nickel and his coauthors ask whether we can make sense of the notion of "trustworthy technology." Their clear-minded answer is: "not really." In ascribing trustworthiness to technology, "this would have to be a thin notion of trustworthiness. It would differ significantly from the full-blown, motivation-attributing notion of trustworthiness" that they take to characterize interpersonal contexts (Nickel et al. 2010: 443; for dissent, see Weckert 2011). I endorse their point. Although permissible, using "trust" to refer only to security concerns misses out on the richer notion applied in other contexts, including interpersonal ones.

Nor should one use of "trust" be allowed to obscure other permissible uses. Consider what is lost if the security specialists' use of "trust" is allowed to predominate to the exclusion of others. Equating trust with security risks overlooks the point that security can never guarantee trustworthiness. A paradigmatic security concern is the restriction of access to only those who are approved by the system manager. But the system manager must still be trusted, and must also

---

[6] Microsoft Word 2010>Quick Access Toolbar>Word Options>Trust Center.

trust those whom they approve not to abuse this access. This is a general point about trust: although trust can be shared across a group of people or minimized by using a third party as surety, there can never be a point at which it "bottoms out" (see O'Neill 2002a: 5–6; Weckert [2005: 108–109] independently relates this point to computer security). Another perennial security concern is ensuring robust identification of the server or person with whom I am communicating. It certainly restricts my ability to place trust if I do not know who I am talking to. But simply knowing their identity does not suffice for rational trust; it might have been Muammar Gaddafi. Although the security of computer systems is likely necessary for people to interact with confidence online, it is hardly sufficient.

Furthermore, the security specialists' usage may have perverse consequences, if it is construed as the only legitimate use. Helen Nissenbaum points out that "boxing people in" is generally a very bad strategy for fostering cooperative, trusting relations with them. She observes that demonstrating trust through accepted vulnerability shows others that you think well of them, which itself leads to people being more trustworthy (Nissenbaum 2001: 124). Empirical research corroborates the point; introducing "extrinsic" reasons for trustworthiness tends to displace "intrinsic" ones, and can lead to an overall decline in contribution to public goods (she cites Kramer [1999: 591]). Too much security exhibits distrust, and when people think it unwarranted, they react by being less trustworthy. So "the pursuit of trust must be decoupled from the pursuit of high security; trust will not ride in on the coat-tails of security" (Nissenbaum 2001: 130).

Grounding Trust in Technological Contexts

This final section is concerned with the practical implications of the genealogical account, namely its consequences for the search for trust. I do not answer the search for trust directly. That task is beyond present scope. Instead, I offer some outline remarks about how philosophers might contribute to that task and illustrate how that contribution may proceed.

Recall that a reason for elucidating trust is the hope that an analysis of the concept will answer the question of how trust can be restored in a technological context. The principal result of this genealogical enquiry is that this hope is forlorn. There is nothing about "the concept of trust" per se that dictates an answer to that question, because there is no single concept to address. The genealogical account is quietist, in the sense that it is neutral regarding the possible bases of trust.

The quietist result does, however, have a more positive implication for that more substantial enquiry. Although there is no single concept of trust that, when read off the world, tells us the answer to the search for trust, there are some distinctive *forms* of trust which are particularly noteworthy, some of which I have identified. Stipulating that *this* is the concept that is on the table for a particular discussion provides a starting point for addressing this larger, diffuse inquiry. Once this is done, there is no reason to be suspicious of an analysis of that particular form of trust. Although the analysis will be stipulative, insofar as it describes an actual phenomenon, it has value. So often the simple invocation of trust fails to be sufficiently perspicuous. Clarity in philosophical debate requires specifying which type of trust is at issue.

One important form of trust is that which I previously called "cognitive trust." Cognitive trust is a belief about another's future trustworthiness and can be used as an analytical basis to evaluate the instrumental effectiveness of contemporary technologies. It conforms to an evidential principle – that is, A's trust of B over X is justified only if it is proportioned to the evidence that B will be trustworthy over X. The evidential principle applies because belief is rational only if it is proportioned to the evidence. Cognitive trust is the appropriate form of trust to adopt in situations in which one has no special moral obligation to trust the other, and in which there is some good at stake that requires accuracy. Such goods may be practical, epistemic, or moral goods.

The evidential principle has wide application online. There is frequently some such good at stake and I have no specific moral obligation to trust another, so my trust is permissibly and sometimes obligatorily cognitive. But identifying the implications of the evidential principle cannot be done in one grand systematic sweep which takes in the whole of the technological world. Instead, it requires piecemeal application to specific contexts as new issues arise. I have done so to the utility of robots in war (2011a) and of online reputation systems (2011b). Here I wish to highlight briefly its application to the epistemic evaluation of search engines.

Here is the question: ought inquirers trust search engines to return an objective string of results in response to an inquiry? I argue not; there is evidence that they are untrustworthy in this respect. The evidence is this: personalization of search engines threatens objectivity. Yet most search engine results are personalized. There is an explanation to this problem.

Personalization is a wider trend in how services are provided over the Internet than just the provision of search results. It consists of the use of algorithms to profile individual users, based on their past browsing and information consumption history, to predict what kinds of online content they will prefer. As profiles "deepen" over time, so the variance between what you and I are provided with when we go online increases. The idea is well captured by a quotation widely attributed to Mark Zuckerberg, founder of Facebook: "A squirrel dying in front of your house may be more relevant to your interests right now than people dying in Africa." If you really are more likely to follow a link that takes you to a squirrel dying in front of your house, personalized Web products therefore prioritize that rather than the people dying in Africa. Personalization on Facebook means that, in your news feed, it prioritizes information about the friends you contact and follow the most. The Amazon recommender system will be known to nearly all present readers, and similarly works on the principle of personalization: "people like you have also bought . . . ".

Pertinently, search engines now personalize your results. Entering exactly the same query, I will get a different set of results than you will. In practice, this means that sites you have previously visited will be prioritized in your search results pages; call this *individual personalization*. Additionally, sites which are visited by other people whose browsing histories resemble yours in ways picked out by the algorithms as relevant are also prioritized; call this *profile personalization*. Google rolled out personalized searches to signed-in users (those with Gmail or Google accounts) during the summer of 2005. In late 2009, it announced that personalized search would be the default option for all users, and this is the current situation.[7] Although you retain the power to turn the feature off, "the devil is in the defaults" (Kerr 2010), because the significant majority of users are either unaware of changes to defaults, do not know how to change them if they are, or do not care. Although we do not know the numbers – Google guards their data closely – the legitimate presumption is that the great majority of searches now are personalized.

How does personalization threaten objectivity? It is a contingent psychological fact about humans that we suffer from confirmation bias. That is, people are generally more likely to find reasons to discount evidence which goes against their antecedent belief and not to subject it to similar scrutiny evidence which confirms their existing belief. They are also likely to view evidence which is consistent with their belief as confirmatory, even though it is also consistent with competing possibilities. Francis Bacon observed the problem: "Once a man's understanding has settled on something (either because it is an accepted belief or because it pleases him), it draws everything else to support and agree with it" (*New Organon*, section 46. The claim is empirically demonstrated. For classic studies, see Lord et al. 1979; Wason, 1960. For an overview, see Nickerson 1998). Confirmation bias means that we are, generally, more likely

---

[7] See Google (2005, 2009). The differences between "signed-in" and "signed-out" personalized search are explained at Google (2012).

to seek out testimony that supports our existing beliefs, rather than testimony which contradicts it.

The problem is that personalization reinforces confirmation bias. Suppose on past queries you have followed links only or predominantly to testimony with which the snapshot suggests you will agree. Links to these sites are then promoted in future searches, which, broadly, will offer testimony with which you are likely to agree. Therefore, pages that contradict or challenge your existing views are likely to be demoted in the rankings.[8] Personalization, therefore, threatens objectivity. The more personalized the results, the less they represent the sides of the argument with which you disagree, and the less objective they are. Thus it constitutes evidence that inquirers ought not (cognitively) trust search engines as a tool for the objective orientation to new sources of information. The corollary is that, insofar as this is a kind of trust we desire to be well-grounded, so there is prima facie reason to constrain personalization in which there is an epistemic good at stake. This result shows how philosophers can contribute to the search for online trust: by piecemeal consideration of the varied kinds of evidence for trustworthiness putatively available, and how that evidence may be restored or strengthened.

---

[8] I am not the first to observe this. Eli Pariser has recently coined the phrase "the filter bubble" to describe the effect of personalization across the Web, including search engines, and he gives a number of (admittedly anecdotal) examples (2011).

6

The Worry about Trust

Olli Lagerspetz

Introduction

The main thesis of this chapter is: trust in the context of the Internet, and elsewhere too, is usually best understood as a continuation of the normal run of life, not as an exception to it. We need to look at those usually unchallenged background activities, contacts, and commitments that, at some point, lead up to situations in which questions about trust are asked. This is not to say that we constantly trust each other, but it means that the question only has an application in particular situations, and that the meaning it has must be understood in the context of the situation. As a further, methodological remark, continuous with the previous point, I suggest that what trust "is" is best seen in situations in which "trust" *is raised* as an issue. To understand trust, we should not be looking for a mental state, attitude, or behavioral pattern "out there" for which the word stands. We should focus on the various kinds of worry that invite talk about trust; on what prompts us to apply the vocabulary of trust in certain problematic situations; and on how applications of that vocabulary contribute to solving, creating, or transforming those situations.

This also invites the question to what extent particular worries about trust are specific to the use of the Internet, as opposed to being continuous with what happens in other walks of social life. There exists a misleading picture that represents the Internet as a world unto itself, an incorporeal realm facing us with a specific set of philosophical and ethical conundrums. This looks to me like a romanticization of the Internet. It is more fruitful to think of our various uses of the Internet as so many extensions of our off-line practices.

Trust: Assessing the Debate

Trust entered as a theme for the English-speaking philosophical mainstream only in the 1980s. The work published at the time is still widely cited and

120

used as a starting point for research.[1] Much of it had a background in rational choice theory. The main question addressed there concerned *risk-taking*: how to account for the rationality of cooperative relations between parties who are not transparent to one another. The volume *Trust: Making and Breaking Cooperative Relations*, a collection edited by Diego Gambetta[2] (first published 1988) was influential in establishing the parameters of the debate. Gambetta sums up his definition of trust:

> In this volume there is a degree of convergence on the definition of trust which can be summarised as follows: trust (or, symmetrically, distrust) is a particular level of subjective probability with which an agent assesses that another agent or group of agents will perform a particular action, both before he can monitor such action . . . and in a context in which it affects his own action. . . . When we say we trust someone or that someone is trustworthy, we implicitly mean that the probability that he will perform an action that is beneficial or at least not detrimental to us is high enough for us to consider engaging in some form of cooperation with him.[3]

This definition locates "trust" in situations in which a choice must be made between "cooperating" and "defecting." A further point Gambetta makes is that our need of trust will increase with the decrease of our chances actually to coerce and monitor the opposite party.[4] Given these parameters, he claims, it can sometimes be "rewarding to behave *as if* we trusted even in unpromising situations."[5]

An obvious objection, however, can be made here. Considerations about possible payoffs might give us reason to behave as if we trusted. But the conviction that it would be a good idea to simulate trust does not translate to trust.

The political theorist Russell Hardin takes up this point and argues that trust implies genuine belief in the other's trustworthiness. He proposes to analyze trust on the model of "encapsulated interests."[6] When I trust you, I believe that you will act in ways that lie in my interest, because it lies in *your* interest to promote mine. I can conclude that you will be trustworthy if I know that

---

[1] See also the overview and critique of existing research presented by Thomas W. Simpson, Chapter 5 in this volume.

[2] Gambetta (ed.) 1990.

[3] Gambetta 1990: 217. Similar positions are endorsed by Dasgupta 1990: 55–56; Good 1990: 33; Schneier 2012: 5; Taddeo 2010, 2011; and Williams 1990: 8. For critique of Taddeo, see Simpson, Chapter 5.

[4] Gambetta 1990: 218–219.

[5] Gambetta 1990: 228. Gambetta is, in particular, referring to results presented by Axelrod (1984). See also Kohn 2008: 23–39.

[6] Hardin 2002: 1–3.

you derive some benefit from our continued relation. Thus Hardin's analysis is presented in terms of beliefs rather than strategies, but it is still firmly rooted in game theory.

As Gloria Origgi has pointed out, one advantage (if you like) of game theoretic approaches is that they involve a kind of anti-ideological justification of cooperative relations.[7] Cooperation is neither good nor bad in itself but its value depends on payoffs to the agent. The values of different outcomes are determined on the basis of the agent's preferences, not on the basis of a normative system with claims to universality. However, it may be responded that this view is not ideologically neutral at all, because it privileges *Homo oeconomicus*, man as utility maximizer, above other perspectives on human nature.[8]

In her essay, "Trust and Antitrust" (first published in 1986),[9] Annette Baier takes exception to the Hobbesian background of game theory and contemporary ethical theory. The essay, and the further treatments of trust included in her subsequent books,[10] are now a central point of reference in the literature. According to Baier, mainstream ethics has been hostage to what she describes as "male fixation on contract."[11] Ethical relations have been understood on the model of quasi-contractual arrangements between parties who are roughly equal in power. But our most important human relations have a connection with family life. Those relations inescapably involve trust, dependence, and vulnerability. According to Baier, ethics needs to address questions about the soundness of our various forms of interpersonal dependence.[12] She suggests that trust should be analyzed on the model of entrusting. We grant the other with discretionary powers to look after something that we care about, and we should now ask what reasons we have for accepting or rejecting such dependence.[13]

Baier's treatment of trust differs from that of the game theorists because of her emphasis on its "warm," emotive aspects.[14] On the other hand, they still share some important background assumptions. They think of risk-taking as

---

[7] Origgi 2008: 17. Also see Hardin 2002: 74–78.
[8] A case in point is the example which Hardin (2002, 1–3) chooses for illustration. He discusses the economic dealings between Verkhovtsev and Trifonov in Dostoevsky's *Brothers Karamazov* (Book III, Chapter IV). Most readers of the novel would not jump at this particular case as an example of trust. It looks more like one of those shady manipulative relations that Dostoevsky was fond of describing.
[9] Baier 1986; reprinted in Baier 1994: 95–129.
[10] Mainly Baier 1994.
[11] Baier 1986: 247.
[12] Baier 1986: 252–253.
[13] Baier 1986: 236–237, 240.
[14] Origgi 2008: 102.

the basic model for trusting. The preferred case for Baier is one where the agent consciously takes a risk, "along with confidence that it is a good risk."[15]

> When I trust another, I depend on her good will toward me. . . . Where one depends on another's good will, one is necessarily vulnerable to the limits of that good will. One leaves others an opportunity to harm one when one trusts, and also shows one's confidence that they will not take it. Reasonable trust will require good grounds for such confidence in another's good will, or at least absence of good grounds for expecting their ill will or indifference. Trust then, on this first approximation, is accepted vulnerability to another's possible or expected ill will (or lack of good will) toward one.[16]

The analysis implies that when we trust a friend – at least, supposing our trust is "reasonable" – we believe there is a risk that she may willfully let us down. But I find this description problematic. If we merely believed that our friend is *probably* not hostile or indifferent, wouldn't it be more correct to say we *distrust* her? Thus one might object that Baier is not describing trust at all, but only a kind of cautious reliance on the other's good intentions. A more benign interpretation would be that her description fits one form of trust – deliberate entrusting – but not the kind of trust typical of the intimate human relations that initially interested her.

Baier's emphasis on accepted vulnerability, or risk-taking, seems to stem from a conflation of two distinct perspectives on the trusting relation – something that, in the quote, shows in her easy change of pronoun from "I" to "one." On the one hand, from our position as observers, we would typically not *describe* a relationship as one of trust unless we could think of a risk of some kind in connection with it. On the other hand, it does not follow that *the person who trusts* must believe that she is making herself vulnerable. Perhaps no question has arisen for her about her friend's trustworthiness. If challenged, she might respond that she knows her friend and hence, that there *is* no risk. From our position as observers, we may say that her trust in her friend is expressed precisely in the fact that she would dismiss the idea that she is making herself vulnerable.

On the whole, it seems to me that important cases of trust will get distorted if we insist on analyzing trust on the model of risk-taking. This was a point I made in my book, *Trust: The Tacit Demand*, published in 1998. I was partly building on Wittgensteinian argumentation presented by Lars Hertzberg in his 1988 paper, "On the Attitude of Trust."[17] I have been asked why these

---

[15] Baier 1986: 236.

[16] Baier 1986: 235. Govier (1997: 4) and O'Neill (2002) express similar views.

[17] Hertzberg 1988; Lagerspetz 1998. See also Lagerspetz & Hertzberg, 2013.

considerations have not been more generally heeded.[18] Or, supposing we made
our cases badly, why haven't related ideas by others[19] made their way into
mainstream debate?

One possible reason is that the work on trust by moral philosophers mostly
has a normative or action-guiding intent. It is expected to have some bearing
on the question on whom we should rationally "place"[20] our trust in an increasingly complex society. The search for guidelines for action naturally goes
together with the assumption that our behavior in the relevant area is based
on decisions – of which we are in full control – which in turn easily motivate
analyses that assume conscious planning on the agent's part. This tendency is
further connected with deeper commitments concerning the nature of rationality. Practical rationality is supposedly expressed above all in choices we make,
not in the ongoing flow of our lives. Practical rationality, on that view, is not an
aspect of human sociality, but a faculty that stands outside of it and which we
apply to it. Hence, it would simply appear irrational or naïve to doubt that we
could (and perhaps should) be prepared, at any given moment, to undertake an
unbiased review of our relations with others according to independent rational
standards.

One way to understand these intellectual tendencies is to consider in what
ways studies of trust bring in, or more frequently, fail genuinely to bring in,
a time perspective. We should consider the ways in which human behavior –
rational or otherwise – is embedded in practices extended in time.[21] I now turn
to this theme.

Trust and Time

Consider an online medical forum for children's illnesses.[22] If my daughter has
caught a fever, I might go there to get in touch with other parents with similar
concerns. They might recommend home remedies or share their own practical

---

[18] A question posed by Richard Harper, personal communication, December 10, 2012.

[19] I am thinking of some work in the philosophy of testimony (e.g., Coady 1992 and McMyler
2011) as well as some earlier, relatively well-known work in sociology (e.g., Garfinkel 1967),
psychology (e.g., Erikson 1977, Bowlby 1969), and theology (e.g., Løgstrup 1956). These
authors by no means each say the same thing, but they all offer alternative understandings of
the rationality of trusting.

[20] O'Neill 2002, Lecture 1.

[21] In a related analysis, R.J. Anderson and W.W. Sharrock (Chapter 7) stress the continuities of
institutions and practices, as opposed to the "bare psychology" of mainstream theories designed
to show how trust is supposed to emerge de nihilo in dyadic relationships. See also David Clark,
Chapter 2.

[22] An example initially suggested to me by Ali Qadir.

problems and solutions. Why should I trust their postings? A skeptic might point out that I have never met them. I would not even know for sure they are real parents and not advertisers for medical companies.

As a matter of empirical fact, such worries are not going to be high on my agenda. Whatever doubts I have regarding the reliability of the postings on the site, they are likely to be quite continuous with similar questions I sometimes face in the outside world. We normally rely on quite a large number of subtle and not-so-subtle prima facie ways to judge the reliability of those with whom we have to interact. I assess the contents of the postings on internal evidence. Once logged in, I can classify some of them as well-researched, emotional, commercial, and so on. This is not very different from how I would relate to statements by people I encounter somewhere else – even though, of course, there are fewer cues on which I can rely (for instance, no visual cues).

These continuities highlight the fact that, on the whole, our Internet contacts are embedded in communities that are also physically present in our lives: at office or school, in the family, with friends sharing information about various Web sites. Perhaps other parents I know have initially directed me to the children's illnesses forum. A wider community is implied despite the fact that, in a narrow physical sense, typically just *one* person will be sitting and typing in front of the screen. Such communities also extend beyond the sphere of personal acquaintances, to what Benedict Anderson has termed imagined communities.[23] On the whole, our social lives are characterized by participation in such communities. These include Anderson's main example, the nation-state, but also, among other things, political, professional, and religious communities and informal groups with which we feel connected. Those communities are imagined, not in the sense of being unreal, but in the sense that they embrace people whom we have not met but with whom we connect via the perception of some common background, some shared interest or goal.

It seems to me that continuities between "off-line" and online communities and practices are often overlooked in debates about trust and security on the Internet. Perhaps for the sake of simplicity, the focus usually lies on "man versus machine" – instances of a *single* person connecting, via the Net, to other persons or agents – or perhaps, on "man versus man via the machine" – a single person who faces another through a kind of digital mist. The focus on the heroic, lone user tends to overemphasize our vulnerability, and hence both our need of trust and its exceptional and precarious character.

This state of affairs is no doubt encouraged by a desire to keep things simple, but it is also a result of the intellectual tendencies I have mentioned. Theoretical

---

[23] Anderson 1983.

approaches often study trust in the light of specific "one-off" scenarios. In a typical scenario, an agent needs to arrive at decisions about whom to trust and how valuable goods to entrust to them.[24] This approach is connected with the fact that theories of trust are typically expected to deliver *guidelines* for distinguishing between reasonable and unreasonable cases.[25] The task has a more manageable appearance if answers can be developed in the context of isolated test cases.

Some treatments of trust explicitly address the simple case of two strangers thrust together in neutral surroundings. Basic models inspired by game theory, such as *Prisoners' Dilemma*,[26] are built around that scenario. To be more accurate, the assumption is not that the two agents *must* be strangers, but rather that the question whether they are strangers is irrelevant. The relevant information concerns their *present* preferences and beliefs, regardless of their previous history.[27] More advanced games, such as the iterated Prisoners' Dilemma, incorporate the agents' earlier and possible future actions. However, I would still maintain that this research in a certain sense aspires to be context-free and ahistorical. To see the point more clearly, consider the following remark, included in economist Partha Dasgupta's analysis of reputation for honesty as a capital asset.

> You do not trust a person to do something merely because he says he will do it. You trust him because, knowing what you know of his disposition, his information, his ability, his available options and their consequences, you expect he will choose to do it. Commitment on his part merely alters the game that is to be played, and therefore alters your expectation of what he will choose to do and, what is subtly tied to this, simultaneously alters his expectation of what you will choose to do.[28]

---

[24] E.g., Gambetta 1990: 222; Govier 1993; Good 1990: 33; Williams 1990: 7.

[25] E.g., Baier 1986: 232, identifying the question as, "Whom should I trust in what way, and why?"; and Govier 1993a: 156, identifying the question as "When, why, and to what extent trust – or distrust – was reasonable or right?" According to Jones (1996: 4), philosophical accounts of trust should "[set] constraints on what can be said about justification conditions of trust." Hollis (1998: 124) suggests that the important question is, "not why people do trust one another but whether and why it is rational for them to do so"; i.e., the "Enlightenment question of who merits trust" (105).

[26] A full description is found in any standard work on game theory. See also, for instance, Gambetta 1990: 216; Hollis 1998: 68–69; Schneier 2012: 51–53; Williams 1990: 3. For a critique, see Grant 1993: 425–430.

[27] See also, e.g., Hollis 1998: 22 (and passim). I would rather side with Coye Cheshire (2011: 52) who suggests, on the contrary, that non-repeated interactions between previously unrelated individuals qualify as acts of risk-taking, not of trust – even if I do not believe we must insist on any specific language use here.

[28] Dasgupta 1990: 55–56.

The factors that we are invited to consider in this passage are described as various *present* conditions. The consequences of history and context are acknowledged, but their relevance is distilled into whatever impact they have on the agents' dispositions and abilities at the present moment. However, this work is context-free only in the sense that the examples are deliberately left vague. Consider the Prisoners' Dilemma. Who are the "prisoners"? How did they end up there? Do they have any reason to trust the promises of the "police"? If the details are not filled in, it is not clear what we should think of the scenario. But once they are filled in, it would be less tempting to treat it as the general blueprint for rational choice.[29]

Not only formal models of trust, but also non-formal attempts to approach trust are often construed on the tacit assumption that the time dimension can be stuffed into a black box. In one of her papers, Trudy Govier invites us to consider under what circumstances we should accept the help of a stranger on a busy street. This particular problem of course would arise precisely because, for want of previous acquaintance, we have no obvious reason to think one way or the other about him. Govier concludes that our degree of caution should be proportionate to the value of what is at risk. Thus "[t]o accept a man's help carrying packages across a busy street, a woman needs to trust him, but slight trust will be enough – unless the packages contain exceedingly valuable items."[30]

I hasten to add that Govier discusses more complex cases too. Some of her examples concern trust between married couples and friends, where their shared history will obviously be the central source of their beliefs about each other. Govier's general view is that our judgment of a person's trustworthiness will be based on available information (if any) about his or her past actions and intentions.[31] Yet I would say this approach is still timeless, rather in the manner of the one I previously cited from Dasgupta. It is built on the paradigm of two strangers incidentally thrust together – the more complex cases being derived from it by throwing in detail. Govier is not an exception here. The nature of the normative inquiry itself easily forces a kind of timelessness onto it. Some decision is to be made *now*. The relevance of the past supposedly lies in its role as a source of information about the agents' interests, beliefs, and

---

[29] Above all, the game must assume that the rules of the game and the possible payoffs are fixed and well-known to the participants. This presupposes some stable organized background.

[30] Govier 1993: 167. Cf. Jones 1996: 21: "Domain and consequences interact to determine which default stance [with regard to trust versus distrust] is justified and how much evidence we need to move from that default stance."

[31] Govier 1993: 169.

competence, but the situation itself must be understood as a snapshot, on its own contemporary merits.

What is then wrong with the snapshot conception? I would say the problem is that it distorts our understanding *even* of the reasoning that *does* go on within the limited time frame in question. Consider Gambetta's comment on his definition of "trust" that I quoted earlier:

> This definition . . . tells us that trust is better seen as a threshold point, located on a probabilistic distribution of more general expectations, which can take a number of values suspended between complete distrust (0) and complete trust (1), and which is centred around a mid-point (0.50) of uncertainty.[32]

Here Gambetta envisages a situation in which we make some kind of assessment and, consequently, a decision to either cooperate or withdraw. This is a possible scenario, even though it obviously reads more like an idealized model than a messy real-life situation. The game theorist's response would be that the model is not supposed to describe in detail how we arrive at specific predictions. It is only meant to state, in a general way, a central feature of rational cooperative behavior. We should rationally be prepared to cooperate only insofar as we have arrived at a sufficiently favorable view of the other party. But the central problem becomes apparent if we ask the natural question: How do we then assess the probabilities? In the model, the relation between assessment and trusting is supposedly *external*. In other words, there is some agreed, putatively neutral way to arrive at a probability value, independently of any previous tendency on anyone's part to trust or distrust the other party. The problem here is that there is no context-free method to assess the implications of someone's earlier behavior for what he is likely to do in the future. The *relevance* of the record of the other's past performance – the kind of use that we should make of his record – cannot be assessed separately from the question whether we are prepared to trust him. Here the importance of a time perspective comes in.

Our perception of the other is shaped in the course of our ongoing relations. Our tendency to construe the "probabilities" of a situation in one way or other – or perhaps more frequently, simply not to think of them at all – is already indicative of our trust or distrust.[33] Consider why we trust a colleague or a friend. It is true that we could normally, if challenged, produce justifying

---

[32] Gambetta 1990: 218. For a similar view, see Taddeo 2010, 2011.

[33] In her essay, "Trust as an Affective Attitude," Karen Jones describes trust as an attitude of optimism about the goodwill and competence of the other (Jones 1996: 7 and passim). The actions of the other are "viewed through the affective lens of trust" (12). Thus she acknowledges that our judgments of "evidence" about the other are not independent of our existing relations with them. However, Jones presents this as a source of *distortion*, implying that there is (or could be) a context-free way to determine what degree of optimism is the rational one.

"reasons" or "evidence." We could, for instance, say that we know our friend. But while our judgment of someone as trustworthy is sometimes literally a conclusion we draw from his or her earlier record of punctuality or honesty, we would not even be *looking* for those qualities in him or her unless we were basically open to the possibility (or fact) that this person can be trusted. Thus if it is suggested that the only alternative to strategic calculus is blind trust, what is ignored is that *both* alternatives presuppose a stable background in which we are already connected with each other's lives, or in which we at least have general ideas of what is involved in "normal" interaction with the individual in question.

The role of such normality was illustrated in some of Harold Garfinkel's ethnomethodological experiments. Here is one:

> [S]tudents were asked to spend from fifteen minutes to an hour in their homes imagining that they were boarders and acting out this assumption. They were instructed to conduct themselves in circumspect and polite fashion. They were to avoid getting personal, to use formal address, to speak only when spoken to.[34]

On the whole, the experience was quite unsettling to those concerned. The students' family members did not find them polite at all but, on the contrary, arrogant or ironic; or they suspected they were ill or troubled in some way. The experiments illustrate that we cannot simply go ahead and decide to take up this or that attitude in a human relationship. I can certainly behave in ways that, in a sense, would be the "same" as those that signify politeness in my relations with someone *else*. Yet our shared past will place constraints on what my behavior can possibly mean in the context of family life. This is not to say that humans are constantly engaged in intellectual acts of social construction and interpretation ("skillful" or otherwise), but simply that human behavior acquires the meaning it has because it bears a relation to past interaction.

In his work on the ethics of trust, the theologian K. E. Løgstrup highlights these issues. He points out that, while we can choose to withdraw from some trustful relations and dismiss invitations to trust, on the whole we have not *chosen* to live a life in which we trust others and are trusted by them in turn.

> [W]e have this strange and unself-conscious idea that the world where the other leads her life is something to which we really do not belong. . . . However, in reality it is quite different: we are each other's world and each other's fate.[35]

> If trust and the openness that is part of it were just something to be arbitrarily chosen by us, we could do without it and not lose anything. . . . But it is not so. Trust is not

---

[34] Garfinkel 1967: 47. On Garfinkel, also see Watson, Chapter 8.
[35] Løgstrup 1956: 25–26. All quotes from this work are my translations.

up to us. It is given. Our lives simply are, not by any design of our own, shaped in such a way that they can only be lived so that the other is offered up to us in showing trust or asking for trust, delivering more or less of her life into our hands.[36]

Løgstrup's talk of "delivering" one's life in the hands of the other perhaps involves unnecessary dramatization. The important point is that we already figure as elements of each other's worlds. We can decide what to do about it, but we cannot ignore it without bidding farewell to ordinary human life. In this perspective, trust arises from our ongoing lives with others. On the whole, we do not treat our relations with others as something that requires us to pass judgment about their trustworthiness. In the particular cases in which such judgments are called for, we think of the alternatives against a general background of "normality" that we are not questioning.

How to Study what Trust "Is"

My second claim is that we see what trust "is," not by identifying some mental state or behavioral disposition for which "trust" stands, but by looking at how *claims* about trust enter ongoing situations. To see the import of this suggestion, consider again a quick sketch of the current theoretical mainstream. Two ideas about the role of trust in human life are frequently put forward. They can also be combined by single authors, as they indeed mostly are.

On the one hand, as we have seen, trust is approached in the context of specific "one-off" scenarios in which it is the outcome of a balance between various beliefs and desires. This suggests the idea of trust as a specific undertaking, an exception. On the other hand, more or less everyone who writes on this topic also adds that social life by definition involves mutual dependence.[37] One cannot imagine organized society without a complex net of trust relationships. Considered this way, trust looks more like the normal state of affairs than the exception. Something like this has been a truism for sociology from its very inception amid debates about the sources of social cohesion. It is slightly odd that philosophers and political scientists should feel the need to argue for it and to develop fresh arguments for it. No doubt this impulse is a reaction to the predominance of "beliefs-and-desires" models of human motivation, stemming from the individualist and rationalist bias that easily creeps into a theoretical endeavor.

---

[36] Løgstrup 1956: 27–28.
[37] Baier 1986: 234; Fukuyama 1995; Govier 1997; Hollis 1998, passim; Kohn 2008; Luhmann 1990; O'Neill 2002.

I am offering this sketch of the literature to make a limited point: there is ambiguity in the literature about how to think of the *presence* of trust in the cases discussed. Should we think that trust enters our deliberation in particular cases only, or should we think of it as a constant background of our lives – like the air we breathe, unnoticed until it turns scarce or polluted?[38] Both alternatives are problematic.

Consider the case of online dating, brought up in a paper by Coye Cheshire. We would typically be proceeding from an initial stage of cautious interaction, with minimal commitment, gradually toward greater risk-taking and openness. If all goes well, we finally meet off-line "where physical and personal risks are arguably more numerous."[39] What interests me in Cheshire's description is its perspective. Meeting someone in the flesh comes across as a major step. This is a very natural reaction. But although it is indeed natural, one may still ask what would make us think that the meeting involves *physical risk*. I move in urban space every day, with people all around me, mostly with no sense of physical threat. Why should I feel threatened in this particular case? To put this in another way: If I must trust my date in order to see her at a lunch restaurant, why don't I feel threatened by the others who also sit there?

One response to this might be: "You need to trust the other patrons too – only this is not something you are likely to be thinking about." Similarly, one might argue that we trust that the food in the corner shop is not poisoned and that our fellow library users are patrons looking for books, not murderers looking for victims.[40] What this response really comes down to is that all normal life among people involves features that might, by giving them some particular twist, be described as instances of trust or risk-taking. I am not suggesting that we *ought* to do so; only that typically no information about existing physical possibilities would refute such descriptions if someone were to insist on them. One might, for instance, point out that nothing prevents anyone at present from slipping poison into my tea. But to present that as a genuine possibility, not as an idle thought experiment, would be to suggest that someone at present might *want* to harm me. Clearly, no consideration of what is physically feasible would in itself be sufficient to give me a reason to suspect foul play. On the contrary, we can see such possibilities as genuine only if we already think there is reason for suspicion. The interesting question here is not what we might imagine in the abstract to happen but, instead, why we sometimes feel the need to bring up such scenarios.

---

[38] Baier 1986: 234.
[39] Cheshire 2011: 51.
[40] Baier 1986: 234.

Why is it that we might naturally want to pick out my meeting with this particular person as involving "personal or physical risks"? This is where my methodological suggestion comes in. We gain an understanding of what kind of a thing trust is by investigating the kinds of worry that make us use this concept.[41] In other words, what is it we *do*, in the present case, if we evoke notions of trust, vulnerability, and betrayal? The bottom line is that "trust," and the vocabulary related to it, are used to make a difference in a situation. They are our ways to organize our understanding of it. In the present case, the difference between my date and the other patrons at the restaurant is that I see her as a potential companion. I have an idea of what our future relationship might be. She is in a position to accept me or to reject me, which is not true of the others. When I reach out to her, I am conscious of my situation as someone who has delivered some part of my life into her hands. If she rejects me now, my understanding of our relation in the past will also change. In that sense, there is no immutable *evidence* here that points to one direction only, regardless of the overall flow of our relationship.

Is the Internet Inherently Deceptive?

If there is some general question about the role of trust in the Internet, it will be about how technology enters our relations with people. But it may not be fruitful to think of this as just *one* question, because our use of the Internet is not one thing either. The Internet is a conglomerate of various ways to access people, companies and institutions, databases, libraries, and so forth. Consider some areas in which problems may arise: communicating with friends you already know; befriending new people on the Internet; and security issues, surveillance, and identity theft.

Suppose I email my wife about today's shopping arrangements. I might just as well be leaving a note on the kitchen table. Nothing beyond mundane practical questions hangs on my choice of medium. The relative simplicity of this case depends on the fact that we have an established contact from before (and we have no reason to think that an outsider might intercept the message and somehow use it against us). My wife has no reason to wonder who is sending her the message or what ultimate reasons might lie behind it. If she were to suspect foul play of some kind, the reason would be something more complex than just the fact that the Internet is involved.

But there are more complex cases – for instance, that of befriending someone in the "blogworld." The question here is how this is different from other ways

---

[41] For a rather similar approach, see Richard Harper, Chapter 1 in this volume.

of getting to know people. Many questions may be asked generally about what is involved in getting to know people, but most of them are not specific to *where* and *how* this happens. What about making friends at a wedding, in a post office, or in a supermarket? Should there be a separate treatment of each of these themes, and should we insist that each presents problems quite unparalleled in the others?[42]

One possible source of concern, typical of the Internet but not present in these other cases, lies in the fact that Internet communication is *disembodied*. It involves contact with someone who is not physically present.

Bjørn Myskja has addressed this theme. His work is interesting because he offers a discussion of trust that does not follow the usual beaten path. His interest in digital communication goes beyond that obvious theme of security issues. Nor does he want to reduce trust to cooperation in the manner of the game theorists. He thinks trust is a genuine ethical relation that cannot be cashed out in terms of predictability. And he asks what the prospects and challenges are for the development of trustful relations in a digital environment. Myskja's general view is that the Internet as a medium creates a problem because of what might be called a lack of fit between the content and the medium. On the one hand, the Internet enables us to communicate deeply personal thoughts and feelings in real time. On the other hand, it disconnects personal relations from the types of face-to-face setting where trust naturally develops.[43] The communicating parties cannot rely on behavioral cues that typically regulate trust and distrust in face-to-face interaction.[44]

Myskja emphasizes the role of bodily presence in trust. The reason is not that we need to keep an eye on each other.[45] Myskja is not part of the research tradition that presents trust as a response to difficulties of monitoring the behavior of others. Drawing on the work of Løgstrup, he believes that the trustful human relationship is primordial. The role of trust in human life is not reducible to some other, more fundamental function.

Bodily presence usually makes a profound difference to how we think of others. For all kinds of reasons, we often tend to relate to people not directly, but via preconceived ideas or "pictures" of *the kind of* person that we suppose the other to be.[46] However, as soon as we meet in the flesh, the real person at once

---

[42] Questions by Camilla Kronqvist.

[43] Myskja 2008.

[44] Also see Cheshire 2011: 49: "the social cues we rely on to detect risk and uncertainty in the physical world are often unreliable when we do not know who is behind the digital curtain of anonymity."

[45] Cf. O'Neill 2002.

[46] Løgstrup 1962: 22–23; Myskja 2008: 214.

sweeps away the picture. For this reason, the Internet looks like a problematic medium. It allows a degree of confidentiality that normally indicates solid trust, and yet does not involve the actual meeting that usually accompanies such relations. Myskja concludes that only partial, not "unconditional," trust will be realistically possible over the Net.

One objection needs to be made here, for the record at least. Myskja does not seem to be quite right in thinking that confidentiality and trust are somehow unnatural in written communication. It is possible sometimes to be more open in a letter than in face-to-face interaction. (There is a Roman saying to this effect: *litterae non rubescunt.*[47]) In the late eighteenth century, private letters were sometimes called "soul visits."[48] Romances and friendships sometimes arose and persisted exclusively in writing, without the correspondents ever meeting.[49] But of course the idea of a soul visit still trades on the understanding that personal presence – the visit – is the quintessential form of togetherness. Physical distance takes some heat off the relationship and sometimes allows for more candor, precisely because presence is such a powerful influence on us. To consider an intermediate case, it may feel easier to broach an embarrassing topic if we avoid direct eye contact.[50] Thus these examples, although they may look like counterexamples, might also be interpreted as indirect support for stressing the difference that bodily presence makes. You *long* to be with a friend, you long for them to be with you at least from time to time (but probably not all the time). Friendship without presence feels unfulfilled. It is a tragedy when close friends are forcibly prevented from seeing each other.

It may also be objected that it is sometimes easier for us to talk personal issues with strangers than with close friends. But this, too, is really an indication of the fact that closeness matters to us. Friendship pulls us toward greater confidentiality, but also the consequences of rejection and misunderstanding appear greater.

But while it can be maintained that close personal relations typically at least exercise a kind of "pull" on us toward physical contact, it does not follow that written communication has the opposite "pull" toward *deception*. This is where I am skeptical of Myskja's approach.

For Myskja, the Internet is, by definition, a form of make-believe. It creates a *virtual reality* in which people can assume roles they do not have off-line. This amounts to nothing less than conscious, mutual deception. Nevertheless, he believes that it may also foster trustful relations (albeit not "unconditional"

[47] "Letters don't blush," i.e., it is easier to say things in writing than face to face.
[48] "*Seelenbesuch.*" Friedell 1960: 739.
[49] Friedell 1960: 739.
[50] A point made by Lars Hertzberg.

ones), as long as the parties are aware of the fictitious character of the virtual reality where they meet.

> The online world is a fictitious world, a product of art. Like art, it resembles the real world, but can only function because we know it is not. We act within online worlds as if they were real, and interact with each other as if others are who they present themselves as, even when we know that this is not the case.[51]

Myskja's description of "online worlds" as instances of deception is based on his contention that any kind of fiction (for instance, telling a joke) is a form of *lying*. He goes so far as to imply that communicating one's "meanings and intentions" constitutes lying whenever it assumes any other form than that of stating straight out what is true by "the literal meaning of our words."[52] The natural upshot is that lying necessarily belongs to social life. In the Internet, pretense is made into a *systematic* feature of all interaction. Now let us test Myskja's thesis by considering some instances of what he might mean:

a) Someone assuming the identity of a "High Elf" in *World of Warcraft* (a multiplayer online game).
b) Someone, possibly a "Troll,"[53] professing political views, under a pseudonym, on a discussion site.
c) A possibly suspect Web site offering prescription medicine for reduced prices.
d) A fifty-seven-year-old man posing as a fourteen-year-old girl to get in touch with girls of the same age.
e) A friend posting untruths on Facebook.

The details of the examples are my own, with the exception of (d), which comes from Myskja.[54] However, they are all modeled on his descriptions of how the Internet blurs identities.

---

[51] Myskja 2011: 133.
[52] Myskja 2011: 124–125. Myskja attributes this definition of lying to Kant and argues that "lying" may, *pace* Kant, in fact be morally innocent or even morally recommended. Hence, he states, "Kant's demand of absolute truthfulness is problematic in regard to our everyday communication" (125). He claims furthermore (Myskja 2008: 216) that Kant himself does not hold on to this demand in some of his writings other than the *Groundwork* and *Critique of Practical Reason*. An alternative reading of Kant's position – which I favor – would be to define "lying" strictly as "asserting what one believes to be false in order to deceive someone" (Jackson 2001: 149). This allows for jokes, stories, and also the mere avoidance of issues one does not wish to bring up for discussion. This would also be in closer accordance with what people in general would mean by "lying."
[53] A "troll": someone who enters an Internet debate deliberately to disturb or distract it.
[54] Myskja 2011: 132.

The first two items of the list – (a) and (b) – are not clear-cut instances of *deception*. To act a role in a game – as in (a) – belongs to the game and involves neither deception nor truthfulness. Moving down on the list, a discussion site – as in (b) – is, in some sense, a *public* site. In a public political debate, whatever message is conveyed must be taken on its own merits. A posting may involve deception insofar as the writer conceals his or her real motives, for instance if the writer is paid by a government agency to disrupt debate. On the other hand, this possibility, too, is part of the given parameters of public debate and hence not specific only to the Internet as a medium. On the whole, the relation between pseudonym and identity looks like a possible source of problems. A pseudonym is more anonymous than someone I encounter "in real life," even if I do not know their name.

The next item may be a case of deception. Here game theory may be the right tool: one should weigh the risks against possible benefits.

The fifty-seven-year-old con man – in (d) – is an obvious case of deception. Our reaction may be: "What a dirty/silly old man." Or, if we are more cynical: "Told you so." Cases like this are easy to imagine, because the identity of the person "at the other end" cannot be verified. But is this a case of mutually recognized pretense? We would not necessarily think that girls who are fooled by the con man somehow ought to accept this possibility as part of the bargain.

The last item raises an obvious problem about trust; not because it specifically concerns the Internet, but because it concerns falsehoods between friends.

These examples are imaginable, with suitable modifications, in "non-Internet" life as well. Probably the interesting continuities are mostly to be found between online and off-line cases (such as live action role-playing and online role-playing) and not between the various examples of online activities that were cited.

One distinctive feature of the examples is that they involve written communication. In his further treatment of the "deception" involved in online communication, Myskja cites a paper by John Weckert:

> At the keyboard you can concentrate only on yourself, your words, and the feelings you want to convey. You don't have to worry about how you look, what you're wearing, on those extra pounds you meant to shed.[55]

[55] Myskja 2008: 217, quoting Weckert, J. (2005), *Trust in Cyberspace*. In Cavalier, R.J. (ed.), (2005), *The Impact of the internet on Moral Lives*, Albany: State University of New York Press, 95–117, at 111. Weckert is in turn quoting from Wallace, P. (1999), *The Psychology of the Internet*, Cambridge: Cambridge University Press, at 151. Emphasis added by Myskja.

Myskja's interpretation immediately follows:

> There exists a kind of trust online that depends on the fact that we exercise this self-censorship or deception. The fact that we deceive and know that those we communicate with know that we deceive and *vice versa* contributes to an open communication on subjects that both parties find important. The implicit reciprocal acknowledgement that we are not completely honest in all respects may promote reciprocal trust. We know that we communicate with the other not as he is, but as he wants to be (or as he wants to be perceived to be), because we present ourselves in the same way.[56]

Myskja implies that written communication is necessarily less direct, less open, and more deceitful than oral and visual, face-to-face communication. But this is not obvious. Løgstrup also discusses an opposite case.[57] In this example (from E. M. Forster's *Howards End*), there is a meeting between the chief protagonists, Leonard Bast and the Schlegel sisters. Their relation is disturbed because of their preconceived ideas about the "sort of" person the other clearly is. They rely on stereotypes supported by visual cues such as dress, furniture, and general demeanor, signals of social status in a highly class conscious society. Thus even "the body," considered in this wide sense, may keep us from encountering each other.

But Løgstrup has more to say about the body. Most of the time, he is not speaking of the body in so many words, but he does say much about the *voice* – about our responsiveness to a tone of voice.

> [I]n the mere act of addressing someone – regardless of content – a certain tone is struck, in which the speaker, so to say, goes outside himself or herself, so as now to exist in the relation of the address to the addressee.... Not hearing or not wanting to hear the tone that the speaker has struck is, therefore, to ignore the speaker's self, insofar as the speaker himself or herself has ventured forward in it. The fact that all speech is embedded in such elementary trust is also shown by the fact that even a completely trivial remark will ring false if the speaker does not believe it will be received in the same spirit as it is meant.[58]

The last sentence is not an empirical thesis about how the speaker's voice *sounds*. (In that case it would be a false one, because it is obviously possible for a good liar to talk in a convincing way.) Løgstrup is making a point about

---

[56] Myskja, 2008: 217.
[57] Løgstrup 1956: 20–23.
[58] Løgstrup 1956: 24.

the nature of the relation between the speaker and the addressee. The suspicion of ulterior motives brings into it a sense of loss of immediacy. My voice sounds awkward because the *situation* is awkward.[59]

This "voice" is something that one may also see in writing. We are present in our written words too. This is for good and ill: spelling, ways of conducting arguments, and so on, make social class visible. Handwriting is perhaps an intermediate case. It can be used as authentication of the writer's identity. It also has a more direct connection with the physical movements of the body. It perhaps indicates your age and how frequently you write things by hand.

My general point here is that the description of digital communication as "disembodied" must be qualified.[60] It is disembodied in the sense in which all written communication is independent of immediate presence. But it does not exist in a world of its own separate from the concerns and practices that characterize human interaction elsewhere. Online communication, like all communication, can be both sincere and deceptive. As with all communication, we have developed ways to differentiate between prima facie reliable and suspicious instances. Although bodily presence makes a profound difference to the communicative situation, the difference cannot be articulated as a contrast between truthfulness and deception.

Different kinds of media have their own modes of operating, presenting us with various opportunities and risks. Questions will arise about, for example, how much to trust pictures on blogs. If there is any sense in speaking of the deceptiveness of the Internet, here is one example. Suppose you want to get an idea of how people generally think about this or that. The quantities of expressed opinions one way or other may give you wrong ideas of what "the general opinion" is. It is possible for someone to write, under different pseudonyms, a number of supportive comments to his own blog, creating the impression of massive agreement where there is none. But if one were to claim that there must be something inherently inimical to truthfulness and trust in Internet communication, *simply* because it involves the Internet, one should wonder whether that person would be prepared to accept *any* form of communication as truthful.

---

[59] Garfinkel (1967: 51) reports a somewhat related experiment. He instructed his students to engage in conversation with someone and act on the assumption that the other person was acting on hidden motives and did not really mean what he/she said.

[60] See also Harper 2010: 47, 76, for some caveats about the contrast between embodiment and disembodiment in digital communication.

Privacy

In Chapter 2, David Clark treats trust issues from the point of view of user security. He is using "trust" as a tool to highlight issues about identity theft and security-based constraints on the Internet traffic. To sum up what I see as his main point, his analysis implies that the Internet involves a security problem that is endemic. The Internet must accommodate two potentially conflicting strivings: our hope to access as many other users as possible and as much information as possible and, on the other hand, various concerns for security and privacy.[61] In other words, can we keep the "Inter" of the Internet going and yet feel safe in our use of it? One solution is to grant service providers controlling powers so that they can fight spam, viruses, untoward postings, and similar problems.[62] But our responses to that suggestion will depend on whether or not we trust the service providers.

Myskja argues[63] that regulations and security measures – or "institutionalized distrust," as he puts it – are needed for creating a stable framework, or online society, that allows for the development of trusting relations between individuals or companies online. As he points out, "not all kinds of checks and controls undermine autonomy." The implementation of quality controls, inspections, mandatory reporting, and so forth can make our use of public services less complicated and less risky.

> The fact that there exists institutionalised distrust ensures that we can trust the transportation systems, the health services and other central aspects of modern life.... As Luhmann ... famously has pointed out, this aspect of trust reduces the complexities of living in a modern society.[64]

This positive view of control presupposes that the control in question is morally neutral or benign.[65] But of course, the merits of Internet surveillance are now being widely debated. Our views on control will naturally reflect our attitudes toward the instance(s) that would exercise control. They are also likely to mirror

---

[61] Privacy issues are structurally built into the Internet because the users' personal data are no longer contained only in their PCs but in servers around the world (the Cloud). Anyone who can gain access to the Cloud may imaginably find out a way to pry into what is stored there.

[62] Naughton (2012) suggests that there are both political (286–288) *and* technical reasons (284–285) why Internet service providers are facing demands to limit openness. He raises the spectre of a dystopia of *1984* and *Brave New World* combined.

[63] Myskja 2011: 123–124; Myskja 2008: 219.

[64] Myskja 2011: 123–124.

[65] For a less favourable view, see O'Neill's (2002) critique of the "culture of accountability."

our general ideas about vulnerable technology. These are instances of policy and security issues that we face in a society grown larger than life.

One thing we learn from these debates is that "trust" can be profitably used as a tool for highlighting a legitimate worry – security issues – without claiming that there is nothing else to it. Another thing we learn is that the forms that these worries take for us are strongly dependent on our views about the surrounding society; for instance, whether we are inclined to view government agencies with suspicion.

At the bottom of the worry about surveillance lies the realization that personal data can be exploited for manipulating and harming people. But this is true of any archive, whether it be digital or kept in a filing cabinet. The ethical and political issues that arise are specific to the use and control of records, not primarily something that arises with a particular recording technique.[66] Here we need to consider: What are the historical changes brought about by the Internet; in what ways is the current situation qualitatively different from what was the case earlier? One obviously new development concerns the sheer volume of available information and the cost-efficiency of data assemblage. Messages left behind by individual users are all ultimately interconnected. They may conceivably be retrieved by an unexpected third party even years after the event.

Historical Comparisons

When reflecting on our current predicament, we easily think in terms of contrasts with a uniform, generalized "past." Things used to be in a certain way, and the Internet is now changing it all. We might think: "Diaries and letters used always to be private, whereas now emails and blogs are semi-public." We tend to project a certain understanding of privacy onto the past.

I suggested earlier that we should try to understand trust not by developing a general-purpose definition, but by trying to see what kinds of worries our questions about trust are expressions of. But now we should apply the same treatment to privacy. Privacy is also something that is best understood by looking at the kind of worry to which our concern for privacy amounts. "Privacy" is not a given thing.

One dominant approach to privacy arises as a natural consequence of Liberal political theory.[67] As liberal political theory would have it, there is a preexisting natural sphere of privacy that encloses each individual. Each of us relates

[66] A point made by Antony Fredriksson.
[67] See Mill 1956, chapter 4.

to the world in the form of ever widening circles, with ourselves and our bodies (especially their "private" parts) closest to the center. The different circles of separate individuals, and individuals and institutions or governments, touch. The question is where these intersecting circles go deep enough for the individual at the center to fend off further incursion. This is admittedly one possible way to think of privacy, but we should not think of this as a stable picture. "The sphere of the private" is not a given area of life (the area positioned closest to us) but it is something defined in our responses to encroachment. We do not feel that our privacy has been violated because someone has entered this sphere unbidden: on the contrary, we feel that someone has entered unbidden because we feel that our privacy has been violated. Or, to put this still in another way: what *is* "close" to us is defined by the fact that we react to certain actions as encroachments.

Our currently "traditional," but now challenged, view on privacy is largely based on practices that prevailed in the late nineteenth and twentieth centuries. It has been normal, for instance, to think that diaries were meant strictly for the eyes of the person who wrote them. Letters were directed to the addressee and no one else. Against this background, current Internet practices around blogs and email undoubtedly signify a break with earlier ideas. On the other hand, we should also recognize that these ideas are in constant flux.[68]

Johann Wolfgang von Goethe tells us that in his youth it was normally expected that private letters might be read aloud in company without anyone thinking it was a breach of trust. In a sense, letters were the blogs of the time. The first volume of his autobiography was published 1811, forty years after the events he describes. At the time, he clearly felt that attitudes had changed so much that he needed to clarify earlier practices to his readers. The general openness of the time doubtlessly presupposed a society that was closed in other ways. (It would presumably have been seen as a breach of trust to show someone's letters to a servant.) Goethe speaks of his sojourn in Coblenz in 1772. A guest, Herr Leuchsenring, brought with him several caskets containing letters by friends.

> [A]t the time there was such general sincerity between people that you could not talk to one person, or write to him, without considering your words as being directed to several people at once. We searched our own hearts and those of others.... Such correspondences, especially with important personages, were meticulously collected and extracts were read at meetings with friends. And hence, while political debate had little interest for us, we were fairly well acquainted with the wide range of the moral world.[69]

---

[68] On the development and earlier functions of the "private" letter, also see Harper 2010: 13–20.
[69] Goethe 1925: 593.My translation.

At this juncture, Goethe also relates an incident that he would doubtlessly have characterized as abuse of trust – he says it won't receive general approval.[70] Herr von Laroche, the friend with whom Goethe was staying, was in his youth (in the mid-eighteenth century) engaged as the private secretary of Count Stadion, a German diplomat. He was trained to imitate the Count's handwriting so as to spare him the trouble of writing fair copies. But Laroche was also employed to compose passionate love letters that would be dispatched to Stadion's mistress. Chuckling to himself, Stadion would read the letters and choose the ones he wanted to send off.

These examples show that there are different possible ways to understand the "private versus public" distinction and also, that many problems and ambiguities connected with this are not only specific to online communication. What is, then, the same as before, and what is not? In what ways are the rules of the game in the Internet the same as those offline? There seems at least to be one important difference that directly connects with the forms in which the Internet is organized. If you write something on a commercial site (say, Facebook) the site will *own* it. For instance, the company will be allowed to conduct searches on what you have written. Thus, an important aspect of the worries that the Internet may be causing is connected with the *political* question of what is involved in handing over important parts of our communication to an agency that remains accountable to no one except its owners. The question is not whether this technology is pernicious as such but how it is organized and who controls it.

Conclusions

I have suggested that worries about trust are something that arises from breaches in our ongoing relations with others. As a response to ruptures of this kind – actual or conceivable – we perhaps describe a relationship as one of trust. Trust in this everyday sense is neither a one-off thing nor a constantly operative background assumption about those with whom we interact. It is not generally useful to think that every communicative relation is characterized by some *given* degree of trust or distrust. These questions arise because we wish to make a point of some kind. Perhaps we wish to say that a certain relationship is valuable and not to be violated.

---

[70] Goethe 1925: 594–595.

The Internet is not a world unto itself. We should think of the Internet not as a unitary phenomenon but as a set of practices, or – more correctly – as a set of extensions of practices that also exist elsewhere. The worries that communication practices in the Internet may be causing us are largely the same as those that provoke worry in corresponding practices outside it. However, the sheer volume of the material and the enhanced efficiency of surveillance create a demand for addressing some of those worries politically – that is, by way of collective decisions, and not just in private.[71]

[71] Thanks are due to Richard Harper for asking me to write this piece and for valuable suggestions throughout the writing process. An earlier version was read at the Department of Philosophy at Åbo Akademi University on October 22, 2012. It has benefited greatly from comments by the participants (especially by Camilla Kronqvist, Ali Qadir, Ylva Gustafsson, Antony Fredriksson, Jonas Ahlskog, and Lars Hertzberg). I have received financial support from *the Finnish Society of Sciences and Letters*.

7

The Inescapability of Trust: Complex Interactive Systems and Normal Appearances

Bob Anderson and Wes Sharrock

Introduction

As the contributions to the first and last sections of this volume indicate, trust is a problem for those who build Internet services and those who are tasked with policing them.[1] If only they had good models and even better specifications of users, use, and usage, or so they seem to say, they could build systems that would ensure and enhance the privacy, security, and safety of online services. Understandably (but perhaps not wisely), they tend to be impatient with what appears to be overly precious concept mongering and theoretical hairsplitting by those disciplines to which they look to provide these models and specifications. But perhaps an understanding of the provenance and distinctiveness of the range of models being offered might give those who wish to deploy them deeper insight into their domains of application as well as their limitations. Each is shaped by the presuppositions on which it is based and the conceptual and other choices made in its development. No one model, no individual summary of requirements can serve for all uses.

Awareness of this "conceptual archaeology" is especially important when the model's presuppositions are orthogonal to those that are conventional in the field. In such cases, it is critical to understand both why different starting points are taken and the benefits that are felt to be derived thereby. Difference is rarely an expression of simple contrariness but usually reflects deliberate choice made in the hope that things might be brought to light which otherwise are left obscure.

There is a third point to be made here. Although a particular frame of reference or research mind-set might seem to be the natural and obvious one

---

[1] Turilli et al. (2010) provide a general introduction and summary of the issues. The general reactions range from those such as Cerf (2010) and Spafford (2009), who are very concerned, to Odlyzko (2010), who takes a more low-key view.

to adopt and, indeed, be widely used, from the point of view of research method, no particular initial standpoint is mandated. We are not required to base our research investigations on any given set of presuppositions. The test of presuppositions is their fertility as a way of thinking about the research problem in hand, not the fact that they happen to be popular in the research community.

All this signals our intention to adopt a frame of reference that is somewhat unusual in studies of trust and computational systems. We will start not in what might seem to be the obvious place, namely with trust as a feature of the individual user's mental model or cognitive state, but with trust as a constituent feature of a sociotechnical system in use.[2] We start, then, in the same place as investigators like David Clark (Chapter 2), Thomas Karagiannis (Chapter 3), and Angela Sasse and Iacovos Kirlappos (Chapter 10 and Adams and Sasse, 1999) with the system as a configuration of interacting users, services, and other technical objects. We start, however, with a concern for users' experience as they are immersed within this sociotechnical system and engaged in a flow of activities. From this departure point, we will eventually arrive at the issues that preoccupy Clark, Karagiannis, Sasse, and others, but will get there by a somewhat different route with, we hope, something distinctive to offer. Our intention is not to undermine, correct, or criticize more conventional approaches. We see them as having much merit. However, in the collective conversation represented by this volume, we believe there should be a place for a distinctive voice and its alternative contribution.

To aid engagement with our proposals, our first task is to summarize the key elements of the conventional approach so that we can contrast it with our way of reconceptualizing trust. We illustrate just what this reconceptualizing makes available through an extended examination of trust in a technologically dense environment, namely air traffic control, as well as through a briefer description of some features of using Internet-based technology, such as email. We finish with some recommendations for designers of Internet services.

The Challenge of Trust in Context of the Internet

Like many others who have a deep grasp of the Internet and its technologies, in his stage-setting contribution to this collection, David Clark bases his warning regarding the need to exercise care in their use on the distinction between actual and perceived risks. It is the gap between actuality and perception in which

---

[2] Although we have deep respect for the studies of The Tavistock Institute (see Emory & Trist [1972] and Mumford [1996] for examples), we do not want to be heard as adopting their definition of this term. What we take it to denote will become clearer as we proceed.

the problem lies. There are risks everywhere and even the most technologically knowledgeable among us may not know or understand them all. Certainly, those of us without such a level of knowledge neither appreciate nor know how to mitigate them. The gap between perceived risks and real risks is the challenge of trust in relation to the internet. Sara Bury and her colleagues (Bury et al. 2010), for example, report that many (even most) people are aware of only some of the dangers that the Internet poses and are particularly concerned about the security of personal information, images and photos, business information, and so on. Although they do not put it in these terms, she says, they are preoccupied by the risks of phishing, spoofing, identity theft, malware, and data vulnerability. They are, however, wholly unaware of other risks such as those identified by David Clark. Like Clark, Karagiannis and Sasse, and Danezis, the general reaction to this is to advocate for the development of a twin track response. By means of one-time passwords, public key encryption, smart cards, strong authentication, and other technical devices, technologists should develop ways of addressing the vulnerabilities of current technologies. This will make the technology more trustworthy. At the same time, major Internet organizations and public agencies should undertake programs of education and consciousness-raising so that users are much more aware of exactly what the dangers are and how to reduce them. This will make the public less trusting.

This twin track approach is "the conventional wisdom." It has led to research which conceptualizes and models trust in terms of levels of perceived vulnerability. Its starting point is an assertion such as this: once we understand how and why we think we are safe when using the Internet, we should be able to design technologies and associated practices which could make us more secure. Examples of such studies have shown that users of Facebook and other networking sites differ on demographic and other dimensions in their sensitivity to security issues and that these differences can be modeled by social contract theory (Fogel & Nehmad 2009). We know that the perception of trustworthiness is driven by perception of likelihood of betrayal, social preferences, and risk preferences, which have implications for the use of Behavioral Economics as a theory to drive design (Fehr 2009). We know that users have two kinds of trust beliefs based on their perceptions (Lankton & McKnight 2011): beliefs about technology and beliefs about other people. In relation to Facebook and other Internet services, these beliefs are aligned. Users define interactive services both as a technology *and* as a quasi-person. Thus, they view such services in terms of the pairings: competence/functionality; integrity/reliability; and benevolence/helpfulness. The result of all these analyses enables us to explain – or so it seems – why popular techniques like posting photographs of those delivering a service do not appear to make us more trusting of that service (Riegelsberger et al. 2003).

There are several common features to these analyses. First, they are over-whelmingly cast in terms of what we will call "bare psychology." By this term we do not simply mean that they are motivated by reduced versions of explicit and formalized psychological theories. In addition to such simplification, trust is presumed to be obviously rooted in an individual's mental state. Trust is taken to be, first and foremost, as an issue in relation to individuals and their interactions.[3] What David Clark, for example, refers to as the network level issues of trust are, on the conventional view, decomposed into the psychological properties of individuals. Parameterizing these properties and controlling for those parameters is the modus operandi of the research.

Second, the studies are not really about trust at all. They are about *distrust* and how there is not enough of it. To talk about trust, investigators feel the need to frame their questions in terms of what people do or don't trust or what they should or shouldn't find suspicious, risky, or dangerous. The concept of trust is determined by its supposed complement, distrust. It is as if we cannot get a view of trust unless we go through distrust and risk.

Third, while everyone agrees the issues are interpersonal and essentially social, because trust has been taken to be a component of an individual psycho-logical state, it is assumed the state of trusting must be the outcome of some entrusting action(s) we individually have taken or are currently taking, which complement the ostensible actions in which we are engaged. In using an ATM to draw out money, when posting photos on our Facebook site, or ordering books from Amazon, we are both drawing money, posting photos, ordering books *and* trusting. But although event logs, keystroke capturing, and screen scraping allow us to see what we do when we do the buying, posting, and so on, the trusting goes on "in the background" as what Gilbert Ryle (1949) once referred to as an "occult process" in our heads (or somewhere) and is beyond direct (empirical) reach. It is for this reason that trust has to be surfaced by asking about its absence.

Trust as a Bare Psychology

Faisal and Alsumait (2011) provide the most stripped down version of the psychology of trust. They see trust as a (mental) state in which the actor pre-sumes he or she will gain expected results from an encounter without suffering negative consequences. Al-Ani et al (2012) develop this into a pair of trust components: cognitive trust (i.e., that the other has the knowledge and skills

---

[3] This much, then, we have in common with Lagerspetz's (1998) original critique of the concept of trust as that is usually defined in philosophy and the technological disciplines.

to do what is expected and reliably will do so) and affective trust (that is, that the other will satisfy the user's emotional and social expectations). Siau and Shen (2003) elaborate on this central idea and propose three core components to trust.

1) Trust occurs in dyadic relationships. There are two parties who rely on one another for mutual benefit.
2) Trust involves uncertainty and risk. There can be no guarantee that the other will prove to be trustworthy.
3) The trustor has faith in the honesty of the other who is being trusted.

The way the problem of trust is conceived here might be summarized as follows. When two parties come together to engage in an exchange or extended interaction, trust must be built. To understand trust, we must model its build-up (or is it accretion? or, perhaps, even construction?) from a position in which it does not exist to a position in which, through our interaction, we come to trust each other. Under this view, trust is a layering of assumptions or expectations we hold about competence, predictability, and goodwill (Shau and Shen 2003) or competence and affectivity (Ani et al. 2012), reputation and identity (Clark Chapter 2), or the compliance budget (Beautement et al. 2005).[4]

The trouble that all commentators acknowledge is that the value of this analytic idealization is undermined by users who seem to assume the basis of competence, capability, goodwill, affectivity, reputation, and identity is already in place when the proposed processes for assuring that outcome have not been gone through. As a consequence, people trust the technology, or the other or both, too readily. In other words, people resolutely refuse to behave as the conventional conception of trust proposes they do (or should).

This refusal by users is the situation that the conventional approach to trust seeks to remedy. When faced with a disjuncture between what people do and what the theory says they should do, however, our response is to focus even more on what people actually do and to seek an extensive description of the circumstances within which their actions are embedded. What is it about the context as they see it that allows them to be so trusting? Given that we start from the point of view of the user, the central distinction of the conventional view between perceived risks and actual risks has little analytic edge for us. Users only orient to risks of which they are aware. The focus turns, then, to how, from within the ordinary technologically enabled courses of action in

---

[4] As antediluvians, it is of some comfort to us to find the contemporary avant-garde reinventing the sociological wheels of our youth. Beautement and colleagues' compliance budget looks for all the world to be a reconstruction of the "effort bargain" first described by Baldamus more than fifty years ago (Baldamus 1957).

which they are engaged, users take such contexts to be trustable. How is the ordinary, daily experience of using technology constructed so that trusting is the normal state of affairs it clearly is for most people most of the time?[5] We like to think of this kind of description as a "third person phenomenology."[6] In place of the contradistinction between *real* and *perceived* risks, we put a venerable sociological maxim, that of W. I. Thomas (Thomas & Thomas 1928): if men define situations as real, they are real in their consequences.[7] For us, the question becomes how trustworthiness comes to be defined as real in any given situation and so has the consequences it has.

Apart from the centrality of the *perceived* and *actual* risks dichotomy, the standard account of trust has two additional core elements:

1) Actors are defined as effectively *asocial*. Encounters, engagements, and transactions happen between pairs of decontextualized and abstract *agents* and not between members of social groups, communities, or institutions. Obviously there is recognition that people do belong to groups, communities, and collectivities but these are viewed as the consequence of individual actions not as their frame. The emergence of technological and social networks is, for example, where David Clark's analysis ends.
2) From this, it follows that the psychology invoked to motivate actors is a somewhat bare one. The social dimensions of actors' psychological states are absent.[8]

We ask what happens if one takes trust to be effectively (rather than consequentially) social in character and, therefore, to be rooted in our membership of groups, communities, and collectivities. From that position, we ask exactly the same question that David Clark and most other commentators do. But in asking it, we attend to the social rather than the individual psychology of

---

[5] None of which should be taken to imply that users are *always* at home with the system, *never* have moments of doubt about who they are dealing with, and so on. The point is that such "breakdowns" are not the typical users' typical experience. As we will see, it is on this typicality that normal appearances rest.

[6] This is a somewhat different approach to that of Pieters (2010) and Ess (2010 and Chapter 9) in their phenomenological reconceptualizations of risk and certainly to Don Idhe's "postphenomenology" (Idhe 2009).

[7] It should be noted that this is a *methodological* (for want of a better word) point, not a philosophical one.

[8] Let us be really clear what we are (and are not) saying. We are *not* saying that the model that motivates conventional studies of trust should be expanded, extended, or "filled out" to include the social psychology we seek. We fully recognize that models are ways of reducing complexity with the reductive strategy being very much a matter of choice. We do not want to add anything to the bare psychology. We want to start from a less-bare psychology, namely a social one.

technologically mediated social interaction.[9] Such a social psychology treats trust as a routine, obvious, known, and taken-for-granted feature of ordinary social technologically and non-technologically mediated interaction. For short, we will call this *commonsense social psychology*. The aim is to bring out what it is about social life that allows people to act on the basis of a generalized assumption of trust and to assume that others are too. To put things slightly differently, we ask: What are the features of normal appearances in the ordinary (technological and non-technological) interactions of everyday social life which enable people to trust?[10]

Hopefully by now it is clear that contrast between our approach and the conventional view is not simply that it sets aside the *real* and *perceived* risks distinction and departs from a position that takes sociality as central. In addition, it demands that attention be focused first and foremost on descriptions of users' experience rather than the generalized explanations of their trust behavior, whether those be couched in terms of individual psychological traits, demographic characteristics, or, as with Simpson (Chapter 5), the structural properties of modern society.[11] Although we have a wealth of information about who is more trusting than whom and with regard to what, and we have a panoply of accounts of why people of modern industrialized societies are (or are not) disposed to be more trusting, we know very little about what trusting looks like as a feature of commonsense psychology, and especially commonsense psychology in regard to ordinary interaction with technology. Because this notion of a "commonsense" social psychology is the pivot on which our analysis turns, we will now spend a little time explaining just what we take it to mean.

Trust and Commonsense Social Psychology

Our view is one that sees trust as a routine collective *frame of mind* rooted in *experience*. It follows that sociality should be premised in an assumption of a shared *intersubjective* world. The social actors with whom each of us interacts are social beings, much as ourselves. Our actions are based on the

---

[9] This is, then, a very similar conception to that of Watson (Chapter 8).

[10] This could be seen, then, as an attempt to provide the kind of psychology which Olli Lagerspetz (1998) asks for. Whether it is tainted by the "romanticised Hobbesianism" he sees in other sociological accounts, we will leave others to determine. Suffice it to say, we think not.

[11] Philip Pettit (2008) provides a philosophical interpretation of the implications of these changes. Ulrich Beck's (1992) well-known volume develops a broad sociological position, and a set of responses are contained in Zinn (2008). An attempt to define a possible "middle range" approach is given by Cook & Gerbasi (2011).

assumption they have the same order of understandings, feelings, and attitudes as ourselves and act on the basis of them much as we do. They also share with us a common understanding of how social life is organized and of the rules to be followed. It is on shared understandings and shared intersubjectivity that the normal appearance of routine daily life is based.[12]

A number of additional points are worthy of note:

1) Intersubjectivity is a condition of social life and our experience of it begins in media res, in the midst of the flux of daily life.
2) The unity of the social and material world[13] is pre-given for us. We are just as much "thrown" (to use Heidegger's expression) into the ongoing and pre-given social world as we are into the material one.
3) As fully competent participants in this social world, we all possess repertoires of skill for managing our actions and interactions. However, as with all skill, our skillfulness is rendered invisible most of the time. The fluency, deftness, and elegance we typically display when managing our social lives hides the skillful practices we use.
4) It is these social practices which are the routine joint deployment of these skills which coproduce the normal appearance of ordinary social life which we take for granted and rely on.

The research challenge is to find a way of bringing these skills into the open to describe how they are organized. To borrow a phrase of Harold Garfinkel's (2002), who was responsible for developing this approach, we have to "extract the animal from the foliage." If we define successful social interaction as the outcome of skillful deployment of sets of shared practices, then, by examining the flow of the action itself, we can try to identify the practices and the skills by which they are deployed. This enables us to treat the smooth flow and seamless interconnection of actions in the social world as the jointly produced accomplishment of routinely used and methodical practice. Moreover, anticipation of the use of such skills becomes a key component of intersubjectivity and the commonsense psychology which motivates the socially organized strategies whereby trust is accomplished.

[12] Again (we will stop this now), this is *not* to say that people always understand one another, always hold to the same shared expectations, and so on. All we are saying is that social life is grounded in a presumption that this is normally so – a presumption that holds until further notice. If it turns out the presumption needs to be revised for *any* occasion, then, as normal social actors, we have ways of discovering what that requires. See Watson (Chapter 8).

[13] Edmund Husserl's term for this world is the *lebenswelt*. As we discuss later, Alfred Schutz's (Schutz & Luckmann 1973) interpretation of Husserl's analysis is one of the inspirations for our approach (Husserl 1936).

We should enter an important caveat here. Nothing is being said about the goals, purposes, or aspirations participants might claim for themselves or attribute to others. These are only of interest to us as they surface in the flow of action and its outcomes, the achievements of those in the setting. Whatever the outcomes are, whatever the participants take the interaction to come to, our analysis treats the participants as "coproducing" those outcomes with just the normal appearances they take them to have. Because our topic is "trust," this is analyzed as an accomplishment, and participants are viewed as "coproducing" trust. With this stance, we can look at how those achievements are organized and analyze the mutual orientations, expectations, and understandings that ground them.

Some Working Concepts

The Phenomenological Epoché

The term epoché (or "bracketing") is used to describe that part of the phenomenological method or attitude whereby the appearances or properties of the object under study are investigated. The analyst takes some object, say the tree outside the window and, to reflect on it, brackets off the-tree-in-our-field-of-consciousness from the tree about which we have experience, knowledge, understanding, presumptions, and theories. The object "the tree-in-our-field-of-conscious" sets aside, for example, its species, the memories we have of sitting under it, what the use of its wood might be, its relationship to other trees around, the effect of the shade thrown on the vegetable patch nearby, and so on. The phenomenological epoché insists simply that we address this particular tree only as a datum of our experience here and now. Thus, the tree appears (or is "appresented") as a locale of sensations and functions which are *egologically organized*. What this experience means, what it connotes, how it relates to other experiences we have, and the myriad of other no doubt important questions are not dismissed. They are simply set aside for now as not being relevant while our attention is turned to the tree as a phenomenon of immediate experience. The aim of this method is to move, step by step, through the levels of our experience, constituting each "higher" level from those on which it is premised.[14] In this way, what is taken for granted or assumed at one level can, in its turn, be

[14] The quotation marks here are important. The phenomenological method begins by withdrawing subscription to an ordering such as this. That we can point to hierarchies of experience reflects our capacity to organize and construct the facticities of the world, not any essential character the world must have.

subjected to scrutiny at another level. In phenomenological analysis, each epoché is associated with a distinctive "attitude" toward the world-under-view and a set of "relevances" that shape the way the world is viewed. Some examples of "attitudes" that have been examined in this way are philosophy (obviously), logic, mathematics, science, art, fantasy, theater, and religion. Each constitutes a different framework with a distinct attitude and set of relevances that bring different sets of "objects" into view and puts others aside. As we will see, commonsense understanding in the ordinary wide awake world is an important attitude with its own distinct relevances.

The Epoché of the Natural Attitude

When turning to the examination of social life, phenomenological analysis noted that social actors adopt what is described as "the epoché of the natural attitude" (Schutz 1982). This epoché involves suspending the possibility that the world is not as it appears. We assume the reality, facticity, veridicality, naturalness, or obviousness of the world we experience to get on with ordinary social interaction.[15] This assumption is, of course, "until further notice." The epoché of the natural attitude is the commonsense basis for social life and the requirements of engagement with others in social life provide its relevances.

If we apply these ideas to the problem of trust in sociotechnical systems, it soon becomes clear that it is the epoché of the natural attitude (i.e., what users "bracket," take for granted, assume to be the case), which causes the distinction between perceived and real risks to collapse. For someone engaged in a flow of activity using a system, perceived risks are the actual risks.

Asking how the normal appearances of trustability are constituted as the taken-for-granted facticities they are seen to be is an attempt to answer the same questions that David Clark asks at the end of Chapter 2. As we have just discussed, the commonsense properties of any social phenomenon (just what they are *for those in the setting*) can be treated as the jointly produced outcomes, or the achievements, of those participating in that setting. With this as our frame of reference, analysis of the social character of trust becomes more tractable.

Three general analytic themes can be used to provide the description we seek. In the next section, we offer a little elaboration of them and how they might be used to analyze trust in relation to internet services. In the succeeding

---

[15] The important contrast here is with the *scientific* or *analytic* attitude, which begins by accepting the possibility of doubting just these things in order to focus on how they are produced or what lies "behind" appearances. Of course, in doing so, scientists bracket other things such as the dependability of their instruments, the stability of the properties of materials, and so on.

section, we will examine them in more detail in a very different domain – namely, air traffic control. The themes are:

1) *The natural metaphysics of a setting*: What "objects" are oriented to and deployed in the setting and how are they organized, related, and recognized? For example, what, from the flow of interaction, can we say are such things as the Internet, the user, a rendered Web page, a broken link, a friend, malware, a site, or a posted entry? How are they constituted, recognized, oriented to, organized, and related? How are they classified, grouped, and arranged in this setting for the tasks that are underway? The metaphysics so described is, of course, a culturally given one.

2) *The situated reasoning of the setting*: What sets of relevances do social actors have and how do they recognize and account for similarities and differences, relationships, and discontinuities between objects and classes of objects, projected and actual outcomes of actions, and so on? How are causal and other sequences of actions produced so that a train of events becomes recognizably "an attempted phishing," clearly "a broken link," demonstrably "a friend's comments," and so on. Here two distinctive clusters of notions are important; "local historicity" and "natural accountability." The former refers to the precise course of actions and treatments through which some particular phenomenon passes on any particular occasion. The latter is the set of practices whereby the sense or meaning which some phenomenon has, what it "really" is, emerges in the context of particular events as the "local historicity" of that object unfolds. In the ordinary flow of activity, what some object "is" becomes the potentially revisable outcome of the interaction so far. The qualification is important because, if, as the interaction develops, things turn out to be different to what was anticipated, what the object "is" undergoes revision.

3) *The specifics of the context*: How is the activity in hand produced so that it is obviously and recognizably *really that* activity and not a charade, mock up, spoof, scam or other construction? How do cultural objects display their "normality" so that they are immediately recognizable by any user. What are the "thises and thats" which demonstrate that this object is just what we take it to be.[16]

We now provide a brief sketch of how these ideas might be applied to the description of very familiar aspects of Internet interaction mediated by

---

[16] In a previous discussion, we have indicated how the psychological notion of "affordance" (Gibson 1986) could be reformulated to provide the basis for this kind of description (Anderson and Sharrock 1993). Of course, those with malicious or mischievous intent trade on the recognizability of the specifics of the context.

technology – namely, managing email. This acts as a bridge to a broader description of trust in a dense technological environment – namely, air traffic control.

Trust, the User and Email

Imagine the following scenario. You have a set of documents to send to an organization. They concern the estate of a relative or some such matter. You are not sure if the package is oversized and what the postal cost will be. You take the package to the nearby post office and ask the counter clerk. The counter clerk weighs the package, calculates the cost, and puts stamps on it. He then puts the package in a sack. You pay and walk out.

This is an episode, we hope, everyone recognizes. If we look at it from the perspective we have been outlining, a number of facets surface.

1) Your actions and those of the counter clerk are premised in *sets of relevances* given by your different situations. You have documents to send. He has a job to do. This set of paired relevances is shaped by your and his reasons for acting.

2) You assume that these relevances provide *typical* and *dependable motives* for the counter clerk and others whom you expect to be engaged in the projected trajectory of action (various workers for the post office, the members of the organization who will process our documents, and so on). These motives complement yours. This assumption sets your *expectations* of what will happen.

3) These motives are associated with *types of social actors*; personal types such as the counter clerk and anonymous course of action types such as whoever processes the documents.

4) Given such expectations about typical relevances and motivations, you take for granted that these others, these typical actors, will do what you expect of them and so do not feel the need to ensure the clerk has calculated the cost correctly or has put the package in the right sack. You do not seek reassurance that the post office employees will carry out their roles and take the package where it is supposed to go.

5) In addition, you anticipate they will hold expectations about yourself as a course of action type, someone who wants to post a package, and so you shape your behavior to fit with their expectations. You write the address legibly and give the post code. You pay the price of the stamps and so on. You *design* your actions to fit with your projection of their actions.

6) You do not feel the need to check that the documents have arrived or that they are being processed, although of course you *can* do this, and sometimes you

might. This time, though, the situation does not call for it. Your experience of the interaction allows you to take it for granted that the normal trajectory of actions will be carried out.

7) Finally, you expect to be able to do much the same thing any time you need. The typicality of the action just is that we can do it again.

So much; so trivial. But it is in the trivial that we trust. The points we have just made are what "trust" in the sending of a package comes to. In any course of action, it is the relevances we and the others engaged with us have which determine the patterns of typification we assume to be in place. The intersubjectivity of social life is the interlocking interpretations of these patterns of typicality. It is only when normal appearances fail with objects and relationships missing or used in ways we do not expect (the counter clerk throws the package in the air and calculates cost on the loudness of the "thump" it makes when it lands) or projected courses of action do not materialize as we anticipate (the package never arrives) that we reach an "until further notice" point and question what we have otherwise taken for granted. Commonsense rationality consists in following typical courses of action in expectable ways; in doing the same thing the same way, again and again. Being rational in ordinary life, then, means trusting the counter clerk, post men, and officials in the processing organization to do what we expect them to do.

We have chosen the posting of a package as our example simply because email systems attempt to capture much of the familiar processes of the postal system. When we send email, our relevances shape the patterns of typification we have. We assume "someone" has designed the system to enable mail to be sent where we want it to go. We assume "people" working for the network will keep the systems running to allow the mail to be delivered. We assume they have no interest in our mail per se and simply facilitate its passage through the system. We assume the designated recipient will receive the note and will read it. We assume the motivations of all these actors are complementary to our own and their relevances dovetail with ours. Because "this time" it goes the way it always has, we take it that this is just another ordinary mail note being sent or received. Moreover, and this is crucial, the system has been designed on the presumption we will trust it. Our trust in the system is pre-given in that the patterns of relevance we, as users, are assumed to have and the patterns of typification derived from them. The system works *because* we trust it.

A key term in the description we have just given is the *typicality of our experience*. This is experience as we expect it to be. But how do we expect the experience of sending email to be? Once we ask this question, what appears to be a fundamental and natural metaphysical distinction – that between the user (considered as a bundle of social, cognitive and biological properties) and the bundle of hardware and software properties designated as the email system – can be brought into focus. As is shown by both Banks (Chapter 11) and Sasse and Kirlappos (Chapter 10), design of the user interface, be it command line, wimp, voice, or whatever, is the explicit attempt to manage this deeply ingrained distinction. Putting it another way, those user interface designs which are successful (in whatever ways one wishes to measure such success), are so because of their capacity to solve the problems engendered by this separation. Somehow or other,[17] our experience consists of reaching across the divide to manipulate the system or to communicate through it in some way. The affordances they provide for closing the gap between the user and the system underpin the attractiveness of the most widely used metaphors for designing email and other interactive systems.

When we look at email use as a stream of experience, the natural distinction between the user and the system dissolves. Instead, the system-and-user is foregrounded as a cultural *object*. What, at any particular moment, is the system *for* the user and where the boundaries of *the-system-in-use* might be for those working with it can be brought into view. When composing an email, we do not think about what the system is doing. Neither do we ask where the writing takes place. On the keyboard? In the mail window? Where? Just as writing with pen and paper is only rarely experienced as having a thought, moving the pen, and expressing the thought, writing email is not pressing keys and watching bitmaps. It is thoughts flowing through words. When scribbling a note to a friend, we are at one with the pen and paper. When typing email we too are at one with the system. In the experience of the task, there is no *perceived* difference between the user and the system. The commonsense reality of using email is that the system and the user are one. Because of their own distinctive relevances, our technical ways of describing the use of a system fail to capture this. Distinctions such as user and system are important in technical talk. But do they matter for the user in the midst of using the system? Does the practice of using email depend on holding to a system-user dichotomy? Questions such as these indicate how we can make the distinction between system and user move from being a given in the design to a topic for analysis in the service of design.

Bringing the ideas of relevances, typifications, and commonsense realities to bear upon interactive systems such as email raises a number of possible lines of investigation. The first is that any description of the setting/working system becomes a description of the system-as-seen-and-produced-from-within flow of

---

[17] As Harper and Odom (Chapter 12) demonstrate, because our knowledge of their success remains so vague, it has to be "somehow or other."

action. Second, and closely related, the constructs around which that system is organized (such as the unity of the user and the system) are resources for users in their sense making of the working system. The working of the "working system" produces and reproduces the reality, validity, and veracity of these constructs as the normal, ordinary, and routine things they are. Immersion in the flow of action brackets questions about the dependability of the system or its trustworthiness.

Here lie the key insights we think our approach offers. First, it suggests that trust is the default mode of ordinary social life. We assume things are as they seem to be. Moreover, when we do call things into doubt, we do not suspend doubt tout court. It is not possible to doubt everything at once. To scrutinize some things, we still have to take other things for granted. Second, it follows that if we want to reshape our encounters with technological systems (such as email) so that we are less trusting, we will have to design them in ways that do not, either overtly or tacitly, call into play the structures of typification we deploy in ordinary life. The metaphors and analogies that seem natural or intuitive and that allow for ease of use are precisely those that allow commonsense rationality to be deployed. If we don't want users to trust the system, we have to find ways of breaking the frame on which trust relies. In the next section, we show just how hard this is to do.

Air Traffic Control: A Technologically Intensive Environment

Richard Harper's introduction to the volume summarizes how the sheer complexity of modern technological (especially Web-enabled) systems and services seems to have made the issue of trust intractable. However, although the technologies might be different as technologies, as places where interaction is managed through technology, they do not appear to be all that different to the environments and locales of work which we and others have studied in the past.[18] To demonstrate this similarity and further illustrate how the issue of trust in a technological system might be reconceived, we will revisit research carried out more than twenty-five years ago at what was then the London Air Traffic Control Centre at West Drayton.[19] We show the detailed social organization of trust to be a constituent feature of ordinary computationally mediated work practice. Because the character and recognizability of ordinariness is embedded

---

[18] See Button (1993) for an introductory overview.
[19] The West Drayton Centre no longer exists. Its functions were transferred in 2007 to a new facility at Swanwick near Southampton. For the original research report, see Hughes et al. (1998) and Harper & Hughes (1993).

in the local physical and organizational detail, we begin by summarizing the setting as it existed then and how air traffic control was carried out (and, by and large, is still today). For ease of reading, we set our description in the historical present. We are not concerned to mark how air traffic controlling has or has not changed; nor are we concerned with its contemporary use of the Internet as an infrastructure. Our interest is simply describing how, when we studied air traffic control, the routinization of trust was evident all around.

The Setting: London Air Traffic Control Centre

The organization of air space above The British Isles is somewhat complicated. The simplest division is that between "controlled" and "non-controlled" air space. In the latter, aircraft are largely free to move at will. In the former, all aircraft must be controlled by an appropriate air traffic controller (ATC). Controlled air space takes three forms: en-route sectors, where planes are at or approaching their cruising heights and speeds; Terminal Maneuvering Areas (TMAs), where streams of planes seeking to land or take off are organized; and Aerodrome Approach, where planes are taken into land.[20] The control of en-route sectors and TMAs over England and Wales is located at London Air Traffic Control Centre (LATCC).

The suite at which a controller sits consists of buttons surrounding the circular luminescent green radar screen. Above these are screens displaying information of various kinds. To each side are clacking line printers. Each controller is hooked into the suite by the trailing cable of a headset and microphone. In the center sits what is possibly the only anomalous feature, a wooden tray holding printed "strips" with hand written notes scribbled all over them.[21] To ATCs, the strips are the key to good controlling. As one controller said: "You have got to have a complete picture of what should be in your sector and what should be in your sector are on those strips." He went on to describe their use:

> It is a question of how you read those strips.... An aircraft has called and wants to descend. Now what the hell has he got in his way? And you've got ping, ping, ping, those three. Where are those three? There they are on the radar. Rather than looking at the radar. One of the aircraft on there has called. Now what has he got in his way? Well, there's aircraft going all over the place, now some of them may not be anything to do with you. It could be above them or below them. Your strips will show you

---

[20] With the move to Swanwick, there was some change in nomenclature. TMAs became Terminal Control Areas; however, the TMA abbreviation was retained.

[21] One critical change between ATC when we studied it and today has been the digitization of paper strips. Nonetheless, that provision has been made for them to be used as a fall back in case of computer failure reinforces our view of the importance of the information they provide.

whether the aircraft are above or below, or what aircraft are below you if you want to descend and aircraft, and which will become a confliction.... You go to those strips. You pick out the ones which are going to be in conflict if you descend an aircraft, and you look for those on the radar, and you put them on headings of whatever. You find out whether those, what those two are... which conflict with you third one. It might be all sorts of conflicts all over the place on that radar. But only two of them are going to be a problem. And they should show up on my strips.

Flight data strips are about one inch wide and eight inches long. They specify the flight path of an individual aircraft. This includes the aircraft name or "call sign" and type, its departure and destination point, its preferred route, and its height and speed. In addition, the estimated time of arrival at certain navigation points in the sector is printed at the side. Each sector has three or four key navigation points, a new strip being printed for each aircraft relative to each point. The strips are placed in racks or "bays" just above and behind the radar screens. Strips are printed ten minutes or so before an aircraft is due at a point. Strips record the aircraft's passage through the sector. As each point is crossed, the relevant strip is discarded.

This record is what controllers attend to and use in their work. It is the material instrument and worksite of controlling. The strips, however, do not determine the sequence of actions that controllers perform in the same way that whatever comes along the production line determines what the line worker has to do next. Instead, the controller has to organize the strips so they can become a resource to help organize the work of controlling. Strips are "glanced at," "searched for," "taken heed of," "ignored," and "revised" – not just when they first arrive, but continuously. This is the work of organizing the "doing" of the work. As a result, the strips provide the controller at any moment an "at hand" and "in hand" sequence of actions through which to create "order in the skies. Management of the strips is, then, a very large part of management of the traffic.

The Controller's Problem

At its simplest and most general, the controller's problem is a scheduling one. For any controller controlling any segment of air space, the traffic has to be taken as and when it arrives and threaded together into an orderly pattern before each individual plane is handed off to the next sector or controlling segment.[22] All of this scheduling and traffic management has to be achieved in and through making the traffic flow. Airplanes cannot be "parked" for a couple of minutes; nor can traffic jams be allowed to occur. Even when they are put into holding patterns of various sorts, aircraft are still on the move, part of the flow of traffic.

---

[22] We have discussed this in Anderson et al. (1987).

The controller utilizes a number of different resources to solve the scheduling problem. Two are, in essence, technologically determined because they are related to or constrained by the hardware and associated software of the suites themselves:

1) *Information resources*:
   a) the radar screen and its displayed data
   b) the flight strips
   c) screens of weather conditions and other data
2) *Communication resources*:
   a) radio/telephone (RT) to aircraft
   b) telephone links to other controllers, and others
   c) face-to-face communication with the suite team

In addition, a further vital resource is the controller's working knowledge of the system itself. This accumulated, know-how, know-what of years of experience is brought to bear on the technologically provided resources to determine at any particular time what appropriate courses of action should be.

The point is obvious and well-known (Reason 1986). The Air Traffic Control system comprises numerous complex subsystems, instantiated in hardware, software, regulations for controlling, working practices, and the like. In the face of the ordinary contingencies of practical working life, conflicts, inconsistencies, and incompatibilities among these subsystems are bound to arise. These constitute "the normal, natural troubles" (Garfinkel 1967) of the controller's working life. In dealing with these troubles, the controller displays "normally competent controlling." Being able to recognize them as the "normal, natural" phenomena they are is, to some extent anyway, what being a competent controller involves. Because these troubles can occur both with the traffic and with the technology, their solution is achieved by managing the traffic through managing the technology.

The skills required for this management (i.e., "working with the technology") are multilayered and interwoven. Moreover, they often seem to lack the sense of planfulness, deliberation, cogitation, task-definition, specification, calculation, and solution seeking that conventional approaches to system design presume. Instead, the process is an interpretive one but in a somewhat different sense than normal. The controller just *knows* what to do. Here, "knowing" means "interpreting the conditions at this suite at this point in time against a background of what has gone so far, what time of day it is, where everything else is currently, what has yet to arrive, what is going on in neighbouring sectors, and everything else that the controller takes to be relevant" to the task in hand. The whole is a *gestalt contexture* which provides the meaning of what is going on. The problem the controller faces is *this* problem here and now where *that* is obviously the appropriate course of action to take. The controller experiences problems and their solution, then, as part of a flow of work.

Trust and Air Traffic Control

Air Traffic Control as a Division of Labor

At LATCC, control of air space is managed within an extensive division of labor. This fact is known and used by all who work there to explain and interrelate the activities of controlling. Controllers, managers, and others encounter LATCC as a working division of labor and depict the organization of tasks accordingly. Consequently, the division of labor is a commonsense construct oriented to and used by controllers and others (Bittner 1965). Viewed in the midst of its operation, the division of labor is encountered as a body of fragmented tasks and activities. Working within a division of labor, controllers encounter it not analytically as an integrated totality but practically as a stream of differentiated tasks to be performed. Tasks unfold as things to be done now, things that can be left until later, things that are tied to the completion of other tasks, and so on. We can think of the division of labor as having almost a *transcendental presence*. Any individual task gets its sense from and hence contributes to achieving its overall structure. Seen from within the division of labor, the overall structure is not a unified and totalizing rational scheme. Instead, it appears to be organized around a principle of *egological determination* in an environment which is information saturated.

The organization of activities around any control suite consists in a number positions occupied by particular persons. Exactly how those positions are distributed is locally determined to best fit the management of the work in hand. From the point of view of any of these positions, the work to be done appears as a continuous, impersonalized stream. Within the bounds of training and regulation, it is immaterial who occupies what position. In other parts of the division of labor, of course, this might not be so. The differentiation of tasks and the related hierarchy of responsibility (as is depicted in the rational organizational scheme) is embedded in the flow of activity as an institutionalized structure of "decisions-I-can-make" and "actions-I-can-take" together with those that others deal with (hence our description of it as "egological"). Processing the endless stream of tasks means no more and no less than doing-what-I-do and passing things on so they can do what they do.

The egological principle is centered on the location of the individual within that structure of activities. The boundaries to spheres of operation vary from those that are permanently open and those under view, hence *near to hand*, and those which are *at remove* and so taken for granted. The distinction between tasks which are near to hand and tasks at remove is expressed in a number of ways.

1) There are tasks together with their associated rights and responsibilities whose performance are never a matter of inquiry. Other tasks, however, must be constantly appraised. Individual controllers need not concern themselves (in fact, cannot concern themselves) with the state of activities on a neighboring sector, even one whose interaction with their own is intense. Similarly, it is of no concern why the upper limit of a holding stack may have been lifted from its normal setting at FL 130 (13000'). Surmises can be given from what "everybody knows" about controlling, but doing what has to be done does not require these issues to be even minimally investigated. The operating division of labor rests on a presumed *symmetry of structure* and *reciprocity of location* without the need for an understanding of the precise detail. Controllers assume the organization of work for others is much the same as it is for themselves.

2) Correlated with the presumed symmetry of structure and reciprocity of location is an *horizontal structure of relevances*. There is every reason for the inbound controller of the Heathrow northern TMA[23] to ensure that the "squawks" (calls signs) displayed on the screen are correct by requesting identification from the aircraft when initial contact is made. Equally, it is crucial to ensure the statements of height transposed from the screen match those marked on flight strips. There is much less need to know if the code for the airport from which the aircraft departed is correct. The correctness of this data is, literally, someone else's problem.

3) The egological principle provides a working solution to the problem of *task performance*. The division of labor specifies just which tasks one has to embed one's own activities within and which tasks are institutionally taken care of, so to speak. Competence is the achieving of such embedding or the calling into play of the institutional structures.

4) Coordination within the division of labor is both *ecological* as well as *egological*. Activities are performed in organizationally specified zones and niches. Some are technologically fixed; others are not. During busy periods, high work load sectors can only be really managed by further dividing the sector and allocating two controllers to the same screen. Similarly, the Sector Chief can only supervise the sector if he can see both screens and

---

[23] Terminal Maneuvering Area (i.e., the sector of air space that manages the approach to an airport).

can manipulate the associated flight strips. Other activities are freed by technology. Because of telephone links, a geographically adjacent sector of sky with which a sector has a lot of interaction need not be a neighboring suite. Indeed, fluid management of traffic requires that transactions between suites are independent of the layout of the Operations Room. At the same time, those who know the layout have a geography of institutionally specific locales in which things get done. Thus, even the spatial layout of the Operations Room is saturated with information.

To summarize: from within, the division of labor is experienced as a fluid *gestalt contexture* of task performance. Tasks move back and forth, from foreground to background with an associated restructuring of their relevances. The elements of this gestalt are tasks performed, those in process and those awaiting take up. All are thematized by the egological structures of relevance just described. This gestalt is evidenced in innumerable ways and is available at a glance to the competent controller and is what grounds the controller's trust of the system.

So far, we have been describing how immersion in a division of labor is both a feature of and reproduces trust-in-the-system – doing things normally, competently, and routinely and appearing to do so is trust-in-the-system. To use the term we used earlier, the normal, natural attitude of competent controlling is premised in a bracketing of all sorts of matters which could, of course, be enquired into but are not. Trust in the normal, routine, expectable working of the division of labor allows the controller to embed tasks to be done now into the orderly flow of activity and thus to reproduce that orderliness. Being a competent controller means taking that trust for granted. Trust, then, is a given for the sociotechnical system of air traffic control. Were that status, that bracketing of trust, to be withdrawn, normal, routine, competent controlling would become impossible.

We now want to turn away from general descriptions to look at two particular activities in which this taken-for-granted character of trust can be exemplified. Both involve the collective or social use of technology to perform complex tasks.

Silent Handovers

For any particular controller, management of the "blips-on-the-screen" and strips in the bay is the management of planes in the sky. The order on the screen and in the bay is proxy for the order in the sky. Controlling the progress of these objects is instructing the plane. This is the controller's task; a task that is completed with the transition of the object across the screen, down the bay, and the plane out of sector. At such transitions, the task of controlling is passed on to someone else. One of the most striking things about routine controlling is the extent to which such transitions are managed with minimal or even nonexistent exchanges between the controllers concerned. These transfers are called "silent handovers."

The accomplishment of a silent handover is evidence of the normal working of the system. Blips and strips appear on the relevant screens and in the relevant bays with the right codes and values, in the right order, and at the right time. "Right," of course, means in correspondence with standard procedures and practices (or with whatever exceptions are in force). As the receiving controller, the routine controlling work done somewhere else has made your task unproblematic. We are not saying that all handovers are silent nor that explicit and extensive coordination work is never required. However, such explicit transitioning work is itself institutionalized, so that the "repair work" required on the routine can be effortlessly undertaken. At times, such repair work is itself managed "in the background," as when the Sector Chief accepts into sector a military crossover or an uncontrolled aircraft using visual flight rules (VSF).

The silent handover demonstrates that controllers can and do manage traffic flow secure in the knowledge that planes will be picked up and safely managed, whereas receiving controllers can be assured that the blip-on-the-screen *is* the relevant aircraft-in-the-sky and that it has arrived there in all the expected ways it should. Silent handovers are testimony to the way normal appearances are used for the effective management of the system. In fact, given traffic loads and complexities, silent handovers are a *necessary* way of managing the system. They are made possible because trust-in-the-system is built into the culture of air traffic control. Without silent handovers, managing transitions would impose more work on controllers and therefore require more time to deal with individual aircraft. This in turn would make the system less efficient and less trustworthy than it is.

Stack Jumping

Stacks are located in the London Terminal Maneuvering Area (LTMA), a sector of the airways roughly coinciding with South East England. For controlling purposes, LTMA is divided into a North and a South sector, each of which is further divided when required. The primary task of LTMA controllers is to separate outbound traffic leaving Heathrow and Gatwick and climbing to the levels stipulated by their Standard Instrument Departure (SID) patterns from aircraft inbound to the same airports. At busy periods and to ease congestion, in-bounds are sent to one of several locations, or holding points, where they circle until space is available for a landing approach. These locations are the "stacks." Heathrow has four (over Lambourne, Biggin Hill, Ockam, and Bovington). Gatwick has two (north of Burgess Hill and over Mayfield). The number of aircraft in each stack and the number of stacks in use varies with how busy the sector is. As airspace fills, aircraft enter – or are "stacked" – at higher and higher levels. Each plane is separated from those above and below by 1,000 feet. As planes leave the bottom of the stack, those above are directed down one level.

The purpose of stacking is, of course, to turn varied pulses of aircraft coming from all directions into a coordinated and predictable stream of planes that airports can handle. The controllers only have to direct aircraft to the top of the stack while Approach Control (situated at the airport) takes them out from the bottom. On the other hand, departures consist in a continuous stream that has to be distributed across the various route ways. The LTMA Controllers receive traffic from the main airports and must direct it around the in-bounds before allowing it to turn away onto its designated routes. In practice, this involves threading planes around, through, or over the stacks.

As one would expect there are sets of procedures for these tasks. Within LTMA sectors, the most important of these procedures relate to the standard profiles of aircraft inbound and departing from the airports and related stacks. These procedures are laid down in the operational manuals and take the form of

1) SIDs, which detail the exact trajectory of outbound traffic and are designed to satisfy noise abatement requirements and ensure no flight conflicts with in-bounds.
2) Standard Arrival Procedures (STARs), which are designed to coordinate in-bound traffic. As with SIDs, STARs reflect the destination and route of the aircraft.
3) Agreements between LTMA and neighboring sectors on which levels aircraft should be handed over.

From both the controller's and the aircraft's points of view, the standard procedural flight rules may not always be the most expeditious way of managing the plane or the traffic. Nor do they necessarily ensure safety. STARs and SIDs are complex and somewhat restrictive because they have been designed to weave traffic through but away from all other traffic. In addition, they do not take account of the differences in performance of aircraft. They are general-purpose specifications that any aircraft can follow. As a consequence, following an SID can result in delaying the ascent of an aircraft to its optimal cruising level and speed, thus prolonging the flight, increasing cost, and creating extra pilot work. This can also create more work for controllers because planes on STARs and SIDs can be in a sector for much longer than necessary, using up airspace and RT time and requiring extended controller attention.

Not surprisingly, then, controllers have developed well-known and shared procedures for dealing with the "troubles" created by the conflicting demands of STARs, SIDs, and stacks. These procedures are an essential part of professional competence and controlling skill. They – and the techniques associated with them – avoid delay, reduce work-load, and contribute to increased safety by reducing the time an aircraft remains in a busy sector. They are ways in which expert controllers apply their expertise by working within the system to manage the system. When faced with the possibility of – if not conflict, then certainly inconsistency – between sub-goals of the system (i.e., segregation of traffic and expeditiousness), controllers use the resources provided by the system to achieve working and workable solutions.

"Jumping" a plane through the stack can only be done because the controller trusts in and is at one with the system. Being at one with the system is a crucial element of trust in the system. Although the aircraft remains at a low speed to satisfy noise requirements, from the configuration of in-bounds (both in the stack and on their way to it, as well as those under the control of the Approach Controller), the controller senses there is enough "space" for the plane to jump through the stack. The value of "enough" here is "enough to satisfy the requirements of safety and competent handling." The former are defined by the Air Traffic Control Manual and the latter by the practices of ATC at LATCC. For example, two planes are circling in the Biggin Hill stack, one at 7,000 feet and one at 8,000 feet. An out-bound on its way to the Daventry sector would only have to climb to 9,000 feet before or by Biggin Hill to be safely clear of the stack and able to continue its climb out of the LTMA before it has reached the northern geographical boundary. Such a maneuver allows the out-bound to "jump" all the in-bounds under TMA control and will, almost certainly, allow it to continue its climb in the relatively empty sector above the TMA much sooner than allowed in the SID.

On the face of it, the practice of "stack jumping" looks to be a relatively straightforward tactic. Just what you might expect experts to do. However, the point is not that controllers produce a "simple and easy" solution to a problem (which they do), but that the work and skill allows them to *see* and *feel* just how and where the system affords a solution to problems it has itself created, and that their trust of the working sociotechnical system enables them to employ it in the ways in which they do. Effortless though it appears, this work – this expertise – is by no means simple to describe nor easy to acquire.

To begin with, stack jumping requires a complex series of judgments about the changing structure of the traffic flow, the performance characteristics of particular aircraft and an awareness of everything else that might be relevant to the current state of the traffic flow. Controllers refer to this as their "picture." The need to hold this complex gestalt in mind when deciding whether to "jump" a plane is the reason stack jumping is rarely practiced by novice controllers or those who have been off duty for some time. When jumping a stack, previous out-bounds have to be considered in case they are slow and thus likely to be in the way of subsequent, faster planes. Or there may be too many planes converging on the stack at its top level indicating that it could have to be raised before a possible "jumper" could get there. On the other hand, there may be the possibility of creating space at the top level by slowing down all the planes approaching the stack. Added to this is the fact that the speed of modern planes is such that often there are only moments to notice an opportunity and decide which out-bound to jump.

The advantages of stack jumping for both controllers and the system are obvious. It ensures quick exit of aircraft from the sector. It frees RT time, gives the plane to the en-route controller earlier, which can ease the handling problems of in-bounds. It enables planes to reach efficient operating height and speed quicker and, because it is a simpler trajectory, often increases passenger comfort. So keen are some pilots to jump that on their first contact with LTMA they "offer good climb rates" to controllers. On occasion this creates a situation in which the issue of "trust" (or lack of it) becomes explicitly visible and managed in the flow of controlling. Because of the efficiency and cost gains from stack jumping, pilots may offer climb rates that the controller knows or suspects are technically or practically infeasible. Given what depends on the rate being achieved, under certain circumstances the controller may decide not to trust the pilot and so refuse the climb rate offered and direct the aircraft on another route.[24] In addition, many aircraft do not have the capability to climb as fast as jumping requires. However, pilots know that informing a controller early that such a climb rate is possible greatly increases the likelihood of being offered a chance of being put on that vector.

As is to be expected, stack jumping operates under limitations. Apart from the need for quick assessments of such situations, the most troublesome is

---

[24] Pilots from particular countries and particular airlines are well-known to be especially "untrustworthy" in this respect.

the failure of the plane to reach its directed climb rate. There may be various reasons for this, but it has serious consequences. A controller may be depending on an outbound to climb in front of an in-bound, and if the out-bound does not climb fast enough a possible "confliction"[25] may occur. Other problems relate to the distribution of controlling responsibilities between the Approach and the LTMA Controller. Occasionally, an aircraft might be directed to a sector of airspace without prior coordination. Rather than take a plane over the stack, the LTMA Controller, for example, may choose to route it around the middle of it and hence through the flight path of those emerging at the bottom of the stack (remember the aircraft in question is climbing all the time). On other occasions, a plane may be taken from midway up the stack. In such cases, one or both planes may have to be redirected.

Stack jumping requires intimate knowledge of the routines of the sector and of the aircraft currently being controlled, traffic management requirements, an awareness of the amount of attention the controller must give to any one maneuver, and much, much more. Such knowledge is sector-specific. This knowledge has to be applied and honed time and time again to allow the procedure to be effective, smooth, and trouble-free. It requires exact assessment of the progress of aircraft along their given vectors and where "in the sky" they are in relation to one another. These assessments are based on information "seen at a glance" with the appropriate course of action being "executed' immediately and without deliberation.

Stack jumping not only depends on trust in the system, it *is* trust in the system. For all these reasons, novice controllers generally shy away from it. The skill and the work by which it is brought off are made invisible by the very effortlessness of the achievement. That experienced controllers do not vacillate and ponder the possibilities; that they act smoothly and efficiently to produce the space for a jumper to jump through with no hiccoughs, finger crossing, wood touching, drastic changes of mind, or direction make it difficult to see the artful and professional handling of the system that makes it all possible. This is all the more so because such artfulness and skill are to be seen only ephemerally in the orderly progression of planes-on-the-screen, strips in the bay, inscriptions on the strips, and exchanges with aircraft, controllers, and so on. This skill of competent controlling through stack jumping involves working the system to satisfy the procedural rules of air traffic control, where what counts as satisfying the rules is the production of smoothly flowing traffic

---

[25] A confliction is the merging of the trajectories of two aircraft to violate the minimal requirement of two miles horizontal and 5,000 feet of vertical separation.

and demonstrably competent controlling of whatever aircraft are in the sector at any moment.

Conclusion: What to Do about Trust?

We have no doubt that the concerns that many commentators point to in relation to trust and computational systems are real and potentially dangerous. Like them, we think that technology providers, public agencies, and those in relevant responsible positions have a duty to raise general awareness of the range of the threats we face. However, we do not think that the approaches being advocated for the design of complementary technological solutions are likely to work. In fact, they could even make things worse. This, we suggest, is the consequence of the limited construal of the notion of trust which is adopted and the "bare" psychology that motivates it. We have suggested an alternative approach, one which is rooted in a particular social psychology in which the users of technologies are conceived ab initio as social beings sharing an intersubjective social world.

Adopting this point of view has allowed us to suggest that trust is not optional for normal social life. It is a given for and the basis of enacting the social relationships and functions with which we are all familiar. It is, we suggest, the default mode in all routine activity. Two things follow from this. If we want people to be less trusting in certain circumstances or in regard to particular types of technical object, then we will have to think very carefully about the use of what appear to be especially "natural" metaphors and analogies when designing systems for use in those settings. The resemblances we trade on in using such tropes predispose the user to take for granted the relevances and typifications associated with them. This taking for granted is designed *into* the system and enables the systems to be used as they are. If we want to make the issue of trust more overt in the daily use of technologies, we will have no option but to question some of the core tenets on which usability as a design goal has been enshrined over the last half a century. That will be a severe challenge.

Second, even if we succeed in designing so as to reduce the level of trust we place in some technologies, we cannot design for its total suspension. In distrusting certain kinds of message, certain orders of instruction, certain types of location, and certain types of technology, we will have to trust others. This will mean being very specific about when, where, and with what and whom users should be careful, knowing full well that elsewhere and with others they will not need to be. Of course, this is just another way of saying that design will continue to be an endless game of catch up. As we engineer withdrawal of trust from some activities and technologies and so make them safe, others which are still trusted, will be at risk of being suborned.

Third, the panoply of activities that are underway in any complex operational sociotechnical system constitute a multidimensional, tightly embedded mosaic. Designers would be wise to design for the whole mosaic rather than seeking to partition off of a particular enclave, because introducing a policy of distrust in some part of the complex will undoubtedly generate turbulence for the entire system. An organized and orchestrated management-endorsed-and-promoted policy of systematic distrust in an environment such as Air Traffic Control will generate far greater difficulties than the normal, natural troubles that controllers and dealers are used to and comfortable with. If they cannot trust the system, they cannot make the system work. The same also goes for email, Web browsing, or Internet banking. If we withdraw trust when using these systems, we cannot make them work. Because we can't solve the "problem" of trust once and for all, trying to do so will, in all likelihood, simply generate other, perhaps catastrophic, problems instead.

Finally, we have made great play with the suggestion that different departure points and different modes of reasoning bring out different features for examination. We recognize that, at one level at least, this is trite. But at another level it is important. Too often in research, traditional ways of framing problems come to be unquestioned. As a consequence, we are blinded to possibilities and insights they do not encourage or permit. We have suggested that we need not hold to the unquestioned assumption that our understanding of trust in relation to technical systems should be framed by contrasts between real and perceived risk, users and the system, or psychological and social characteristics of the user, or investigated solely by the search for explanatory factors. Such assumptions may be the taken-for-granted aspects of our research, but they don't have to be. But, as with trust, that does not mean we can proceed without any assumptions at all.

8

Trust in Interpersonal Interaction and Cloud Computing

Rod Watson

Trust and Formal Analysis

I came to the consideration of trust not because it is currently a public issue, nor because it seems to be in vogue in sociology. Instead, I was dismayed at some of the recent sociological treatments of the subject and, in particular, at these studies' cursory treatment of one of what many would consider to be the leading foundational modern study of trust in social interaction, that of the late Harold Garfinkel who, in 1963, published a paper titled "A Conception of, and Experiments with, 'Trust' as a Condition of Stable, Concerted Actions," (Garfinkel 1963b).

During the time that he was Professor of Sociology at the University of California at Los Angeles, Garfinkel devised a radically innovative approach that he termed "ethnomethodology." This meant "members' methods." By this, then, Garfinkel intended not a technical or professional research method per se but, instead, a topic for study; namely the study of society members' interactionally deployed cultural methods of making sense of the everyday contexts in which they find themselves, methods also of sharing this sense and incorporating it into their joint projects of action – in a phrase, sense-making-in-action.

Garfinkel's ethnomethodology was methodologically radical. It challenged the very foundations of major schools of sociological thought and, in doing so, created reactions ranging from confusion at its new, "obscure" terminology to outright hostility and attempts at marginalization. Nonetheless, ethnomethodology and its spin-offs refused to go away and gradually gained a foothold within sociology and cognate disciplines. His study of interpersonal trust was conducted in the formative phases of ethnomethodology, and once the furor about it died down, the study came to be increasingly (and quite undeservedly) sidelined, particularly by more contemporary treatments.

172

Even those more recent treatments of trust that do mention Garfinkel often do so in a way that largely rely on secondary source-based, shorthand characterizations of his work, which afford only a simplistic or reductive and often downright distorted view of his work.

Of course, this shallowness (or worse) is attributed to the lack of background being provided. This is because these commentators' intention is to "boil down" Garfinkel's work so that they can extrapolate it to the study of trust in other contexts (e.g., trust in abstract systems or major social institutions). In this, they can cite a powerful, indeed classic, precedent – that of Georg Simmel, who, in typically formal terms, treated trust as a precondition for social exchange (Simmel 1978: 178ff.; Simmel 1950: 318ff.).

With reference to knowledge, symbolic meanings, and the like, Simmel attempted to set up a single, formal frame of reference for the analysis of all kinds of trust, both "interpersonal" and "abstract" (e.g., trust in money). Because Simmel conceived of society as a network of forms of interaction, his work has, rightly or wrongly, often been taken as positing interpersonal trust as a form that is analytically prior to other forms and – in some respects – is the paradigm for them. On this view, the formal features of interpersonal trust are extensible to, say, trust in a national currency.

Alternative Approaches to Trust

This move set up a basis for many sociological approaches in what Garfinkel, in his later work, termed "formal analytic sociology," which relied on formal abstraction in its characterization of social order. Throughout his career, however, Garfinkel has insisted that an opposite approach (devised by him) is more profitable, namely to develop a set of analytic resources that apply to interpersonal trust and no other kind – no wholesale extensibility, no extrapolation, no "standing on behalf of" what are purportedly more "abstract" or more "institutional" cases, and so on.

My concern too is not to inquire what is common to trust in all forms (trust is a multifarious phenomenon), but to ask: "What is distinctive about face-to-face trust-in-interpersonal relations?" I think that this approach helps avoid the pitfalls of reductionism and methodological irony. It is such reductions and ironies that have resulted in the simplistic view accorded by many secondary commentators to Garfinkel's article.

In this chapter, I propose a sociological rather than, say, a directly philosophical or linguistic treatment of trust. (Of course, some philosophical or linguistic sources may be pressed into sociological service). Garfinkel himself counts largely but not exclusively on phenomenology; but among British sociologists, the later philosophy of Ludwig Wittgenstein has informed our considerations. Although restrictions of space prevent much of a focus on the latter, I try to indicate some of those relevances as they come up. By and large, Wittgenstein's later work has furnished ethnomethodologists with another "analytic mentality" for approaching matters such as trust.[1] I shall try to move away from formal analytic and purely normative approaches within sociology and to reinstate, update, and develop some of Garfinkel's concern with the "constitutive" features of interpersonal trust (i.e., the role of trust in persons' conjoint sense-making practices). As I have already observed, Garfinkel was the founder of ethnomethodological analysis within sociology, and his article on trust comprised an early move in establishing some of the lineaments of this approach. It was an approach that highlighted both constitutive and praxeological aspects of social life – trust in action. I hope to offer at least a few examples of how to analyze trust and mistrust from an ethnomethodological point of view. One advantage of ethnomethodology, particularly ethnomethodology conceived from a later Wittgensteinian point of view, is that it allows us a non-reductionist, anti-cognitivist view of trust, neither methodologically individualistic nor holistic/reificatory in character.

Of course, there are other approaches that might claim to address interpersonal trust as, at least nominally, a socially organized matter. Several are themselves formal-analytic in character. One group of these approaches comprises rational choice (or rational action) and game theories, to which some exchange theories might be added. In these, we are typically invited to consider parties' calculations concerning the conditions under which trust is justified. Trust, here, is seen as being essentially a calculated risk that is taken concerning the future performance of others, given limited information, the time-lag involved, and that each party is acting in his or her own self-interest.

Such elements are often incorporated into a coded formula, such as that devised by James S. Coleman. It is just as easily and precisely expressed in ordinary language. His formula expresses that ego will trust in alter if the likelihood that alter is trustworthy or not is greater than the prospective gain or loss respectively. Some types of "rational action analysis" are designed to be extensible to other, apparently quite different, forms of trust. Indeed, extrapolation and extension are instruments through which formalism as an analytic mode is produced.

---

[1] For some comments on the Wittgensteinian analytic mentality in ethnomethodology, see Watson 2009. I have drawn extensively from this article in writing about Garfinkel's Schütz-based approach.

From an ethnomethodological point of view, what is wrong with the rational action approach and associated game-theoretical models of trust? What's missing?

I have argued more extensively elsewhere (Watson 2009) that the first difference between ethnomethodological and rational choice and game-theoretic approaches to interpersonal trust is that the former focalizes the actual, concrete phenomenal detail of the particular social settings in which trust pertains, whereas these other approaches tend toward a decontextualized and highly formalistic (or) schematic analysis. Moreover, ethnomethodological approaches eschew what Garfinkel conceives as the "cultural (or judgmental) dopery" that still pervades classical and conventional sociologies in which social actors are, by and large, seen merely in terms of the passive behavioral playing-out of the norms, rules, and social controls of the society. Garfinkel observes that there exists a wide range and variety of cultural dope models in orthodox sociologies. There is idealization, simplification, and reduction in this dopery.

By contrast, Garfinkel's model of membership presents social actors as active practical reasoners who, in interacting with each other in specific situations, conjointly and artfully constitute (i.e., make sense of) those situations. Such constitutive practices are, or should be, central topics of interest for sociology. For Garfinkel, social actors are conceived in terms of their capacity for social action and interaction and for the flexible use of this capacity in concert with others.

Despite game theory's apparent treatment of social actors as calculative decision makers, Garfinkel still treats game theory as a version of cultural/judgmental dopery. The social actors as conjectured by game theory still act only on the basis of game rules and limited potentials, choosing only on the basis of limited game-furnished options – rules and options that, in fact, the game theorist affords them (and game theorists' conception of games is also highly reductive).

As Garfinkel (1963a: 157) puts it:

Such an assumption is treated as though its conditions were satisfied when the theorists thinks of an actual player as a person who knows and never loses sight of the definitions of relevance that (the theorist's rules – Ed.) describe, that a player's environment does not contain events that the rules do not cover and that the player acts under their exclusive jurisdiction. Call such a player a game-dope.

In other words, "reasoning" as given by game theories, rational action theories, and similar approaches offer us an attenuated, leeched-out version of the phenomenon (this also applies to the thinned-out, lightly schematic versions of choices that game theory gives us). For instance, there is no provision for players' ad hoc practices or improvisation. Garfinkel's critical description of game-theoretic (and other) approaches applies a fortiori to Coleman's characterization of the very highly restricted choice that figured in whether an actor will trust another actor. Of course, the more simplistic the model and the more elementary the characterization of the actor, the more extrapolable and generalizable that model of trust seems to be. In this respect, formalism and (over)simplification seem to go hand in hand; much is ruled out, and much that is artifactual is ruled in.

Both ethnomethodological and game-theoretic or rational action approaches treat trust as part of social order, but – from the ethnomethodological point of view – those characterized by formal abstraction tend to dissolve or lose the phenomenon, because in vivo, in situ formalization bleeds out the distinctive character of settings. Indeed, game-theoretic/rational action approaches sustain a highly minimalistic, even skeletal characterization of social order, and much of this is a result of the methodological individualism incorporated in their models.

One of the many ways in which such formal abstraction is produced is through the use of planned misnomers such as similes and metaphors – "games," "information games," "theater," "on and off-stage," and so on. Such images may help raise into visibility some of the taken-for-granted, unnoticed elements of the flow of everyday life, to "allow the goldfish to become aware of the water it swims in" as Garfinkel puts it. However, when images like these are used, the risk of "methodological irony" or descriptive falsification is added to the loss of characterization of salient detail. That is, we are saddled with a stance which is set in competition with the ordinary conceptions people hold in the attitude of everyday life.

Concretely, the image is set against the intersubjective conceptions of actual parties to the setting. For instance, there are plenty of settings in which the investment of trust is, for participants, anything *but* a "game," or a strategy, or is anything *but* onstage acting and cannot be faithfully rendered by these images. One can think of many studies of medical settings, for instance, where this is the case; one example is the telling of bad news to a patient by a doctor, typically a person with a trusted identity.

What else is lost or dissolved in the rational action or game model of trust? One thing that disappears (but is still tacitly counted on) is the ordinary constitutive aspect of trust. In such studies of trust, particularly in strategy models, information often figures greatly. Garfinkel would argue that there can be no "information" without a shared, in situ endorsement and commitment by participants to a given "definition" of the local setting concerned. Without such a definition, information cannot make "local" (situational) sense of or be "locally relevanced" or locally embedded and cannot provide grounds for action. Therefore, we need to examine participants' constitutive practices in arriving at and maintaining a shared definition of the situation. Trust is, characteristically, woven into such practices, often as a background feature. Indeed, medical settings again furnish some salient instances in which, for example, the patient about to undergo an operation must not only trust the doctor but also all participants – nurses, anesthetists, porters, and so on – as part of their "definition" of the various phases and aspects of the operation.

What has been lost in these games and other models of trust, then, is a whole sphere of constitutive practice – that is, a whole array of sense-making practices whereby all parties to a given setting and its interwoven constituent projects conjointly define and identify players, project, and setting. What is lost is their ways of making sense of how to act within the setting and how to coordinate their actions. This applies even to those special situations in which trust might (at least partly) take on some game-like qualities. The "how" of constitutive practice is important and comprises the focal point of ethnomethodology. Ethnomethodologists ask: "How, by what cultural knowledge and through what knowledge-based 'methodic practices' do members jointly constitute a given local setting?" The nature of the setting-as-constituted is important and later I characterize that as a "gestalt contexture." It is important, as I have indicated earlier, not to reduce issues of the nature of constitutive practice (and of trust) to the individuals concerning who take part in a given contextual weave.

By contrast, so far as rational action, game-theoretic, and associated models of trust are concerned, we are left with a skeletal conception, what Abraham Kaplan (1964) terms an idealized "reconstructed logic" of a given social setting, one that misses out on the practices that constitute or compose that setting and which accord it meaning. This selective, reductive, attenuated, and out-of-context formal-analytic approach comprises idealizations that fail to capture participants' own interlocking practices in the trust-based, coordinated production of a given setting as a sensible, recognizable phenomenon. Consequently, in the rational action or game-theoretic model, interpersonal trust is presented as a unitary, standardized, transposable, interchangeable phenomenon, stable across all sets of contingencies and eliding participants' conjoint reasoning or sense-making on the matter. It also elides, of course, the gestalt properties of the setting thus produced – a crucial issue in the analysis of the workings of trust in such settings.

Of course, the extraction of such apparently standardized features of trust might be seen as a strength in the formal-analytic sociology of which rational action, game-theoretic, or exchange-based theoretical models are examples; but for ethnomethodology, such extensions lead to what Schwartz and

Jacobs (1979) term an "anaemic" characterization of trust in just any particular setting.

I tend to agree with Olli Lagerspetz's argument, although not his imagery, that trust is not just a description of a state of affairs but a "tool" of interaction (Lagerspetz 1998). I share Lagerspetz's concern to locate trust within a consideration of routine human agency. I should prefer, however, to locate this consideration more firmly within the phenomenon of members' own competence, within their commonsense social descriptions, what symbolic interactionists term members' shared, ordinary "definition of the situation." Such lay description is itself a social activity, a "tool" of interaction, and trust is part and parcel of the assembling of a sensible description of a given setting and of the activities that produce it. This point leads us to the ethnomethodological alternative – an alternative that, it is to be hoped, leads us away from methodological individualism and cognitivism (attenuated or reductive characterizations of social action) and toward characterizations that are free from methodological irony and that place constitutive practice in a central position.

The Ethnomethodological Alternative

For ethnomethodologists, the focal question is: how can we attempt, at least, to recapture the phenomenon with which we started out?[2] That is, how do we reinstate the constitutive, contextualized nature of trust? How do we do this in a faithful, genuinely naturalistic way? It seems best to begin with Garfinkel's 1963 article in which he not only derives a particular conception of trust that is largely derived from Alfred Schütz's phenomenology, but also tries to set up some empirical "demonstrations" or "interventions" – his infamous "breaching experiments" – that were meant to render his conception visible (Garfinkel 1963b). These comprised a certain kind of "interruption" in the familiar, recognizably normal flow of ordinary action in everyday situations – giving those students who consented to the intervention what Garfinkel termed "a nasty surprise." In so doing, Garfinkel rendered familiar events "anthropologically strange," thereby rendering those events visible and available for analysis. To use another phrase, Garfinkel employs in a different context, the interventions were designed to "get the animal to stand out from the foliage in which it is hidden." Because trust is so embedded in a wide variety of particular contexts and takes its shape from those contexts, there needs to be some way of focalizing trust. For a brief time, Garfinkel thought that these interventions would do just that.

---

[2] This is the overall theme of Schwartz and Jacobs (1979).

The interventions comprised teaching devices quite as much as research ones, though the two concerns are not necessarily so distinct in ethnomethodological inquiries. Garfinkel asked his undergraduates to do such things as violating a rule in naughts and crosses ("tick-tack-toe") – that is, placing a naught on a line rather than in a box. He also went beyond such game-based interventions by, for instance, getting student volunteers to act as though they were strangers in their own homes, bargaining in stores with fixed prices, or pursuing a conversation in a way not given in the normal or typified forms of acceptable talk. For instance, when some student's friend mentioned in conversation that his car had had a flat tire, the student would persistently pursue the matter: "What do you mean, a flat tire? How was it flat?" "What part of it was flat?" and so on.

For many non-ethnomethodologists, these interventions came to define the research "technique" of ethnomethodology, although they were in fact very far from that. The interventions do not define the fully fledged ethnomethodological approach to research at all. Garfinkel used them mainly as teaching devices and abandoned them after a few weeks. Why? After all, he drew some interesting observations from them. The indications are, though, that he came to regard them as artifactual, especially for a radically naturalistic approach. What might Garfinkel have meant by this?

We may say that where breaches occur in everyday interaction, their normal form is minimization rather than pursuit and escalation. Indeed, some breaches involve an indication in advance that they are about to occur, and can thereby be preempted altogether. In any case, when breaches do occur, not only are they minimized, but co-participants collaborate in using ordinary knowledge-based methods to repair the breach at the earliest possible moment, thus precluding the kind of escalation on which Garfinkel insisted. Certainly, if we adhere to Lagerspetz's insistence in his important study (Lagerspetz 1998: 1ff.; and Chapter 6 in this volume), that we adhere to the experience of ordinary humans (an insistence, I wholeheartedly endorse and which, of course, Garfinkel would also), then the interventions are somewhat problematic.

But with this caveat in mind, it might still (arguably) be worthwhile to look at the consequences of these breaching interventions. Some students simply felt unable even to initiate any interventions (and of course, were not forced to; in any case, their accounts of their inhibitions comprised relevant data in themselves). One can imagine that they seemed, literally, like a breach of trust, a breach of faith. Others, often after much hesitation, reported great inhibition in pursuing the breach while also reporting that those with whom they interacted made strenuous efforts to normalize the form of the interaction; and, when these efforts met with failure (often because the subjects became confused), they were less able to define the situation, were more likely to ask "what's going on here?" and were less able to answer that question. Moreover, the student was often confronted with anger, hostility, moral indignation, and other negative sanctions – injunctions to avoid being silly, to act properly, and so on. These were part of broader efforts to repair the situation, to return it to normal.

Students also reported their discomfort and feelings of guilt at having to act like a cultural stranger, having to breach a trusted categorical identity such as "son," "daughter," "customer," and so on.

Garfinkel's "breach experiments" acquired a certain notoriety, and occasioned a highly moralistic reaction from not a few po-faced sociologists, many of whom were themselves not otherwise particularly known for their high moral tone; Garfinkel's "experiments" were nowhere near as taxing on his students as were, say Stanley Milgram's[3]. In fact, the moralistic reactions were, by and large, a shibboleth used against intellectual rather than moral divergence.

What, then, do these "anthropologically strange" renditions suggest to us about trust, and the whole paraphernalia surrounding trust, in those settings? First, the confusion of the student experimenters' co-participants and the concomitant disorganization often bordering on anomie shows how central is participants' ordinary trust in the normal forms of interaction (including, of course, speech exchange). By the same token, it shows how important is the process of making and sharing the sense of any specific situation, that is, their constitutive practice. Finally, the interventions showed that adhering to the "normal forms" of interaction and to the standard sense of that interaction was sanctionable – that is, morally enforceable.

Garfinkel expresses these interventions as breaching what Schütz conceives as the co-participants' taken-for-granted "background expectancies." Such "expectancies" – although I use the term purely as a temporary placeholder – comprise part of persons' "commonsense knowledge" of normal forms, of "what everyone routinely knows (as a competent member)" of his/her everyday world. One might, however, prefer to refer to "normal form" typifications, as Cicourel puts it (Cicourel 1972: 252–256).

Each participant trusts that the others share and adhere to the same background expectancies that he/she endorses; and that they not only share but adhere to them. This is what the "culturally methodic" or patterned practices of making and sharing the sense of a particular situation consist of. The notion of "background" is very important here and is frequently underestimated by commentators on Garfinkel's interventions. The expectations are oriented

---

[3] I am referring, of course, to his famous – or notorious, depending on your view – "experimental studies" of 1963.

to by participants but are usually not explicitly so, except in the violation – hence, of course, the interventions. The interventions were conceived as a "methodological" way of achieving what Schütz (1982) termed (following Husserl) "the epoché of the natural attitude." This is where the observer "brackets off" some feature of the routine flow of everyday life, raises it from the background to the foreground and thus renders it visible and available as a topic for analysis. Items in this taken-for-granted stream of everyday life may include "participating in one's family," "making a purchase," "conversing with others," "receiving counseling," "changing a wheel," and so on – all topics in Garfinkel's "interventions."

Garfinkel characterizes participants' shared sense-making in terms of what he calls "constitutive rules." These are participants' rules, used at the level of ordinary commonsense, in the coproduction of sensible features and events concerning a situation. Constitutive expectancies are, essentially, determinations of (some of) these rules. His interventions were designed to produce environments that are "specifically senseless": they are, as Garfinkel put it, "atypical, causally indeterminate, without a relevant history or future, means, character or moral necessity" (1963: 194; See also Garfinkel (1967): 53–55). In this quotation we can see, in some respects, the phenomenologists' technique termed "the epoché" of the natural attitude. In a sense, they are also somewhat akin to the pragmatist Kenneth Burke's (1954) "perspective by incongruity," which shows up as a taken-for-granted situation by contrast.

Secondly, these constitutive rules and the practices to which they are integral are treated by the parties to a social situation as morally enforceable. That is, they are required for the production of a jointly perceived environment of normal objects and events. Garfinkel draws a distinction between constitutive and preference rules, where the latter are treated as discretionary. An instance may be given from club tennis, and from a more patronizing era in the game. In mixed doubles, a constitutive rule is that any player can hit the ball directly at either opposing player. However, the preference rule in earlier times was that male players would not aim the ball directly at an opposing female. Another preference rule is that of kicking the ball into touch in football/soccer to allow a player (often an opposing player) to receive medical attention. Such rules of preferred play are, Garfinkel says, discretionary. Garfinkel focuses, however, almost entirely on constitutive rules and practice.

For Garfinkel, trust is a condition of such constitutive practice. For the coproduction of a sensible social setting, each party must be able to trust that her/his co-participants reciprocally endorse the constitutive rule, or the constitutive accent of the rule and the expectancies that are part of these. "Trust," here, is that all parties can count on each other's commitment and adherence to the constitutive expectancy and the practice. Each party must assume that every other party "sees" both the practice and the situation in the same way, and must assume that were any of the parties to swap positions in the interaction, they would still see the rule, the expectancy, and the practice in the same way. In other words, Garfinkel located trust within what has been termed "the reciprocity of perspectives" or the "interchangability of standpoints" – part of the architecture of shared sense, shared understandings.

Trust, then, has the twin features of being both a *condition* in making sense of a situation and a *requirement* that parties are committed to producing the same sense of that situation, that they are for all practical purposes "on the same page" irrespective of their biographical differences, interests, and so on. Indeed, persons' "explicative transactions" (i.e., exhibitory practices through which they display to each other their specific orientation to a given setting) are part of exhibiting trustworthiness in this respect. By contrast (and analyzing members' explicative transactions concerning trust may sometimes be a less artifactual way than intervention "breach experiments" of examining interpersonal trust), preference rules seem to be, for Garfinkel, of largely normative significance – norms of preferred conduct (again, in the final analysis, discretionary rather than required).

Garfinkel, then, quite definitively removes the phenomenon of trust from an exclusive location within what sociologists have termed "the normative paradigm" and, without denying its normative relevance, places it in the constitutive arena. When he refers to "stable concerted interaction," he is primarily referring to the conjoint stabilizing of the sense that is integral to that interaction – a mutually endorsed, trusted sense of the situation, as it were.

Despite what I feel are some conceptual and methodological problems attached to Garfinkel's re-emplacement of trust (see, e.g., 1967: 13–14), this is his big contribution. Certainly, this was so at the time when he wrote his paper on trust, when few of his contemporaries in sociology wrote about trust, and almost all who did treated it virtually exclusively in terms of the normative paradigm. For instance, Talcott Parsons, Garfinkel's eminent doctoral supervisor, treated trust as predominantly a normative element, in terms of normatively structured expectations. But, like Garfinkel, he usefully led us toward a conception of trust that does not refer to the "whole person" but to a particular performance or course of action. But for Garfinkel, interpersonal trust is a naturally situated phenomenon, one that is part of the familiar stream of everyday life as participants themselves know it. Trust is also a practical matter, part of our practical everyday affairs, located in specific contexts and attuned to those contexts. We may, then, speak again of "trust-for-all-practical-purposes," to use a classic ethnomethodological formulation. We cannot speak of perfect trust any more than perfect rationality – a problem for some rational action theorists of trust (Good 2008).

In these respects, game-based interventions may not be the best way to pursue the study of interpersonal trust, just as game theory may not be. In games, constitutive and preference rules can (sometimes) readily be separately identified, whereas in non-game situations, the "same" rule might be said to have both a constitutive and preference accent.

Moreover, as Lagerspetz quite properly points out, Garfinkel tends to tie his analysis to the notion of expectancy – "background expectancy" – to be specific (1998: 140). This may be a carryover from his Parsonian days as Parsons, too, focalized "expectation" in a more normative conception. However, we are not sure that Lagerspetz's suggestion that ordinary, trusting interaction involves a "lack of expectation" quite captures the situation either. To expect is a very specific activity, not a diffused, generalized one. If we accept Lagerspetz's general point, I think we should avoid the logical grammar of the term "expectation" altogether, even in its negation. Probably, the situation is better rendered by reference to participants' reciprocal commitment to "normal forms" (including "normal projects of action" such as those itemized earlier in this chapter). That is, each party to a social setting can, through trust, assume that the apperception of these forms is the same irrespective of any person-specific characteristics, or that she/he will define the normal form (for all practical purposes) "in the same way": this is the strong sense given by the reciprocity of perspectives. Thus, the subjects of Garfinkel's experiments might be said to repair the breached normal form of the interaction – to reestablish the student experimenter as a closely familiar member rather an apparent stranger within the family.

More Recent Ethnomethodological Approaches Relevant to Trust

By the time he published his now-classic book *Studies in Ethnomethodology* in 1967, Garfinkel had long abandoned the "breach experiment'" or interventions. What, then, tended to take their place? One increasingly used approach was to use what are (often) minimally invasive techniques such as using audio or video-recorded data and transcripts of these data as derived from natural settings – work settings, domestic settings, and others. One way – not the only way but, arguably, a starting point, at least – is to focus on situations in which trust has been explicitly mentioned.

In this sense, we can treat trust as an ordinary, commonsense conception and put it through the set of operations recommended by Erving Goffman: "(the concept) must be traced back to where it best applies, followed from there to wherever it seems to lead and pressed to disclose the rest of its family. Better, perhaps different coats to clothe the children well than a single splendid tent in which they all shiver" (Goffman 1962: xiv and cited by Watson 2009). We feel Wittgenstein might have approved; ethnomethodologists certainly will, in their analyses of members' ordinary uses of concepts.

We can, for instance, then establish how the term "trust" is localized or particularized by co-participants, how it is adjusted to a particular "local" situation. Observe, for instance, how this specification or contextualization occurs in a transcript from a legal tribunal investigating police corruption (cited in Watson 2009). The Police Officer is "A" and the informant/suspect is "D":

D: No, I discussed with Sergeant McKee and we felt it wasn't the appropriate thing to do and that you couldn't trust O'Brien.
A: You mean you couldn't trust him to keep his mouth shut?
D: No. That's not what I'm saying.
A: You couldn't trust him not to tell somebody that two members of the Armed Robbery Squad had allowed him to keep twenty-five thousand dollars which might very well be the proceeds of an armed robbery?
D: No I'm not saying that.
A: What are you saying?
D: He was a person that would say one thing and then he would change his mind and renege on what he was saying. (continues)

Here, we can see that D, the informant, arrives at a specific determination of "trust in-this-case" by denying that O'Brien would intend from the start to deceive, but that he would say one thing and change his mind later. In this respect the suspect is also working toward a definition of trust-in-this-case that he *and* the police officer can reciprocally understand and perhaps, endorse – again, establishing a reciprocity of perspectives. This reciprocity is central to the issue.

We might see this sequence as consisting of a set of "explicative transactions" (Pollner 1979) concerning the determination of trust-in-this-case. Those transactions are part and parcel of arriving at that determination as a practical matter, here and now. In this sense, we must even take care not to espouse a conception of "interpersonal-trust-in-general," let alone extrapolate it to non-interpersonal (in the sense of face-to-face) situations such as trust in information from "the Cloud." There is no "across-the-board" determination of trust, only specific local adjustments of trust to particular "local" situations such as determining the particular way in which a given person may be deemed to be untrustworthy, as we have just seen. These specific determinations of trust in a range of "local" situations may be "connected" by family resemblances, but they are certainly not coterminous.

We can, of course, also examine how trust operates in situations in which it is not explicitly mentioned – that is, queues or waiting lines or the close ordering of vehicles on a motorway. Here, one can frequently find perspicuous settings that show the local operation of trust (e.g., "saving one's place" in queues, and the like).

In these cases, trust refers not, of course, to trusting the person or the "whole person" so much as trusting that a given performance will be issued by a given actor within a given, jointly oriented-to, participation framework (Goodwin 1981 passim), and that the performance will be competently, responsibly, recognizably, and completely issued. Here, we may think of trust in its prepositional form: "... trust to (+ some performance)." Thus, as in Lumet's film *Serpico*, a set of police officers may not trust one of their number (Serpico) to accept bribes, which places him outside the cohort in which reciprocity of perspectives may be presumed to operate. In other words, we are working toward a course-of-action model of trust, or rather a course-of-situated-action, where, of course, the "situation" includes, but is not coterminous with, the participation framework. For instance, in the participation framework of flight crews, we need only to trust the pilot to fly us to our destination airport, rather than trusting her/him as, say, a parent or taxpayer. Here the notion of "actor" (or "social actor") is restricted to "she/he who issues a particular course of situated action," and is oriented to and, reciprocally, acted toward as such by co-participants and witnesses, and, again, "trust" to the reliance on those actors to issue a particular course of action within the framework of a given context – the gestalt or configurational nature of the framework as participants apprehend it, is important: it's not just to do with rationally cognizing individuals, especially when these are conceived in idealized terms.

Put another way, we trust "persons" as incumbents of a given membership category (i.e., a form of person – reference such as "captain," "second officer," and so on) operating within a given participation framework (and a given instance of that framework) in which the framework itself is partly constituted in terms of a given configuration of membership categories – "flight deck crew" as a participation framework constituted through the categories "captain," "second officer," and so on. With reference to some person identified in terms of a given category (see Sacks 1972: 332–340) within a particular instance of a given participation framework, we may say that trust refers to all participants taking it "as read" or "as given" that the incumbent will produce what they regard as a satisfactory course of action, one that is situationally appropriate both in single-category and framework terms. This is especially so when, say, some "category-bound activity" that some categorized actor performs (idem: 335–338) occurs within a participation framework that is duplicatively organized – that is, it has a team-like quality (idem: 334). In these cases, trust is also underscored by the requirement to be a "team player" (e.g., in a family or on a flight deck); taken-for-grantedness of these elements is a central feature of trust.

Taking a performance predicated on a category "as read" is one thing. Of course, this performance is disjunctive with a given social actor's category – incumbency can be quite another thing. It can occasion a challenge to this implicit trust, or it may generate suspicion. For instance, as Michael L. Williams (circa 1972) has observed, if a police officer in the street notices someone "categorizable" as a "respectable businessman" suddenly stops on the sidewalk and gets involved in a cash transaction with a "street person," then the officer may suspect that the event is, in fact, a drug deal. This in turn, may occasion a putative re-categorization of the social actor from "respectable businessman" to "drug dealer" because he has involved himself in an activity that appears disjunctive with the original categorization. Such a re-categorization will furnish grounds for further action by the police officer: we might say that the officer's action is category-based.

Moreover, the re-categorization involves a shift from a more trusted categorical identity (respectable businessman) to a less trusted identity (drug pusher). At the moment of this writing, the late Jimmy Savile is in the process of being re-categorized from the trusted categorical identity "charity worker" to that of "pedophile," a process that bears many similarities with what Garfinkel, in an early analysis, calls a "status degradation ceremony" (Garfinkel 1956: 420–424). One axis of such "ceremonies" is the relegation of a person from a "trusted insider" (or "one of us") to a mistrusted outsider.

One way in which doubt, suspicion, or mistrust are occasioned and publicly manifested, then, is in the re-categorization of some actor. Of course, we may see this as occasioned too by the membership category "street person," where "involving him/herself in a drug deal" might be seen as conjunctive with that category. We may, then, speak of the "categorical order of trust (and mistrust)." Of course, setting appropriateness is also important. If that area of the street is known for drug deals, what is someone apparently categorizable as "respectable businessman" doing there?

However, we should bear in mind that the occasioning of doubt, suspicion, or mistrust is relatively rare in interpersonal relations. As Edward Rose (1992: 170, also cited by Watson 2009) states it: "Doubt interrupts and is rare. Trust commonly prevails. . . . Trust as a rule is the rule, doubt the exception. As a rule, people have to do with things through the exercise of trust pared by doubt occasionally, hardly ever by the exercise of doubt relieved occasionally by trust." Rose's quotation is a salutary caution for situations of interpersonal trust, but whether it applies to the same extent to trust in information (e.g., person-information) derived from the Cloud remains to be seen. At the moment, it probably remains something of an open question; after all, one does not require a password for most forms of face-to-face interaction. However, we should not be overly swayed by the occasional moral panic or media revelations concerning some major breach of trust on or in the Internet/Cloud. We must recall that millions of specific uses of the Cloud/Internet are perfectly routine and unproblematic, where issues of mistrust do not occur and trustworthiness is taken for granted. For instance, we routinely trust that we can access a Web site or our email and can transport the most mundane and unremarkable online activities. It remains to be seen whether the intentional overloading of, say, Web properties will begin to strip away this taken-for-grantedness. This, then, brings us to a brief but more explicit consideration of whether or not the stated features of interpersonal trust are extensible to "trust in the Cloud."

Extrapolating Interpersonal Trust?

We have expressed skepticism about the treating of interpersonal trust as a primitive or extensible case and have pressed the case for ethnomethodology's approach as ideally suited to this "non-extensible" quality. We consider that this argument about non-extensibility applies a fortiori to the case of trust on the Internet.

Phillip Pettit has argued, in his paper "Trust, Reliance and the Internet," that the extension of interpersonal trust to Internet "relations" is unwarranted (Pettit, 2004). He claims that the conditions for the extension of interpersonal trust are simply not present in the case of Internet relations: there are no means whereby we can establish a belief in their trustworthiness, because – on the Internet – the "pegs" of our personal identity (including, we should add, our categorical identities) are frequently invisible or unavailable – no "face" (no facial expressions or gestures), no "frame" (no evidence from others) and no "file" (no past record). Beyond these very general, rather thin characterizations, we get no real consideration of interpersonal trust; and this is a drawback in Pettit's analysis.

Although Pettit does not quite state it in the same way, we cannot trust the Internet – or, we might add, the Cloud – in the same way that we might trust co-present others because we do not have access to evidence that might lead us to mistrust them, either. Again, we might say that the features of face-to-face interpersonal trust cannot be extrapolated.

Pettit is still closer to primitive case and to individualistic rational action analysis than I consider to be healthy, but we think we can take his general point on the nontransferable quality of features of interpersonal trust, so far as trust on the Internet or trust in the Cloud are concerned. It is not just a problem of "evidence" as Pettit puts it (although it is that too, as we shall see), but also of the fact that the whole "cultural apparatus" for interpersonal trust – the reciprocity of perspectives is by no means unequivocally or firmly in place for Internet/Cloud contacts. As ethnomethodologists might say, we need to start from scratch in examining issues of trust on the Internet.

In any discussion of extensibility – from the interpersonal situation to the Cloud, we must begin by establishing exactly the features of the interpersonal situations, or, perhaps better, "face-to-face" interaction. As I have indicated, discussions of extensibility seldom seem to start at this obvious point.

We can establish such a starting point by filling in what Pettit leaves out (no matter how much we may agree with his overall argument) or presents in only attenuated form. Pettit does not furnish anything but a most adumbrated characterization of interpersonal settings. In so far as such a characterization is provided at all, Pettit glosses it as involving "face" and "frame" (evidence available from how the person interacts with others).

Once more, we see from this checklist of features that Pettit inclines toward a methodological individualism, tending to emphasize, in various ways, per- ceived "personal" characteristics. Of course, this is part of the picture, but it is not a generic part. He does not fully consider the interpersonal situation not as purely composed of individual persons but as an interactional setting with its own social organization and its own gestalt properties – "gestalt contexture," as Garfinkel, following Aron Gurwitsch, terms it. In focusing in a reductive way on the perceived characteristics of individuals, Pettit gives far too much away to his potential adversaries, such as rational action theorists. Of course, he is far from alone in this: studies of trust and the Internet/Cloud have all too frequently been methodologically individualist in character, and to a far greater extent than Pettit. Many have reduced issues of security or trust to, say, individuals' cost/benefit calculations (see, for example, Beautement et al. 2008).

What, then, are the organizational features of interpersonal settings, consid- ered phenomenologically, within which interpersonal trust is a constituent? Of course, we do not wish to make particular parties to these settings "disappear." Instead, we want to consider them as actors within a given framework or set- ting, in terms of the setting (relevant courses of action they issue), and within courses of action that build into the interaction that in turn produces interper- sonal settings. Pertinent as perceived personal characteristics may be, it has to

be acknowledged that they can only operate within the weave of gestalt properties of the interpersonal situation per se. Indeed, the very specific here-and-now
pertinence of this or that personal characteristic is conjointly construed in terms
of the nature of a given situation.

It is odd that, given the massive amount of sociological work on interpersonal
face-to-face interaction, very few analysts have actually addressed this crucial
issue head-on. George Psathas and Frances Waksler (1973) deserve credit for
being amongst those few. I shall invoke their work extensively, although I
shall present my own version of and additions to the properties they advance
rather than their more unyielding and over-formalistic insistence that they are
"essential features." Instead, I consider these properties a feature of a gestalt
contexture that, depending on the specific instance and its local organizations,
variously foreground some of these features (e.g., the "we" feeling) while
relegating others to the background; but this does not mean they are inoperative.

Although Psathas and Waksler refer to "background features" (background
understandings and knowledge), they do not mention either trust or Garfinkel's
1963 study. This is a regrettable lacuna, because trust is clearly engendered in
and by many of the features of face-to-face interaction the authors adduce. It
is up to us to do what they do not – that is, explicate how trust figures in each
feature.

In an ordinary, face-to-face contexture, the parties involved are in immediate,
direct bodily co-presence with each party, vividly available to the other(s) in
terms of "raw, unmediated senses" (not just vision). This yields direct, rich, and
broadly based mutual availability and feedback. It involves eye-to-eye contact
and other kinds of reciprocal, situation-relevant monitoring, including "ritual"
features and symbolic endorsement of co-presence and of specificities of *this*
situation, here and now. The reciprocal orientation of parties to each other is
expressed in meaningful actions, and, indeed, the interpersonal situation is a
configuration of meaningful actions. Such situations may well involve a shared
pro tem "we" feeling and relation.

Within this "we-relation," each party's acts come to be sensitively attuned
and constantly re-attuned to those of co-present others, just as, reciprocally, the
acts of those others are attuned to that party among the others. We might add
to Psathas and Waksler's description of features that this reciprocal attuning
clearly requires trust.

This finely tuned interlocking of normative and constitutive reciprocities –
again, we might add, not least those relating to trust – involves mutually aligned
understandings and expectations. That having been said, the "we-relation" may
vary on a "scale" of intimacy, focus, and directedness. The most heightened
interpersonal interactions are what Goffman termed "focused interactions."

Those interactions with an intensely shared focus are also, typically, rich in communicative load and content. This produces what Goffman terms a "bounded field" of face-to-face interaction in any specific instance, a mutual orientation to shared time, space, circumstance, project, and so on. A significant part of all this is how to initiate and close down these situations, and such openings and closings are, frequently, heavily marked as such.

Clearly, this is not a complete characterization of interpersonal situations, but I hope to have given sufficient detail to suggest that there is a plenitude as well as a singularity to these kinds of situation. The properties of such situations cannot be "automatically" assumed to be extensible to any other situation, and certainly not in the particular configuration they collectively take. It is only through providing formalistic, schematic, theoretically reduced, overly selective, limited and thinned-out simplistic versions that the illusion of such extensibility can be sustained. Indeed, it seems that extreme analytic formalism of, say, the Simmelian type can only be created and sustained by a thinning out of the salient detail, the "content" of the setting to be formalized.

One among many examples of the formalistic thinning-out of the characterization of interpersonal situations is given in what Garfinkel has termed the "game dopes" of game and rational-action theories. It is clear, too, that the properties given previously are organizational features of settings, not properties of individuals. After all, what is relevant concerning an individual's personal record is given by the set of relevances in terms of which the particular interpersonal situation is cast: the suspicion that a person cannot be trusted in terms of marital fidelity may not be specifically relevant to the negotiation of a business deal.

It is evident then, that the description of the interpersonal setting I have given involves a competence model of interaction – that is, the participants' reciprocal recognition and ratification of cultural competence as the basis of action and where competent actors form constituents of a gestalt contexture. The properties of such complex contextures would not, *could* not, be produced through the interaction of game dopes.

Given a fuller rather than a theoretically simplified conception of interpersonal situations, it seems evident that the configuration of features per se is not to be found in the use of the Internet or the Cloud. To be sure, some features might to some degree be "transposed" in considerably transfigured form (see following discussion), but that is very different from asserting that the configuration of the properties of the interpersonal situation is identical or can be transposed wholesale to the situations of Internet/Cloud use.

If, however, we decide to eschew such extreme analytic formalism and instead choose to preserve the phenomenological integrity, the experiential "intactness," of the face-to-face setting, then our conception of trust will, and must, change accordingly. We shall have to see trust as minutely interwoven and sensitively attuned to just this situation, here and now, in all phenomenal detail. We shall need a conception that treats trust as not only "underwriting" each feature of the face-to-face situation but which is minutely intertwined into and expressed in that situation as participants intersubjectively experience it. Garfinkel's early "trust" paper allows us to begin this task, but his later work provides the conceptual apparatus that allows us to go far further along these lines (Garfinkel 2002).

One fundamental difference between the interpersonal and cloud computing situation is that, although we can "directly" apprehend a given feature of the contexture in the interpersonal situations, we rely on "information" in a very specific determination in the cloud computing situation. In a recent paper co-authored with Andrew P. Carlin, we invoked Wittgenstein's characterization of the logical grammar of the term "information" (Watson and Carlin, 2012: 331; Wittgenstein 1958, para. 356). If I look out of the window and declare to my companions that it is raining, I do not tell them: "My eyes give me the information that it is raining"; or "I have information that it is raining." If I say "I have information that it is raining," it is indicated is that I have not directly observed first-person that it is raining but that, for instance, someone else has reported to me that it is raining, and that I am, so to speak, conveying that report. It is a second- or third-person conveyance.

To illustrate this point, this local grammar is evident in the following excerpt from an article in *The Guardian* by the journalist Giles Richards, in which the Formula I racing driver, Lewis Hamilton, had criticized his teammate Jenson Button for a perceived slight:

> Earlier in the week Hamilton had reacted to being informed that Button had unfriended him on Twitter by posting: "I thought we respected each other but clearly he doesn't. He had been misinformed and apologised soon afterwards.
>
> *(Richards 2012: 27)*

The logical grammar of the term "information" quite evidently lends the lie to the computationalist models of mind that derived from Alan Turing's conception of artificial intelligence, insofar as these models depend on conceptions such as "the processing of information taken in through the sense-organs." More importantly for our purposes, it shows that the term "information" applies not only to materials derived from the Internet or the Cloud and not from those directly apprehended in face-to-face interaction.

In turn, this shows that the "type" of trust that is lodged in – and is, indeed, a condition for – face-to-face interaction will not be extensible (certainly not extensible in toto) to the Cloud situation, nor will the "type" of trust in the Cloud situation be identical to interpersonal trust. The type of trust in the Cloud situation will certainly involve "information" in the sense intended earlier, whereas the interpersonal situation will not. We may then speak of "finite provinces of trust[4]," but what I later call (following Wittegenstein, of course) a "family resemblance model" militates against any over-reification that some might, erroneously, see in this phrase.

The fact that "information" is "received" or reported rather than "directly" apprehended in a first-person sense, provides, of course, for the possibility of "misinformation," (see the "Lewis Hamilton" example, discussed previously). Of course, lay users of the term "information" know this: consequently, the potential for mistrust of information received is omnipresent, but by no means always activated – even on the Internet or in the Cloud, mistrust is not invariably the norm. Nonetheless, producers of information may be orientated toward the possibility that they potentially be read as "misinforming" recipients and may, as a consequence, seek to present their information as "authoritative," "factual," "*the* actual version of events," and so on. For their part, recipients of this information may seek cues as to its "authoritativeness." As Luc Sante (1993: 78) expresses it, admittedly with more than a touch of hyperbole:

> Information . . . strives for certainty, or rather its purveyors do, whether quixotically or disingenuously. The police tipster, the industrial spy, the political clairvoyant, the highly-placed source – all are in the business of pretending infallibility. And their commerce, once a small-time traffic, is in the process of becoming ever more institutionalised, increasingly central to a global economy as it moves from nocturnal alleys to glass-walled offices. . . . [The] commerce of information is descended in part from augurers who advised military leaders in antiquity. It has merely been dressed up with technology and soft science . . . for the benefit of contemporary rationalists.

As analysts, may we therefore keep an eye open for the culturally based methods information-producers use to imbue their information with authoritativeness? As Dorothy E. Smith informs us in a justly celebrated article, information may be presented as independent of the wishes, intent, or interests of its producer, where, indeed, the producer may present him/herself as having been forced to acknowledge the information and its implications (Smith 1978: 33–37). Such presentations comprise what Smith calls "authorization procedures." To use Emile Durkheim's phraseology, the information is presented as "external" to and "constraining of" the observer, in that it overcomes any resistance to acceptance on the producer's part. The materials presented in information terms may be authorized in a first-person "I was there: I saw it" sense.

---

[4] A phrase I attribute to Roger Slack.

Such ordinary cultural methods as these may be referred to as "'authorization procedures." This class may also include presenting the information as coming from more than one origin and as corroboratively "cross-checking" across independent sources; alternatively, the information may be presented as having been ascertained by more than one witness, independent witnesses, or by someone with a putatively trusted identity – say, a priest or a judge. Of course, recipients of some item of information orientate toward these selfsame authorization procedures in extending trust to that item. They may, indeed, seek to validate some item of information by using such procedures.

These authorization, validation, or objectification methods are to be found in ordinary, face-to-face interactions in which information (again, in the sense of information being reported by one or more of the co-participants) is being conveyed between co-present persons. Interpersonal interaction is perhaps the primary site of these procedures, the site in which they are found in their richest, most detailed and vivid forms, but they may also be found, with a *mutatis mutandis* rider, in textual incarnations including, of course, on computer screens.

This rider points to the fact that the authorization procedures, if present, will appear in transformed ways, ways that are adjusted to the Internet or the Cloud context and machine-based activities rather than the interpersonal one. Any links between the authorization of procedures in these two very distinct settings may be treated as what Wittgenstein terms "family resemblances," however distant (see, in another context, Heritage, 1978: 83–88).

To sum up, interpersonal situations and cloud computing situations cannot be treated as identical and interchangeable. One cannot be treated as an extension of the other, nor can interpersonal situations be transposed to the cloud computing ones. It is only by artificially reducing the salient detail of the interpersonal situation to "fit" the cloud computing situation so that they can be forced by violence into a false equivalence that the two situations might be conceived as "identical" (and, obversely, we might note, this forced relation also involves the simplification of cloud computing situations).

One axis of difference between the two sets of situation is, as I have observed, that of "information." The cloud computing situation invariably turns on information, whereas the interpersonal one does not, necessarily. When interpersonal situations involve the conveying of some item of information, some of the procedures or methods used to warrant that item are also found in the conveyance of information of "the client": the example of authorization procedures was given. However, given the generic differences in interpersonal and cloud settings, it would be misleading to treat these procedures as "identical" across those settings. Instead, the procedures are finely adapted to the specificities of the setting in which they occur, and, again can thus be seen as, at best, connected in terms of "family" resemblances.

In these comments about information, for the purposes of brevity and exemplification, I have focused on producers' and users' ways of attempting to establish its trustworthiness. Of course, there are other issues too concerning information as others in this volume have shown (e.g., Karagiannis on privacy and the transporting of personal information).

Of course, we may see some analogous methods of establishing the authority or trustworthiness of a given item or body of digital information. There is certainly a perceived need for such methods, not least in scholarly life. Indeed, Carol Tenopir and colleagues are currently involved in a (non-ethnomethodological) project on trust and authority concerning, for instance, digitally available scholarly sources (at the University of Tennessee, Center for Information and Communication Studies). This project, however, shows no appreciation of the potential of ethnomethodological analysis in that area, despite the demonstrated potential of that mode of analysis in, say, human-computer interaction.

In Chapter 2, David Clark gives us some examples of what we might term online authorization procedures – downloading a "trust" profile from third party (with a trusted identity and who is trusted for his/her expertise, independence, reputation, and so on) or the provision of third-party credentials. As Clark shows, there may be references to brokers, intermediaries, and others for the purposes of assuming trustworthiness. Clark's paper is rich in such examples, but what we get from reading his paper on the technical detail of these authorization procedures is that while they bear a general, sometimes remote, "family resemblance," to authorization procedures in interpersonal settings, their digital incarnation also renders them very different in nature and form from interpersonal ones. The resemblance is there in the "'basic logic" of the procedures, but they are nevertheless very remote in the two contexts.

Local Contexts of Trust in Cloud Computing

We might also consider the situation in which computing, or cloud computing, operations are placed within particular participation frameworks in which co-participants already know each other and trusted identities (including categorical identities) are already in place. We might, here, see cloud computing in terms of a simile: current computing with its local-physical base of operations is akin to exchange by local bartering; cloud computing is akin to exchange through a country's currency. This, of course, involves de-localization in that, as Nicholas Carr (2009: 117) claims, cloud computing will displace private systems as the preferred platform for computing as it expands. The shift into the Cloud will, then, lead to reductions or restrictions in the household's own physically based, local data centers. However, this shift will not and cannot extinguish local features of computing; it will only re-contextualize them.

The key considerations concerning trust will, in many respects, still be local-situational ones, in the sense that computational work (also) remains part of the situated, often face-to-face, interactions (between people in, say, a household) and thus may play some part in building, underwriting, or detracting from trust that people qua actors in what has been termed a given "participation framework" have for each other (Goodwin 1981).

Here, we might say that cloud computing is (re-)localized, or interlaced into a broader set of activities in the participation framework. We might also conceive of trust as fine-tuned to each participation framework, and to each instance of a given framework, at least in what we have already called a "family resemblance" sense. So what part does computing play in the normal, routine everyday operation of each of these frameworks so far as trust – that is, interpersonal trust – is concerned? Because there is relatively little research bearing directly and extensively on this issue, we shall simply suggest a protocol for further study that might be well-conceived, or it might not. I shall take a prototypical example of family household interaction and make some suggestions about the frame of reference within which such a study might proceed. Indeed, Microsoft Research UK and ParisTech are initiating a pilot study of Information and Communication Technologies (ICT) use in domestic settings from which we might begin to add a little more to the existing research literature on this issue, with special reference to cloud computing.

In domestic settings, computer-based systems clearly have to be integrated into the normal, typical, frequently interpersonal activities of the household. Designers of these systems have to pay attention to how the system is *actually* used, for what purposes and in what circumstances it will or (importantly) will not be used, and so on. To properly look at the operation of such systems, we need thoroughgoing field data on the often complex, detailed nature of the "interaction" between the system and the various overlapping participation frameworks that comprise the household – not least in its local ecological (spatial) aspects. The details making up these settings, including the local ecological settings, must be shown to be oriented to by members, even in "background" ways, and salient to their setting-specific practical purposes. The details are not to be simply arbitrarily imputed by the analyst.

There is, then, a distinction we are making between trust in a computer-based system (in the sense of, for example, trusting the cloud-based information it provides) and trust both as a constitutive feature of a particular participation framework and as overlapping set of frameworks into which the computer system might be incorporated. In the former case, the "natural home" of the trust is on the Internet or in the Cloud; and in the latter case, the "natural home" of trust is in the particular framework of face-to-face, interpersonal interactions.

Of course, the two types of trust might blend in some respects on particular occasions, but I am here focusing on the latter. Doing so leads to questions about whether computer systems can serve to underwrite, reinforce or (re-)build trust within those frameworks. By "overlapping frameworks" within the household, we intend such situations as when the family is all at home, or perhaps when the family or some segment of the family have guests and the like, and it has been noted that the current ICT systems are not necessarily "guest friendly." They may actually exclude guests. David Randall (2003: 234–238) has noted that one priority that families have is "connectivity," and the task for us is to specify the particular nature and pattern of connectivity in each participation framework and the different determinations of trust that each specific framework-related mode of connectivity entails. It is within each framework, and each instantiation of a given framework, that "trust" has its specific determination.

Most of the design for users concerning personal identity operates on the "(specific) personal identification" – "anonymity" axis. This simple, linear characterization works for some limited purposes but remains "interactionally flat" – that is, it is simplistic as a description of what happens interactionally in a complex locus such as a household. We require a more sensitive, more complex view in which, for instance, ICT provisions adapt "communication flow" to multiplex, overlapping participation frameworks and particularly to the range and diversity of membership categories, plus the actions and the activities predicated on those categories. Trust that the parent(s) reciprocally understand some item of information or some activity is different from trusting that children or guests will do so: again, there is a categorical order of trust in that trust, here, is differentially organized and "distributed" according to the membership category – incumbency of the persons in a given participation framework.

Such variable reciprocities of perspectives will, clearly, have different manifestations depending on the particular categorizations and their specific configuration in each participation framework. We may here refer to the *categorical specificity* of the design of information within these household frameworks. For instance, as Sommerville et al. (2006: 186) observe, the maintenance of privacy and confidentiality (and *trust* in privacy and confidentiality) are much more problematic when those categorized as "elderly" or "disabled" are subject to a monitoring technology that informs relatives about potential problems than when children are subject to that technology. The preference of the elderly or disabled person for privacy will mean that such monitoring systems cannot be construed as fixed or interchangeable across all frameworks and all categorical relations. Again, they must show participation framework-specific design, where, for example, provision for privacy is relevant in one framework but not another.

Whatever the empirical ethnomethodological study of such participation frameworks in home-sites, worksites, or whatever, the characterization of the setting must incorporate a full and rich characterization of the phenomenal properties of face-to-face interaction. Sad to say, some thinly "ethnomethodological" worksite and other studies have not done this; but I am recommending what I consider to be best ethnomethodological practice.

Conclusion

I contend that such framework and instance-specific design should be based on rigorous ethnographic field observation concerning the operation and relevences of each framework, and, in particular, based on a radically naturalistic approach such as ethnomethodology. It is one situation in which system designers and social scientists can complement each other, for a much-improved understanding of "ICT use in the life-world," the real world of people as they themselves collectively experience it in its salient phenomenal detail.

In this chapter, I have attempted to set out the nature of interpersonal trust. I have also tried to set out the best methodology for capturing and analytically explicating the features of that form of trust. My argument has been that various strands of enthnomethodology are the most adequate approach to this task. Following the ethnomethodological approach, I have argued that the features of face-to-face interpersonal trust are not extensible to trust in the Internet or the Cloud, or are certainly not extensible or transposable in any wholesale way; again, I have sought to show that ethnomethodology, as opposed to (for example) Pettit's approach, is the best way we have of characterizing this non-extensibility and non-transposability. Finally, I have made a few cautious comments on how the incorporation of ICT into interpersonal interaction may bolster trust, reliance, and confidence. To adequately demonstrate ethnomethodological claims about this, we must locate our analysis in a rich (rather than impoverished) conception of face-to-face relations. Consequently, we need to analyze these things not in terms of individuals but in terms of socially organized interaction patterns and frameworks as persons themselves collaboratively make sense of them in the course of their production.[5]

[5] I thank Richard Harper (Microsoft Research UK), Anne Warfield Rawls (Bentley College), Andrew P. Carlin (St. Columb's College), Andrew J. Goldsmith (Flinders University), Bernard Conein (University of Nice), and Anita Alzamora-Watson (formerly of Bradford University) for their inputs into my research on trust. I am grateful to the artist Sonia Boyce for suggesting readings on some aspects of this paper. I thank Andrew J. Goldsmith, too, for furnishing me with the transcribed data from which I have drawn the illocutionary sequence on trust in Section 4 of this chapter, and for permission to use these data in various ways in this and other papers. I alone am responsible for the trade-offs in their advice.

9

Trust, Social Identity, and Computation

Charles Ess

Introduction: Two Literatures on Trust

I approach the topic of trust from two converging directions. The first derives from work primarily in the domains of Information and Computing Ethics (ICE) –work that also includes perspectives from phenomenology and a range of applied ethical theories.[1] The second draws from media and communication studies most broadly, beginning with Medium Theory or Media Ecology traditions affiliated with the likes of Marshall McLuhan, Harold Innis, Elizabeth Eisenstein, and Walter Ong. In these domains, attention to communication in online environments, including distinctively virtual environments, began within what was first demarcated as studies of Computer-Mediated Communication (CMC). The rise of the Internet and then the World Wide Web in the early 1990s inspired new kinds of research within CMC; by 2000 or so, it became possible to speak of Internet Studies (IS) as a distinctive field in its own right, as indexed, for example, by the founding of the Oxford Internet Institute.

Drawing on both of these sources to explore a range of issues at their intersections – most certainly including trust – is useful first of all as the more empirically oriented research constituting CMC and IS work thereby grounds the often more theoretical approaches of ICE in the fine-grained details of praxis. At the same time, the more theoretical approaches of ICE, as we will see, help us complement the primarily social scientific theories and methodologies that predominate in CMC and IS. By taking both together, I hope to provide an account of trust in online environments that is at once strongly rooted in empirical findings while also grounded in and illuminated by a very wide range

---

[1] In these ways, I begin philosophically in what are characterized as continental philosophy and history of philosophy – i.e., as sharply distinct from the analytic starting points taken up in this volume by Tom Simpson and Olli Lagerspetz.

of theoretical perspectives. This approach requires at least one important caveat, to which I return shortly.

I begin with an overview of what trust online "looks like" – first from within the domains of CMC and IS, and then from within the domain of ICE. Taken together, these sources give us a fine-grained account of how trust in online environments faces both significant problems as well as (perhaps surprisingly) significant advantages. That is, we see that against the background of (especially) the hard dualisms of the 1990s, between the online and the offline and between the virtual and the real, online trust is clearly problematic – first because of the affordances of anonymity and then because of easy identity deception. At the same time, however, we see that CMC and IS research increasingly moves away from such hard dualisms to the now decade-long (if not longer) set of viewpoints and findings that rather highlight how our off-line and online lives – most certainly including our senses of identity and selfhood – are, for the most part, inextricably interwoven rather than radically disparate. Turning then to recent work in ICE on trust in online environments, I first explore a taxonomy of diverse philosophical accounts of trust. These lead us to a philosophical anthropology that refines our understanding of how trust works from especially phenomenological perspectives. These perspectives further link trust in a strong sense with human capacities for autonomous choice and a particular kind of reflective judgment called *phronesis*; these in turn are illuminated especially through contemporary accounts of virtue ethics as frameworks for analyzing online phenomena (such as friendship) that depend, obviously and crucially, on trust. A key distinction introduced here is between such strong trust, on the one hand, and reliance, on the other hand. Briefly, reliance describes relationships that lack choice. Simply, I (ideally) have a choice whether or not to trust another, and the Other has (ideally) a choice whether or not to fulfill my hopes and expectations, thereby reinforcing or betraying my trust. My use of "dumb tools" – that is, artifacts that have no meaningful choice – is described as a kind of reliance. This distinction will be critical for the core question of the article – a question that emerges only fully at the end of the next section. That is, given the kinds of selves that we are becoming, will such selves continue to enjoy capacities for trust in online environments, and/or will such selves instead be increasingly coerced into relationships more accurately characterized in terms of reliance (as most appropriate for dumb tools), not trust (as a relationship of choice between autonomous agents)?

To see more fully why this is a question, in the next section, I take up two sorts of problems that online trust encounters. The first is the problem of embodiment. One of the most influential accounts of trust, that developed by

K.E. Løgstrup (1956), highlights the essential role of embodied co-presence in the establishment of trust. But especially in early, primarily text-only environments, as thereby (largely) disembodied, such trust thus becomes especially problematic. We will see, however, that some of these difficulties can be overcome, in part by taking on-board the rather novel appreciation of precisely how deception online (as well as off-line) can foster the emergence of trust in a "virtuous circle" or "bootstraps" trust in ways otherwise difficult to account for. A second, more fundamental problem is evoked by what I argue to be changing senses of selfhood – namely, from more individual toward more relational selves. Recall the collocation between trust in a strong form, human autonomy, and *phronesis* in contrast with reliance as a relationship marked by the absence of choice. Where more relational selves appear to move away from the sorts of autonomy affiliated with strongly individual senses of selfhood – and where these relational selves are increasingly interwoven with and interdependent on both human and computational/communication networks – our core questions thus emerges with full force: will such relational selves still be capable of trusting relationships – most especially with the both human and artificial agents (AAs) that increasingly make up the networks defining their sense of selfhood and identity – and/or will such relational selves be increasingly entangled in coerced relationships of reliance, rather than trust?

In the fourth section, I return to recent developments in both ICE and IS that suggest the possibilities of sustaining trust in a strong sense for such relational selves. These recent works argue that such relational selves will be more accurately understood as hybrid selves (i.e., ones that sustain both strongly individual as well as relational emphases). Insofar as the individual emphasis is retained, in short, we may then be optimistic that our future selves will further retain the autonomy (and *phronesis*) required for trust in the strong sense.

But first, a caveat. We will see in the opening exploration of CMC and IS literatures that "trust" is a consistently mentioned point, either of celebration and/or of concern: but "trust" is rarely lifted up to a central focus of attention or investigation. Instead, trust is characteristically noticed along the way to other places and themes. Although this might seem a disadvantage in some ways, in the examples I bring forward, I hope it is clear that they have the advantage of attending to trust in conjunction with one or more other significant elements of online communication. They thereby illuminate the phenomenon of trust within a rich context. As a primary example, Shannon Vallor undertakes one of the most significant and influential analyses of the *virtues* fostered and/or hindered by Social Networking Sites – including the core virtues of patience, perseverance, and empathy. These virtues are central to almost any conception of the good life – the life of contentment and well-being (*eudaimonia*) that is inextricably tied to harmonious relations with one's larger community – first as these virtues or capacities are required to enter into, sustain, and develop deep friendship (2010). Vallor further mentions "trust" in conjunction with specific virtues, beginning with patience: "Patience helps to express to the other the depth of one's commitment to the relationship and builds trust and confidence in its future, by showing that the relationship's continued existence is not wholly dependent on its momentary rewards" (2010: 165). Vallor goes on to mention that the virtues of honesty (2010: 166) and empathy (2010: 167) likewise contribute to trust in our important relationships. As we explore more fully later in this chapter, at least the forms of trust in play in deep human friendships and other intimate relationships are thereby dependent on our capacity to practice and sustain such virtues, including the core "meta-virtue" (my term) of *phronesis*, a particular form of practical judgment or wisdom immediately interwoven with our capacities for autonomy and choice. At the same time, Vallor's account brings forward the essential roles of these virtues in the development of nothing less fundamental than our very characters and thereby our primary behaviors. She notes that how far we learn – or fail to learn – these virtues may shape our "moral character as predominantly honest or deceptive, *trusting* or *suspicious*, as these dispositions strongly influence the likelihood that we will become perpetrators or victims of fraud. (2010, 165, emphasis added; cf. Ess 2010, 294).

Again, what we might think of as an indirect glance toward trust is nonetheless quite valuable for showing us how trust is inextricably bound with other aspects of communication, our communicative lives, and – in Vallor's view – nothing less than our contentment, our hopes for a good life, and our very character. The upshot is thus a more holistic approach. As I think will be clear by the end of this chapter – as part of the larger convergences here between ICE, CMC, and IS, this more holistic approach offers distinctive and novel insights that we might not otherwise acquire.

A Brief History of Trust

A. "Joan," "Rape," and Embodiment (CMC/IS)

Tales of identity deception have taken on an almost mythical quality in writings about the internet. The same stories are told over and over as cautionary tales to inoculate the unwary.

(Kendall 2011: 318)

Lori Kendall's comment on the core thematic of identity deception in the literatures of CMC and IS directly points to one of the earliest accounts of identity deception and – thereby – the connection between (disembodied) communication, its possibilities for deception, and the problem of trust.

As many readers will know, the story of "Joan" – the online female persona of a person later revealed to be a male psychologist – has figured prominently in the literatures of CMC and IS as one of the earliest and most influential accounts of online interactions. The account is telling, however, not only as a primordial example of online deception, but also for what Lindsey van Gelder conveys regarding the high hopes for online environments in the earliest days of online interactions. So she comments:

> Many of us on-line like to believe that we're a utopian community of the future, and Alex's experiment proved to us all that technology is no shield against deceit. We lost our innocence, if not our faith.
>
> *(1991: 534)*

And we can add our trust, at least in the persona of "Joan." In particular, "Joan" "introduced" one of his women confidants to his real-world self, resulting in an affair. This woman later described the deceit and betrayal as "mind rape" (1991: 534), thereby prefiguring a still more prominent example of identity deception in the earliest days of the Internet and the Web, namely the (in)famous "rape in cyberspace" (Dibbell [1993] 2012). Most briefly, as participants in LambdaMOO (where MOO stands for Multi User Dungeon-Object Oriented) entered (virtually) a shared living room, the unfolding texts portrayed how two participants' avatars were being sexually assaulted in graphic and sadistic detail. For the real-world owners of these avatars, despite the disembodied character of such texts, the experienced sense of violation evoked real tears.

As I have detailed previously (Ess 2011), prevailing conceptualizations and discourses surrounding online environments as "cyberspace" in the 1990s defaulted to a strong dualism between the online as virtual versus the off-line as real: cyberspace versus "meatspace" – a dichotomy rooted in William Gibson's defining science fiction novel *Neuromancer* (1984) (and from there, it is clear, in both Cartesian and Augustinian dualisms further rooted in what Nietzsche aptly critiqued as contemptus mundi, contempt for the world, as a thematic metaphysics in especially orthodox Christianity). Again, the significance of this episode is not simply that identity deception is possible online, as facilitated by disembodied communication as either anonymous or pseudonymous. Equally important, this episode is the primary exemplar for how these easy dualisms, however orthodox for the time, were quickly challenged by the real-world experiences of those victimized in purely online and disembodied environments – in good measure, because these experiences involved profound violations of *trust*. Most simply, the power of such experiences directly contradicts a putative hard line between the online and the off-line, the virtual and the material, and begins a gradual thread of both critical discourse and empirical findings that, over the course of the 1990s, gradually rejected these dichotomies in favor of conceptualizations that stressed (as they had to, in light of increasing evidence) perhaps unavoidable if not simply indissoluble continuities between these two experiential domains.

In particular, succeeding waves of research in what can now be called Internet Studies has brought to the foreground the role of the body and thereby *embodiment* in our online presentations of identity. In this way, this work thus intersects with some of the earliest philosophical analyses of trust – namely those of Knut Erik Løgstrup (1956, 2007), who emphasizes precisely the role of embodied co-presence in the establishment and sustaining of trust (cf. Myskja 2008). (We return to this connection more fully in the next section on philosophical approaches.)

So, by 2004, for example, some of the earliest work on the now overwhelming popular online environments provided by Social Networking Sites showed that trust online could be fostered precisely by already established relationships of friendship and acquaintanceship. So Nancy Baym, referring to some of the very earliest work on SNSs (Donath & Boyd, 2004), points out that such SNSs

... are grounded in the premise that both online and offline people would rather connect with those who share acquaintances. This can create trust and, at least in the abstract, render the dangers – and opportunities – of online anonymity passé.

(Baym 2011: 288)

But such off-line webs of relationships, of course, inevitably included the embodied co-presence of the individuals and groups involved. And so, perhaps not surprisingly, other IS researchers highlight precisely the role of the body – including the body as gendered – in how we present and sustain our identity in both off-line and online environments. So Lori Kendall notes that "in most long-standing communities, [identity] deception is minimized. The formation of community depends upon consistent identities" (2011: 319). In particular,

... most people in virtual communities wish to represent themselves in consistent and realistic ways. People do manage to perform consistent identities online. Among other things, this means that the aspects of identity that some hoped would become insignificant online – such as race, class, and gender – remain salient.

(2011: 319)

So it is, for better and for worse, the dreams of bodiless liberation in cyberspace in the 1990s, as depending on a radical split between the online and the off-line, are increasingly pushed to the margins of most persons' everyday experiences and usages. To be sure, there are still virtual spaces that allow participants important possibilities for exploring, say, sexual identities and preferences not easily accepted or pursued in their off-line communities – whether the rural GLBTQ youth documented especially by Mary Gray (2009, 2010), or, more darkly in my view, continued fascination with male domination, female subordination, and its various expressions (e.g., female "submissives" in the *Second Life* World of Gor [Bäcke 2011] or the various "altporn" sites and related environments that include thematics of BSDM [Paasonen 2010; Thorn and Dibbell 2012].) Whatever we may make of this in terms of sexual ethics, embodiment remains a thematic precondition for online as well as off-line presentation of selfhood and identity. So Janne Bromseth and Jenny Sundén note, precisely in the context of their overview of IS research on GLBTQ spaces and environments: "our bodies hold us accountable for our actions, in the sense that they are our physical representations of selves" (2011: 279). Reinforcing Kendall's observation, such embodied presence, finally, is critical precisely for creating *trust* – most especially in such environments as these may present their participants with greater risks. So Bromseth and Sundén add that the processes of building community in online environments requires precisely "the development of trust and predictability through social responsibility," (2011: 279) where such responsibility, as we have just seen, rests in large measure on (more or less) authentic (re)presentation of our embodied selves.

B. Trust, Reliance, Autonomy, and **Phronesis**: *Philosophical Approaches*

In recent work (Ess 2010b; Ess and Thorseth 2011), I have sought to develop an overview of how trust is further taken up within the literatures of Information and Computing Ethics. Here I will draw briefly on these sources to first sketch a philosophical taxonomy of accounts of trust. I flesh out this taxonomy with more extensive accounts of trust as developed by several philosophers – primarily with a view toward how these further contribute to what I call a philosophical anthropology of trust. As we will see, this anthropology draws on Kantian epistemology, virtue ethics, and phenomenology, and thereby returns us to our thematic focus on embodiment and embodied co-presence as critical to at least strong forms of trust. But we also see a critical distinction emerge between *trust* (in a strong form) and *reliance*: most briefly, a strong form of trust between human beings entails our capacity to *choose* whom to trust – a choice that further implicates our judgment (*phronesis*). This allows us to further distinguish between the sorts of trust we may freely take up with other human beings as free agents, and the sorts of (sometimes grudging) reliance we are increasingly forced into by way of our ever-growing implication in communication and computer networks. At a first level, we readily accept that may have to rely on these to move forward in our daily lives: such reliance, however, by no means implies that we trust these technologies. But as we will see, the conception of trust that emerges here, as bound up with strong notions of human freedom and a distinctive form of judgment (*phronesis*) helps elaborate this initial sense of difference between trust and reliance.

Briefly, we will see arguments for artificial agents (AAs) and multi-agent systems (MASs) as acquiring increasing degrees of autonomy and choice in their interactions with one another – and with us. At this point in time, we can make at least a temporary distinction between a strong form of trust that issues from full human autonomy and *phronesis* and a somewhat weaker form of trust that may more accurately describe our relationships with AAs and MASs. Whether or not this distinction disappears at some future time when such agents may acquire a "fully functional" equivalent to human freedom and *phronesis*; the distinction will be at least temporarily useful for the final section in which I consider the implications of our changing sense of selfhood for our basic conceptions and experiences of trust in both robust and less robust forms.

Trust is Said in Many Ways: A Taxonomy with Examples

For our purposes, we can organize understandings and conceptualizations of trust into four categories, beginning with cognitive or rational accounts of trust. These accounts take up trust as a form of rational choice, one depending on a fairly straightforward accounting of pro and con reasons for trusting a person, institution, or other. In the canonical definition offered by Coleman, such deliberations amount to what "a rational actor applies in deciding whether to place a bet" (1990: 99, cited in Weckert 2005: 101; cf. Pettit 1995: 209). We shall see quickly that such accounts are strongly limited; but they are especially useful in a context that is critical for us – namely, the many forms of networks and computer-based decision making constructs that increasingly define both the contents and essential infrastructures of our lives. For example, Mariarosaria Taddeo takes up such a rationalist account of trust in her analysis of how trust is to be defined as a relationship between artificial agents and multi-agent systems, such as stock-trading programs. Such "e-trust" enjoys the advantage of relying on reasons and information that are relatively straightforward to quantify and submit to algorithmic processing. Taddeo further sees her account as resting on the "Kantian ideal of a rational agent" – that is, one capable of choosing its own best options in light of specific goals (2011: 76).

At the same time, however, Taddeo highlights what is missing – for humans at least – in such accounts. Broadly, trust in human relationships implicates contexts and situations far more complex than those defined for AAs. Specifically, AAs, as Taddeo notes, lack "mental states, feelings, or emotions" (2011: 76).

But such factors are central to a second class of trust definitions – precisely *affective* accounts of trust. Such accounts are necessary, as John Weckert points out, because purely rationalist accounts fail to encompass two familiar forms of trust: children's trust of their parents and trust between friends. The latter example is especially important for us as it brings to the foreground Aristotle's account of friendship (Weckert 2005: 101) – the account we first met in the introductory discussion of Shannon Vallor's analyses of trust as interwoven with the virtues necessary to friendship.[2]

Moreover, Weckert introduces the core distinction between trust and *reliance*. The latter, in his analysis, more accurately describes our posture toward inanimate objects such as tools. Weckert develops this distinction first around the element of *choice*. Whether we have the choice to rely on our tools and instruments (i.e., the commuter must rely on a bicycle, a bus, or a metro to arrive at work in a timely fashion), such instruments and tools have no *choice* as to whether or not they will perform in ways that will satisfy our expectations. By contrast, trust deriving from and working between human beings depends centrally on choice and thus autonomy: whatever the role of emotions (as in the case of children and new lovers, for example), human beings choose whom to trust and under what circumstances – and our trustees have choice in whether or not they will live up to the hopes and expectations that ride on our trust. For Weckert, trust then emerges as a kind of hermeneutical framework that shapes our perceptions and experiences of others: trust thereby stands as a kind of disposition, ultimately based on choice accompanied by non-cognitive and emotive elements. I am "disposed" to trust my trustee, we can say; but especially given the core role of choice for both the trustor and the entrusted, trust remains an "epistemic uncertainty" – that is, something that can be broken. For that, as Weckert sees it, precisely because trust operates as a hermeneutical framework reinforced by both reason and emotion, human trust is robust. Trust can, of course, be violated; but especially among children and friends, to begin with, broken trust can often be restored, even in the face of a reason that, on

---

[2] In Chapter 5, Tom Simpson has characterized Taddeo's (2009) work as an example of a popular approach to trust in philosophy that focuses precisely on trust as rational choice – an account he then critiques. What we see here, however, is that Taddeo (2011) acknowledges the limits of exclusively rationalist accounts insofar as the rationalist account, while working well for AAs, misses precisely the complexity, including the emotional complexities, of trust in human contexts. And from here, the reader will see, I build an account of trust that issues in critiques of purely rationalist accounts that are at least parallel with Simpson's.

It is probably fair to say that this account is not popular in contemporary philosophy, and so Simpson's opening characterization may hold. Still, this account stands as at least as an alternative one that is largely rooted in philosophy. Moreover, insofar as this account echoes Simpson's in highlighting both the affective and the conative, it may offer interesting parallels and resonances with his in turn.

a strictly rationalist account of trust, would compel us to never trust the Other again (Weckert 2011; cf. Ess and Thorseth 2011: xiv).[3]

Weckert's analysis leads to a core question: in what sense, if any, can we *trust* software agents – that is, not simply rely on them as we would inanimate tools? Weckert argues that at least some software agents are possessed of a degree of autonomy significant enough to qualify as the sort of autonomy required for his definition of trust. Indeed, Weckert concludes that "autonomous software agents can be trusted in essentially the same sense in which humans can be trusted" (2011: 100; cf. Ess and Thorseth 2011: xv).

How far this is so, it should now be clear, turns on just how far such agents are indeed autonomous. This question is further complicated – but in an ultimately helpful way – if we add a third sort of account of trust. Such accounts derive from phenomenological perspectives and analyses, including one provided by Annamaria Carusi (2008). Carusi is interested in the highly practical problem of how to establish trust between practitioners from divergent disciplines, such as computer scientists, mathematicians, and biologists. Such trust is necessary, obviously, for the sake of interdisciplinary research projects: but such trust is all the more problematic for now familiar reasons – that is, especially as these collaborations often proceed all but entirely via online and thereby largely disembodied communication, how do we, in Carusi's helpful phrase, "bootstrap trust"? Carusi highlights the role of visualizations – for example, of heart processes – that are created through extensive collaboration among these three disciplines. Carusi argues that such visualizations are especially important as they catalyze trust. To make her case, Carusi draws on yet another aspect of Kantian thought – namely, Kant's analysis of our aesthetic experiences as bringing into play both imagination and a shared *sensus communis* (literally, a "commonsense" – a *shared* sense or sensibility). Such shared aesthetic experiences are inextricably bound up with the rational dimensions of our knowledge. In both ways, what emerges is a shared intersubjectivity, a shared universe of knowing that is at once rational *and* affective. As visualizations derive from and reinforce the *sensus communis*, they thus both draw from and contribute to our shared knowledge and experience. In this way, "visualizations contribute to building up the intersubjectively shared framework of agreement which is basic for trust" (2008: 243; cf. Ess 2010: 291).

Carusi thus reinforces Weckert's account by highlighting the role of both the cognitive and the affective in our understanding of trust, and thereby reinforces the limitations of a purely rationalist account of trust, as Taddeo first pointed

---

[3] Weckert's emphasis on trust as robust in these ways reinforces the conceptions of trust developed in this volume by Anderson and Sharrock (Chapter 7), and then Watson (Chapter 8).

out. In this direction, Weckert refers to Annette Baier's early analyses of trust, as emphasizing precisely that trust involves the affective, the cognitive, as well as what Baier calls the conative (1994: 132, in Weckert 2005: 102; Ess 2010: 291). Furthermore, as Carusi later builds on this analysis, she provides yet one more strong critique of holding strong distinctions between the virtual and the real (2011: 109). Most importantly for our purposes, Carusi's account of trust not only provides an anchor in Kantian epistemology, but also in virtue ethics. As is well known, purely rationalist accounts of trust run the risk of leading us into what is called the vicious circle of security. That is: if, say, my online banking system appears to become untrustworthy (or, depending on its utilization of AAs and/or MASs, unreliable), a tempting response may be to give me more *reasons* to use it, by way of offering new security measures (e.g., an additional range of "security questions" that must be answered every time I subsequently log on). But the growing complexity of both security and regulation mechanisms often inspires the opposite of what is intended – namely, a growing lack of trust – as the very complexity of such systems seems inevitably to render them more unstable and thus (even) less trustworthy (Carusi 2011; cf. Thorseth 2008: 130; Ess and Thorseth 2011: xv).[4]

This sort of vicious circle helps highlight one of the primary difficulties attached to strictly rationalist accounts of trust. Presuming a "zero-trust" state, if you wish to argue that I should trust you and begin to offer me the reasons for doing so, all of this is instantly stopped by the simple observation that I have no reasons in the first place to trust you, and hence even less reason to accept or trust the reasons you may want to provide me for trusting you. The problem of trust thus becomes a kind of moral bootstrapping problem: if there were a complete absence of trust, it is difficult to see how trust might ever be established on strictly rational grounds. By contrast, Carusi's account of trust can resolve the bootstrapping problem by beginning within an already established, shared cognitive-affective framework – that is, as part of the basic cognitive/affective apparatus of (more or less) all human knowers who thereby encounter one another within a shared intersubjectivity.[5] Moreover, this shared

---

[4] This notion of the vicious circle of security exemplifies Clark's core insight that "technical mechanisms, by themselves, do not give assurance of correct operation. Only when security is combined
with trust do we get a network where we can hope for secure, reliable, robust operation" (Chapter
2). Danezis makes this point precisely: insisting on more "security" in the absence of trust
only leads more restrictions that strongly tend to disable rather than enable trust (Chapter 4).

[5] Carusi argues that trust is in part, so to speak, "pre-given" in our everyday social existence with
one another, as this existence rests on a shared intersubjectivity that emerges in part through
a shared sensus communis. In these directions, she reinforces the arguments of Anderson and
Sharrock (who, perhaps not accidently, share with Carusi a phenomenological starting point),
which highlight how far trust is a given or starting point in ordinary life.

intersubjectivity, most especially as it includes the affective dimensions of trust, allows Carusi to argue for a *virtuous circle* of trust. In many instances, at least, in such intersubjectively shared worlds we begin – as the example of children highlights – with the presumption of trust; we act *as if*, to use another Kantian phrase (brought forward by Bjørn Myskja, 2011), the Other is trustworthy. Once trust is bootstrapped in this way, it opens the possibility of further experiences with Others that will either reinforce or, perhaps, undermine our initial presumption. But especially as trust emerges in this account as something of a disposition (to echo Weckert) that can then, in effect, be practiced, reinforced, and expanded (whether in online or off-line environments), trust thereby appears as a *virtue* – that is, precisely a capacity or habit that we can develop and improve upon over time.

To recall the opening discussion of the work of Shannon Vallor, trust is already recognized as closely implicated with the virtues required first of all for friendship (again, as initially following the Aristotelian analyses). In particular, Vallor at least hints that trust functions as a virtue in its own right, as she articulates her concerns as to how contemporary SNSs may foster and/or hinder the develop of such virtues as patience, perseverance, and empathy. So, to recall, she comments that "we must also understand how, for young people, particular online practices may contribute to the shaping of their moral character as predominantly honest or deceptive, *trusting* or *suspicious*, as these dispositions strongly influence the likelihood that we will become perpetrators or victims of fraud" (2010, 165, emphasis added; cf. Ess 2010, 294).

More broadly, building on the works of Taddeo, Weckert, Carusi, Vallor, and Myskja (among others), along with May Thorseth, I have proposed a philosophical anthropology that conjoins Kantian epistemologies and ethics, phenomenological accounts of embodiment and embodied knowledge, and virtue ethics (2011, xix–xxvi). A crucial linkage here is provided by Thorseth's complement to Carusi's use of Kant's *Critique of Judgment*, as Thorseth brings forward Kant's notion of reflective or deliberative judgment. Most briefly, such reflective judgment directly contrasts with what Kant calls determinative judgment. The latter is a familiar form of deductive or algorithmic judgment that begins with accepted first principles or reasons, and deduces particular consequences from these with the addition of particular premises defining, say, a given context or circumstance. By contrast, reflective or deliberative judgment works, so to speak, from the ground up – that is, from an initial knowledge of given circumstances and contexts, in the effort to discern which general principles or reasons may be relevant in our assessment or decisions (our *judgments*). For Thorseth, our capacity to undertake reflective judgment is critical first for our ability to take into account "the possible judgments of others," as this is part and parcel of our communicative presence (whether online or off-line) with others. Echoing Carusi's use of Kant's *sensus communis* to establish a shared affective/rational intersubjectivity, for Thorseth, Kant's reflective judgment is necessary for the kinds of (ideal) communication required for deliberative democracy (2011: 163).

More broadly, Kant's notions of reflective or deliberative judgment thereby bring forward still more foundational accounts of *phronesis* as a kind of practical wisdom or judgment highlighted by Socrates and then Aristotle as a core capacity for human beings as moral agents (Ess and Thorseth 2011, xxiii). *Phronesis* is at work precisely in those contexts in which we are unsure ethically. That is, much of our day-to-day ethical experience is relatively non-problematic. We know, to the point of not having to think or reflect about it, what "the right thing to do" is, at least in most circumstances. With regard to the kind of judgment in play here, this is because we can in most circumstances employ a relatively straightforward determinative judgment. For example, while bicycling to work, I can be infuriated by another cyclist who may carelessly or even dangerously cut in front of me. But whatever levels of self-righteous anger may arise – most especially if such a cyclist puts human beings at risk – I am not seriously tempted to whip out my concealed pistol and shoot him or her down. It's a simple determinative judgment: do not kill (general principle) – to shoot at the offending cyclist might kill (specific circumstance) – therefore do not shoot. (Indeed, because such judgments are so simple and straightforward, they almost always operate all but unnoticed in the background of consciousness.)

Happily, most of our moral and ethical experiences work this way – again, to the point that we rarely have to think about such reactions. By contrast, many of our ethical challenges arise precisely because the specifics of a given situation do not immediately allow for straightforward determinative judgments that would resolve our ethical choices. Instead, the specifics of a given situation – to use Carol Gilligan's example, the high school girl who discovers that she is pregnant – may invoke a range of general and often conflicting general principles. So she finds herself confronted with conflicting ethical demands, including perceived duties of obedience to family and/or church, the specific wishes or desires of her boyfriend, her own wishes and desires, and, of course, perceived duties or ethical requirements attributed to the growing life within her. To make the judgments needed to resolve such terrible dilemmas, there appears – at least so far – to be no algorithm, no "über-general" or meta-general principle to help us straightforwardly deduce the correct conclusion or resolution. Instead, such judgments are precisely reflective judgments that must first determine which obligations and duties take highest precedence. That is, we must discern – again, from the ground up – which general principles are called into play here, and – precisely because they conflict – which will take priority. Hence such judgments are so difficult: precisely in the absence of a straightforward determinative judgment, one driven by a simple algorithm or "über-algorithm," initially we are left fumbling about trying to discern what general principles might come into play.

The difficulties here may be further compounded insofar as such judgments appear to implicate tacit and embodied forms of knowledge – knowledge that thereby stubbornly refuses to be made articulate and thereby a component in our more determinative ratiocinations. As Plato put it:

> . . . a first-rate pilot [cybernetes] or physician for example, feels [diaisthanetai] the difference between the impossibilities and possibilities in his art and attempts the one and lets the others go; and then, too, if he does happen to trip, he is equal to correcting his error.
>
> *(The Republic, 360e–361a [Plato 1991])*

"Feels" translates here *diaisthanetai* – literally, a sensing (aesthesis) through (dia) a given situation so as to discern what is possible and what is not. Such a sensing appears to entail both the affective and the cognitive – and thereby, I suggest, brings into play the more tacit, pre-reflective, precognitive dimensions of our knowledge and so points to an embodied form of knowing/feeling.

In all events, *phronesis* is thus inextricably tied to our radical autonomy as human beings. That is, our sense of quandary and paralysis in such situations, in this light, is not simply a matter of "not knowing what to choose." It is more fundamentally a matter of being free to choose from multiple paths, as guided by reflective judgments that are usually multiple, ambiguous, and uncertain – that is, not determinative.

This means, to begin with, that we should distinguish between two forms – or at least degrees – of trust. The first is the sort of affective-cognitive trust between human beings as autonomous beings – that is, capable of *choosing* whether or not trust one another, whether or not to behave in ways that will sustain and fulfill the trust that others place in us, and whether or not to try to recover trust if it has been betrayed or broken. Such trust further requires the non-determinative forms of reflective judgment or *phronesis* tied to human autonomy. As we have seen, what we can think of as "dumb objects" – that is, instruments or tools without agency or choice, are not objects of such trust, but rather reliance. By contrast, as Weckert has argued, at least some AAs may be thought of as trustworthy. So far as I can gather, the current state of the art gives us AAs with a degree of autonomy that is still quite limited as compared to humans; moreover, whether or not such agents can be programmed with capacities that would fully reproduced *phronesis* is currently under fierce debate (e.g., Sullins 2011). My point here is not to close out the possibility of AAs developing the equivalent of autonomy and *phronesis* that humans currently may claim: that remains to be seen, quite simply. Instead, insofar as we can distinguish between degrees of autonomy and *phronesis*, the less such capacities are at work in AAs and MASs, the less we may say we can choose to trust them in a primary sense, and the more we must say we (choose and/or are forced to) rely on them.

More broadly, we should now be clear on how trust stands among an array of critical virtues – habits and capacities that we may choose to develop and or leave nascent. But such virtues – perhaps most importantly, the virtue of *phronesis* – are critical to our conceptions and choices regarding the good life, as a life of contentment and harmony. Most fundamentally, as Vallor helpfully reminds us, our choices in determining what virtues we will foster or neglect are nothing less than choices as to *who we will be/come* – specifically, whether we will develop into more trusting or more suspicious and thereby more or less like to be either the victims or perpetrators of fraud (2010: 165). Insofar as this is true, we would be well advised to pursue the virtues of *phronesis*, trust, and so on, and to be wary of those contexts and instrumentalities that may frustrate or hinder their development.

We will return to these choices in the last section, where we examine the choices available to more individual and more relational selves

Trust and Online Environments: Two Problems

As this volume attests, the range of challenges and possible resolutions to (re)establishing at least some form(s) of trust in online environments is extensively analyzed and well documented. In this context, I wish solely to highlight the two sorts of problems that our account of trust – that is, as a disposition or virtue both presumed and chosen by autonomous and embodied human beings capable of *phronesis* – bring to the foreground.

A. *From Embodiment to Disembodiment (1990s) and Now Mediated Embodiment*

The first of these difficulties is presented precisely by the role of embodiment and embodied co-presence as essential components for our experiences and choices of trust. That is, as pointed out with especial clarity by Bjørn Myskja, in his phenomenological and Kantian approach to trust in online environments, beginning with the work of Knud E. Løgstrup, trust is at once at the center of "the human condition as such" (Myskja 2008: 214). This is first because we, as embodied beings, are thereby vulnerable and dependent on one another. At the same time, it is precisely in contexts of embodied co-presence that we may learn to entrust others with our vulnerability, to take the risk that they will take responsibility for our well-being, without, of course, having "any guarantee that they will" (Myskja 2008: 214).[6] For Løgstrup and then for Myskja, it is in "the personal meeting," the face-to-face encounter of embodied co-presence where we learn to trust one another. Prior to and in the absence of such encounters, we tend to develop or accept prejudgments about others that incline us against trusting them. "These judgments will normally break down in the presence of the other, and this proximity is essential for the eradication of these preconceptions" (Myskja 2008, 2, with reference to Løgstrup (1971: 195), 22f.; Ess 2010, 292).[7]

In this light, the difficulty with online communication is not simply that it affords anonymity and thereby identity deception: more fundamentally, especially in the days of text-only communication, such encounters were largely (but not entirely) *disembodied.* Absent the embodied encounter with the Other – in which, as we now know much better than ever before, we gauge and take our measure of one another in a wide range of tacit, non-verbal, and non-reflective ways (Stuart 2008) – we are thus deprived of the multiple ways in which the face-to-face encounters can help us move from wariness and uncertainty to at least a modest willingness to risk trusting the Other.

Of course – again, as contributions to this volume attest – a host of strategies have been developed and deployed to encourage greater trust online, despite these limitations. Here we can note that approaching the problem of trust from a phenomenological perspective such as Carusi's also helps (perhaps dramatically) shift the problem, insofar as this perspective highlights a shared intersubjectivity from the outset that allows us to "bootstrap" trust in ways otherwise difficult to imagine. For his part, Myskja argues for a similar sort of bootstrapping – one that, surprisingly and strikingly, begins precisely from the possibilities of identity deception online. That is, drawing on Kant's later ethical work, Myskja points out how deception can serve important *virtuous* ends. Most briefly, deception for Kant is acceptable as part of a self-presentation that shows ourselves as better than we really are. This view depends on an account of human beings as strongly tending toward "moral weakness." But given this

---

[6] This focus on *risk* as interwoven with our choosing to trust one another recalls the point made by Clark in his opening essay – that society is based on a kind of risk insofar as every interaction resting on trust thereby rests on a trust that can be (chosen to be) violated. See Clark, Chapter 2.

[7] In Chapter 6, Lagerspetz critiques the emphasis in both Myskja and Løgstrup on the role of the body and embodied co-presence as salient to trust. However the debate on this level might turn out, it is sufficient to point out here that Lagerspetz's critiques do not directly address the elements of Myskja's analysis that I bring forward here – namely, his use of Kant to defend at least some forms of deception (both online and off-line) as the bases of virtuous circles.

view, deception that hides such moral weakness can, again, help bootstrap us toward more morally commendable behavior:

> If others saw us as those villains we all really are, this would only serve to corrupt everyone; simply, we would get used to bad and immoral behaviour as normal. Pretending to be better than we really are is not only deception; it makes us act as better humans.
>
> *(2008: 217; Ess 2010: 292)*

For Myskja, the sorts of online deception made possible by especially more disembodied forms of communication can thus foster virtuous development, including the emergence of trust. Specifically, we know in a strong way that we do not tell the whole truth and nothing but the truth – for example, in a SNS profile, an email, or a tweet. But Myskja points out that this "reciprocal acknowledgment that we are not completely honest in all respects" may foster trust nonetheless:

> We know that we communicate with the other not as [s]he is, but as [s]he wants to be (or as [s]he wants to be perceived to be), because we present ourselves in the same way. On this non-ideal Kantian morality we may deceive others both in order to protect ourselves against their negative judgment, but also in order to promote the moral improvement in the society. Deception is an integral part of social intercourse and mistrust is prudential.
>
> *(2008, 217; emphasis added,* CE; *Ess 2010, 293)*

Between Carusi's and Myskja's suggestions of how trust may be bootstrapped and fostered in online environments, it is perhaps less surprising that there is as much trust online as we can discern. In any event, over the past decade (and more), rapid technological developments – including the ever-greater diffusion of ever-greater bandwidth – have served to increasingly bring the body back into online environments. Whether by way of simple VoIP video and audio calls – such as Skype, iFace, Google videochat, Viber, and others – or more sophisticated virtual worlds (such as *Second Life*), more and more dimensions of the embodied co-presence first pointed to by Løgstrup as necessary to trust become more and more available in online environments as well.

None of this is to say that the problems of trust in online environments will devolve to the simplistic or simply go away altogether. As millennia of human experience demonstrate, we can be very effective at deception and the destruction of trust in fully embodied contexts; bringing more of the body online thereby allows us to bring along our full suite of abilities for both vicious and virtuous deception. But these developments seem to ameliorate to a very large degree at least the early problems of trust-building in especially more disembodied online environments.

B. Changing Nature of Selfhood and Identity

In my view, a still more fundamental challenge to the problem of trust is evoked by apparent changes in nothing less foundational than our very conceptions of selfhood and identity.

Most briefly, our discussions of trust in "Western" societies – along with most other ethical discussions until the past two or three decades – have turned on a series of conceptions of human beings as primarily *individual* entities. This is at work here first of all in the Kantian emphasis on human beings as *autonomies* – that is, as moral agents radically free from (mechanically) causal determination, including determination by others. To be importantly fair to Kant, it is arguable that his notion of the self as a rational autonomy is already less radically atomistic than the conceptions of selfhood developed in early modernity by Thomas Hobbes and then John Locke. As Charles Taylor makes exquisitely clear in his magisterial *Sources of the Self: The making of the modern identity* (1989), Locke's "punctuated self" or radically "disengaged self" especially emerges in early modernity as precisely the sort of self that is no longer dependent on Others – whether family, community, or the larger institutions of church, state, and customs as conveyed and enacted by culture. Instead, such a self is thereby radically free – to determine for itself and by its own lights what "the good life" consists of and how it is to be pursued (Taylor 1989, 159ff.).

Whatever its shortcomings and moral failings, those of us still attached to democratic processes and the ethical norms affiliated with the modern liberal state, beginning with norms of equality and gender equality, must be grateful for the emergence of such a self. As Taylor elaborates, such a self both requires and justifies the modern liberal state – that is, the state that does *not* define the good life for its citizens. Moreover, it is most especially in Kantian arguments for respect for the autonomy for others "always as ends in themselves, never as a means only" (Kant [1785] 1959: 47) that we can find the strongest arguments for equality and gender equality. More broadly, the prevailing ethical frameworks of modern Western ethics have turned on the assumption of a singular moral agent: whether we are deontologists or utilitarians, we presume that the moral agent who must decide about and thereby take responsibility for his or her moral decisions is first of all the autonomous individual capable of such deliberation and responsibility (see Figure 2).

But all of this has begun to change – first somewhat slowly, beginning within the traditions established, for example, by Kantian ethics. As Soraj Hongladarom has pointed out, both Kant and Hegel already shift from radically atomistic conceptions of selfhood to what we will now call more relational conceptions (2007). In particular, Jürgen Habermas's theory of communicative action (which also builds on phenomenology) takes up a notion of "communicative reason" that is intrinsically relational. As his expositor Thomas McCarthy puts it, our identity is from the outset a social identity, one shaped by our interactions with others, and is thereby "from the start interwoven with relations of mutual recognition" (1978, 47).[8] To be sure, much of feminist thought at the time was deeply critical of Habermas for putting forward an account of rationality that was easily deconstructed as excessively masculine and exclusive of *emotion* as a critical component of knowledge and ethical decision making (Benhabib 1986). Nonetheless, the turn toward these more relational understandings of selfhood was accelerated precisely by early analyses of ethical decision making with one's "web of relationships," beginning with the work of Carol Gilligan (1982).

These various shifts toward more relational conceptions of selfhood can be seen in a host of other ways, beginning with Georg Simmel's analyses of the self as a "sociable self" (1955, 1967), followed by what George Herbert Mead inaugurated as "the social theory of consciousness" ([1934] 1967: 171). In turn, Erving Goffman developed an account of the self as defined by its roles and relationships that are then performed and managed in different ways (1959) – an account that predominates in contemporary Internet Studies. This relational – but still also individual – self is further apparent in more contemporary work in IS, beginning with the widely used conception of the self as a "networked individual" (Wellman and Haythornethwaite 2002). At the same time, however, more overtly relational conceptions of selfhood have also come to the foreground (e.g., Gergen 2009; Harper 2010). Still more recently, feminist philosophers have brought forward notions of "relational autonomy" that seek to accept these important recognitions of how far our sense of selfhood and agency is interwoven through and defined by our relationships with others, but without abandoning entirely earlier understandings of moral agency and responsibility as tied to more individual notions of selfhood (e.g., Mackenzie 2008). Additional developments along these lines – by philosophers precisely focused on computation, networked computing, and the networked communications these make possible – have been most recently articulated by Judith Simon, who articulates how such networks embed us in a "distributed epistemic responsibility (2013). Finally, Luciano Floridi has provided both a theoretical account for and practical examples of what he calls distributed morality and distributed (ethical) responsibility (2012).

---

[8] This interdependence, moreover, "brings with it a reciprocal vulnerability that calls for guarantees of mutual consideration to preserve both the integrity of individual persons and the web of interpersonal relations in which their identities are formed and maintained" (ibid.).

To see what all of this has to do with emerging problems of trust, however, we need to turn quickly to two more sets of perspectives. The first set is historical and cross-cultural; the second is contemporary and has to do with our expectations and practices regarding *privacy* and private life.

Historical/Cross-cultural. Very broadly, these recent turns to more relational understandings of selfhood would not seem surprising either to either ancient Greeks or medieval Christians, Jews or Muslims; nor would it be surprising to those raised up in societies and cultures shaped by Buddhist or Confucian thought. Instead, from a historical and cross-cultural perspective, whatever its boons and deficits, the modern individual self is something of an anomaly. So far as I can gather, all of these non-modern cultures and settings would rather insist that the self is first of all relational. Indeed, for much of our shared history globally, this emphasis on the relational self has been so extensive as to push awareness of individual selfhood largely to the margins.

An important and representative example of this can be seen in ancient Confucian understandings of selfhood. As is well-documented, within Confucian tradition (and in ancient Chinese cultures more broadly), you *are* your *relationships* – where these relationships are first of all your various familial relationships: your parents and grandparents, your aunts and uncles, your siblings, your children, and so on. This emphasis on relationality as defining our sense of identity is perhaps most strikingly illustrated by Luria's interviews with pre-literate peasants (where relational selfhood goes hand-in-hand with *orality* as a first stage of human communication). When asked "who are you?" Luria's informants uniformly replied that they were not able to answer such a question. Instead, he would have to ask the members of the surrounding community: it was their views and opinions that were decisive for determining who one was (Ong 1988, 52ff.). (Although it is too long of a story to recount here, it is just through the emergence of *literacy* and then the conjunction of *literacy* and *print* in the modern West that facilitates the emergence of the radical *individual* conception of selfhood that we have seen previously. See Ess 2010; Foucault 1988).

The consequences of this view for our conceptions of *privacy* and *private life* are fundamental. Most briefly, for relational selves the only positive notions of something like "privacy" exist only for groups, not individuals – as in the ancient Thai recognition of the notion of familial privacy (Kitiyadisai 2005). And in the Chinese case, the only word for something like "privacy" in a Western sense – *yinsi* – was defined (until 1985) as something negative or bad, something that the individual felt needed to be hidden from the larger group (Lü 2005). Although these notions may not seem intuitive to contemporary "Westerners," they make perfect sense. If your sense of identity is inextricably interwoven with the multiple relationships that define your identity, what good reasons would you have for ever wanting to be alone? Ostensibly, no good ones, only bad ones.

In this light, on the one hand, we can start to understand how modern Western conceptions of privacy as primarily *individual* privacy and as positive goods emerge only alongside foundational understandings of the self as radically individual self. Again, the story here is very long and complex one (for an overview, see chapter 2 in Ess 2013a). For our purposes, however, it will suffice to note that one index of the shift away from more individual toward more relational understandings of selfhood is precisely the shifts now well-documented in especially younger people's expectations of privacy. For example, Patricia Lange has documented how young people using Facebook are able to carve out "publicly private" and "privately public" communication strategies –where these shared spaces are neither fully individually private nor fully public (2007). At the same time, such spaces closely cohere with recent notions of privacy as contextual (Nissenbaum 2010). Importantly, none of this means that young people are necessarily abandoning more traditional conceptions of individual privacy (Boyd and Marwick 2011): it does mean, however, that they are moving precisely toward the sorts shared "public privacy" of relational selves, as prefigured in the Thai conceptions of familial privacy, for example.

This brief review of relational selfhood from a more historical and cross-cultural approach now helps bring forward a core issue for the question of trust in online environments. As a last point: one of the features of relational selves – whether in the pre-modern West or non-Western and indigenous societies – is precisely their radical dependence upon the larger set of relationships that define them. At the same time – at least historically – such selves have always only been intertwined in hierarchical social structures and nondemocratic forms of power and governance. It hence becomes a critical question: as our "Western" sensibilities continue to shift from more individual toward more relational (and with it, from more rational toward more emotive) understandings of selfhood and identity, will we likewise thereby become more comfortable with more hierarchical social structures and more nondemocratic processes? Correlatively, and more centrally for our purposes, will we become less and less individual selves marked by autonomy and *phronesis* and more and more relational selves dependent on the responses of others for our sense of identity?

This second question then opens up to our core question: what is "trust" for an increasingly *relational* self, especially one forced to engage in networks both human and computation that are beyond one's control or even capacity to fathom?

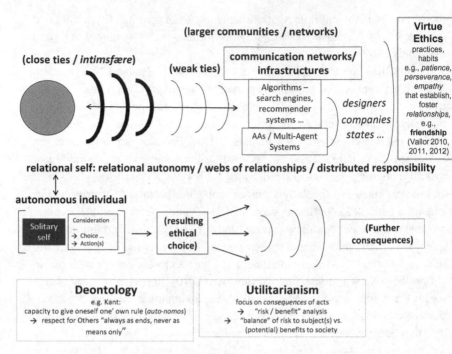

Figure 2. The relational self versus the autonomous individual.

C. Do Relational Selves Trust and/or Rely?

It may be helpful at this stage to review this shift in a pictorial way. Figure 2 indicates the shift from more individual toward more relational senses of self-hood, as the latter is inextricably interwoven with a range of networks, beginning with one's close relationships. Moreover, in the contemporary developed world, these networks include computational devices and computer networks – indicated here in terms of AAs and MASs – and we can add a host of others (e.g., the hybrid networks of SNSs; hybrid because much of the content is generated by humans, but most of the communicative functions are defined within and carried out, of course, by computational systems that include AAs). Finally, as is indicated in the figure, this shift is accompanied by the turn toward virtue ethics. That is, as indicated by the lower portion of the diagram, modern Western ethics – specifically, both deontology (as we have seen in Kant) as well as utilitarian ethics – both turn on the high modern conception of the individual as a rational autonomy and thus singular moral agent. Whether this agent draws more on deontology and/or on utilitarian approaches to choose among possible acts (indicated by the arrows) – once a choice is made, it is the individual moral agent who is seen to be responsible for the choice and thus morally accountable. By contrast, virtue ethics has emerged alongside relational conceptions of selfhood globally (as manifest in the orally-based ethical systems of Confucian thought and Buddhist traditions, as well as in Socratic teaching and, arguably, the teachings of Jesus). In this light, it is no surprise that the diverse conceptions of more relational selfhood, beginning with early social science conceptions and ranging through contemporary senses of the relational self as entangled in networks of distributed responsibility, for example, is accompanied precisely by the renaissance of virtue ethics as well.

Figure 2 may help us further sharpen our sense of the question raised here. Again, relational selves are historically more at home – and unquestionably more dependent on – the hierarchical social systems constituting the relationships that define such selves. As a second reminder, we saw earlier that we can distinguish between a strong sense of trust as it emerges in part out of autonomous choice and allied judgments (*phronesis*) regarding whether to trust and/or to sustain trust, – that is, reliance on tools and instruments that have no choice. It is certainly arguable that this distinction may be better conceived as a continuum with a mid-point demarcated precisely by AAs that can demonstrate at least a limited range of autonomous choice, if not quite (yet) *phronesis*. However these technologies may unfold in the future, for the time being, we can acknowledge that as members of contemporary societies we – whether as more individual and/or more relational selves – are increasingly entangled in networked webs of relationships that include both human and artificial agents.

For the most part, we have little choice but to do so. For example, we may choose (up to a point) whom to friend in a SNS: but especially for adolescents these days, there is little choice but to be on such an SNS (Livingstone 2011). Add to this the recognition that our networked webs of relationships are increasingly composed of and dependent on AAs and MASs, so it seems that the range of relationships within which we are free to exercise a strong sense of trust, as anchored in autonomy and *phronesis* (and, so far, with human agents), is increasingly giving way to a range of relationships within which we have little choice but to *rely* on networked computational technologies. As but two prominent examples: (1) Facebook users have no choice but to rely on the algorithms that determine the various feeds of information from family and friends – algorithms that are entirely proprietary and, for many users, puzzling; and (2) even more broadly, search engine algorithms – perhaps most notoriously those deployed by Google – are likewise entirely locked up as proprietary and so beyond user insight, much less control. But again, to use such search engines means we have no choice but to rely on – while not overly trusting – such algorithms and related processes.

Again, some sort of middle ground exists here insofar as the AAs and MASs included in these networks may exercise some version of choice and some version of *phronesis*. I may, for example, choose in at least a weak sense to trust the recommendations created for me by Amazon's AAs that review my purchases, but not (it still makes sense to say) necessarily rely on these. But should AAs and MASs become increasingly autonomous and capable of strong *phronesis* – in some future version of the Turing Test it is not unimaginable that both human and artificial agents will make strong choices and judgments as to whether to trust, not simply rely on, one another.[9]

On the other hand, these developments also point in darker directions – broadly toward decreasing choice and increasing interdependency. One approach to this is to consider how far democratic norms of equality and gender equality might survive in more hierarchical societies that are likely to emerge along side more relational selves. I have argued recently, drawing on the work of Pak Wong (2012) and Mary Bockover (2010), that the analogs offered by contemporary Confucian societies as they democratize suggest that some form of democratic processes, as depending on and enabling more individual autonomy and choice, may well be possible in such societies, but they will almost certainly exclude strong norms of equality, most especially gender equality (Ess 2013b).

All is Not Lost: Sustaining Trust and *Phronesis* in a Hyperconnected Era

These broad patterns, however, are countered in part by recent work in both philosophy and IS.

A. Philosophical Perspectives

As we have seen, at least since the emergence of second-wave feminism and ecological ethics, a number of philosophical accounts have emerged that circle around the notion of a more relational self: most especially, the contemporary accounts of relational autonomy (Mackenzie 2008) and distributed morality (Floridi 2012) highlight new (or perhaps more accurately in light of the deep and extensive historical precedents, renewed) ways of thinking about human beings as moral agents who share ethical responsibility across their networked webs of relationships.

---

[9] The Turing Test was proposed in its original form by computer pioneer Alan Turing as an alternative way of approaching the question "can machines think?" Turing described instead the "imitation game" as played between three people – a man (A), a woman (B), and an interrogator of either sex (C), all placed in separate rooms. The interrogator communicates with the first two – perhaps through a teletype – and asks questions intended to determine the gender of (A) and (B). Turing proposes that if we replace (A) with a machine, and the human interrogator *is not able to detect any difference* between the communication with another human and the communication with a computational device, then, in effect, the computational device has accomplished the functional equivalent of human intelligence. See: Turing, Alan. (1950).

At the same time, however, none of this necessarily suggests the complete loss of more individual senses of selfhood, and thereby the complete loss of (high modern) conceptions of individual autonomy and *phronesis*. Such a direction would have seemed likely especially in the 1990s, during the heyday of postmodern conceptions of identity as multiple, fluid, and ephemeral – and as facilitated most especially in networked communication environments, as the work of Sherry Turkle (1995) made especially clear. But as we saw in the opening section, such conceptions of the 1990s – beginning with a radical distinction between the virtual and the real, the online and the off-line – began to give way to understandings of these that rather stressed their inextricable interconnections. Caught perhaps most tellingly in the phrase "The Internet in Everyday Life" (Bakardjieva 2005), these turns increasingly emphasized how online identity performances were rooted in and usually reflected off-line identity with great accuracy. In particular, as we saw in Section 2, understanding identity as rooted in our singular, distinctive bodies became a prevailing understanding, as rooted in a range of empirical studies in IS (e.g., Kendall and others).

Similarly, more recent philosophical explorations of our sense of identity in online environments reiterate more classical, high-modern notions as well. As just one example, a recent special issue of *Philosophy and Technology* is devoted precisely to questions of online identity, primarily as explored through prominent theories of identity, including Locke's psychological continuity theory (which would allow for notions of "uploading consciousness" to computer systems for example, with our sense of identity more or less sustained), physical continuity theories (that rather insist on identity as inextricably interwoven with body), and more recent narrative theories that are especially helpful in accounting for a *unity* of identity as distributed across off-line and online venues (including, for example, one's sense of *identification* with one's avatar; Schechtman 2012). Broadly, this collection reinforces the understandings of identity in IS over the past decade or so – namely, of identity and selfhood as more singular than multiple, more continuous than fragmented, and more consistent than discontinuous between online and off-line expressions. These findings point, in short, toward sustaining individual notions of selfhood and identity alongside more relational ones (Ess 2012: 280 ff; cf. Floridi 2011).

B. Internet Studies, Redux

Finally, recent work at the intersections between philosophy and IS also suggests that what we may see emerge is a conjunction of both more individual and more relational emphases on identity.

As a first example, in her analysis of a prominent Danish blogger and her audience, Stine Lomborg highlights the negotiation processes that emerge here, ones that work to both preserve *individual* privacy (and thereby autonomy) alongside a co-constructed and shared "personal space" that is thereby neither fully individually private nor fully public. Lomborg draws in part on Germanic senses of *privatlivet* (private life) and the *intimsfære* (the intimate sphere) in which these terms designate precisely the sorts of spaces and experiences made possible by and for close relationships, in contrast with more strongly individual foci on "privacy," for example. At the same time, she finds that Georg Simmel's understanding of "the sociable self" – that is, a form of the relational self – helps account for the communicative processes, including the negotiation processes that she observes. In these two directions, the "personal space" demarcated through online negotiation processes thus emerges as precisely a collocation between more individual and more relational senses of selfhood. So she writes:

> To maintain the blog as a personal space, self-disclosure plays an important role through the personal, even intimate, experiences and emotions revealed in the blog conversation. By this means, both author and readers balance a fine line between, on the one hand, pressure to reveal personal issues as a preamble for developing relationships among participants and, on the other hand, a norm of non-intrusiveness to protect each other's [individual] privacy.

> *(2012: 423)*

The sense of self that emerges here is at once an individual self that retains (traditional) notions of individual privacy, but at the same time, is a relational (or, in Simmel's terms, a sociable) self that is further "attuned to the norms and practices within the network of affiliation" (2012: 432).

In similar but more overtly political terms, Maria Bakardjieva has analyzed how "third spaces" of what she identifies as "subactivism" emerge in online environments. Such spaces occupy a distinctive place between the larger "grand narratives" of either utopian dreams (for example, of realizing greater democratization on a planetary scale) or dystopian nightmares (most starkly, of Orwellian big brothers capable of perfect surveillance – and thus perfect control – through increasingly diffused network communications). We encounter the emergence of these third spaces by attending as closely as possible to the "the private sphere" or "the small social world" which blends ethics and politics for both the individual subject and collective identities (2009: 96). These ongoing micro-interactions and conversations surrounding work, home, and parenting are distinctive; they are "not about political power in the strict sense, but about personal empowerment seen as the power of the subject to be the person that they want to be in accordance with his or her reflexively chosen moral and political standards" (2009: 96).

Bakardjieva's conception of subactivism, as focusing on microlevel efforts rooted in individual and small group interests, does not necessarily rise to the level of grand (if utopian) visions of global (or even national) democratization – for example, as in the Arab Springs. But subactivism further falsifies Orwellian visions of the complete loss of individual autonomy. In this way, subactivism thereby closely resembles Lomborg's third or "personal space" – that is, spaces that conjoin a (still protected) individual privacy with larger, but by no means indiscriminately public, networks and relationships. In particular, these spaces allow individual participants to negotiate what they share for the sake of sociability and subactivism at the microlevel. In doing so, they thus sustain a high modern Western sense of individual privacy as protecting individual agency and autonomy – precisely for the sake of the project of being/becoming "the person we want to be" (Bakardjieva 2009: 96).

Most broadly, such third spaces appear to preserve individual notions of identity and autonomy alongside sociable or relational selves interwoven with larger networks. Insofar as such spaces likewise sustain and foster *phronesis*, they thereby allow for the ongoing cultivation of trust in the strong sense, not simply reliance.

Concluding Remarks

The account of trust that we have seen emerge from a strongly philosophical perspective foregrounds the essential role of individual autonomy and thereby reflective judgment (*phronesis*) in the *choice* to trust and to respond to trust with further choices and behaviors that either fulfill or betray it. I have further argued that such trust remains an option, despite the threats to strong trust posed by selves becoming more relational and thus more dependent upon increasingly complex and more hierarchical networked webs of relationships.

I have not been able to develop this point at length, but here I can note that a core tenet of the Medium Theory[10] that stands behind much of this work is that our sense of selfhood correlates with the media technologies we employ – whether the technologies of orality (favoring strongly relational selves), literacy, and literacy-print (that lead to high modern notions of individuals as rational autonomies), or the technologies of "electric media" and the "secondary orality" (and secondary textuality) they bring into play. As may be surmised from this,

---

[10] Medium Theory – Meyrowitz (1985) – is affiliated most prominently with the work of Harold Innis (1951, 1972), Marshall McLuhan (1964), Elizabeth Eisenstein (1983), Neil Postman (1985), Walter Ong (1988), and, more recently, Naomi Baron (2008) and Zsuzsanna Kondor (2008). Rather than focusing primarily on the content of a given communication medium, Medium Theory attends to the affordances and characteristics of basic communication modalities, beginning with orality, and then literacy, literacy-print, and the secondary orality of electric or electronic media. For further discussion, see Ess (2010).

the rise of networked communication is especially well-suited to fostering the emergence of the more relational sense of selfhood evoked by the secondary orality of such communication and electronic media more generally (Ess 2010; 2013a; 2013b).

Additionally, this means that our futures – most fundamentally, the kinds of selves we will become – in some measure will depend precisely on important choices we can now make between which forms of media technologies we will most fully embrace. The choices here are not trivial or inconsequential. I hope it is obvious by now that to sustain strong forms of trust, so we must sustain the sorts of more individual senses of selfhood and identity that make such trust possible. But this also means sustaining the media technologies of literacy and print, as the medial foundations of such individual sensibilities and autonomy. I am somewhat optimistic that we will choose to do so – and not at the cost of engagement with and enjoyment of contemporary communication technologies and the more relational selves they afford. Instead, as Medium Theory has long argued (and was argued even earlier by, for example, Riepl 1913), new media technologies never supplant (so far) older ones. Manifestly, as we learned to write, we did not forget how to talk. Similarly, alongside the shifts especially among young people toward more relational forms of selfhood and thus of more "familial" or shared notions of privacy or *privatlivet* as "publicly private" and "privately public" networks, these same young people retain an interest in individual privacy (Boyd and Marwick 2011: 1). It is additionally clear that the seemingly casual attitudes toward *individual* private property, as manifest in illegal downloading and multiple other behaviors that fall under the "sharing is caring" mantra, are precisely consistent with relational selfhood as well (Ess 2013a). But just as with attitudes toward privacy, there is good evidence that young people remain quite capable of making informed choices about whom to trust in such environments (Boyd and Marwick 2011: 10–14).

At the same time, however, I hope our media choices can be more fully informed by reflections such as these, so that we are clearer, to begin with, as to the core importance of media technologies and our deliberate uses of these in shaping the sorts of selves we may become. Moreover, the consequences of our choices will not only determine (at least in large measure) whether or not robust forms of trust may be sustained among increasingly relational selves. Alongside such trust also reside our commitments to democratic processes and norms of equality, including gender equality, as core norms for autonomous – even relationally autonomous – individuals (Ess 2013b).

Part Three

Trust in Design

10

Design for Trusted and Trustworthy Services: Why We Must Do Better

M. Angela Sasse and Iacovos Kirlappos

Introduction

When the first e-commerce services emerged in the late 1990s, consumer trust in online transactions was identified as a potential major hurdle. Researchers of human-computer interaction (HCI) started to investigate how interface and interaction medium design might make these services appear more trustworthy to users. Jens Riegelsberger (then a doctoral student) and the first author were part of that first cohort (Riegelsberger and Sasse 2001). We soon realized that much of the HCI research was very much focused on increasing user trust in Web sites through design elements, but did not consider (1) existing substantive knowledge from other disciplines on the role and mechanics of trust, and (2) existing methodological knowledge on how to conduct valid studies on trust formation and its impact on behavior. To address this, we reviewed and integrated existing knowledge to prepare a foundation for HCI research, which was published in two research papers: to address point 2, a prescription for valid HCI methods for studying trust, *The Researcher's Dilemma* (Riegelsberger et al. 2003a); and to address point 1, a framework for HCI research and *The Mechanics of Trust* (Riegelsberger et al. 2005).

The key message from the latter paper was the need for HCI researchers to engage with technology developers to create trustworthy systems, rather than focus on influencing trust perceptions at the user interface level. In the worst case, the latter could lead to manipulating user trust perceptions to place trust in systems that are not trustworthy, which would be socially and ethically irresponsible. The way forward, we argued, was to design systems that encouraged trustworthy behavior from all participants, by creating the right economic incentives and creating reliable trust signaling. In the current chapter, the authors summarize this prescription and reiterate the argument for it, because it is still valid today. We then review progress over the past eight years to consider to what extent the prescription has been implemented. Although our conclusion may seem sobering, it really is not: the security signals offered by service providers are not accurate enough and require too much user effort. "User education" on how to stay safe online is usually prescribed by technologists as a way to improve human decision making; they ought to pay attention to what David Clark so clearly states in Chapter 2: "technology is only the foundation" for human activity in cyberspace, and it must to be designed to support human activity. Trusting behavior is a particularly important part of productive human activity, and the reading of trust signals is a habit we have formed through years of socialization – learning and experience in the physical world. Humans will have to learn a few new tricks to use the brave new world of cyberspace to their advantage, but it is unrealistic to expect them to learn a completely different set of trust signals and rules from those that serve them well in the physical world. Our argument is that technology and interaction designers must do better: they have to work together to create online environments in which humans can easily detect and interpret trust signals, without learning a complete new set of signals and rules. In the remainder of this chapter, we provide a summary of the framework on how to design systems that support human trust decisions. We then discuss a series of examples of trust that users encounter in online transactions today. Many existing systems and services do not offer effective support for their trust decision making. We finish with a call for a step-change in designing more trustworthy interaction environments.

Trust, Risk and Uncertainty in the Physical World, and Online

Trust plays a vital role in the world: most economic and societal agreements depend on the ability of two or more parties to trust each other so that they can collaborate to mutual benefit. Mayer et al. (1995) define trust in social interactions as: " the willingness to be vulnerable based on positive expectation about the behaviour of others." This "willingness to be vulnerable" (or, as Clark puts it in Chapter 2, to assume that the other party will add in my best interest) may seem reckless when my financial assets or sensitive confidential are at stake. But the willingness to do this needs to be seen in the context of my expectation of the benefits from that transaction: I take a risk because I hope to gain a benefit as an individual. From a collective point of view, the economic benefits of trust-based transactions lie in the savings made if we do not need legal frameworks, enforcement, and technical security mechanisms (Flechais et al. 2005). As long as everyone sticks to the rules, individuals or organizations can benefit from saving this cost; but when the rewards from not playing by the rules are significantly higher than the consequences of not doing so, and increasing numbers of people do not play by the rules, we need to put assurance (security) mechanisms in place to change the risk-reward structure. But, as David Clark correctly points out, security mechanisms – such as whitelisting of email senders – may reduce risk, but they do not enhance trust. We not only pay a cost for their operation, but also create constraints for honest participants, which David Clark brilliantly compares to the Victorian convention where people "will not talk to anyone unless they have been introduced first." We whole-heartedly agree with Clark that "better technical security mechanisms cannot make a secure Internet." Use of assurance mechanisms means we cannot reap second-order benefits of trust, such as enhanced cooperation, goodwill, and creativity (Handy 1995). This is why we need to create environments that incentivize trustworthy behavior, rather than rely on assurance mechanisms; the aim of this chapter is to discuss how this can be achieved through better design, which is why need to examine the detailed functioning of trust in more detail.

The need for trust arises when we cannot be sure about the *risk* and *uncertainty* associated with transactions. *Risk* arises for the *trustor* (the transaction partner who moves first) because he/she cannot control the *trustee* (Giddens 1990). By "making the first move," the trustor stands to lose something of value – money, time, or credit card information, to name a few The less a trustor knows about the *ability* and *motivation* of the trustee to hold up their end of the bargain, the higher the *uncertainty* he/she faces (Deutsch 1958).

Uncertainty and risk can, therefore, be reduced by providing information about the trustee's ability and motivation to fulfill – in the physical world, for instance, when entering a shop for the first time, you would register signs such as significant investment in premises, high stock levels, knowledgeable sales staff, and the presence of other customers. In the online environment, users are drawing on similar signals.

Since the creation of the Internet, increasing numbers of interactions between humans (shopping, banking, dating, gaming, and health consultations) are mediated by technology, and in many cases, the participants never expect to meet face-to-face. Technology-mediated interaction (TMI) offers many benefits: it significantly widens availability of potential interaction partners, increases competition in commercial environments, and provides access to otherwise unavailable services. The spread of e-commerce, for example, created ample opportunities for local businesses to expand their potential customer basis on a country-wide (or even international) scale, which in its turn results in increased competition and lower prices. Despite their advantages, TMIs significantly increase the complexity of the trust development process: participants

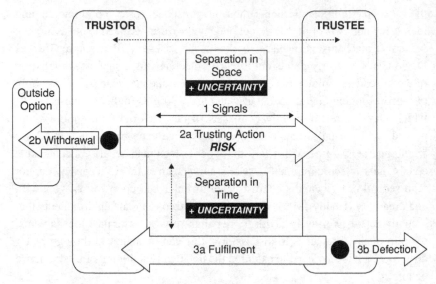

Figure 3. The basic trustor-trustee interaction (Source: Riegelsberger et al. 2005).

need to reach a transaction-enabling level of trust over a medium which makes the trust signals they rely on meaningful and easily to manipulate. This presents new opportunities to attackers, who also like the Internet because if offers access to increased numbers of potential targets and a safe geographic distance (Schneier 2012). Fear of not being able to tell the difference between trustworthy and non-trustworthy transaction partners leads some people to stay away from the online environment altogether, because the perceived risks and uncertainty outweigh the potential benefits. This was a problem in early days of e-commerce, when lower prices were not enough of an incentive to persuade many consumers to shop online (Egger 2001; Grabner-Kraeuter and Kaluscha 2003). This underlines the need to develop systems that support trustworthy action and user ability to distinguish between trustworthy and untrustworthy actors in TMIs (Fogg 2003).

The "Mechanics of Trust"

The steps of trustor-trustee interactions in a TMI trust exchange were brought together in the framework developed by Riegelsberger and his colleagues (Figure 3), which provides a summary of all factors designers can draw on to design for trust in TMI environments. During the first phase of a TMI, the

Trustee's net benefit = Transaction Rewards – Effort invested for fulfilment.

Figure 4. Trustee benefit equation.

trustor and trustee exchange signals to assess each other's *ability* and *motivation* to engage in a successful transaction. After the initial signal exchange, the trustor has the option to either proceed with the trusting action (2a) – which makes him/her vulnerable to the trustee's behavior – or withdraw (2b). (In the latter case, no transaction takes place, and both parties are unable to reap the potential benefits.) But the trustor's decision is not solely based on the exchanged signals; his/her own risk propensity (tolerance for risk), under-standing and perception of exchanged signals, and other external factors (e.g., how easy it is to withdraw) also influence the decision. After the trusting action takes place, the trustee has full control over the interaction and he/she can choose to either fulfill (3a), or defect (3b). The trustor needs to have the ability to fulfill– that is, be able to deliver the goods and competences advertised – and be motivated to do so (because he/she now hold the benefits of the transaction, she could "'take the money and run").

Trust-Warranting Properties

So why would a trustee fulfill, instead of doing exactly that? Any effort to fulfill their part requires the investment of additional resources that will reduce their net benefit compared to the pre-fulfillment state (Figure 4).

So what would motivate a trustee to fulfill and how would a trustor perceive that motivation to make themselves vulnerable to their actions? This motivation for fulfillment for a trustee can come from a set of trust-warranting properties (Bacharach and Gambetta 2001), the long-term effects of which outweigh immediate non-fulfillment gains. Effective signaling of those during a TMI can significantly affect a trustor's decision between *trusting action* or *withdrawal*. Riegelsberger and his colleagues (2005) distinguish between two different types of trust-warranting properties (Figure 5):

- *Intrinsic properties* are relatively stable attributes the trustee possesses cre-ating their *ability* for fulfillment, but also providing them with *motivation* to fulfill. *Motivation* relates to factors internal to the trustee (e.g., personal costs of breaking trust) and provides non-monetary rewards to the trustee, such as personal satisfaction. It can be a result of *internalized norms* (leading to ful-fillment without any external incentive) or *benevolence* (contributing to the well-being of people – for example, what companies do under the banner of

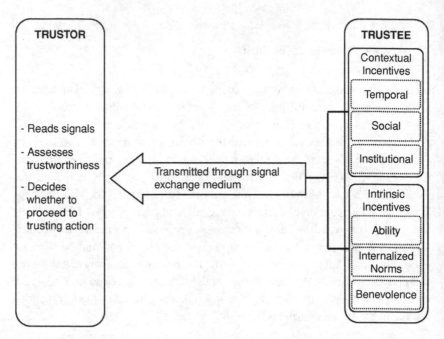

Figure 5. Signaling trust-warranting properties (adapted from Riegelsberger et al. 2005).

"corporate social responsibility").[1] *Ability*, on the other hand, refers to possession of the resources required for fulfillment. Long-term fulfillment based on intrinsic properties results in the development of social capital, creating environments in which cooperation benefits everyone (Schneier 2012).

• *Contextual properties* are attributes of the context of the interaction that provide motivation for trustworthy behavior by dis-incentivizing non-fulfillment, leading to self-interested actors fulfilling (Raub and Weesie 2000b).

There are three different types of contextual properties:

• *Temporal embeddedness* is the prospect of further interactions becomes a shadow of the future (Axelrod 1980). Non-fulfillment in a transaction may damage one party's potential to engage in future ones.

---

[1] In specific transactions, companies also occasionally show benevolence to individual customers – for instance, accepting a return of a product that is not faulty, but just not what the customer expected. Or an insurance company may settle the claim of a long-standing customer even when, on a legal technicality, they could refuse to do so. They exert this type of benevolence because it creates grateful and loyal customers, equals future transactions, and benefits for the company. Therefore, this is usually done as a calculated trust-building move.

- *Social embeddedness*: Performance information about a trustee's past behavior can be shared amongst trustors, damaging their reputation as a trusted transaction party if they fail to fulfill a transaction (Corritore et al. 2003).
- *Institutional embeddedness*: External enforcement exists that penalizes non-compliance; obvious membership to a trusted group or a society in which defection is penalized increases perceived trustworthiness (Schneier 2012).

The essential difference between intrinsic and contextual properties is in whom the trustor places trust. Intrinsic properties result in *party trust* (i.e., to the trustee), while contextual to *control trust*: to the mechanisms that dis-incentivize non-fulfillment by the trustee (Tan and Thoen 2001). Compliance attributed to control trust does not imply a trustee is trustworthy, but in most cases it is "*good enough*"; even if it is not proper to call someone who fulfills because of contextual properties "trustworthy," this behavior still leads to successful transactions (Riegelsberger et al. 2005).

There is an additional stage in trust formation that is particularly relevant to TMI: after a few successful transactions with a particular trustee, the trustor's stance changes from trust (in which he/she is aware he/she is vulnerable) to an expectation that this particular trustee will deliver in future transactions – a state Bernd Lahno (2002) calls *reliance*. In a state of reliance, trustors are even less willing to spend time examining trust signals in much detail – and this is something attackers exploit online (as we shall see).

Space and Time Separation Effects

The Riegelsberger framework successfully captures the *asynchronous* and *asymmetric* nature of TMIs and the problems in signaling trustworthiness that make them challenging to design for:

- Signals lose meaning. In real-world interactions, the signal exchange is rich and at multiple levels, without distinct separation of the different transaction stages presented in Figure 3. This makes many of the trustee's properties easily obvious to the trustor (e.g., the ability of a physical store to provide a buyer with an item is obvious to the buyer when an item is physically available in the store). In a TMI, the steps of a transaction are well-defined and without overlap, and the same properties are now indirectly observable via signals that may be unreliable or require more effort to understand (*channel reduction*, Whitty and Joinson 2009).
- Fulfillment is no longer immediate. The increased time and space separation increases the delay between trusting action and fulfillment resulting to increased uncertainty on the transaction outcome (Giddens 1990).

- Fulfillment may be indirect. The presence of intermediaries that aid fulfill-ment (e.g., technology as a fulfillment medium, such as postal systems) may cause delays or failure in the transaction completion that can potentially reduce the trustor's level of satisfaction from the transaction; also impacting the potential of engaging in another transaction with the same trustee (or through the same medium) in the future.

The identified challenges increase the trustor's perceived uncertainty on an interaction's outcome, which can result in reduced willingness to engage in TMIs. As a result, the more TMI systems grow (e.g., e-commerce expansion) the more effective trust signaling systems are required (Schneier 2012). The increased risk and uncertainty can be balanced out by the implementation of technological solutions that accurately transmit trust signals, but also allowing fast and accurate party identification to reduce the need for a trust assessment "from scratch" for every new interaction.

Technology in TMIs

Technology plays a dual role in TMIs. It can be both the transmission medium over which trustor and trustee exchange signals for trust development, but it can also be the medium over which the whole interaction takes place. In both cases, accurate trust signaling is important to enable correct trust placement and increase the willingness of parties to engage in TMIs.

Technology as a Signal Transmission Medium

As previously discussed, prior the trusting action, both parties transmit signals about trust-warranting properties, which result in expectations on the behavior of the trustee, leading the trustor to either *trusting action* or *withdrawal* from the transaction. The decision of a trustor to proceed to the trusting action is solely based on their *perceived* trustworthiness of the trustee (Corritore et al. 2003). This is formed by the assessment of the trustee's trust-warranting properties based on the emitted signals of trustworthiness. Those signals can be divided in two categories (Riegelsberger and Sasse 2003b):

- *Symbols* have arbitrarily assigned meaning and were designed specifically to signal the presence of trust-warranting properties, so the trustor needs certain knowledge be able decode them (e.g., trust seals in e-commerce).
- *Symptoms* are trust signals that were not specifically designed to signal trust-warranting properties; they are given off as by-products of past fulfillment instances to honest actors, and come at little or no cost to them (e.g., reputa-tion information).

Signal Manipulation – Mimicry

Humans overestimate their ability to read trust signals. They consider themselves able to detect lying and untrustworthy actors, but do not perform well on those tasks (see, for example, Horn et al. 2002); attackers exploit this by emitting manipulated signals to appear trustworthy (Bacharach and Gambetta 2001). This involves an emission cost because attackers need to invest time and effort in identifying the signals that trustors perceive as trustworthy, and faking them – mimicry. As David Clark points out, in the real world, we rely on trusted agents such as policemen and banks, but if attackers can impersonate policemen, this is not a good strategy. In the real world, mimicry can be costly – for instance, building a fake cash deposit machine and stationing a fake security guard next to the real cash deposit machine to direct customers to the fake one, owned by attackers – and faces the risk of being caught. Online, trust symbols are often easy to fake – trust seals or company logos are easily copied; and because users do not inspect the link or credentials (see Section 6.1), the technical protection incorporated does not work. Mimicry of trust symptoms requires significantly more effort; they are by-products of trustworthy trustees doing what they are supposed to do – for instance, shipping goods – and an adversary needs to invest in mimicking that behavior – for instance, start shipping empty boxes.

Designing online environments that prevent (or at least significantly reduce) an attacker's ability to mimic trust signals should be at the center of any trust-enabling implementation. Raising user awareness of potential mimicry attacks (as we shall see) – through, for example, the kind of "user education campaign" to which security professionals want to resort – can backfire because it can scare off users (Riegelsberger and Sasse 2001). Awareness campaigns would not be needed if the transaction environment enabled users to read signals of trust-warranting properties and to correctly place their trust. We need trust signals that are reliable and easy to read. It is unreasonable to expect users to "stop, look, and listen" every time they open an email or Web page. They must also be cheap for honest actors going about their business, but expensive to mimic by attackers.

Technology as a Channel for Trusting Action

In other situations, technology may not just be the signal exchange medium, but also the medium over which the trust interaction takes place (e.g., delivery of electronic goods). The success of TMIs affects perceived trust in the Internet in general, and the willingness of individuals to engage with services based on it in the future (Lee and Turban 2001). But technology is not a moral actor; therefore, any trust or mistrust is based on the experience with the sociotechnical system formed around the use of technology. This includes a number of entities: (1) the trustees that use technology as a fulfillment medium, (2) the institutions that regulate their behaviors, and (3) the intermediate channels that aid fulfillment or signal exchange. To ensure smooth completion of transactions, systems that support trustworthy behavior must aim to encourage trustworthy behavior from both trustors and trustees, but also ensure all intermediate mechanisms operate in a way that makes correct fulfillment easy.

Designing for Trust

To improve on current systems, we first and foremost have to provide reliable trust signaling. Currently, humans transfer trust interpretations from other environments to TMI, unaware that the same signals they rely on successfully in the physical world are easy to mimic online (Kirlappos and Sasse 2012). Second, solutions must encourage trustworthy behavior, and technology/domain-independent to be widely applicable across current and future different technologies and contexts, because too many or constantly changing trust signals are not usable (Riegelsberger et al. 2005). Because the economic benefits of trust are based on its fast, low-effort nature, solutions which require users to know and check many trust signals in detail are non-starters.

Case Study: E-Commerce

The launch of e-commerce since the early 2000s created the need to reach a transaction-enabling level of trust in commercial environments in the absence of the traditional trust development medium face-to-face interaction (Seghi 2012). Adversaries were quick to exploit the new opportunities this setting created by setting up fake online stores and pretending to sell popular products at tempting prices to attract customers. Consumers shop online because it provides significant benefits over traditional shopping: access to a wider range of products, time and money savings, and opportunities to acquire something they would otherwise not be able to afford. Direct marketing and online advertising further encourage the notion of "terrific bargains"; attackers are extremely skilled in using this to tap human needs and desires:

- Tapping into "Need and Greed" (Stajano and Wilson 2011): If I love Tiffany jewelry, but cannot afford it, I want to believe that "75% off Tiffany jewelry bargain" is genuine. Once attackers know what consumers want, they tempt them with such "too good to miss" deals, but ship either counterfeit products or nothing at all.

- "Time principle" attacks (Stajano and Wilson 2011). By emphasizing the limited duration of an "offer," attackers put pressure on consumers, who then let their defenses down to seize the "un-missable" deal. This is a particular problem with online ticket sales for sporting or music events for which tickets sell out fast.
- Mimicking a trusted trustee (Dhamija at al. 2006). Most consumers trust search engines. Attackers place advertisements and/or manipulate search engine rankings to direct users to fraudulent Web sites. This type of attacks exploits potential customer *reliance* on trustworthy trustees(such as search engine or apps store providers); the problem is compounded because consumers expect these providers to carry out more far more stringent checks on linked sites or apps these actually carry out.
- Mimicking *institutional embeddedness* by adding fake trust seals on their sites, or *social embeddedness* by adding fake customer reviews on their site (Kirlappos et al. 2012). Both can result in increased perceived trust by consumers, which can lead to incorrect trust placement.
- "Good actors turning bad." After building positive reputation acquired by small transactions, attackers default after a series of big ones, exploiting the trust effects created by *social embeddedness* (eBay 2012). This is another form of exploiting reliance; another way is building a good reputation through low-value or fictitious transactions. A similar approach is account takeover attacks which take over reputable retailers' accounts (Riegelsberger et al. 2005; Lee 2002). In this case, attackers exploit reputation and reliance of consumers on a retailer based on its past behavior.
- Use a trusted platform (like eBay or Amazon marketplace) to defraud people, exploiting potential misconceptions of consumers, who have already developed trust in the specific platform (*institutional*).

All of these attacks are rooted to the economic problem of *information asymmetry* (Akerlof 1970). This is the absence of face-to-face interaction results in reduction in the meaning of the exchanged signals in the trust interaction. Trustors are thus unable (or less able) to infer whether or not the trustee is willing to fulfill. The retailer, on the other hand finds themselves in an advantageous position, as trusting action and fulfillment now take place with *space and time* separation: a retailer is expected to wait until they have received full payment before shipping out any products (Tan and Thoen 2001). This provides adversaries with enough time to disappear before a customer may realize they did not fulfill the interaction. In other cases, non-compliance cases may even go unnoticed as a consumer may never realize they have received counterfeit goods![2] The purpose of any trust-enabling technology for e-commerce should be to either reduce the asymmetry, by providing consumers with enough to allow them to make informed trust decisions, or ensure that potential misbehavior is not possible in the design of the system.

A number of different approaches have attempted to address the online scams problem. Anti-phishing tools, trust seals, and user education were introduced to reduce miscalculated trust placement.

Anti-Phishing Tools

Anti-phishing indicators provide users with cues to help them assess whether or not a Web site is safe. They are implemented either as security toolbars, providing consumers with indications whether a Web site is identified as scam (*Spoofstick*[3] *Trustbar*[4]) or as tools that change visual elements of the interaction, like the browser background (Dynamic Security Skins; see Dhamija and Tygar 2005). Despite many proposed approaches, no solutions have managed to reduce trust misplacement. Zhang and his colleagues (2006a) found that even the most effective available tools have unacceptably high false-positive rates and all heuristic-based anti-phishing tools can be circumvented using relatively simple attacks. Wu and his colleagues (2006) also report that in empirical evaluations, even after explicitly telling experiment participants to pay attention to anti-phishing mechanisms, they either failed to do so, or could not interpret them correctly. Those problems suggest that anti-phishing tools fail to effectively aid correct trust placement.

Trust Seals

Trust seals are extra-legal, symbol-based trust-signaling mechanisms, created by Certification Authorities to provide trustworthiness information about a retailer to potential customers (Ba et al. 2003). They are added in Web sites as logos, signaling that a certified organization (Trusted Third Party, or TTP) has granted the right to use those based on some rules of conduct (e.g., past trustworthy behavior, private data handling, or presence of a secure payment

---

[2] In a UK police operation, "Operation Papworth," seven out of the top ten Google results for a popular brand of boots were found to be fraudulent Web sites (Internet Marketing News, Operation Papworth highlights the UGGly side of Google. December 8, 2009. Retrieved from: http://www. browsermedia.co.uk/2009/12/08/operation-papworth-highlights-the-uggly-side-of-google/).

[3] www.spoofstick.com.

[4] trustbar.mozdev.com.

system). Research on the effectiveness of trust seals suggests that they can significantly affect consumer trust placement (Bakos and Dellarocas 2002; Firon et al. 2005; Hu et al. 2003; Kimery and McCard 2002), but evidence suggests they fail to support *actual* trustworthy behavior (Kirlappos et al. 2012; Kirlappos and Sasse, 2012) for two reasons:

- They do not protect against the most common attack, yet more mimicry, in the form of fake trust seals. Consumers only glance at seals, and assume everything is well; and if they are tricked by a fake trust seal, their trust in seals is undermined.
- They do not improve on consumers' ability to make accurate trust assessment of Web sites. Consumers interpret the mere presence of a trust seal as proof of a Web site's competence and expect much more significant protection that the seals actually offer – that is, they create a false sense of security.

User Education

For security professionals, user education is seen as the "first resort" to improving consumer trust decisions. They want consumers to read extensively about general and specific risks (e.g., Google's "Good to Know,"[5] or StaySafeOnline[6]), providing a range of advice on what consumers can do to protect themselves, such as keeping their antivirus and browser up to date, checking merchants out before first-time purchases, check for *https://* indicators and closed padlocks, and only provide a Web site with information necessary to complete a transaction. The existence of multiple sources and varying to conflicting advice can cause confusion (NCSA's StaySafeOnline mentions nine Web site properties that each require three to four verification checks). Consumers try to reduce the information pushed at them into a manageable set of rules, but the process can be haphazard (Harvey et al. 2000). In addition, research has shown that the advice given by current awareness campaigns is not effective (Schechter et al. 2007, Kirlappos et al. 2012) – for example, the majority of consumers do not check for *https://* indicators, padlocks in the address bar, or who the Web site's owner is. The advice to "only provide a website with the information required to complete the transaction" is not helpful: credit card information is sensitive, but is also required to complete a transaction. Consumers can follow advice of awareness campaigns and still be scammed (e.g., "always check for the presence of trust seals"). This results

---

[5] http://www.google.co.uk/goodtoknow/online-safety/shopping.
[6] http://www.staysafeonline.org/

in loss of trust in awareness campaigns as competent sources of accurate information (Twyman et al. 2008), reducing consumer willingness to follow the communicated advice. As a result, Cormac Herley (2009) argues that rational users will ignore any user education advice, because even diligent application of what is being taught offers users only limited protection against the current attack methods.

Conclusions: Improving Trust Signaling to Incentivize Trustworthy Behavior

The ineffectiveness of current ways to protect consumers is evidenced by the number of scam Web sites and the reported losses, which are still at alarmingly high levels. UK card fraud crime amounted to £365.4 million in 2011,[7] and in the United States, online retailers lost $2.7 billion to fraud in 2010 alone.[8] Those failures can be attributed to their inability to capture the dynamics of trust development and accommodate for the actual trust-assessment signals people use (Kirlappos and Sasse 2012). Trust symbols (the main properties of a Web site that users are told to look for) are *just a subset* of the trust development process. The second type of signals, *trust symptoms*, is equally important, but seems to be ignored by trust-signaling approaches. Those symptoms can be widely varying and developed as a form of *trust assessment heuristics*, based mostly on past interactions of users with online and high-street retailers, but also general past computer and browsing experience. A number of those heuristics have been documented by past research (Egger 2001; Jarnenpaa et al. 2000; Kim et al. 2008; Kirlappos and Sasse 2012; Nielsen et al. 2000; Sasse and Kirlappos 2011; Shneiderman 2000):

- *Perceived amount of effort invested in a Web site.* Inferred by consumers using factors like aesthetically pleasing design, Web site's ease of use, and well-formed Web site layout.
- *Company information.* Presence of information like physical location, contact details, and its presence at easy to find positions in a site can increase the perceived trustworthiness for a Web site.
- *Variety of products available and amount of information on a product of interest.* Those lead to the belief that the site belongs to a big retailer and when combined with rich media representations of it (such as images and diagrams) significantly impacts a consumer's perceived trustworthiness.

---

[7] http://www.theukcardsassociation.org.uk/media_centre/press_releases_new/-/page/1323/.
[8] http://www.internetretailer.com/2011/01/18/fraud-losses-fall.

- *Inclusion of Terms and Conditions/Privacy Policy.* Consumers seem to relate the mere presence of terms and conditions to trustworthy entities.
- *Well-formed URLs.* Consumers believe that scam Web sites have long, non-meaningful URLs (this was only true in the early days of phishing).
- *Indicators of past trustworthy behavior.* Name and reputation of a company can form a positive expectation on its potential behavior. Recognition of brand names with which a consumer has dealt in the past (online or in the real-world) results in higher perceived ability of fulfillment. User reviews, presented inside the Web site also affect perceived trustworthiness, but those are easily manipulated, and consumers rarely attempt to verify their authenticity.
- *Trust transfer.* Inclusion of other recognizable entities affected the decisions of participants; for example, claims by a Web site that they are subsidiary of Ticketmaster (UK's biggest ticket retailer), links to social networking site, advertisements of known companies, and links to known charities all affect perceived trustworthiness of a Web site.

The trust symptoms all point to the same problem: trust development is much more complicated than what the designers of solutions to aid well-placed trust assume it to be. Consumers do little to verify any of the Web site properties presented earlier, which leaves them vulnerable to a much wider range of attacks than those currently covered by user education, anti-phishing or other trust-signaling mechanisms. A significant shift is required to effectively communicate the risks involved in user decisions. Technology needs be introduced to aid correct trust placement by automatically performing any verification required, alerting consumers when potential risks are identified, aiding their accurate assessment of the dangers; eventually resulting in more informed trust decisions and reducing the potential of consumers to be victimized by online scams. The following developments could help to improve trust signaling.

Use of Trusted Third Parties (TTPs)

TTPs are intermediaries in trust transactions that provide incentives for fulfillment to the trustee and assuring the trustor on the success of the transaction, essentially improving the reliability of the intermediate medium used for compliance. TTPs already play a significant role in digital environments: certification authorities are used to certify public key ownership for encrypted communication, PayPal holds credit card information of buyers obscuring it from sellers, and eBay and Amazon offer their own platforms over which people can buy and sell products (they also have mechanisms to protect consumers from scammers),[9,10] promising to refund purchases when things go wrong (most credit card companies also follow this approach). Despite not resorting to *intrinsic* trustworthy behavior, those mechanisms provide assurances for trustworthy behavior that can result in increased trust to the trustor, the TTPs, but also the internet as a TMI-enabling medium. Similar approaches need to be implemented on an Internet-wide shopping scheme to enforce trustworthy behavior from retailers, which can positively affect user experiences.

Automatic Identity Verification

We agree with David Clark's comments on the necessity for automatic identity verification. Automatic verification approaches can be used to verify a site's authenticity based on a set of predefined properties and alert consumers when a problem is detected on the site. Phishing attacks becoming ever more sophisticated – for instance, spear phishing attacks on employees that refer to (publicly announced) events in the company (for instance, of impending redundancies). Even general spam messages contain increasingly detailed and plausible information, designing to make them seem trustworthy (see Figure 6), and designed to panic consumers into action.

Solutions like the SOLID,[11] which identifies unauthorized use of symbols registered by their original owners, or McAfee's SiteAdvisor,[12] are already used to provide authenticity information or potential maliciousness of a site, by scanning the Web page's content. VeriSign's Norton Secured[13] mechanism provides information on the Web site owner, enabling the potential to implement a Web-wide *mutual authentication* mechanism between consumer and retailer (Zhang et al. 2006b). Those, or other similar systems, can be used as the basis of a larger implementation, developed in collaboration with Web browser creators, which will automatically alert consumers when scam Web sites are detected, but also inform crime prevention authorities and Internet Service Providers (ISPs) who can then act to block traffic to those and take them off-line. Automation is important in this case as the amount of effort a user should be asked to invest to identify or report a site should remain minimal. In addition, the success of any attempt to implement a mechanism like this requires the involvement of all interested stakeholders (retailers, certification authorities, ISPs, and crime prevention authorities, to name a few). A solution

---

[9] http://pages.ebay.co.uk/ebaybuyerprotection/
[10] http://www.amazon.co.uk/gp/help/customer/display.html%3F;nodeId=3149571.
[11] http://https://www.solidauthentication.com.
[12] http://www.siteadvisor.com/.
[13] www.verisign.com.

Dear Customer,

Within PayPal's latest security checks, we recently discovered that today there were 3 incorrect login attempts to your account.

For your safety, PayPal set your account status to limited. For your account status to get back to normal, you will have

to Sign In correctly at: https://www.paypal.co.uk-cgi.bin.web/webscr?cmd=_login-run

Due to our latest fraud attempts, the following IP addresses were recorded:

Invalid login from:

..53.59 3d-ed.uk

Invalid login from:

..220.153 3drapidprototyping.uk

Invalid login from:

..215.156 40kfightclub.uk

Protect Yourself from Fraud: Don't send money to someone you don't know. Find out how to help safeguard your transactions and your personal information to avoid online fraud.

This message is mandatory, if you do not complete it in less than 24 hours, your account may get deactivated.

Copyright 1999-2013 PayPal. All rights reserved.

Figure 6. Example of spam email imitating company communications, with "plausible" details.

developed with all legitimate stakeholders in mind can significantly improve the public perception of e-commerce as a safe and trustworthy service.

Non-Compliance Detection Using Intermediate Parties

Non-compliance detection can also take advantage of intermediate fulfillment mechanisms to reduce the problem of asymmetric information (see Section 3.2). In an e-commerce scenario, logistics are the first entity in the fulfillment chain and can be used as an indication of the seller's behavior. A trustee who receives many payments but does not ship a broadly corresponding number of goods is suspicious. Tracking mechanisms are already offered by shipping companies to provide feedback to individual customers, but are currently not used as a communal feedback mechanism of the type David Clark suggests in the Chapter 2. There is, of course, the *empty box scam* in which the buyer and courier end up with a delivery receipt that invalidates any claim by the buyer for non-receipt of a product.[14] A potential solution to could be the implementation of RFID labels on high-value items, which allow detection of a genuine item included in a posted parcel (Schneier [2012] reports that a similar approach has been used by hotels to prevent customers from stealing towels). Whereas there are potential workarounds for attackers, the increased cost would make them unattractive to most attackers, who are always looking to maximize their cost/benefit ratio (Herley 2012). Approaches like this can also protect sellers against consumer-side scams (e.g., buyer receiving a packet using untracked delivery, then filing a not-received request on PayPal and obtaining a refund from the seller's account,[15] or the empty-box scam in reverse.[16] Once again, industry-wide adoption is required for the success of this approach. To encourage this, the benefits of participation should be made obvious to retailers; although, in the long run, they may find themselves under social pressure from their customers to implement mechanisms like this anyway, as customers could move to one of their competitors that uses a more secure delivery system.

Better Reputation Dissemination

The importance of *social embeddedness* in a widely connected environment like e-commerce should not be overlooked when trying to design effective trust enabling mechanisms. In well-connected social settings, where reputation information is easily disseminated, a trustee's reputation is essentially a hostage to the hands of the trustor (Raub and Weesie 2000a). Dissemination of negative information on a retailer's behavior can affect all the trust-warranting properties, and thus act as a deterrent for non-trustworthy actors. To take advantage of the power of reputation, systems need to be created that make reliable reputation information easily available to potential customers. In this case, the major hurdle to overcome comes from the fact that reputation information dissemination is costly, without any immediate benefits to the individual that disseminates that information. A satisfied buyer, for example, needs to invest time and effort to share their experience with other potential buyers. This creates a *free-riding* problem as some trustors may take advantage of the available

---

[14] http://www.zoklet.net/bbs/showthread.php%3F;t=17090.
[15] http://reviews.ebay.com/ITEM-NEVER-RECEIVED-SCAM%3F;ugid=
      10000000003801615.
[16] http://www.lovemoney.com/news/scams-and-rip-offs/scams/12513/watch-out-for-this-ebay-scam.

reputation information without contributing to enriching it (Cornes and Sandler 1996). Despite that, a number of occasions exist where the trustor may be incentivized to contribute to reputation information dissemination:

- A trustor may also benefit from contribution (e.g., eBay mutual feedback: When a buyer leaves feedback for a seller they also get rated by the seller; the more positive feedback you have, the more trustworthy you are considered by other eBay members).
- Existence of rewards for feedback providers (e.g., restaurants offering discounts on next visit if a customer provides them with feedback).

A successful example of how incentivizing reputation contribution can be implemented comes from Couchsurfing,[17] a Web site of backpackers on which people post their availability to host people, but can also travel around the world and stay with other members. To reduce the risks associated with hosting strangers/staying in strangers' homes, the Web site has references for both the host and a visitor posted after each stay. People with good references are more likely to receive more requests both for hosting and visiting. Those who break the trust relationship between host and visitor get a bad reference, which severely impacts their attractiveness to future hosts and visitors.

In addition to providing incentives for disseminating information, new reputation mechanisms should also aim to automate the process as much as possible. This can reduce the costs associated with dissemination, resulting in increased willingness to provide it with relatively minimal incentive. Numerical ratings can work better than text, as trustors get to click on a number and then accompany their rating with a few comments if they wish. To reduce the potential for mimicry, reputation holding mechanisms need to be managed by TTPs, but not by the individual trustees – a retailer should link to reviews from a reputable review site, not host those on their own site on which manipulation is easy.

Security Indicators that Don't Interrupt Users (Unless Absolutely Necessary)

Another problem with security indicators is that their continuous presence at the same position in browser interfaces results in a habituation effect – even users who intend to pay attention forget after a while. Wu and his colleagues (2006) suggest that active interruptions can be more effective than passive ones; an indicator may be present all the time, but its behavior changes when a potentially risky site is identified (e.g., displaying a pop-up window asking the user to make

---

[17] http://https://www.couchsurfing.org/.

a decision). Active indicators need to provide consumers with warnings relevant to the goals they are pursuing when they need to make a decision; asking them to interrupt their main activity until they acknowledge the content of a warning can ensure that they have consciously taken a decision, even when they decide to take a risk and compromise their security. Such warnings should only appear when absolutely necessary to avoid creating routine behavior patterns, such as consumers just clicking "OK" to swat the alert. In addition, indicators like this must communicate effectively to the consumers the risk of each of the available options, and also make sure that a safe option is selected by default (Gutmann 2009).

Refocus Awareness Campaigns

Awareness campaigns need to be refocused to better capture the true dynamics of the interaction between buyer and seller in e-commerce. Despite telling consumers to look for specific trust signals, they currently do not help to verify the authenticity of those signals, and do not protect them from any potential mimicry. Future campaigns need to focus on correcting consumers' misconceptions by using simple messages: threats when shopping online (e.g., a Web site you access may be fraudulent and you may receive nothing for the money you pay) and what consumers need to do to protect themselves (e.g., if in-browser Web site verification is implemented – *make sure your browser is up to date*). Combining this with automatic Web site verification mechanisms can significantly reduce the amount of information that needs to be communicated to consumers; also reducing the effort they have to make to check the authenticity of a site. This can result in a significant decrease in the confusion amongst them and aid safer decisions when shopping online.

Improved Trust-Signaling can Benefit Everyone

Trust-signaling is currently not effective. Scams still happen and will happen, and some consumers, sometimes, want to take risks. The introduction of technology in many aspects of everyday life turned correct trust placement to a severely challenging task for both individuals and organizations. The effectiveness of current attempts to encourage trustworthy behavior can be significantly improved by improving the understanding behind human behavioral drivers that shape current trust-related behaviors, essentially placing the users in the center of designing trust-enabling systems. Using the improved understanding technology can be used to aid correct trust placement, reducing user confusion and effectively communicating the risks associated with their trust-related decisions. Risk cannot be entirely eliminated in TMIs unless everything is turned to a controlled environment, which is both expensive and undesirable. Providing adequate incentives to ensure trustworthy behavior can aid the creation of an environment where well-placed trust is encouraged and non-trustworthy behaviors impose adequate costs to make those economically inviable. Major online retailers have found ways to protect their customers, either taking the risks themselves (Amazon's approach), or by putting safeguards around the trustee's actions (as eBay has done). But we need to devise mechanisms that protect everyone involved in TMIs. This can improve the competitiveness of both small and large commercial retailers, widen consumer options, and lead to the creation of a low risk, high benefit environment for everyone involved in TMIs (both trustors and trustees).

11

Dialogues: Trust in Design

Richard Banks

Introduction

If you've used a PC, a mobile phone or some other digital device, you've experienced the output of my discipline of interaction design, the field in which I've worked for the past seventeen years. The goal of an interaction designer is to design digital tools that help people achieve a task in their life, be it sending an email to a colleague, making a phone call to a friend, or creating a Web page for everyone to see. Interaction designers make choices about what a person sees on screen, when they see it, and how it reacts to their mouse clicks or finger presses. We design experiences that are intended to lead a person successfully through the stages of their task, hopefully in a way that feels effortless and even delightful or fun.

Design is a processional discipline. Designers start with an often vague set of needs and technologies; their goal is a gradual prioritization and synthesis of these and a narrowing down to something specific and buildable. This process, which is an iterative one based on constantly testing ideas, is primarily visual. We use tools like sketching, modeling, and prototyping to test these ideas and make choices of those we think are most successful.

In this chapter, I want to talk about the illusion inherent in most of the processes of design because of the gap between a sketch and reality. I talk a little about the seductiveness of the process, and particularly the untrustworthiness of the things that designers produce. From there I go on to talk more specifically about my own discipline of interaction design and the slippery nature of the pixel. Finally, I want to talk about recent shifts in the nature of digitally designed experiences, and the impact they are having on our relationship with the digital things we own.

The Seductive Image

Architectural books and magazines are full of beautiful renderings, sketches that imply wonderful new spaces, and jewel-like scale models. They form part of a seductive narrative that implies that prototype forms *are* architecture – that is, that the built form will map to the illusion. But when a building is constructed and placed in context, it often fails to live up to the promise shown in the rendering. Testing ideas through the creation of images, of prototypes, is incredibly powerful as a method. Indeed, to a great extent this *is* the design method. The fidelity of what is produced during this process, however, matters a great deal. Hi-fidelity renderings that imagine the finished artifact, particularly, can be extremely seductive but ultimately untrustworthy, because they can gloss over the complex issues that emerge during production or avoid placing items in correct context.

I went to Brunel University for my undergraduate degree, and the architecture of the main campus followed some of the worst aspects of the Brutalist style of the 1950s and 1960s. I'm not an opponent to this style. The National Theatre in London is a favorite building of mine, although it is still a contentious and challenging structure. The Brunel campus, however, was full of poorly weathered concrete buildings which were overbearing and quite depressing. I remember thinking at the time I was a student that the architectural renderings that were developed to imagine the final built environment must have been quite compelling to convince decision makers that building should commence. Perhaps they were rendered in pen and ink, as many were during that period, showing the buildings as strong geometric shapes surrounded by trees and lawns. A modern educational idyll that unfortunately didn't quite live up to its potential. To be fair to Brunel, since I was a student they have worked hard to develop both their built environment and its landscape. As the Guardian puts it "the brutal architecture has been softened somewhat by landscaping and greenery" (Guardian 2004).

Technology has developed a great deal since the 1960s of course, as have the tools that are used to design. The accessibility of 3D modeling software, for example, has helped democratize the product development process by helping smaller, less well funded teams work through the process of production. But these same tools have exacerbated the power of the model or sketch by making it relatively straightforward to render conceptual ideas in a way that is highly realistic – to all intents and purposes, real. It can lead people to believe that the building or product that is shown is already built.

Kickstarter, a Web site that enables crowd-funded product development, have banned project proposals that rely too heavily on beautiful renderings of their idea, and not enough on the reality of their business and technical plans. In a blog post announcing this ban they clarify that by "rendering" they mean "photorealistic renderings of a product concept. Technical drawings, CAD designs, sketches, and other parts of the design process will continue to be allowed. Seeing the guts of the creative process is important. We love that stuff. However renderings that could be mistaken for finished products are prohibited" (Kickstarter.com 2012). There's a sense in which these highly realistic renderings deprecate the process of manufacture, and make it seem like a simple jump from a digital thing to something physical. There's also a sense that other, lower fidelity or complex forms of image have an honesty to them that works to support reality, rather than undermine it.

Part of the process of design is picking the appropriate level of abstraction for visually working through ideas at different points in the development of a product. Designers have to resist the urge to rush ahead and attempt to get a sense of the artifact that they are designing before it or they are ready. The design process is processional, even as it involves tighter and tighter loops of iteration. Selection of fidelity plays an important part in that procession, and this can lead to a frustratingly long, but necessary, reveal. Things need to be presented early on that encourage the right kind of response, they should be sketchy and deliberately vague; then, as a more cohesive idea reveals itself from the whole, the representations of that idea become more and more real, too. Going hi-fi too early can be a distraction that encourages the bypassing of important work.

Electronic Abstractions

With the design of physical products, there is a separation between the material of design tools and the material of the final product. Most experienced designers know that there is a huge gulf between seeing a beautiful rendering and holding a real object, made of plastic, metal or other material in their hand. The rendering often deceives others – the client or potential customer – but not the designer who understands that there is still a long road to reality. The rendering works on their behalf to gain trust and buy time.

With interaction design, the material of concepts is the same as the material of the final product, both of which are rendered using pixels. This makes the borders between concept and reality more vague. A mock-up of a Web site done in Adobe Photoshop can literally look the same, pixel for pixel, as the website itself. It can be easy, then, to trivialize the work needed to make the Web site something with which others can interact – something that actually works.

Designers can more easily deceive themselves because the rendering and reality are indistinguishable.

Much of the engineering of software is hidden. A piece of software will run on a digital device, a computer, which, under the covers, is unimaginably complex and mysterious. Electronic devices have gone from being room sized, made of large discrete components whose relationship was at least visible, if not immediately apparent, to tiny indivisible components, each of which may contain thousands of pieces of circuitry in just a few square millimeters.

What an interaction designer presents on screen has no relationship to the innards of a device at all. Let's take buttons as an example. The on-screen button is a fundamental element in user interface design, one to which I'm sure you have grown very accustomed. Whereas a physical button is a part of a circuit, actually closing a loop, for example, to free electrons for some task, with the digital version what you are pressing is an abstraction.

The button itself is a visual illusion, assembled through the magic of tiny dots of light on a screen. Early buttons in user interface design were honed to have some sense of physicality. I remember working as a designer on Microsoft Office in the mid-1990s, for example, and carefully applying a light line of pixels to the top and left edges of a button, and a dark line to the right and bottom, to create highlights and shadows that would make it pop out as if it had depth. The button is a Trompe l'œil, a two dimensional image with pretentions of reality. Today, the button is so commonplace that I barely have to put a simple box around it for people to know that it is an element that needs pressing.

When you press one of these non-buttons they often respond to your touch, seeming to depress, and extending the illusion through time. Any sense of physicality ends at this point. Deep in the machine, a cascade of digital cogs is triggered that act so quickly, and in such volume, that they are incomprehensible. Unlike, say, driving a car for which there is still a primarily direct relationship between pressing the accelerator pedal and feeling the car go faster, with a computer, that relationship becomes a nonsense. We don't act on anything directly. What we influence, through our button press, is activity in a world of polarized electricity, of ones and zeros, of switches embedded in silicon, that is so strangely alien that presenting its reality to us would make no sense.

Even programmers, who are closest to the world inside the microprocessor, chose not to communicate with it directly. Whereas early programmers dictated the specific movement of ones and zeros within the machine using "machine code" – instructions that are native to a particular processor – modern programming languages are abstractions, reliant on a stage of compilation to translate what is written into a form on which the machine can act. "Low level" programming languages are most like machine code – closest to the language spoken natively by the machine. But most modern programming languages are "high level" and are optimized for human understanding rather than understanding by the electronics embedded in a device. That is not to say that these languages are easy to learn. It is more that the electronics embedded inside our devices have got so complex that they have pushed us to find ever more abstract ways of coming to terms with, and directing them.

Metaphor, Mental Models, and the Reassurance of the Icon

So all software interfaces are an illusion – abstract systems built on an unimaginably complex foundation. Does it matter that we can't understand what is going on inside the device? Perhaps not. The act of designing user interfaces is all about choosing from an infinite number of illusions, none of which come close to expressing the deeply complicated nature of what's going on in the machine. You could argue that no interface is trustworthy, in terms of what you see versus what is actually taking place; yet as long as the illusion itself has its own internal logic, we are able to get away without understanding what is going on behind the curtain. We are willing to suspend our disbelief and pretend that the interface *is* the machine.

We could think of language as providing the closest parallel to the choices that designers make in the creation of digital experiences. Words are not dissimilar to the digital materials that designers use in terms of their illusory qualities. We make choices in the use of words to represent an idea or create a world, just as interaction designers make choices with their use of pixels. We have an infinite number of ways in which we could use words or pixels to do this, to represent what we want to communicate. Once we arrange some words or draw some pixels, we make a commitment to the tone and direction of the world we are creating. The ball starts rolling, and other words and pixels become more likely for us to select, just as some become less likely. Some support and enhance the illusion we are trying to create, just as others undermine and even break it.

For what it's worth, designers can be strangely suspicious of words, particularly in the relationship between description and action. Maxine Naylor and Ralph Ball describe how "words are delicious, powerful and tenacious. They are valuable, fabulously seductive and dangerously diversionary, all at the same time. They are so persuasive that they can conspire to convince many people that just talking and writing it down is the design process" (2005: 30). There's a sense here that words form a veneer and distract from action. The implication is that the design process is about the manipulation of stuff, about the authenticity of what is produced, and we should be suspicious of anything that comes between us and action. Yet I wonder whether somehow digital experiences are no less seductive, are attempting to be just as persuasive, and deserve the same level of suspicion as words, because of the way they mask the system they purport to represent.

Designing interfaces is choice in abstraction, and once choices start to be made, they lead in a certain direction, one directed, among other things, by the expectations they create in others. An interface designer's job is the creation of a system of logic, grounded as it is in illusion, which "makes sense" and the mental model of which can transfer itself successfully into the head of another. Pattern spotting is a part of human nature. We try and understand a system's logic, and from that logic make inferences about how the system might work in circumstances that have not been experienced yet. We project forward, in anticipation of things with which we have not yet interacted. This is true for the systems we happen across in the real world, just as it is true for abstractions.

Consistency has always played an important part in software design because of this goal of reinforcing the logic of a system. Making things that look the same behave the same helps strengthen the illusion of the system, giving it firmness through a foundation of standardization. Every time the user has an expectation of the system, and that expectation is successfully met, they trust it a little more.

Consistency therefore becomes a key constraint. Stay inside the constraint, reinforce the rules that you've, perhaps unconsciously, started creating for your users and you can gain their trust and carry them with you. Stray outside, undermine your own rules, and the abstraction becomes a distraction. The user no longer trusts that you can make the right choices on their behalf.

The role of an operating system like Microsoft Windows, or OSX from Apple, is to package together a consistent set of rules, elements, and behaviors, providing a foundation for a specific set of consistent experiences. The first few weeks of using an operating system with which we are not familiar involve the testing of the rules of this new environment in a way that is not unlike the experimentation of a child trying to understand the way the world works. We try interacting with it, often tentatively, and develop hypotheses as to the way things work, which we test further. As our expectations are reinforced in a certain direction, we gain confidence until finally we become fluent in the interactive language which describes this digital place.

In this phase of uncovering the rules of a piece of software, many people have a tendency to blame themselves rather than the system if things are not clear. Designers can get away with poor design in their software because their customers often assume that they are the one that lacks the capacity to figure out the intricacies of the interface. I've heard many people say things like "it must be me," and describe themselves as "stupid" when they can't get something apparently simple done with software. To these people, poor design is not at fault. It is their lack of ability that is the problem.

Ironically, poor design can also have its own internal logic. Once the user of a piece of software finds the path through it – however badly it might be constructed – and manages to achieve something with it, it becomes valuable to them. That path becomes something that they internalize and can repeat. Even if that path is poorly designed, they become reluctant to see it change, because they know it, and know it works for them. This makes it hard for designers to revisit it later to "fix" it, because they already have people who don't see it as broken, but instead rely on it for some task.

Operating systems are full of standardized rules and we gradually learn them all. We learn how the mouse works; how to click and right-click; and how to drag, scroll, open, save, and close. We learn the elements that make up these experiences – icons, folders, the desktop, buttons, scrollbars, the cursor, and so on – until they become commonplace, well-understood, and very real to us.

Yet as the recent shift from mouse-based interfaces to those of touch remind us, these worlds are just abstractions, just a series of choices made to create an illusion that helps us achieve some task. Touch-based interfaces introduce a new range of rules and elements. We are now learning new skills – how to swipe, press, and pinch – some of which are compatible with our old ways of interacting with devices and some of which feel strangely contradictory. We've created a world that has become trusted, but whose cracks are starting to show as it becomes clear that other worlds are possible.

Metaphor has been one of the greatest tools at the disposal of interaction designers. With metaphor we have been able to coopt the rules of a preexisting system and apply them to our own. Before we started using metaphor in earnest, we used words as the primary interface to allow regular people to talk to machines. Early personal computers had command lines into which instructions were typed that told the machine what its user wanted of it. This system was not unlike the act of programming, but the command line instructions operated at a level even higher than "high level" languages, packaging together verbs and nouns that told the machine what to do.

Command lines require a knowledge of the language through which the machine is made to act, and for many people this syntax is just too arcane and inaccessible. Metaphor has provided an alternative. As computers grew in power and became visual rather than textual, we moved away from using words to talk with the machine and instead drew on the organizational principles of the office, the domain into which most early computers emerged, to create the desktop metaphor that has sustained the interface of personal computers for the past fifteen to twenty years.

In the case of the desktop metaphor, we've drawn on physical things – on folders, on paper, on an actual desktop – as a way of creating a model for working in the digital world. By many measures, it's been quite successful. The desktop metaphor is an illusion that has seemed acceptable and accessible to all. It has masked the complexities of the microprocessor, and has carried us into an era in which people have been able to embrace computing while computing has changed many aspects of our world.

Strangely, while the desktop metaphor is far more of an abstraction of what the machine is doing than the command line interfaces that preceded it; it has somehow come to seem more machine-like. Perhaps this is only in retrospect as the metaphor has usurped text-based commands, as well as the complex engineering beneath. To many of us, the model of folders and icons is more than just metaphorical. In our minds, it *is* the way the machine works under the covers. When we drag an icon from one folder to another, we imagine that – under the covers – the machine is similarly moving the file that the icon represents from one part of the hard drive to another. The metaphor, then, no longer provides only an abstraction that allows us to use the machine; it has consumed the machine and become in our minds the way in which it actually operates.

File icons are one of the more powerful elements in this deceit. An icon represents an item within the operating system – a document, a picture, a piece of music, and so on. Whereas the icon is really a proxy for a document, a way of accessing its content, it has really come to *be* the document. An icon has a strong, almost physical presence. It is something we can act directly on and manipulate. We can literally drag it around, copy it, and select it in a way that we can't with any other piece of the user interface. We learn to drag icons early in our digital education. It becomes second nature to us. In fact, there are very few other situations in the use of computers in which dragging and dropping is consistently used, yet the icon continues to invite this interaction. People recognize the capacity of an icon to be moved this way, even as they rarely do this with other digital things.

Files, then, have become one of the most anchored of elements on the computer. They have a strong sense of place and can be interacted with in ways that are quite physical, or as physical as a digital thing – represented entirely by pixels and code – can be. Most importantly, they represent our "stuff." While operating systems are full of system representations, of applications and their elements, it is the folders and files that feel like our little piece of it. When we move from one device to another, it is these iconic elements that we want to take with us.

Cloud of Uncertainty

However, the nature and representation of our stuff is changing. When computers were isolated, before they became interconnected by default, the file system was a primary repository for the things that belong to us. If we wanted to move stuff from one device to another we had to use a floppy disk, a zip drive, a USB stick, or some other form of external storage. Now, however, we interact with services that are hosted online and, arguably, they have started to play a more important role in our digital lives than our off-line systems, particularly as they become the place in which our digital stuff starts to live by default.

The World Wide Web has been with us for nearly twenty years, but for much of that time we haven't had a hugely personal stake in it as a place in which our stuff lives. We've used it to learn new things and to share the things we know with others; we've used it as a means for communication; and we've used it as a marketplace. It's only in the past few years, that we've started to both move our stuff to it, as well as create new content directly on it.

We now post billions of photos and videos onto sites like Facebook and Flickr, and use services such as DropBox and SkyDrive as repositories for the documents that we used to keep off-line. We own a diversity of devices – laptops, phones, and tablets – that have made manual management of our stuff cumbersome. It is now more straightforward to pick a place (or places) online for our digital possessions to live, and to access each through our technology so that we are always looking at the same copy.

Yet, whereas operating systems use a consistent, constant illusion for storing and presenting the things we own and create a strong sense of an entity through the use of the file icon, online services are purely internally consistent. Our online content is part of a new Wild West, stored in a way that is purely optimized for the service on which it lives. These optimizations are dictated both by the experiences that the service want to offer through its user interface, and by the efficiencies that it needs to reach to scale to millions of users while still quickly returning content to you.

A digital photo on a PC, for example, is represented as a single item that is self-contained. Both the image data, which allows the reconstruction of the photo onscreen, and the attributes of that photo (such as the time at which it was taken) are stored as part of the file, embedded within it. When I copy the

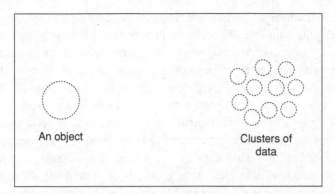

Figure 7. A file as an object vs. a cluster of data.

photo to a USB stick, all of this associated data travels with the photo, which reinforces the idea that the file is self-contained. Under the covers, the illusion of the icon continues to be supported, with the file system doing the work that is needed to move the bits on the hard drive around so that they continue to make sense, metaphorically.

When I post this same photo online, to a service such as Facebook or Flickr, it becomes something quite different. Behind the scenes, on the server, the item is broken into pieces and becomes part of a complex system of databases and relationships that supports both the rapid recall of the item and its properties, and a new kind of experience in which the relationships between items seem to matter as much as the items themselves. The item shifts from feeling like a single entity, technologically supported to maintain that sense of object-ness, to instead being a loose bundle of associated data in which the different elements of the original object are now distributed but connected. It becomes a small cluster of relationships, a mini-cloud in the Cloud (see Figure 7).

Take the Web service Flickr as an example. Flickr is a Web site focused on photography, and, interestingly, one of the first online sites to share newly posted items with everyone and anyone by default. Before Flickr, online photo Web sites (such as the one from Kodak) were primarily personal, and were driven by our need to print our digital photos on paper. They had a simple structure of "albums" that were the equivalent of the old paper envelopes in which newly printed photos would be stored together, with images often from the same event.

By emphasizing sharing by default, Flickr gave its customers a strong sense of community. This social layer has pushed the site away from a more static structure, optimized around virtual "albums," toward a more diverse set of features that are now everyday parts of our online experience. These allow, for example, relationships to be built between the images of different photographers (by creating the same "tags" on different images); images to be brought together thematically in a collaborative way (through the creation of "groups"); for people to create curated experiences of the photos of other Flickr users (through the creation of a "gallery"); for photos to be given a location so they can be seen in the context of place (through the use of "maps"); and so on.

All of these structures create new kinds of relationships between items in which the image itself is merely a node in a huge cloud of interconnected data. The act of using Flickr is to add to this cloud, to reinforce existing connections, or to create new ones. The user's actions, and those of their social network, are focused on the layering of new properties onto newly posted images through the creation of these relationships.

This is quite different from the file system in which properties seem to matter little. Relationships between files in the file system are primarily created through the use of folders, which are external to the file – entity-like in and of themselves – and not treated as an attribute of the item but a structure within which the item sits.

A key distinction between the operating system and a site like Flickr is that the attributes of a file item are not active and actionable, as they are online. Online, these attributes are often represented as links that the user can click on to find out more about an item and its relationship to others.

When a photo is taken on a digital camera, for example, one of many attributes stored in the newly minted image is the "Date Taken," which registers, to the second, the moment the shutter was depressed. This is one of the properties that move with the item. Once the photo is stored in an operating system, this attribute is a little underexposed and underutilized. It can be accessed through the "properties" dialog in Microsoft Windows, where it is visible as a piece of text, and it can be used to sort a set of items chronologically in a folder, but little more. Once this photo is posted online, this attribute comes alive. On a site like Flickr, this simple date is used in myriad ways to connect the photo to others.

For example, it is exposed as a simple link beneath an image on which the user can click (see Figure 8). Clicking the link navigates to a new page on which the user can see all the photos they took on the same day. On this page there are links to show all the photos taken on the same month and year, as well as to shift to a "calendar" view which gives them a grid-layout to view their photo activity.

Each property of an item, therefore, is treated by Flickr's creators as a precious resource with which new experiences, new ways of navigating, and viewing content can be created. Flickr itself adds its own layer of attributes

Figure 8. Active properties underneath a photo thumbnail on Flickr.

Shannon
Click here to add a description

⊕ ⊛ ▣ Anyone can see this photo (**edit**)
Uploaded on **Jun 17, 2010 I Map I Remove**
51 views / **0 comments**

to the image that didn't originate on the camera. These include "comments" from other people (which both connect an image to the commenter because their name is itself visible on the photo, and act as additional links to their profile); the number of times an image has been "viewed" by members of the Flickr community (using this I can see which of my images has been "most viewed," and is therefore the most popular); and "favorites" (a way to simply mark images that stand out, but which again has the knock-on effect of allowing me to see images that are "most favorited").

This focus on relationships, then, creates an incredibly rich web of content and data. To create this kind of experience, so as to be able to, for example, fetch the properties of one image in billions and display them in a timely manner, sites like Flickr have to also store their content in a way that is quite different to that used in the file system. Pieces of the file are plucked from it and distributed into databases and file systems on servers that are themselves scattered around the world in large data centers.

When you upload an image to Flickr from your device, for example, the properties that are part of that image are sucked into a database, while the image itself is duplicated twelve times at differing sizes and aspect ratios. One of these is the "original" image, preserved at the same aspect ratio and size as the version you uploaded. The other eleven images are each provided as optimized versions, fit for different purposes. There is a small thumbnail (always 100 pixels wide). There are two cropped, square versions of the image, which are good for presenting the content of Flicks in a clean, grid-like manner, because each of these has a consistent aspect ratio. There are then two "Small" versions of the image (240 and 320 pixels wide), three "Medium" versions (500, 640, and 800 pixels wide) and three "Large" versions (1024, 1600, and 2048 pixels wide).

The question, then, is: What happened to the file that was uploaded? Where is the unified, manipulable entity, that was mobile and which I was able to manage? Once my file was uploaded to Flickr, I lost some sense of this because my photo become a distributed thing, with many different aspects. The ripple effect of this treatment of my digital objects is a diminishing sense of entity of an item, and a loss of sense of control, and therefore ownership, over it.

Placeness

It isn't just this strong sense of entity that is lost with the move of my content online. I've lost the sense, too, of *where* it is. The metaphor of the folder provides me with a sense of reassurance, of solidity. Folder hierarchies are not necessarily tidy, but we usually have some sense of their content. At home we often have boxes of stuff squirreled away in our attics and basements, and we may not know specifically what is in each of them, but we have both some sense of their content and also a sense that it is within the boundaries of a space for which we are responsible. It is in our place and is ours to take care of. Folders give us a similar sense. Just as the icon has given us a strong sense of physicality and embodiment in our digital things, the folder has given us a strong sense of their digital place.

Part of this reassurance comes from the binding of hardware and software. I can point to a physical thing, my laptop, and know with some certainty that my digital things live on it. By moving that physical object, I am also moving the digital ones that it contains.

These pieces of hardware have become more mobile, too. The desktop PC, trapped underneath a desk in some corner of the home, is a much diminished artifact, superseded by laptops, which overtook them in popularity a number of years ago, and are now being overtaken again by tablets and smartphones. With these new classes of devices, we have the reassurance that our digital things are literally with us, and sometimes even on us.

There is a hierarchy of reassurance of place, then. We trust in our homes as places to keep things. We trust in our computers and devices as artifacts on which we keep them. We trust, finally, in folders to keep them in. This trust isn't absolute, of course. We know that the things we keep often need looking after and that there is risk associated with putting things in their place. There are physical risks – fire, dampness, and so on. And there are digital risks – the hard drive can be a fragile container in which to keep things, and we know that its content needs backing up, a form of tending that is often hard to remember to do. Yet this tending, ultimately, is our responsibility.

We make decisions about where our digital things should live and, in doing this, we get to know where our digital things should go in the future. In that way, our digital things create a pattern of personal responsibility that is not unlike our physical lives. Some digital things feel organized and tidy, just as some physical things do. Some digital things feel messy and disorganized and need sorting out, just as some physical things do.

I wonder, where my digital things live, in a physical sense, on Flickr. I understand that they have a digital home, which I can visit by typing http://www.flickr.com into my web browser. I also understand that I have control over my things on Flickr, but – in a way – that is mediated by the site. Beyond that, I have no sense of where the bits that actually make up my content on the site actually sit. Whereas before, I had a strongly bound sense of the relationship between places, devices, and the digital things that live on them, now that is lost.

Flickr's Web site creates the illusion that there is a place associated with my photos, a digital one, even if I don't get a sense of the physical equivalent. I can visit a specific Web address to get to a specific photo, for example, and this implies that there is one version of that image, the one I'm always looking at. Yet that is unlikely to be the case. For the sake of optimization, to create experiences that are fast and responsive, there may actually be many copies of one of my photos, distributed across the world on many different computers, which are orchestrated to deliver the pieces of my image to me with as much speed as possible, based on where it is that I am geographically. Things live on a service, but that doesn't mean that the service has "placeness" in any fixed sense. Indeed, that service's placeness may depend on all kinds of needs – the need for power, for speed, for security – that result in a manipulation of my data in ways that are quite hidden from me.

By participating in a site like Flickr, or any of the thousands of other online services through which I offer a piece of myself, I am reducing the sense I have of control over my stuff. I put things on these sites and they shift from being entity-like, and therefore touchable, to being nebulous clouds of relationships. They shift, too, from being located and feeling fixed, to being ambiguously distributed around the world. The content I put on sites like Flickr, then, becomes a little less mine. But who owns it now?

Online Acts of Faith

Flickr owns the infrastructure and experience of the site, and certainly has a stronger sense of the actual distribution of my photo across its servers than I could ever hope to have. So perhaps I partly own the image, now, in tandem with the site? Or perhaps the community can claim some sense of ownership over my stuff, because they are able to affect it through their actions, through the way they create new relationships between what I post and other content on the site, or simply through the way they respond to what I upload.

I *can* continue to access my photos, of course, and I *can* continue to exert some control over them because I can manage the access of others to the things I share. Although Flickr is community-focused and encourages the public accessibility of the content hosted on it, I can still make my photos private. This isn't the same sense of control over access that I have with photos in my own home, where a physical disconnection with the Internet is enough to give me the comfort of privacy. This is a sense of control that is developed through trust, through my dependency on the skills and judgment of the authors of the service on which my content is stored. Their promise to me is that, when I restrict access to things that I own, their system will respect and follow my wishes.

Control over the things I own, as I post them online, is now something I wish for, and have to put faith in, rather than something that I can guarantee through my actions. It is negotiated with others. In the case of the social networking sites themselves, I interpret the sense of control I have over my content through the ways in which they describe and offer that control to me in their user interface. In the case of the members of the social network, I can both exert explicit control over my content to prevent them from passing on my things in a way in which I may be uncomfortable; but more often than not, I put faith in them, too, to behave in a way that seems appropriate to me.

More often than not, control over my online content is a balance between action and faith. On Flickr, I can set licensing permission (through Creative Commons) on my photos, dictating whether I allow other individuals or even corporations to reuse, or even edit, my images for their own purposes. There is an interface for selecting which of the range of Creative Commons licenses I wish to apply to my images. I can click a small "edit" link next to my photo, in the section marked "Owner Settings," and a dialog box appears with a number of radio buttons and other elements for selecting one of the six forms of the license. For example, I might explicitly forbid the reuse of my content for any reason, or I might allow its redistribution, but only if I am attributed as the source.

This user interface makes my decision feels concrete and absolute. Yet this isn't like editing other aspects of my photos, like the date, or pressing the delete button, where something explicit happens. Instead, I indicate my preference and hope that the other members of the community notice it and respect my choice. The action of applying a Creative Commons license to my photos results in them being flagged visually with my wishes, but this mechanism doesn't then travel with the image. If someone chooses to copy my image, for example, the Creative Commons doesn't travel with it. I must trust the community to respect my wishes with regards to their use of things which I consider to belong to me.

Oddly, licensing was never something I had to worry about with my pictures before I started to use Flickr. "To license" may perhaps be part of a new grammar of online action in which wishes are expressed, but not in a way that is enforceable. "To keep private" may be another. As we become used to breaches in privacy, perhaps we are accepting that our control is limited, or that the frontline between the public and personal space shifts constantly despite our wishes.

Perhaps I'm over emphasizing the loss of control and the requirements for trust that come with placing my content into the hands of an online service. I just mentioned the act of file deletion as being "absolute," yet this is one particular command that has always been problematic, whether your content is on a local device or online. When you delete a file on your PC, for example, the bits that represent it aren't suddenly wiped from existence, purged from the hard drive. Instead, the system merely removes that file from any indices that might cause it to be exposed in the user interface, and also indicates that the space that the file formerly reserved on the disk is now available for some other file to occupy. As long as other bits don't occupy that newly vacated space, it is possible to recover all or part of the item. This act of vacating, I suspect, doesn't match the absolute sense of the word "delete." People tend to assume that by "deleting" something, it is gone, unrecoverable by them, and certainly unrecoverable by others. Yet stories abound of second-hand hard drives from which sensitive, deleted content has been recovered. "Deletion" may already be an example of the woolly grammar of action that I described previously. "To delete" may be an act of faith already.

New Types of Entity

Most of what I've described comes from a PC/desktop-centric perspective in which objects start offline and then are put online. Through that process, they are dissembled and shift from having a very strong sense of entity, of file-ness, to instead becoming part of a cloud of properties and relationships in which the content of the file – the picture or the text, for example – seems to play a diminished role.

But does this model of the file really make sense anymore? Although files have given us a strong sense of control, much of what we author now is no longer in this form. Instead, we often bypass the local operating system and go straight online. We create content as part of our social networks, for example, and much of this we would be hard pushed to describe as file-like.

Is a Tweet a file, or even file-like? Maybe this question is nonsense, yet Tweets do have a sense of being as self-contained, of being as entity-like, as a file is. The joy of Twitter is often that so much can be said in just 140 characters. Tweets often summarize and encapsulate an event or a thought in a way that has independence, which can be responded to in isolation.

Yet we'd probably never think of opening Microsoft Word to author a Tweet, or of saving all our Tweets in a folder hierarchy so we can manage and control them. Although they make sense in isolation, they also have a continuum to them that makes them part of a whole. A Twitter stream is a constant dialogue, a continual output, in which any one item rarely rises above the rest, and which as a whole gives you a sense of a person.

Instead of being file-like, Tweets feel simply like a part of the cloud of properties and relationships that is common in online services. Is there much that separates a Tweet from a comment, for example, which is similarly brief? We can imagine the database of relationships and entries on Twitter in which a Tweet is only a small constituent part, and around which float a cloud of properties – like time, numbers of "retweets" and "favorites," responses, hashtags, and so on, that easily engulf the Tweet itself in terms of content.

Tweets, too, have a sense of built-in disposability. We tend to trivialize what we write on Twitter, or in our Facebook updates, despite the power that 140 characters can carry. When we author a Tweet and release it into the wild, it becomes one of billions, and there is a sense that if it isn't spotted quickly, and a response to it given by others, it will disappear under the surface, drowned by the "fire hose" of other people's entries.

This creates a strong sense of ambivalence toward our past on Twitter, the sense that this content was created for others but has no value to us in and of its own self. While Tweets often encapsulate quite personal moments or events, or act as a record of a relationship, they are trivialized by their owners who fail to see them as objects that might be insightful in the long term, just as diary entries are. So perhaps this is another aspect that makes a Tweet unlike a file. The sense that it was created primarily for others, or that it is fleeting. Why would you want to control or manage something that lacks a sense of longevity, or doesn't by default feel like it belongs to us?

Likewise, the content we consume on Twitter has a similarly transient nature. There is quite simply a lot of it and it is, relatively speaking, untargeted. It is broadcast to many, and – as a consumer of this content – it feels slippery. We lose our sense of the whole, instead trusting in serendipity to reveal something about the corpus that might be surprising or revealing. Tweets and Facebook posts have an odd relationship to time, in that objects only feel real if they are recent. If they are recent, we have a chance of consuming them. They then quickly become a part of the past. We suspect that Twitter keeps them, but they seem hard to get to.

Much of our online existence has this relationship to time and chronology, in that what matters is recency and a sense of activity. This contrasts quite strongly with the bounded solidity that many file systems give us, which focus on a confidence in stability, the sense that the folder hierarchy gives us that a thing lives in a place, and that that place is accessible and permanent.

Manipulations of Things

This sense of a lack of permanence, in the loss of our capacity to trust in the continuing persistence of the things that we feel belong to us, is not just prevalent in social networks. The shift of our stuff from digital folders into the Cloud gives us a changing sense of ownership over our content that is felt, too, in new experiences of entertainment media. We may have felt we owned our media before but can we say that now?

My music used to be very physical, in the long distant past when I owned a record player, on which I used to play LPs. It then transitioned to a still-physical form, in CDs, which I understood were digital. The analog lanes of the LP were replaced by tiny depressions representing ones and naughts, and were stored on a silvery disk that still belonged to me. The age of the CD is passing, though, and I now play a lot of my music through services like Spotify and Xbox Music, which stream their content to most of the devices that fill my life. Similarly, I now read many of my books through Amazon's Kindle service and watch an increasing number of films through Netflix and Love Film.

My ownership of the content I watch, read, or listen to on each of these services is highly ambiguous. I might buy a digital book on Amazon, but I'm not confident that necessarily means I own it, and I am aware of times when ownership of a book on a Kindle has been revoked (famously, when Amazon withdrew, ironically, George Orwell's *1984* from its service because of copyright issues, and it disappeared from the devices of customers who had purchased a digital copy).

On Spotify, the issue is even more interesting, because I'm not purchasing music from them at all, but instead paying a fee to have access to all the music that they have available in my specific geography. There is an argument to be made that, compared to Amazon's Kindle service, this actually clarifies the state of ownership. I clearly don't own any part of the service's music, but instead pay a fee to access all of it.

Unlike Twitter, which as I mentioned earlier is strongly chronological, Spotify has no real emphasis, in terms of content, on the recent past. For example, there is no particular bias toward more modern music. Albums are not presented reverse-chronologically, for example, with the most recent most visible. The music, the content of Spotify, is exposed and presented on similar terms. There is no real sense of disambiguation, and – because of this – I often feel that I drown in the overwhelming amount of content that I am offered.

I do get recommendations from the service itself as well as from friends. Perhaps these recommendations, rather than Spotify's content, *are* like Twitter in the sense that these are quick forms of communication, and only the most recent of them have prominence. Old recommendations quickly disappear. These recommendations aren't biased toward the recent past, just as the service isn't. My friends may recommend content from random points in the entire history of popular music. This may happen as they use the service and come across albums from their past and recommend them, or as the service itself acquires the rights to the back catalogs of record labels.

Spotify acts to create complex relationships between artists and albums through the biographies they feature about each artist. These describe how a particular band or performer evolved, and the influences that drove them. These descriptions are linked to the content under discussion, so that a web of music is created in which it is quite easy to lose oneself.

How can we act to exert some sense of control over this content, and how can we continue to use music as a way to express who we are, and to connect with tribes of others who share similar interests, when there's simply so much of it, and it is all treated so equally? It is only in the recent past that I had a wall of CDs that acted to communicate my tastes and interests, and perhaps some sense of me, to visitors to my home. Only a short time before that I would carefully craft mix-tapes that arranged and ordered the songs that I cared about most. These, again, evoked something personally meaningful.

There *are*, however, ways that Spotify allows me to personally invest in the service. Although I don't own the music, I do have an account that allows me to do a lot of the things that I might do with the digital music on my computer at home. I can arrange the music I like into playlists, for example, and mark particular tracks as favorites of mine.

Through these mechanisms, I make playlists of things that I want to listen to, of things that I particularly like, and these act to give me some sense of stability, perhaps even some sense of control, in this massive catalog. Just as my box of LPs was precious to me, and acted to tell others about my taste in music, it is these manipulations, these lists of the songs I want to draw attention to, that become a key way of recording my personal relationship to music. They become the mechanism through which I exert control over this archive of songs, and make arrangements that mean something to me.

This is an odd, intangible sense of ownership. I don't own my music anymore. Indeed, Spotify has the right to withdraw it at any point, if necessary. Instead, what I own are a set of lists of songs that help me remember which items in the service I care about. But even these lists are part of the service, in the sense that they are part of the experience that the service owns. They don't persist independently of Spotify.

Perhaps this is a reasonable state of ownership for the right to access the sum of the world's output of popular music (or as good as). Now I have millions of songs at my fingertips, and the capacity to follow the intricate relationships between them to find paths that are interesting. Perhaps the idea of "ownership" of music is simply a phase that we have passed through, that in retrospect will seem selfish and childish. After all, the idea that you can "keep" music is a relatively recent thing. Before the invention of the phonograph by Edison in 1877, the idea of being able to even capture sound in any way that was permanent would have seemed like wizardry. But before this mechanism was invented, did you need to own a piece of Mozart to love Mozart? Wasn't listening simply enough?

This may be one way in which our relationship to content has changed, then, with our move online. We are leaving a world in which we own and keep little bundles of data as "files," and instead are entering one in which we don't manage and manipulate that data directly, but instead create structures that allow us to refer to it remotely. In this world, the "thing" – the book, the music, the film – belongs to someone else. We simply create and leave behind traces of the connections between those things, which are structured in a way that shows how we care for them.

Anchoring the Cloud

Spotify is an amazing resource, then, one that gives me access to a seemingly limitless world of audio. Within it, I am able to create structures and relationships that emphasize the artists, albums, and songs for which I care. Yet these manipulations, my piece of Spotify, only exists in the context of that service. If the service goes, so do these meaningful structures that feel like they belong to me. Is Spotify a service, then, that I can trust not just as a supplier of entertainment, but as a home for the record of my personal tastes, realized through my manipulations of their music?

This is a perhaps unreasonable question to ask of any service on which I keep my stuff, or keep even a history of my digital manipulations. There is simply a disconnect between my interest in the things I keep on these sites, and the interests of the sites themselves.

As I've discussed, part of this disconnect is about my sense of ownership over content. Whereas I may have interacted with my files through my local PC using an interface that was mostly an illusion compared to what was going on in reality at the level of the transistor, I still had a sense of personal responsibility over the content. I understood where it was and what my responsibilities where in terms of taking care of it. Now, with my content online, the responsibilities of tending the things I care about have shifted to someone else, to the service on which that content is kept, and some of my sense of ownership has gone with it.

The other disconnect is in expectations of persistence, the lifespan of my stuff as I think of it, versus the life of a typical service. Whereas a PC in my house may decay or become outdated, it takes effort for me to dispose of it, and I get some reassurance in the sense that I will be able to access its content in the future. As a container, the case of the PC itself acts as a reminder of its content. But if I use an online service heavily, and then start to use it less and less, I begin to lose sight and memory of it. It doesn't persist in my life without use and it therefore ceases to act as a reminder to me of the things that it contains. As it disappears from my horizon, its content disappears too. I'm left with the sense of a trail of abandoned services, each of which contains a little piece of me and my stuff.

The final disconnect I wanted to discuss is the way in which the content I put up on a site is bound to it. On a PC, I could manage and move content around – move it to a new PC for example. On most of the online services I use the things that I own feel locked in. There's no notion on these sites of me "keeping" my content if I chose to abandon the site itself. The value in many services I use is in and through the things I choose to keep and share with them. My data and details are their currency, and – using this asset – they can better understand their customer base as a whole. They might use this knowledge to add value back to their site and their users by creating new compelling and useful features, or they might chose to offer that data on to others. Either way, the details of our lives are something for them to hoard and it is in their interests, therefore, that the content stays with them. Each service is optimized around the data offered by their users, independently of other services, and each creates its own diverse set of rules and structures for accessing that data.

I'm not at all arguing that these services do not add value to our lives. Photo sites, such as Flickr, create a network of interconnected images, knitted together by their users, which result in new ways of seeing the places, people, and events that have been captured through the camera lens. Social networking sites like Facebook create close communities of friends and family who can share their thoughts and offer insights into their day-to-day life that deepen relationships. Media sites like Spotify offer me the world of music and film, allowing me to dip in and out of any point in the trajectory of culture over the past 100 years.

Each of these services has tremendous value to me but I wish both to feel ownership over the things I think are mine and to feel some sense of personal responsibility over them as well. I want to see these services as adding layers of value to my life in a way that is life-long. Instead, I feel like this value occurs in pockets, without persistence, and is left behind once I have left the service it is embedded within. I need a sense of independence of my life from these places.

A new challenge, then, for our online experiences is returning a sense of ownership to the things that make up our online lives. This likely means the making of a space in the Cloud that I can truly call my own, that will persist for my lifetime and beyond, and onto which the online services I use layer new value which also has continuity. In many ways, the question is not the one I raised earlier – that is, whether I can trust services to look after and take care of my content. Instead, the question is whether they can trust me in being an active participant in the services they offer, while also letting me own and take care of what is mine.

12

Trusting Oneself: An Anthropology of Digital Things and Personal Competence

Richard Harper and William Odom

Preamble

Several of the prior chapters in this book allude to the work of Harold Garfinkel and his seminal *Studies in Ethnomethodology* (1967). One of the great lessons that one can take from that book is the idea that society is made up of people who "do" sociological theory or, rather, people who construct and deploy "lay-sociological theorizing" to both interpret and organize the world around them. Their everyday reasoning is a form of sociology Garfinkel would have us believe. Today, of course, the idea that people theorize in this sense, that they reason sociologically, has suffused itself throughout the discipline of sociology and its cognates. Take Michel De Certeau (1984), for example, or another sociologist of the quotidian, Henri Lefebrve (2004). Both argue that the social world is constructed, "enacted" through the deployment of interpretative skills and agency – through people's capacity to reason in particular ways. And consider other social sciences, such as anthropology. Here Tim Ingold (2011) argues that people construct their places of dwelling through conscious acts of "dialogic engagement": they attend to, work with, and reflect on the things and persons around in ways that directs them in new trajectories, lines of action. All of this is a form of reasoning, Ingold claims.

The subtle differences between these various views notwithstanding, that people reason in a way that can be characterized as sociological, and that, as a result, the thing called society has the shape it has, is virtually commonplace in contemporary thinking. The word "theorizing," however, has been ameliorated with alternate formulas by these (and other) authors. We have just listed some of the alternative words and phrases used: people enact their reasoning and they rationally engage their reasoning as part of how they produce dwellings. These and other formula stand as proxy for theorizing. One of the motivations for using alternatives is that many commentators, including those just mentioned, would appear to prefer keeping the term "theory" as a label for their own thinking rather than as one applicable to the non-professional arena. To put it directly, this move allows them to valorize what they do while giving lay persons' actions a more prosaic, less consequential air. More seriously, it is perhaps correct that a distinction is made between the nature of reasoning in the real world and what is evoked by the term "theory" and its natural provenance – that is, in the world of science. In this latter world, the term labels something that a scientist might conjure and then test against evidence. A theory in this context is, say, a hypothesis. Given this, then, if one were to use the term "theorizing" for lay reasoning, one might be led to believe that lay reason is like a form of science and that the theories it holds are testable and revisable. And, if one goes along with this, it is not such a distant move to also accept that such reasoning is bound to be weaker than true scientific reasoning – lay people are not trained, they do not have scientific tools, and so on. In this view, everyday reasoning is poor science. As it happens, this is a conclusion often reached in cognitive science and variants of psychology. One thinks of Patricia and Paul Churchland (1984, 1989).

This is not at all what Garfinkel had in mind when he argued that people theorize or do sociological reasoning. Although one might accept in hindsight that using the word "theorizing" is not helpful, highlighting as it does a contrast that distracts, Garfinkel's real insight was that everyday reasoning is a practical affair: it is most emphatically not a theoretical business. As Garfinkel remarks throughout the *Studies in Ethnomethodology*, although lay people might like to theorize, they cannot do so without jeopardizing their ability to get on with their real world concerns. These affairs are manifold, varying according to context and topicality and are constitutive of the diversity and richness of what people do and the practical concerns that confront them. Careful examination of these practical affairs will show, according to Garfinkel, how they are worked at, developed, made sensible, and directed in some instance through the elaboration of practical reasoning – a kind of situated, accountable logic. That was what he meant; not that theorizing was like hypothesis testing in which the idea in question has a particular relationship to evidence and proof. Instead, lay theorizing is reasoning in action.

Consider Garfinkel's illustrative example in *Studies in Ethnomethodology*: the ways that coroners have to determine how the bodies they are examining end up where they are. Garfinkel characterizes coroners as "theorizing" about these dead bodies because the coroners ask certain things: "How did these bodies end up here, on the slab in their (i.e., the coroner's) office, at this moment in time?" They answer this question, Garfinkel explains, by invoking known or self-evident facts that can become a resource to let them start understanding what they see before them. Use of these in turn lets them refine "the facts" – the facts that pertain to this case. But these facts are also used in particular ways, in ways that fix them or align them to the world known in common. One such fact – that a body in question is, say, young – is visibly, and thus evidently, so; that is, anyone can see this. The fact itself is thus made or treated as a common fact. Another is that such a body, a young one, would not "normally" end up this way – dead. Young people don't die in the normal run of things. Old people do. "Everyone knows this," the coroners say to themselves, "thus, this is the kind of fact I can use." The coroner tries to construct a set of circumstances that might have led to this premature death – foolish drinking and fighting, say, or abusing drugs. The way they construct these scenarios is in accord with what they reason is sensible, accountable reasons to which any normal person would agree.

This is evidently not like the theorizing of a scientist, its constraints and its manner of use are quite particular. To begin with, in this theorizing, relevant data cannot be selected through methods. The relevant data is whatever is at hand. The coroner has to imagine what kind of circumstances would lead to such an unusual end with only the evidence before him or her. They cannot ask to do another experiment, another run through. The evidence they do have is itself of a particular, real-world character. They don't confine themselves to data produced by pure method or means. They use reasonable inferences based on what they know is the world they live in. Garfinkel (1967) proposes calling this reference to the world known in common as the documentary method of interpretation. In this regard, one might say that the theory, at the beginning of the coroner's work, does look like a theory that a scientist might use – something to be tested, altered. What is different is that eventually whatever the coroner comes up with has to stand up to a court; it has to be the truth. Truth here does not mean scientific truth, it means given the information at hand, given what is reasonable.

This is where the distinction between science and practical reasoning is most stark. The important distinction is not that practical means imperfect, however. In a sense, it is the other way around. For the constraints on practical reasoning make it, in some ways, harder than science. Scientists might object to this formula; the point is to highlight the kind of difficulties confronting people in the real world. Practical reasoning can entail work; it can be demanding. Garfinkel shows that this reasoning is not abstract or obtuse; it is grounded, pertinent, sensible, and evidential. Above all, and this is key, it is accountable – it is the kind of reasoning that can be seen as sensible, apposite, and practical – given the circumstances. And in the case of the coroner, it is accountable to a court. In other circumstances, the accountability will be of a different form – in the production of organizational records, for example, the accountability will be of a kind; in the case of sexual identity, it will be different too. It is the diversity of accountable circumstances that Garfinkel emphasizes in *Studies in Ethnomethodology*.

The value that accrues when one looks at social action in this perspective is that it leads one to see how reasoning is bound to place; to practical affairs not in some general sense, but in some real, local, situated sense. Other sociologists, working at a similar time as Garfinkel (the late 1950s and throughout the 1960s, more or less), also drew attention to this phenomenon: to how practical reasoning is bound up in real-world affairs. Aaron Cicourel's studies of juvenile crime (1967) showed how police theorize about how kids end up committing crime not in some general, caricaturing way but in reference to real-world situations. These techniques of reasoning sought to locate the behavior with which police officers were confronted within a broader canvass of typical conduct that allowed those police officers to make sense of that behavior and thus make reasonable, accountable decisions about how to deal with it. In broad terms, these theories took the form of a set of maxims – for example, that teenagers drive too fast, that boys show off, that most kids end up being good folks while it is only a handful that don't, and so on. Through reference to these schemas, police officers were able to make judgments about how they were to deal with any particular instance. Their dealings in any one instance allowed them to develop this reasoning, making it an ever more powerful and refined set of practices; commonsense skills if you like, skills required so that they could work professionally. Similarly, Egon Bittner showed in his own articles on police work, how, for example, police officer's "commonsense knowledge" of different areas in cities develops and refines itself and allows them to make more nuanced interpretations of conduct to be found in those areas (1967). In another, related study, D. L. Weider showed how inmates and staff of a halfway house reasoned about loyalty, trust, and favors owed through reference to a commonsense construct called the convict code (1974).

Practical Reasoning and Trust

Garfinkel was not alone, then, in highlighting the way people reason in practical contexts. Although obviously much of what police officers and coroners undertake does pertain to questions of trust, what we have been focusing on does not seem too concerned with that. Indeed, we do not want to draw on that aspect. The connection we want to draw between these arguments and the ones central to this book have to do with reasoning as it turns out that many of the debates about trust are centered on what is understood as reason.

Mariarosaria Taddeo, for example, argues in various papers (2009, 2011) that one needs to specify the criteria used by an agent to determine whether to trust another. She claims that it is best to approach this task not by looking at how people make such decisions in real contexts of action, but by looking at what criteria are used when not infected by "economic, attitudinal and psychological factors" (2011: 76). She proposes analyzing the rational decision making of autonomous computational agents that stand as representative, she contends, of some kind of Kantian ideal of human reason – a pure form of reason, unsullied by practical affairs. One output of her analysis is the claim that trust is not a first order property of interaction; it derives as a second order feature. Agents ascertain whether they can depend on another and then act accordingly. Their actions produce situations of trust thereafter. Trust is not a starting premise of action, then, but an outcome. In her view, the way that reasoning occurs is rather like the picture conveyed when the word theory is used: evidence is sought, a judgment is made, trustability can be seen or not. A hypothesis ("they are trustworthy") can be tested with an act: the other did behave as predicted, they did not; a trusting relationship does or does not follow on.

The contrast we want to make is not that Taddeo's form of reason is a reduced, clearer form of the reasoning Garfinkel characterizes. The contrast – as we see it – is in how different the stuff constitutive of Taddeo's reasoning is from the stuff constitutive of reason in practical affairs. In our view, they are not mirrors of each other, nor one a reduced form of the other; on the contrary, they are very distinct, very different. Garfinkel's coroners would not look at Taddeo's agents and exclaim "this is how I ought to reason," nor would they say: "If only I did not have to worry about all the extraneous factors – the psychological and the economic." They would say: "What has this got to do with the world I live in? It would make no sense to render decisions in this way. The world I live in does not operate this way." They would not see a reduced set of criteria, they would see a decision making procedure that would not work.

Of course this does not mean that Taddeo's view of reasoning does not fit anywhere, nor that it might have some specifiable relationship to more complex forms of reasoning. But often times, the difficulty of making such links is, in our view, underestimated in discussions about trust. Besides this, efforts to do so are not always helped by some of the rhetoric that one finds in this domain. As a case in point, Taddeo uses phrases like "reduced form." This rhetoric induces the idea that even though some singular instances are being examined, somehow these stand as representative of all instances; that what is being sought for is a kind of scientific fact, a thing that is the reduced form of trust. This also occurs in the work of others such as in Virgil Gligor and Jeannette Wing's *Towards a Theory of Trust* (2011), who compound that rhetoric with another – that is, computationalism, which is the idea that all thought can be articulated through the structure of computer programs. Here, words like "primitives" come to the fore – this is the elemental label in a computer language.

To take up a point from Rod Watson's chapter, it seems reasonable to accept that there are "participation frameworks" used when people reason about any task at hand, and there will be these in relation to computing as there will be to anything else. Such frameworks might also delineate types of engagement: to participate in a context in which financial matters are afoot might be treated, framed as Watson prefers, as quite different from those situations in which simple entertainment is the goal, for example. Indeed, we saw in Angela Sasse and Iacovos Kirlappos' chapter that, in those situations that entail financial matters of some kind (or more generally some kind of security), then the orientation of those involved is of a particular kind. Participants in these contexts behave in ways that may be characterized as rational, meaning that these individuals make judgments about what can and cannot be relied on for the basis of the evidence at hand. Rationality here means acting in accordance with signals of some kind.

Although the word "rational" is a good formulation of the reasoning in question, the claim that Sasse and Kirlappos make is not that this is the universal basis of reasoning, its primitive or essential form; this is not reason that can be found just anywhere. This is the kind of claim that Taddeo would appear to want us to accept. In contrast, what we learn from Watson and from Sasse and Kirlappos is that this is simply a special kind of behavior. To help draw out its uniqueness, one might say it is a calculating behavior. This suggests that the reasoning in question might be distinctive in ways that the term "rational reasoning" occludes; rational here being too all encompassing or just too vague. The kinds of reasoning often characterized as the basis of trust are then only an instance of reasoning, a form it can take. The kind that is most often used to illustrate this is the calculative reasoning we have just described, the one appropriate to, and bound with, the real-world contexts of, for example, e-commerce.

The judgment as to whether this form is essential to or more basic than (and somehow more elemental than) others is – as we say – too easily jumped to. Furthermore, and just as importantly if not more so, the desire to make such a leap often distracts from other important features of the settings in which calculative reason is found.

There are at least four such features. First, this calculative reason starts from the assumption that questions of trust are in doubt in the first place. In this, trust is not even a second-order feature; indeed, one might say, following Bob Anderson and Wes Sharrock, that it is not trust that is the basis of these settings, it is distrust. After all, in these contexts, users need to be alert to the fact that they are in situations in which there is reason not to trust. Things cannot be taken for granted. When people go to a financial service's Web site, to their bank say, they must assume that the bank will want to start its interaction as if they are not who they say they are, as if they might be a villain. Thus people approach their bank willing to answer questions about their identity that turn around the premise that they might not be who they say they are. It is sensible to expect this; they should not be offended. By the same token, the user might also assume that when interacting with a bank's Web site, he or she will put special effort to make sure it is the bank's actual Web site, not some simulacra – a fraudulent representation, an attempt at phishing. Just as the bank needs to start with doubt about the user, then so too do users need to approach the bank with doubts about whether it is in fact the bank they are dealing with.

However, and this is the second feature of those contexts in which calculative reason is appropriate, surety in this regard becomes an opportunity for villainy. The stable form of trust manifests in, for example, a bank Web site (and in the patterns of behavior around it) can become a resource for mischief. And, indeed, it inevitably will as the stability in some such setting provides an opportunity for villains to joyride on the back of what users and organizations come to take on trust. Signs on which users rely to indicate that the site is real can be copied; processes that seem designed to ensure identity can themselves be copied and turned into tools for phishing. This is why Sasse and Kirlappos say that designing trust in systems is a never-ending dance: trust begets opportunities for mischief, the mischief demands new requirements for design.

A third feature in such contexts is this: just as it is the case that there can never be perpetual security about trust, so it might also be the case that at any moment in time a user might misjudge the situation they are in. The user might have the sophistication to know that even the most trusted system will eventually be broken, but they might not realize that it has been broken in the here and now – that is, at that very moment when they are using it. Again, Sasse and Kirlappos note that keeping users alert to the possibility that at any time they might find their trusted system broken is a constant design problem; users are often overly confident.

Finally, it might not be only e-commerce settings that need to be devised to foster an attitude of calculative reason. When David Clark, in Chapter 2, makes a summons to address trust and the Internet, he is not thinking of e-commerce alone. Clark's focus is on the question of identity when the identity in question is between strangers. It was not just banks talking to customers that he was thinking of, in other words, but when people meet through the Internet via any means at all: via a secure bank Web site or via an email, through an instant messaging system or on a social network. He argues that these contacts – wherever they occur – cannot be undertaken with the same largesse of spirit that is applicable in "normal" face-to-face circumstances. Here there are numerous resources at hand that allow people to make richer judgments about the other. The constraints of the Web make these resources limited. And, for this reason, the risks of dealing with someone whose motivations are not good are thus greater. In his view, we should all worry about trusting strangers on the Internet. Clark's concern is that many people do not recognize this and so do not apply the right form of reason, and this reason should be – as we have formulated it – calculative. The chilling effect this might have on certain forms of human contact on the Web hardly needs remarking.

The Culpable Self

Part of the elemental features of this calculative reason, then, has to do with its applicability, its scope, and the determination of where to use it. Thus far we have listed some features that one might reasonably say are requisite in those contexts in which distrust pertains; one of those features has to do with recognizing that one is in a situation in which calculative reason is what one needs to deploy. One might misjudge where one is. There is obviously a difficulty here – that is, knowing whether to apply a way of understanding – and the echoes of Garfinkel ring strongly. Reasoning requires work in the practical world.

Some of this work has to do with subtleties. Clark's concern – and, indeed, the concerns of Sasse and Kirlappos – has to do with interaction between people. But there is also the possibility that issues of trust might relate to questions that don't involve another, a second person. Something about the relationship people have with computing might force them to adjust how they reason with that technology so as to make it calculative. The issue here has to do with whether a user's own practices, mediated computationally, are causing them doubts of some kind; and specifically not as regards to whether they can trust others, but whether they can trust themselves.

Consider this example. Some years ago, mobile phone operators in the UK offered mobile phones to those only who were willing to set up a system with their bank. This system – direct debiting – allowed the operators to demand from the customers whatever was owed to them at the end of the month. Such a system was viewed as a means of ensuring that phone bills were paid – given that they were paid retrospectively. However, there was some pressure, particularly from political activists, that this was prohibiting access to the mobile networks by the less well-off, the economically dispossessed, those without bank accounts. The operators responded to these concerns by saying that they could set up a process by which phone contracts were "prepaid" with some cash amounts being spent in advance of actual phone usage; once the funds were spent, the phone would cease to function. However, the operators were very resistant to going down this path, because they were convinced that people who would really benefit from such a system would not be the economically disenfranchised after all. The mobile operators thought that mobile phones were a luxury, and it seemed odd to set up a system to allow those without surfeit income to indulge in this way. Instead, they felt the system would be used by those who wanted to hide their identity, because – with the prepaid model – no proof of identity would be required; all that would be needed was cash. The operators, in other words, had a theory about this – a lay sociological theory. People who wanted to hide their identity (via living in a cash-only telecommunications world, for example) were villains or crooks of some sorts. Those who wanted prepaid phones would be people that ought not to be trusted, the operators believed.

The use of the word theory here suggests the view was merely a hypothesis. This discredits the richness of what was meant and what was done by the operators. The operators looked at the issues at hand – how to extend the footprint of mobile phone usage – by, for example, trying to imagine the motivations of potential users and then assembling a picture of those users in such a fashion as to predict who would take up a prepaid system. Part of the way they did this was by evoking ideas about normal life: ideas such that "mobile phones were a luxury" and "therefore it would seem odd" to try and set up a system that allowed the poor to have easier access to the technology – not because one would want to stop them accessing the technology, but because they would not take up the opportunity. According to this interpretation, if people had tight budgets, it would not make sense from their point of view to pay for a mobile phone, prepaid or otherwise. Given the facts of their lives, it would not be practical to have a mobile phone. In this respect, the operators were trying to reason through how they thought people with low budgets would reason; they were solving, if you like, the problem of understanding a situation in much the way that a coroner would – that is, by coming up with reasoned accounts of "reasons," reasons in this case to own an expensive product. By the same technique, the operators constructed the kinds of motivations that might account for those who would take up a prepaid system, if not those with tight budgets, motivations that led the operators to imagine it would be criminals who would use this system. The operators constructed the kinds of persons who would want to hide who they were. The operators asked themselves: "What kind of person would this be?" And the answer: "Well obviously, a criminal person."

Leaving aside any further remarks about the nature of this theorizing, how it developed its characteristics, and so on, the operators relented and a prepaid system emerged despite their reservations. This led to a massive uptake in this way of paying for mobile phones in the general. And the scale of this uptake was more than could be accounted for if it was only taken up by those who had either been excluded from mobile connectivity for reasons of economy or if it had only been taken up by the disreputable. If volume was anything to go by, others, too, used this new system.

Who? Why? The operators wanted to know. Obviously their understanding of the marketplace – of the consumers in that marketplace – was being shown to be wrong in some way. At that time, various researchers, including one of us (Richard Harper), were engaged by the operators to investigate this (Brown et al. 2001; Green et al., 2001). The research showed that, for example, parents like to pay the bills of their offspring not because their offspring were poor or had no bank accounts, but because the parents wanted to participate in financial discussion with their children by having the mobile phone bills at hand. Mobile phone bills became a pretext for parenting (Harper et al., 2005). We found that the use of paper bills were also thought of as important for similar reasons – making bills and their payment a public phenomenon in a home, for example (Harper et al., 2003).

We also found that one of the major reasons why prepaid was so successful was because it enabled people to manage their finances in a way that was surprising. At first glance, managing finances would seem to point toward a platitude: people need to budget. But the character of the management we found, the thing that prepaid allowed people to control, was not as it appeared. With prepaid, people found that they could allocate an allowance for their mobile at the beginning of some period – maybe a week, a month, or even a weekend. They used their planned spending as a way of controlling their own behavior in the future. They would make a choice beforehand and use that as a stick to beat themselves when required. Although users could always add to their prepaid at some future point – the operators allowing people to buy more minutes on demand – people liked the prepaid because it allowed them to excise control not over their purse but over themselves. And here comes the rub. The problem that it allowed people to solve was that they could not trust themselves to stop talking or texting; people knew they might become so intoxicated with a call that they could not end it. A chat could too easily turn into a grotesque bill.

Giving Psychological Color to Practical Reasoning about Trust

The point of this historical example is to beg the question of how people reason about trust in practical affairs – technologically mediated, in the case – and to point toward how this theorizing leads to specification of who is involved in trust. It also points toward some of the methods that people devise to ensure trust in circumstances in which it is themselves that are "untrustable."

As we have noted, many of the commentators on the topic of trust and the Internet like to seek primordial features of the nature of reasoning about trust that would apply to any and all situations in which that reasoning occurs. We have suggested that there is a delicate line between making insightful observations about the character of practical reasoning in real-world contexts and offering up what can best be described as caricatures. This is not to say that certain elemental or basic features of variants of practical reason cannot be ascertained, simply that care needs to be used in their determination. The last example shows that what might seem to be an obvious "primordial" can be egregious: two or more persons are not always involved when matters of trust are at hand. In some cases, only one person is involved. The question of trust – of how to reason about it – has to do with trusting oneself.

This points toward what one might call the psychological. Often in discussions about trust, this is invoked as the source of the ineffable, of irrational motives behind action. One can think of Ernst Fehr's work particularly here (2009: 235–266; see also Joseph Henrich et al. 2001: 73–78). What we are beginning to see in this last example is how, even in what one regards as calculative reasoning, there is a concern for the psychological; and although it might be true to say that these concerns might be treated as a given (as in "I cannot trust myself" as a premise of action), it would not be true to say that they are not reasoned about. If one took out the psychological in a characterization of reason about trust, one would not be offering a clearer picture of that reason but a picture that is corrupted through an absence – it would be missing something fundamental. Or at least, it would be missing something in certain situations, in particular "situated logics."

When one thinks of the psychological, there are various starting places that come to mind, of course, one having to do with the self. One thinks of Richard Hallam's *Virtual Selves, Real Persons* (2009) and Charles Taylor's *Sources of Self* (1989). These are attempts to integrate and balance all the things one might say about the self. What we are thinking of is driven, however, by the earlier examples related as they are to consumption and constraint. This leads naturally to the work of Gilles Deleuze (1990). His research looks at what he proposes are the elemental features of the self and its handling of consumption. Deleuze tries to recast the self in terms of the id and the ego – in Freud's conception, in other words – and links that to contemporary concerns related to modernity and especially the politics of consumption. In Deleuze's view, one aspect of self controls another aspect. The consumer is one part of self, a restraining moralist the other. The modern self, Deleuze argues, has to reason through the tension of desire and restraint that reflects this duality. Deleuze highlights this because of what he believes is the intoxicating nature of modern consumerism: the need to deal with the cost of mobile phones while appeasing the desire to talk is a perfect illustration of this concern. Here is a question of how the psychological plays out in issues of trust: the question is not trust in others but in one self. We want to point out that this kind of psychological color, these sorts of concerns, is presumably what approaches (like that of Taddeo) expressly want to exclude from consideration from the start. But if they do so, it seems to us that they might be missing important constituents of what reasoning about trust entails when that reason is examined in vivo, as real, lived, enacted reasoning. Taddeo's view – being treated here as illustrative of a tone and a method in research on trust – seeks to reduce trust to essentials, but what is cast as a result takes important aspects of reasoning about trust in the real world out of view altogether. Taddeo might view this as a virtue. We do not.

Turning again to what everyday reason actually consists in, what we are suggesting is that the psychological may have various inflections when seen as a constituent of everyday reason – one needs to see what they are. Needless to say, this Freudian cast is doubtlessly not the only one, we will find. Consider this quote from a user of Facebook and how she is "theorizing" about the nature of ownership and ownership of digital entities. She had recently experienced a hard drive crash, losing her digital photo collection in the process. As it turns out, many of these photos were also on Facebook, and she had recently taken to copying the online photos onto the local hard drive on her new laptop:

> [T]alking about it made me realize they [digital photos] are high up there. . . . [T]hat's why I feel like I need to copy them somewhere, have them covered. . . . I do that and I've done that and I don't even think about why I do it. I am scared of losing them, but I didn't realize it until I started talking, right here, consciously you know. . . . I use the sentence "I've got some photos," so I've said it, but I don't know really if I possess them, not until they're here [pointing at laptop], at least then I know where they are.

One can readily understand the apparent problem this person has. Worrying about how she will "own" or "have" her archive of photos in the future and relatedly, where they might be, are grounds for practical concerns; understandable ones as we say. What this subject points toward has to do with the relationship between the properties of real things and concepts like ownership and responsibility. The psychological inflection in this case has to do with how these concerns reflect the relationship between things and her self, what she thinks of as herself. Who she is, one might say, is bound to these connections.

The research from which this quote is taken entailed meeting with various people to understand how they dealt with and reasoned about the Cloud, or at least how they reasoned about various services enabled by cloud-like infrastructures – Facebook and Flickr for example (Odom et al. 2012). The research is particularly focused on everyday reasoning about possessions and their digital form. In this case, despite a recent loss of data on her local hard drive, this person moves her things from an online place (created and maintained by a third-party service) to her own local hard drive. In this way, she is better able to "understand where they were." This understanding is evidently related to her experience; this led her to doubt in her own sense of where things are and whether, consequently, they are safe. As a result, she decided to make her digital archive more "at hand" by not only having a place to view her photos (on a screen), but also by having a physical manifestation of where they are kept – by putting them on her hard drive. In this way, she reaffirms a way of knowing where her digital possessions are. Being aware of where something resides, and being able to point to that physical place, enables her to bring a sense of order to her digital archive in a way that fits with her normal everyday life and practices; it makes sense to do so. One might say she calculates that this is so. But one might also say that this gives a psychological certitude to her reasoning; with this sense of location, she can feel more secure.

The example points toward how this way of reasoning – a form of the calculative reasoning mentioned previously – includes a sort of psychological primitivism with echoes of James Gibson's theory of affordances (1979). In this view, things have properties, affordances if you will, and these can be relied on as clues to other things, other properties or affordances. Accordingly, one can assume, for instance, that when an object is pushed, it moves; that things remain still if they are left untouched; and if they are inanimate, they will remain together until something makes them separate – a hand that moves them or takes them apart – and so on. Obviously, things have more than these affordances; moral overtones also come to apply and these cannot be characterized in the concept of affordances – like the ideas of possession and ownership just mentioned.

Before we get to those issues, the Gibsonian primitives can be brought into question with the Cloud. In the physical world, one of the characteristics of the things we possess is that we generally have some sense of what we own and where these things are; this is interrelated. Place and ownership go hand in hand even before we fret about the price of possession. We can reason on the basis of these bare facts – these primitive affordances. So, for example, we structure and organize our things into containers, putting them in special places, and we often bind spaces to particular values: things put in one place have more value than things put in some other place, for example. Think of the contrast between a safe and a drawer. These acts of putting and categorizing, as mundane and practical as they are, are reasoned ways in which people create a sense of order to their lives and the things within it: this reasoning brings organization to the material world. There are various key things salient in this organization, of course. Homes, for example, act as a kind of physical locale that is bounded. It contains many of the material things we possess. Within a home, we may have additional subdivisions or special places to further contain them. These might distinguish between what different members of a household own, as a case in point. When it comes to digital possessions online, however, equivalent structures of place, ownership and ordering cannot so easily be discerned or made. There is even sometimes some ambiguity – a lack of trust seems too strong – as regards the essential status of things: what they are is unclear.

Consider this quote: "Well, when I put photos ... or personal information online, I've come to accept there's no certainty they're here or there, they're just out there." Although providers of cloud services entice people to put their things online for safekeeping and storage, something about the way that content is presented to those people thereafter causes them to doubt in the things they see before them. Their trust in even the most primitive of Gibsonian affordances – that things exist in ways that can be acted on – seems to wane.

As seen in this subject's reflection, remote services can have a disruptive effect on essential, everyday concerns of organizing, or even interpreting, where personal digital things "are." Given this, it was hardly surprising that some of those we interviewed in our various studies of the Cloud and remote storage (Odom et al. 2012; Odom et al. 2013) created various physical representations of their digital stuff: with these at least they had something they could point to. Similar to the example of the Facebook user backing up her online photos locally on her computer, we came to learn that people often use external hard drives and, at times, storage media like CDs and DVDs, to back up their digital things. In these ways, they were able to produce a sense not only of the familiar but of the controllable; a world not only with things, but possessions and all that implies. Thereby, the world at hand can be one with which they can reason, one they can trust. Creating a physical representation of a remotely stored archive, a cloud archive, allows people to mentally take stock of their things and their responsibilities: with this audit in hand they can then act; they can reason.

Giving physical form to the digital was bound up, then, with the practical desire to create some sense of trust in digital things, even if the motivation for this behavior had been negating a lack of trust in one's own competence in the first place. People knew that they could hardly trust themselves to store things safely, but they came to learn that the Cloud and all it afforded did not offer a perfect situation either, certainly not one that avoided profound doubts. And thus, although they might turn to alternative, local storage media that they knew might and indeed probably would degrade over time, making this decision nevertheless made sense. It was rational, accountable. The world is not a perfect place and this included the world of computing. To put it in other terms: the world cannot be made like some scientific experiment, ideal in all respects. People have to reason in accord with what is practical and this means in light of their own failings and the ineffabilities of digital storage, remote or local.

Part of the ineffabilities here has to do with access. When one puts something away in a safe place in one's home, one is trusting that the thing can be brought to hand when it is desired, and that this same thing can be put back in that safe place, by one's own action. But in our interviews, we found our subjects worrying about not having such practical control over the services that host the place(s) where their digital stuff "lived." They reasoned that this might lead to temporary or perhaps even permanent loss of access. For example, consider this subject's discussion of her Facebook content, and her reasoning about losing control:

> I have this fear that all of a sudden it's going to get shutdown and they're going to wipe [it] and I won't be able to get it back. So it doesn't feel like I'm fully possessing it, I mean I feel like it's my information . . . but it's like I'm not in charge of it fully. Like it's at the mercy of someone else.

This sentiment was common; moreover, it was a worry that seemed to develop as people reflected on what they are seeking with cloud-based services. Although those we interviewed had an initial lack of trust in themselves to store all their digital things, and this prompted them to put personal content – such as photos – in the Cloud, over time these same people came to start doubting in their choice. They began to realize that, although it might have made sense to hand over their treasured things to organizations that offered security and reliability, services like Flickr and Facebook are not in the business of safeguarding possessions in ways that, say, a bank might: after all, even if a bank went bust, things in the vaults remained. But, what about Facebook? After all, our participants reasoned, who remembers Bebo? What happened to stuff stored there?

In this manner, several people described their doubts over the trustworthiness of the unseen and largely unknown third-party entities. Consider this subject's reflection on how the deletion of his now departed friend's Facebook account also erased the social metadata his friend created:

> Those comments were a big part of what I had left from him. . . . [H]is personality really came out in them. . . . Now they're gone, just gone and they can't be replaced.

Even if I could get them back, it wouldn't be the same. It's not just the text... it's the time he wrote it, the day he wrote it. It's like this marker of him and it all came together into something special.... [M]ade me realize how fragile things online can be.

This person's initial reasoning about how cloud environments, like Facebook, operate did not thus fully align with the reality of how they worked, and this led him – and presumably others – to doubt in the trust they initially placed in the service provider. More generally, our participants came to reason that cloud environments may not be morally (and not just practically) appropriate places to keep, organize, and give structure to valued digital things. Something about the values in question was too closely related to the persons who were responsible for them.

Beyond Affordances: Morals and Commonsense Reason

What this points toward, then, is how the concerns of practical reason can become complicated in the age of the Cloud and that these concerns might agitate at quite a profound or deep level, one that might be characterized as psychological. It may be that things become a little more difficult to manage, to reason about and deal with, because of this technology. Things and their moral dimensions particularly can get muddled, somewhat lost; even more so when an individual moves from creating and dealing with stuff on their personal machines, their laptop as in the subject described earlier, and starts sharing that stuff with friends and colleagues on social networking sites. This is despite these sites – and the infrastructure they are built on, the Cloud – being evoked as places that allow people to keep things more safely. Think about Thomas Karagiannis' chapter in this book; think also about the much more brash claims in Nicholas Carr's *The Big Switch* (2008).

What should now be clear is that, in reference to everyday reasoning, what we have suggested earlier is often calculative in form: there are various frameworks that are deployed by people to approach and deal with contexts of practical action. Part of these frameworks has to do with relying on, for practical purposes, what we have called the Gibsonian primitives of things, and at the same time with the moral aspects that shroud these things – such as ownership, sentiment, and such. What this evidence suggests is that when shifts in computing architectures occur, it may be that a person's ability to trust in themselves diminishes by dint of losing surety in these counts – on the Gibsonian primitives and also and somehow thereby also the moral shrouds. This leads them to worry about the possibility that some responsibilities – properties endowed on some object – cannot be dealt with in ways they might want or need. After all, sentimental value is not something that can be handed over if one has promised to look after something. It would make no sense to hand that over to some third party if one wants to continue exercising that role. People start to develop doubts about their existential relationship to digital content: they worry about what is theirs, what another's, what they possess and what they cannot own. Questions of trust come to the fore in these doubts, although these have less to do with, say, financial matters, fraud, or identity theft as is often mentioned when the term trust and the Cloud is discussed, as they do with the sense of self and its manifestation in digital things.

The Psychological and the Social

Beyond these concerns, another set arise when things are put online which we have not yet mentioned. Once things go online, they can become the source of sociability and of ways of sharing and giving. For example, one of our participants reflected on the newly formed distinction between her digital photos on her hard drive and the copies uploaded online:

> ... they get comments from my friends and family, and those acknowledgments and stories become part of them. . . . When I think about the photos as my possessions, I think about the ones on my computer and the ones on my Facebook as different. My [local] photos are me saving them for my family, for the future. . . . On Facebook, the photos are me and my family and the connections we have with other people through the comments. I want both of them.

One can readily understand the problem this person is facing. Worrying about how she will "have" both sets of her treasured possessions is entirely sensible for someone who wants to safeguard their cherished things. These things announce who they are and, perhaps, who they want to become. Her concern is bound to everyday affairs of identity production, if you like, and the relationship between her newly valued things – her Facebook photos – and how concepts like possession, ownership, and the social connections that they enable make her who she wants to be spill out in the term "thing": what is the thing here? Is it an essence or some combination of metadata, tags, and the thing itself?

This is not an obtuse philosophical problem. Young and old alike are familiar with how to use digital metadata as a resource to extend a sense of sharing with family and friends. It is what ensues that is the issue. Consider this reflection from one of the teenagers we spoke to: "We write things if something catches our attention or [we] remember something happened in that photo. . . . I posted them, but I put them up there to share and it's like when we all write on them and tag them, it's those things that make it feel like we all have them together." Similar to how one might annotate a photo album to capture a shared experience and then share that photo album when in the presence of those represented in it, social metadata is attached to photos in the Cloud to create a sense of shared significance across and between friends; it is a commonly understood, everyday practice. However, social metadata, and the Cloud environments that enable it, are introducing new reasons to doubt what is meant by the term "possessions," particularly when concerns of ownership and social propriety come into play. Consider this subject's reflection on his Flickr account and the nature of "possessing" content on that site:

> Some of the most significant moments of our lives are in there.... Over time, so many comments and stories and traces of where we've been are recorded.... When I think of my most important possessions, this is at the top of the list. But at the same time, I have no idea how to get them, not just the photos, but everything together.... [T]hat's where "possessing" them breaks down.... I want them, I'm entitled to them, and they're there [motioning to screen] but do I have them?... [I]t feels like there's this illusion that they're mine.

This participant kept his photos on the Flickr service based on an understanding that it would keep his archive safe and that he would be able to share the archive with trusted loved ones as and when he wanted. Even so, while images from his online archive could be summoned on his computer screen, doubts emerged around whether the archive was "real." An image on the screen could be pointed to, but was it really there in the sense that, say, his parents' photo albums that had once sat on a shelf in his living room were real? If the photos (and their attendant metadata) could not be taken out of the account once they were in "there," then would they be owned, possessed, looked after?

Reasoning about One's Responsibilities

This participant's reasoning can be understood as a normal, practical worry that is commonplace. People commonly save important things, store them away, look at them occasionally and eventually pass some of them down to others as a way of ensuring a legacy. Clearly, cloud places, such as Flickr, can be useful for archiving a person's most important digital possessions and indeed recording rich social histories onto them over time. However, these new "places" also raise basic concerns: How can a person trust that they will be able to gain back these cherished things in the future? The question here is not just the "thingyness" of the object, but the cargo of human values that go with it. It is clear, in other words, that services enabled by the Cloud bring into question notions of ownership and possessions that are almost taken for granted in the material world. Knowing where one keeps a possession is often bound to a responsibility to care for and protect it. It is not solely a matter of knowing where things are and being able to bring them to hand. There is accountability implicated in many of the things that one possesses. There can be, for example, a duty to keep objects safe for someone else's sake, or to pass on items to future generations. (This is hardly a discovery, of course, but interesting work on this can be found in Daniel Miller [2009] and in Janet Finch and Jennifer Mason [2000]). Putting things online can cause people to doubt whether these systems of accountability will function as well, or, to put it another way, whether they will be able to act in the accountable ways they want when things shift onto the Cloud.

Some of the most compelling examples of these worries come from people that possessed digital content of departed friends or family members. For example, this subject describes why he now questions the commonsense notion that cloud contexts, designed by professionals with a high degree of competence when it comes to safely storing digital things, ought to be trusted over his own, non-professional competence to deal with these things accountably. He describes uploading digital photos that had belonged to a departed friend to his DropBox.com account:

> My first thought was to put them on DropBox, like if my computer dies, they'll be somewhere else. Then this whole thing came out [about] nothing on DropBox being safe and heaps of people's accounts weren't as private as they thought. . . . I was thinking, you know, they're the professionals here. What do I know? But, turns out I was wrong. . . . I had this wretched feeling, like I was being lazy about [a departed friend's content]. . . . I took them [photos] down immediately. . . . They're backed up on my [computer] hard drive and on a CD. I'm more in command of their destiny.

Another subject describes how her lack of trust in online services complicated transitioning digital photos and documents from her father's computer to the Cloud:

> I felt like I needed to protect it . . . [put] it in a special place. . . . I did think about putting it online, but it didn't feel right. . . . It probably wouldn't [disappear], but who knows? . . . What if it was accidentally erased? . . . Those are chances I can't take.

When we explore further the very real possibility that the hard drive in her personal computer could crash, she pointed to a higher level moral concern:

> I know my computer could die, but at least it would be on me. . . . [I]t's my responsibility to take care of it. Leaving it up to a website, there's no guarantee it's going to stay around. I can't live with that.

The Evolving Socio-Digital Landscape

What is interesting in several examples is how peoples' commonsense reasoning about the trustworthiness of cloud storage contexts change as they seek to bring a sense of social and moral order to some of their most precious digital things. In one example, the subject began reasoning that a cloud service created by professional practitioners ought to be more trustworthy, but then came to the conclusion that his digital content would become vulnerable to an unknown amount of potential villains "out there" online, in the Cloud. These villains might not even know that they are villains. They might not realize how precious something is. In his responses to our questions and interviewing, the subject seems to ask: "How could a cloud provider know this?" All they see is a digital entity, a list of bytes and a stored address. Values are not made incarnate in these properties. In a second example, the subject reasoned that a personal hard drive failure is more morally acceptable than the potential "accidental" deletion of their content by a cloud service. In both of these cases, then, people are left with few viable alternatives other than to revert to trusting themselves with safeguarding their digital things, even though they do this begrudgingly and with anxiety. These choices are practical and motivated by clear reasons not to trust cloud contexts; they enable people to socially order and become morally accountable for their digital things, despite the fact that storage devices and media can and do become corrupted over time, and can do so in unpredictable ways.

One additional aspect of the moral values that enshroud digital entities is worth noting. An aspect of possessing a material thing is that there is some level of control over others' ability to access or use it. If you possess something, you have the right to alter that thing, or to give or loan it to someone else. And, if this is so, it is taken for granted that others have no rights to alter, take, or borrow your possessions without your permission.

Again, the Cloud introduces more complexities to this basic property associated with the phenomena and how we reason about them. Part of this owes to the fact that digital things can be copied and someone other than the original owner can easily control those copies. Consider the following example in which a subject illustrates this through describing an undesirable experience she had on an online dating site:

> I used to be on a dating site and I had a photo of myself on it. . . . after a disagreement, a man I'd been talking to took it from my page. He sent me a message saying, "If I can't have you, at least I can have your picture on my computer." . . . He put it on his desktop [background image]! . . . that was "my" page, "mine," he shouldn't have been able to do that! I couldn't get rid of it [on his computer] because it's not "mine"

anymore. . . . I possess the original copy, but that doesn't feel like mine anymore because of what happened.

Similarly, another participant explained how a lack of understanding the duplicative properties of photos in the context of the Cloud made them doubt in their own ability to fully possess these things:

> [T]he real way you can keep some possession of a photo online [is] knowing who can look at it. . . . [O]nce someone has viewed it they take some possession of it, but if I am the one letting that happen, then it's still mine. . . . [B]ut if someone gets the photo without you knowing, then I don't know if you can ever really get it "back." Because who knows what's going to happen with it once they get it.

These instances help illustrate how peoples' commonsense understandings of possession degrades as these services fail to draw appropriate boundaries that keep their things safe and away from unwanted (or unknown) use. Although our evidence is mostly from the UK, a recent study conducted by Odom and colleagues (2013) found that young adults had similar doubts in South Korea, Spain, and the United States. They found that people across cultures largely shift their view of cloud storage services to be simply temporary platforms while moving their digital possessions between geographically separated computers.

Consider this U.S. subject's account of the reasons prompting him to ultimately take his files out of the Cloud:

> At first I thought it would be great to keep all my files and stuff in the Cloud. I'd hear about the promise of the Cloud and it seemed like a great idea to be able to have access anywhere. . . . But it doesn't work the same way in practice. . . . Because when I put my stuff up there, it's open to it being messed with. Someone I don't know could get a hold of all my information and documents without me knowing it. And, who knows even what the company is doing with it. They probably have access to all my stuff and they're gonna care more about the company than me. I have no idea when they're looking at it. . . . It's not smart to realize this and still keep everything up there. . . . Until I have a better idea of what's going on and that my stuff is actually safe, I'm going to keep it right here [pointing at laptop].

Many other young adults develop this same reasoning. Using cloud services to move their files between computers that they commonly use helps bring a sense of order to their digital archives; it seems also a responsible way that fits with their everyday material affairs and practices.

At the same time, many people are doubtful of the longevity of the computers on which their files are locally stored and so worry about their eventual demise. In some cases, young adults maintain Internet-enabled external storage devices in their homes, as a matter of instilling a deeper sense of trust in themselves and their competence to take care of their digital archives. The everyday uses of these devices are to back up cherished digital possessions and, in a few cases, share these things with other known entities (e.g., family and friends) through remotely accessible folders. Nonetheless, worries commonly persist that center on the vulnerability that even several points of storage are susceptible to corruption when kept in a single geographic location, making it possible to, as one American subject states, "lose everything, years' worth of memories."

The worry that this participant voices is a common, everyday concern that nearly everyone experiences: the question of what few possessions one would grab in the fleeting moments before fleeing a burning house – the small assortment of things could one truly live without. Mental exercises about these questions help people explore what is important to them and why; making sense of them helps them practically interpret and order the world around them and how they want to construct it.

One of the compelling qualities of digital things that seems appealing in this light is that they can be copied and thus, in a sense, stored in more than one location at once. Although this quality clearly causes some subjects to doubt their trust of cloud contexts (duplication begging the question of ownership as we have seen, for example), others leverage this to share and safeguard their digital things in ways they deem more responsible and morally appropriate. Some Spanish and American subjects in the study engaged in similar practices of storing redundant copies of their archives across a select set of networked computers owned either by family or friends, for example. As a case in point, one Spanish participant stored valued digital possessions on his own computer as well as on a shared folder of a close friend's computer. He considered this to be a safer and more private way to practically ensure the safety of both people's cherished digital archives. In another case, an American participant described the significance of creating shared remote folders on his brother's and sister's computers in their respective households:

> I wasn't thinking too deeply about it when I did it, but over time I have really come to value it. . . . [T[here's significance in storing things important to me in places and with people I trust. . . . And I'm doing the same for them, looking over their things too. It's a different way of knowing your things are safe. Something we could never do with our physical stuff."

Another young American adult similarly describes maintaining a remote folder on a computer in his parents' home in which he keeps cherished photos, email messages from a departed friend, and videos of his college graduation:

> [I]t's not just about the things themselves, but also where and how they're kept. . . . [I]t makes sense to keep them in my parents' home right now. It's a safe place. . . . [T]hey watch over a lot of things from my past already.

Discussion

Although these last practices might appear to be undertaken by the technologically sophisticated (and indeed some of the subjects were technically profi-
cient), they present clear illustrations of how people create a level of moral
accountability and control over their digital archives in ways that are not driven
by technological imperatives. The systems they create are social in nature
and reflect what we have suggested are issues of a psychological character.
When we say "psychological," we are alluding to how people themselves cast
certain issues as pertaining to themselves, to what their self might be and
for what it might be accountable. Nevertheless, and as one subject remarked,
these individuals did not "think too deeply" when engaging in these practices:
their reasoning is responsible and "made sense"; it reflected the common understanding of everyday life shared by these individuals, their friends and families,
psychological or otherwise. It is, in other words, everyday practical reasoning.
The particular purposes of this reasoning was to bring order to their digital
archives in morally significant ways – in ways that enabled them to trust in
their own competences.

It is clear nevertheless that people try to assemble a socio-digital context,
a topographical arrangement of their digital stuff, in ways that requires them
to be inventive. They have little experience of the Cloud and what they have
makes them more unsure of how to deal with its properties. One consequence
of this is that people start to doubt in their own ability; their inventiveness is not
sufficient to deliver what they need. We found that users worry over where their
things are, if there are unseen villains prying at the gate of their online places, or
whether the Cloud services themselves are meddling with their digital archives
in unseen and unknown ways. They even worry about whether they know what
their things "are," their essential phenomenological form: an entity or a bundle,
a picture or a picture and its tags; a single thing with metadata or a set of copies
spread around an invisible world.

These newfound worries lead to a range of different behaviors. People
revert back to old habits that, although they think often risky in the long term,
nonetheless enable them to bring some sense of order and moral accountability
back in to their relationship with digital things. In some cases, not mentioned
here but documented elsewhere (for example, see Odom, Zimmerman, and
Forlizzi 2011), people create physical proxies of cloud-based information (e.g.,
printouts of a Facebook wall or Flickr homepage) in attempts to develop a
deeper sense of trust that they knew "where" these things are, even if this sense
of trust is largely false. And, in yet other cases, people develop workarounds
to subvert proprietary cloud services all together, reasoning that their own

networked storage drives could alleviate newfound worries and shift trust back to themselves to take care of their digital archives in practical and responsible ways.

So how then, might we think about new ways to design cloud technology? How could cloud services be designed to support people in ways that brings order and accountability to them? The sensitive and, at times, paradoxical worries brought on by the Cloud suggest we ought to examine how we interact with the Cloud and the archives people keep there in ways that has not been done satisfactorily before. In what follows, we outline several design considerations that present possible ways forward.

Retaining moral accountability and guardianship. Whereas the promise of the Cloud initially led people to reason it would be a safer and more trustworthy place to keep their digital possessions, users over time develop strong doubts over whether the Cloud's promises are true. People worry about the longevity of cloud services as well as possible unknown or unseen actions performed on their digital possessions. Ultimately, trusting one's most treasured digital things with the guardianship of a third-party service "in the ether" conflicts with people's desires to treat their archives with safety and care. Taken together, these practical concerns make it increasingly difficult for most people to reason that the Cloud is indeed the safest context to safeguard their cherished stuff.

One potential way forward is to create cloud architectures with demonstrable properties that make it difficult, if not impossible, to destroy the digital possessions contained within them. The immutable file types embedded in particular cloud applications and enabled by such architectures could work to (1) help people better trust their reasoning that their files would be safe and preserved in demonstrable ways; and, in this way, (2) create a cloud computing context that places control over guardianship more explicitly back in the hands of the people that own the data.

Additionally, the creation of multiple and remote folders distributed across geographically separated computers can be made manifest and thus given social value. Remote folders can mirror digital archives across multiple locations, and can thus provide a sense of assurance that at least one version of the collections in question will endure and be accessible. These examples highlight not only how peoples' digital possessions are safely backed up on their own terms, but also how meaning is attributed to the remote social contexts in which their things were stored. In a sense, people are able to subvert some of the worries introduced by the Cloud and shift trust back to themselves, while retaining some of the innate benefits of networked redundancy that cloud computing offers. This suggests an opportunity for creating new services that more easily enable, for example, family members to create networked folders on each other's computers. There could also be new, embodied forms of these networked archives, which communicate the safety and status of the owners' and their loved ones' digital archives.

Trusting you can share and be shared with. A core motivation to put things in the Cloud is to share them with others. These actions occur through various platforms, such as social networking sites (e.g., Facebook, Flickr) or applications that directly support cloud storage (e.g., DropBox). These services offer opportunities to connect and exchange things with people and in some cases accrue social metadata. The social process of sharing a digital possession online can transform that thing in question when metadata comes to extend the meaning of the exchanged artifact. The thing becomes something that is collectively possessed. Yet, as we have described, this can be problematic, leading to confusion and doubt over where a possession lies and worries over the actions of others in relation to the digital thing (e.g., whether it has been copied and could be used with mal intent). These concerns again come out of an ambiguous understanding of the context in which exchanges in the Cloud happen. The difference is so stark as compared with the act of sharing material possessions that it makes it difficult for one to practically reason about what the outcome might be and how, for example, people can trust that social propriety unfolds in the same ways it does in the real world.

One way forward entails developing a technical capacity for people to retain some sense of the originating possession and of its history in the Cloud. This could enable shared possession, while at the same time point back to the original artifact. In other words, cloud applications could be developed that extend representations of data to people without fully relinquishing the possession to them. We imagine that if it is possible to extend such rights to people for experiences of joint ownership, it must also be possible to withdraw those rights. However, people's practical ability to give up their rights to access digital things is dramatically underdeveloped in the Cloud.

Current architectural design in many systems provides little choice other than letting data persist on the network or removing it completely, which, as we saw, has significant consequences for the people that value these things. There is a need to more sensitively handle the nuanced social connections among people. In some cases, this might give reason to remove connections among some people while retaining others.

Another way forward focuses on providing people with more awareness over the context in which the exchange occurs. This includes developing tools that enable people to query any digital possession they own to view other people's actions in relation to that object. In doing so, they could find out who else has made copies, who has modified an object, who has added metadata, and so on.

Applications in this design space could better support people in interrogating their digital things to see what has happened to them and who has interacted with them. This obviously raises some challenging issues for privacy, and needs to be handled delicately to avoid introducing new doubts and worries. However, these issues could in part be overcome by allowing the owner of the "original" possession to have certain permissions to view subsequent actions on that object, as is the case now with many online services.

Conclusion

These design directions are no doubt only a handful of what could be many. Others, better versed in the architectures of systems that enable computers and networked devices to connect to the Cloud for viewing, sharing, and taking stock of our digital possessions might have supplementary views. However, what we want to emphasize is that our work shows that this emerging technological platform, the Cloud, and all its promises, can cause people to doubt their own competence at taking care of their digital possessions – bringing order and accountability to them, and, in doing so, the world around them. Like physical things, digital possessions play an important role in how people assert their identity, realize their aspirations, and interconnect with the lives of others. Unfortunately, as people increasingly engage with the Cloud, seeking to place their digital things in secure storage and share it with others, they are met with new worries over profound issues they thought these new systems would help alleviate. Questions like "who has it," "where it has gone," and "will it still be there" remain things that people reason about even in the age of the Cloud. These doubts and questions often lead people to revert back to their old practices – even if they reason these are clearly risky in the long term.

We have aimed, in this chapter, to unpack how people's trust moves from themselves, to the Cloud, and often back to themselves through the groundwork of practical reason. This helps make manifest these situations of choice in the context of everyday life. As the Cloud threatens to further introduce doubts and worries into our lives, it is a good time to take a fundamentally different approach to enabling people with the practical tools and competence to trust themselves with their digital possessions. In our view, this approach entails taking peoples practical real worldly reasoning seriously, and not treating that reasoning as somehow an epiphenomenon that needs to be disregarded or even ignored. It seems to us that in much of the debate about trust (and latterly and trust and the Cloud), this reasoning is eschewed. We hope our evidence shows how complex, subtle, and practical this reasoning is. We hope to have also shown that it is dynamic and reflective, and that it is has psychological color: this reasoning incorporates concerns to do with trust that resonate with personal doubt. These psychological concerns also, it should be clear, point back to the social, to a person's ability to act competently in the world at large.

It seems to us that if one looks at reasoning in this way, for its situated practical character, one will stop searching for essentials or reductive forms; if by that one wants some kind of logical computational property or psychological characteristic – a computational primitive in the manner of Gligor and Wing, say, or an aversion to rejection in the manner of Fehr (see also Quervain et al. 2004). Or perhaps one might say that there are essential characteristics to this reasoning, but they are not of this kind. We have seen that, in the world of practical action, there are only real problems that have to do with things that are at hand. Ways of dealing with these things force us, sometimes and often with regret, to make corrigible what was hitherto taken for granted, a basic premise. So, for example, it is sometimes difficult to know *what* possessions are if one can't identify *where* those possessions are. Similarly, it is sometimes difficult to know a thing one possesses, if the social life of that thing surrounds it with competing claims of possession. These are indeed essential concerns, ones dealt with rationally, carefully, and pragmatically; but even when put this way, they seem grotesquely abstract and philosophical. Rational action, however, is always driven by the logic of the situation: if one cannot fathom *what* a thing is, perhaps one ought to reconsider what a thing *might be*. This is not a Kantian question, simply the concern of someone interacting with Facebook.

13

Reflections on Trust, Computing, and Society

Richard Harper

Back to the Beginning

The topics covered in this collection have been wide and varied. Some have been investigated in depth, others merely identified. As we move now to summarize what has been covered, it is important to remember that the goal has been to provide the reader with a sensibility for the various perspectives and points of view that can be brought to bear on the combined subject of trust, computing, and society. The book commenced with a call to arms: Chapter 2 by David Clark. Part of the sensibility in question demands one be alert, he argues, alert to the way issues of trust in society come in by the back door provided by technology and the Internet in particular. Other chapters made it clear that other capacities are required, too. A further sensibility is to be open to the diverse treatments that different perspectives (or disciplines) offer and to have the acuity not to allow those treatments to muddle each other. One has to be sensitive too to how the concept of "trust" is essentially a vernacular, used by ordinary people in everyday ways. Analysis of it must focus on that use and not be distracted by hypothesized uses, ones constructed through, say, theory or experiment – although these treatments might afford more nuanced understandings of the vernacular. Part of these vernacular practices entails inducing fear and worry. Such fear and worry can undermine some of the other aspects of the sensibility already mentioned; such as awareness of differences in points of view, and of course, beyond this, simply clarity and calmness of thought that might lead one to correctly resist the "crowding out" of other explanations that use of the word trust sometimes produces.

So, beyond these high level reminders, what in particular have we learned? In Clark's chapter, we find that his emphasis is not technological. His opening gambit is that, once we can assume that the technology can do what we expect, the next question – the one that arises now – is whether we can trust the people we deal with through that technology. For Clark, the Internet is essentially about a shared experience, the doing of things by people, together, in concerted ways – for exchanging messages, for updating profiles, for doing business. In this regard, there is a scale of trust entailed: for some activities, little is required; for others, a great deal. This reflects how it is in real life, he explains. It is in this respect that issues of trust and society slip in the back door as it were, through the Internet. Clark makes these assertions despite the fact that he is a technologist by trade. In his chapter, his purpose is to show how the technology of the Internet was designed around assumptions about users (these social creatures, as he defined them). These assumptions are now being revisited as the technology transforms itself in ways that were in some respects not imagined when Clark first started his career – that is, when he and others started fabricating the Internet. This revisiting has to be handled carefully, Clark explains, or else there might be sterilization of the creative essence that has driven the development of the Internet, and particularly the Web. When we attempt to redefine these assumptions, we must not put in a frigid alternative. He explains that, when the Advanced Research Projects Agency Network, the ARPANET, was developed (which he was closely involved with), it was taken for granted that users were benign; all users were pretty much of a "much-ness," decent folks simply wanting to leverage computing for their mostly scientific ends. These assumptions have turned out to be as much an opportunity as a problem, all the more so as the Web has evolved on the back of the Internet. Whereas once one could pretty much trust everyone on the Internet – they were after all only other scientist's going about their business; today one is as likely to meet someone who will abuse you as do you a favor. There is a fear that the sociality enabled by the Internet is like a Wild West, with good and bad people being mixed up in indiscernible ways.

Clark argues that the assumptions about trusting others' ordinary lives are based on the information they have at hand when they deal with those others. Sometimes people have a great deal of information before they meet someone, and sometimes they deal with complete strangers. But in either case, they have resources – various resources – with which to interpret the people they deal with, clues as to who they are and what they are about. What is not available is a predetermined certitude that someone is trustable; that what they say they can do is in fact what they will do – even in the most regulated, controlled and preplanned interaction. When push comes to shove, people have to trust others to act as they claim they will. In this respect, Clark's argument is that, in every instance of interaction between people, trust might be violated – the possibility of which (as it were) is natural; it is a feature of normal life. But, and as a corollary to that, to have it any other way would suffocate how people act; regulation, for example, might guarantee trustability, but it could also obviate that aspect of human nature which is almost its genius: to do things in unexpected and thus creative ways. Clark argues that the approach to individual identity cemented in the early design of the Internet reflects a sort of largesse: there was (and still is) an "openness" and "transparency" at its heart, one that assumed that identity had to be treated loosely, in ways that depended on people's willingness to trust. It thus comes at a risk – but that is no more than one natural in ordinary life. But this largesse allows space for creativity – for the genius of people.

Clark explains that he has come to worry, however, that allowing space for this has come under threat. Today he sees two trends that are reactions to this openness and which might tie it up or reduce it. First, the realization that not everyone who uses the Internet is trustworthy has produced demands for prohibitions to be imposed on those who are not trustworthy from getting on to and being on "the Net." For example, if identity is "assured" – which ensures that who one deals with was certain – then one could trust everyone we met on the Web. And if someone misbehaves in unexpected ways, if they become untrustworthy, then – because their identity is certain – some kind of recall would be possible: one could take them to court, say. These sorts of "solutions" (a prohibition on those with criminal records accessing the Web, say, or a guaranteeing of identity) would require a mix of technical regulatory changes.

The second trend is fear, or doubt. The delight and optimism that characterized attitudes toward the Internet in its earliest days is being displaced. Certainly, the large number of books and public debate about trust and the Web seem to suggest that this so, what was once anticipation is now fear. Both regulation and fear need to be countered, Clark says. He lists in this chapter some of the different consequences various regulatory "correctives" imply, some having implications for the functioning of the technology and some for how people experience what that technology allows – what they can do on the Internet. The ease with which email addresses can be set up might be replaced with a treacle-like procedure that requires documentation and references. This, he explains, will simply put people off communicating at all. The sociotechnical change, the first of his worries, would thus drive the second worry – that is, the dispiriting of attitudes.

Looking at the situation generally, he argues that our contemporary computer landscape demands that society pause and think about trust; trust as manifested through and made salient by the ways we have come to use and rely on a technology that Clark himself was instrumental in developing. But this thinking must be careful and restrained, deep and diligent, but not pedantic. There is no simple answer to producing trustable systems. As just illustrated, demanding too much certitude about identity could inhibit user's willingness to venture onto the Web, whereas making the protocols and standards too detailed might curtail the creative "give it a try" attitude that has made the Internet such an exciting technological infrastructure.

In sum, Clark's chapter is – as I say – a call to arms, a summons if you prefer. But it is a careful summons: it is a demand to avoid slipping into the mistaken idea that the Internet can be "fixed"; one should not be led to believe that some kind of simple solution can make it and all who use it trustable. There must not be a rush to "solutions" that tie the technology in excessive constraint or, likewise, tie up in knots the people who use it. Nor should worries about the Internet become so great that the result is fear: our doubts must not sterilize our ambition. We must reason carefully and be both open and thoughtful; we must trust ourselves to move forward in the right direction and after the right dialogues.

Exaggerated Concerns

Clark's chapter is an ideal starting place for the chapters that follow, each of which offers insights and perspectives on this very summons. But before turning to reflect on those, let me now illustrate how easy it might be to slip into the kinds of exaggerated forms of thinking and thus to the "extreme solutions" to which Clark alludes. And, as I do so, let me also choose an example that demonstrates how these concerns about trust are colored by what the Internet and the Web highlight – that is, the things about trust that they draw attention to – a coloring that keeps infusing arguments about trust, society, and computing even in the chapters within this book.

I select as example from the work of philosopher Onora O'Neill. Her investigations of trust are manifold, but I start with regard to a series of broadcast lectures she gave in 2002 – the BBC Reith Lectures – and I supplement them with arguments she put forward verbally at a workshop on *Trust and Cloud Computing* at Cambridge University in the Spring of 2011.[1] O'Neill commences the Reith Lectures by noting that the commotion about trust is not her concern alone, but society's at large. Trust is an issue that has become a focus for all – experts and laymen, philosophers and technologists. From her own view, from one trained in and an expounder of Kantian ethics, she argues that trust always entails obligations, a set of connections that bind two or more persons together: trust, in this view, is social (O'Neill 2012). O'Neill characterizes some of the elements of this framework – manifest in systems of obligation as the basis of action – through all of the Lectures (as she does in her many

---

[1] Unfortunately, O'Neill's presentation remained verbal and was therefore not available for citation or inclusion in this collection. Some of the chapters here were first presented at that event.

books and articles). In the workshop at Cambridge, she expanded on the basic arguments put forward in the Lectures. Whereas she talks in general about obligations in the Lectures, in the workshop she proposes that when people interact via the Internet, they cannot know whether those they deal with abide by an equal set of obligations. Distance, however ameliorated by the digital, makes surety on this point hard to achieve, she claims. We are, she says, depleted of the normal measures by which we stand as equal with another, as "Kantian individuals," equal in essence and obligation. In this respect, her argument echoes Clark (although whether the two are familiar with each other's work is a moot point). But whereas Clark talks about the capacity for distrust reflecting the looseness that allows creativity, O'Neill emphasizes geography. For her, it is distance that weakens obligation; it is distance that depletes the normal measures of equality. To put it crudely, according to O'Neill, the greater the distance between persons, the greater the likelihood that the mutual binding of trust and obligation will not apply. Despite her eloquent qualifications and everyday allusions to the "moral web" of society, her view comes down to the idea that people trust each other when they are mutually co-present, together, side by side. To put this in words that O'Neill herself would strongly resist, her view suggests that the capacity for two or more people to touch each other is as good a source of trust as anything to do with reason. Trust, put thus, can be said to revolve around the fact that people can, when issues of trust require it of them, grasp another at will and be grasped back in turn. This seals trust. This makes it. This marries them to it and thus to each other. They can do this because they are all together, in one place, and thereby can assure each other that they are equal and equally obliged through their hands and arms. To express it summarily, trust turns on cuddles.

This is of course to paraphrase O'Neill. Reference to cuddles on my part is meant to be teasing, designed to bring a bit of levity to what is most often a rather dry discussion. But the credit to my interpretation of O'Neill resides in the fact that problems in trust arise, according to her, when distances are introduced into social relations. Trust is weakened if not dissolved. Mechanisms need to be developed, O'Neill argues, that make ties between bodies separated by space possible. In the Lectures and in her workshop presentations, O'Neill explores various answers to the question of how trust can be made (and indeed has been made) in situations in which distance of one kind or another comes into play. In the Lectures, she considers how journalists act on behalf of readers, for example, or when public intellectuals and institutions (such as herself in the former case, the BBC in the latter) claim to stand for "everyman" when in fact they are remote, physically separated, existing in different spheres. I think this view has a nuance given it by the Internet and in particular the forms of communication it enables – email, social networking services, online gaming, and so on. With these functionalities, the human body comes to be absent – almost conspicuously so – and because trust is said to be made problematic by the Internet, then, by dint of the conspicuous absence of the body in Internet-enabled communications, then the body must be the seat of trust in "normal" (non-Internet) settings of action.

I should add that, although the Internet provided the background to O'Neill's lectures, she does not in fact refer very much to the Internet in the Lectures; even less did she mention the body. There is certainly no mention at all of cuddling. But the Internet and the body were more central to her discussions of trust and computing at the workshop. Leaving aside the question of whether O'Neill would have formulated her views as such if she had written them down, the important point I want to make, nevertheless, is that to understand O'Neill, one does not have to accept the idea that the presence of the body in any universal sense is always essential to trust. One simply has to accept the idea that the absence of the body in acts of communication is a problem in the context of contemporary society, in the society in which the Internet is the new elemental infrastructure she is thinking about.[2] Something about the acts of communication we undertake on the Internet in particular make the location of the body – its presence or absence – salient. The physical absence of the body on the Web creates an extraordinary sense: the ghostly absence of the body of others becomes suggestive of occult-like mischief: the inexplicable, untrustworthy action of disembodied strangers. O'Neill's views bring geographic coordinates, a person's or a set of person's "bodily location," into the center of the arguments about and thinking on trust and society mediated by computing.

But, is it right? Is the absence of the body the thing that ought to worry us? I have alluded to the fact that this example is meant to illustrate the sorts of topics that are brought up in dialogues on this topic; I have also suggested that, echoing Clark, one has to be careful to avoid extreme interpretations. Is this one of those? As Charles Ess and May Thorseth discuss in *Trust and Virtual Worlds* (2011), the idea that it is the absence of the body that undermines trust is something that was argued when the internet began to take off in the 1990s. But since that time, Ess and Thorseth explain, this link between body and trust can now be seen to have been exaggerated. Or instead, close examination of how people use and engage with others through the Internet makes this view seem too simple. For one thing, social connections are rarely – if ever – conducted solely through the Internet; other forms of connection are made too

---

[2] Those familiar with O'Neill's work will know that she has a long-standing interest in bioethics, which might provide a background impetus for bringing the body into other debates. See O'Neill 2002b.

and these often rely on physical presence. Besides this, the kinds of connection made over the Internet are judged and relied on in reference to what can be made of them: if only an Internet rendering of another can be made through some mode of connection then only certain sorts of human affairs will be undertaken. In this sense, O'Neill's case is too strong: it elides these details. A solution to the problem of trust would not consist of, say, providing a sense of the body through some advanced telepresence system. It might in some instances, but not all. There are so many types of connection made through the Internet that "bodyness" doesn't matter. One doesn't need to see a bank assistant to trust in an online bank, for example. Even so, O'Neill points toward something that is important: physical co-presence does matter in some social affairs. At the same time, the absence of the body in social affairs mediated by the Internet highlights aspects of social affairs that cause doubt and concern – when bodies somehow play a role in the production (or perhaps the display of) the obligations that O'Neill identifies. Think of the chapter in this book by Charles Ess (Chapter 9), for example, and those by Tom Simpson (Chapter 5) and Olli Lagerspetz (Chapter 6). They each, in various ways, consider the proposition put forward by the Scandinavian philosopher Bjørn Myskja (2008), who argues that the absence of the body in some activity alters the ethical fabric of action: altering its auspices and allowing a loosening of truth. Disembodied speaking encourages fiction, Myskja claims. His critics point out, however, that fiction does not mean untrustworthy behavior. But it does need to be heard as fiction: without that starting point, trust can be abused.

What Does the Technology Afford?

Explorations of trust are not to be understood by a simple right or wrong metrics, then. That is but a truism. The kind of work required to avoid such excessive simplicity is through investment in grasping what the technology in question actually does, how it works, and what it enables. It also requires diligent specification of the kinds of social acts that relate to these technologies – trust and society are simply too generic categories to allow one to grapple with anything in particular; one needs to think of where, why, and to what ends: these are not general, these need to be fleshed out.

If the chapter by David Clark set forth a summons, a demand to worry about trust and to do so carefully, the next two chapters set out to deal with the first domain of diligence: describing how the technologies actually work. Chapter 3, by Thomas Karagiannis, shows how, in its evolution and development (from basically a system for communicating data into an infrastructure that is allowing new forms of computing to emerge), the Internet has allowed new forms of business, new business structures and new ways of connecting friends and colleagues to emerge. But in addition, especially as the Internet is increasingly supported by the Cloud, new questions are being posed as regards what it is we want computing to do: what business structures can be allowed, what kinds of connection, and what kinds of governance and markets might emerge on the back of new data forms. These questions don't just assume trust in computing to complete the tasks we determine, but also point toward whether we can trust ourselves to make the right judgment about what we want computing to do. Key to this is the balance between the province of human action and the domain of computing. As we noted at the outset, some commentators are doubtful we can make that decision.

These changes unpack trust, then, into a more diverse set of issues and concerns than are pointed to by Clark. Crucially, Karagiannis explains, the Internet is not just a messaging medium: it is not just about bringing people or organizations together. The huge data volumes sent across it can be aggregated in ways that are allowing computer systems to redefine the relationship between the user and the system. This is the world in which search engines can predict a user's typing, for example, as well as map one's friends – one needs only think of how Facebook brings people together via a "graph." What needs to be addressed with these innovations is not merely that some users might find this a bit creepy; it is rather that this creepiness stands a testament to a transformation in what networked, Internet-based computing says or implies about people, about the users. It is not just that in this world human connections are suggested by computer systems; it is not people using computing to mediate their relations, it is computing choosing those who are mediated. At the same time, how these computers construct a view of the users is also recasting what the users themselves think of as themselves. Cloud data, for example, suggests that users reason in massively predictable ways and that their individual actions can be modeled merely as instances of grossly predictable actions. In this light, the users are ant-like. Even some sociologists are beginning to claim this or at least are implying that rendering of human affairs as ant-like offers insights into society as a whole: consider Duncan Watts and his book *Six Degrees: The Science of the Connected Age* (2004).

It is not clear what his approach offers to sociology, let alone society at large: after all, if sociology is the exploration of what social action means to people, then offering studies of actions without reference to meaning is simply a kind of physics: an analysis of particles, their movements, their proximity, their bonds. But these bonds are not ones to do with meanings, culture, social norms; they are merely the products of mathematical models. This is certainly an interesting and creditable subject, but hardly pertains to trust, or the sociology of it. Perhaps the upshot of Watt's enamor with network data (enabled by the Internet) is to recast what sociology is. But one should not forget that although the data that Watts reports is newly minted, the kinds of questions it lets one answer might not be that interesting. As John Hughes and Wes Sharrock note (2007), the failure of the positivistic approach to sociology in the 1940s and 1950s was not because of methodological problems. Sociologists used statistical techniques: the problem was that the answers those techniques delivered were not very interesting. Women do behave differently from men; the economically disenfranchised do vote differently from the economically well-off. But these are not discoveries: they are truisms. Real questions lie beneath or outside the data-capturing techniques implied in the positivist methods. Likewise today: some think that new models of human action offer insights; but it is far from certain just what the limits of these insights are or how valuable they might be. After all, it hardly seems a deep discovery to know that when people enter a search query for Mick Jagger it is a decrepit rock-and-roller they are after, not the dude down the street. Thus search engines should deliver "Rolling Stones" as a possible link before links to someone and something more obscure. People live in a world of common interests. But these prosaic examples of leveraging the Cloud are often displaced by more contentious ones, ones that lead people to think that they will be "read" and controlled by machines. This is what so terrifies the likes of Douglas Ruschkoff and Eli Pariser. This kind of fear might also have the same incapacitating effect on people's ability to be creative; a fear that Clark alludes to without regard to the powers of massive data.

Karagiannis describes how these systems might work, their prosaic as well as their remarkable qualities, and foreshadows what they will enable. A central concern is to show how the question of trust is complex from the point of view of networks and data systems, because trust transforms itself in various stages or steps in the architecture. The trust between a consumer and a provider of a social network is one thing, the trust between the network provider and the companies that provide data storage is another; the agencies offering secure walls around data stores is yet another. In these respects, trust is transitive; certainly a composite. Some aspects of this trust are carried over from forms of trust existing before, others are new. When companies hire "space" on a cloud service, they assume that the security they had when they stored and processed data themselves (on their own relatively expensive machinery) is equal to what they have on the Cloud. The past and today must be equal. But when ordinary consumers turn to the Cloud and put "stuff" there, what is it they are doing? To say that their personal information needs to be secure is to elide the much more profound question of what that stuff might be, how they imagine they relate to it, and what it means to trust it. To assume that a cloud provider keeps a picture safe is one thing, to expect that when one "deletes" it, the file constitutive of that picture is itself destroyed (forever) is another. These are issues that will come to the fore in later chapters. In these respects, Karagiannis simply adds to the burden conveyed in Clark's summons. There is a great deal to think about as we look forward to and occasionally feel fear about the different, but certainly technologically richer, world we are moving toward.

Chapter 4, by George Danezis, explores one side of Clark's concerns, the first of them to be precise. He asks how sociotechnical systems can be trustworthy, or as he addresses it, secure. His considerations have to do with where the nomenclature of "trust" and "trustworthy" is and can be used. The argument focuses on how it is not just engineers who have been burdened with the task of satisfying the growing demands to have systems that are at once "effective" (leaving aside what that might mean, there are so many things done in and through computing that there are many forms and measures of effectiveness) and yet secure at the same time. Alongside engineers, for example, there are also those who claim the right to specify what the perceived threat to some system might be. These might be engineers but they might be many other types of interested parties too – the end user might be only one of these. As Danezis explains, there can be many such people who can claim the right to make such a specification. A consumer might have a view about what needs to be secure while a company providing a service to that user might have a different view. In addition to their views, government agencies might have yet another perspective which, if given priority, supersedes and undermines the goals of the first two. Thus there is no single problem, no single vision of what a security threat is that engineers can attend to; there are many and these are sometimes pulling engineering solutions in different ways.

Nevertheless, the history of security systems is one of remarkable creativity, if not one of "perfect" solutions, Danezis explains. Claude Shannon, for example, came up with a "perfect" solution for securing data exchange in the 1940s, a solution that was somewhat impractical (1949). Many years later, a much more practical approach was devised when Whitfield Diffie and Martin Hellman presented the concept of public key cryptography (in 1976). Two years after that – but still a long time ago – Ronald Rivest, Adi Shamir, and Leonard Adleman came up with the idea of digital signatures (1978). All these innovations have altered the landscape of security and thus the foundations of today's Internet.

Even so, it would be a mistake to imagine that "making things secure" is ever entirely possible; both at an principle level and a practical level, compromises have to be made that allow for insecurity. All solutions have their weaknesses; no current computer is inviolate. Security coding has to be compiled, for example, and compilers are not secure. Furthermore, insisting that all actions enabled by technology ought to be secure comes not only at the cost of various forms of restriction over what the technology can do – a problem resonating with Clark's concerns. More importantly, security – even though it might be imperfect in some respect – always entails a mix of social and technological considerations. The U.S. military's Orange Book, often treated as the first attempt to formulize what computer security might be, assumed that certain human agents would act as secure gatekeepers to the systems in question, for example. Thus, when one says that a system is secure, one needs to know just how secure one means, and recognize that there is some human agency afoot. Technology cannot look after itself, Danezis makes clear. Digital signatures are an elegant way of binding technology to humans, but this does not make the resulting amalgam secure; it makes it secure in degrees. Mixing flesh and silicon can never produce perfect solutions because it widens the scope of possibility; it does not reduce them to zero.

In any case, there is a bigger issue that Danezis dances around. It is one thing to say that there are various ways of defining what the security threat is, but it is another to cast action on the Web (for example) in the light of security issues: for it affects what is seen. To say that government communications need to be secure reflects the fact that what governments say to other governments is not necessarily public; after all, it is part of the business of government to deal in the underworld of diplomacy. Hence such communications may well need to be secure. But to say that chit-chat on mobile phones also needs to be secure by dint of the same logic – namely, that occasionally content is private – is to give a gravity to idle conversation that it simply does not deserve. Once people learn that this gravity ought to be acknowledged, their willingness to chit-chat might abate; they might find they are only willing to use their mobile phones when they have something important to say, something that deserves and warrants security. This shift in attitude is precisely one of Clark's two worries: if people become frightened of the threats hidden within their use of computing, they might find they withdraw from use. Distinguishing between those contexts in which secure systems offer benefits and in which they simply transform the nature of the communications in question is a concern with which the security engineering community has not fully grappled.

Beyond Affordances: The Apparatus of Ideas

The next group of chapters build on these arguments – on Clarks' summons, Karagiannis's vision of reimagining the networked world through Big Data analytics, and Danezis's exploration of the limits of trust. But each of the subsequent chapters takes a different starting point. If the earlier chapters take seriously what the technology does and how it works, soliciting thereby the sensibility we are seeking, then the next chapters offer diffuse views on social context of technology use. Here the perspectives deal with the nature of ideas – such as the idea of trust and its correlate distrust. These chapters gradually turn to ever more empirical investigations of trust-in-action. It turns out that the apparatus of social action is at least as complex as the technologies of the Cloud, of security, and so forth – if not more so. And this apparatus is, perhaps more significantly, not to be treated as mechanistic, and certainly not computationally; nor for that matter is it properly treated as "logical" or its opposite, "illogical" nor, as many would contend, an amalgam of each. The contrast here is of course the one between trust as calculated reason and trust resulting from emotional decision making – a contrast used in behavioral economics, for example, and related theories of decision making, which is used to account for the perplexing forms of action manifest in the "experiments" these approaches rely on. Daniel Kahnemann's work come to mind, (2011). We shall come back to theories of rationality later.

But for now, it is important to recall the title of the next section is *Conceptual Points of View*. The first chapter in this section (Chapter 5), by Tom Simpson, presents the first of a number of views from philosophy. Simpson argues that one of the currently popular approaches to trust in philosophy entails specifying trust in game theoretic and rational actor forms. This is exemplified in Mariarosaria Taddeo's work, *Defining Trust* (2009), but it also echoes James Coleman's more encompassing *Foundations of Social Theory* (1990). This approach somehow makes trust an epiphenomenon, Simpson claims, making it not just subordinate to reasoning (to reasoning based on evidence); it makes trust largely of no consequence. If Taddeo is right, people make decisions based on the information they have at hand; if they don't trust some information, they don't refer to it. In this sense, trust doesn't matter a great deal. What matters is information. Simpson proposes that a better way of grasping the properties of trust as a concept is by explaining and characterizing it through what is called a "genealogical" approach, one that Simpson explains derives from Edward Craig (1990) and Bernard Williams particularly (see his *Truth and Truthfulness* of 2002). Here, trust is approached with a view to the elemental social forms in which trust must be present. Examples from these elemental forms offer perspicuous cases, ways of allowing the analyst to grasp the issue. Through this, Simpson comes to the view that trust reflects the fact that people cooperate – or rather that they assume and rely on people's cooperativeness – as the basis of their own action. This cooperativeness is unconditional; it is the starting point. Nevertheless, this cooperativeness is priced, it is negotiated; to put it in Simpson's own words, it comes in degrees. At the same time, the particular manifestation of trust might be varied, sometimes being cognitive, Simpson claims, sometimes affective, sometimes conative (related to dispositions, say). Nevertheless, the basic facticity of trust under all this, this genealogical source of trust, results in use of the concept having the rhetorical force it does: for although one might accept that trust comes in degrees, when there is none, something foundational is afoot. Everything might collapse. In other words, his gambit is that philosophy can't sensibly answer what trust is if it confines itself to thinking of trust as (merely) a species of concept. Instead, trust needs to be approached in terms of the "function" the concept has in society, in action. In this regard, Simpson is interested in the "forms of life" that generate concepts such as "trust" (although he avoids using the term "forms of life" himself, perhaps because of its association with the linguistic turn in philosophy some thirty or forty years ago with which he has no track), seeking to uncover the elemental structures and root forms of societies that require – demand, depend on – the existence of the phenomena labeled by the concept. This functioning has evolved and developed through time. Simpson's view is thus closely allied with that of Niklas Luhmann (1988), which holds that societies come to make trust a concern at certain historical moments, although his is more concerned to show how the concept itself might have evolved.

In putting forth this view, a number of implications follow on for our topic. One has already been mentioned. When people are confronted by a rapidly changing landscape and the source of that change is often inscrutable, as it is with much modern computing systems (all the more so when infelicitous phrases such as "the Cloud" are used to define their architectures), then people evoke trust to say that important matters are at stake. Failures in the trustworthiness of activities engaged in and through the Web, for example, go to the heart of all practical affairs, not just computer mediated ones. Simpson strongly echoes Clark's concerns but gives them greater gravity: it is not just trust in computing that we need to worry about; we need to worry at a foundational level. Even so, Simpson is sanguine about this and expects the doubts about trust to abate with time and, of course, diligent inquiries.

A second implication seems more modest, even though Simpson assures us that it is consequential. It holds that there is little traction to be gained if we allow investigations of trust to be at too foundational a level – that is, at the point where the cooperative is evoked as a human need. Instead, we have to examine the particular format of trust derivative of this in some instance. He cites his own studies of search engines (2012b) and suggests that the form of trust applicable there is of an epistemic or instrumental kind, where facts are judged against facts, and where that judgment is based partly on issues of trust: Can I trust *this* more than *that*? In this respect, such inquiries "quiet down" the rhetorical power of using the word trust, a power that Simpson admits is important, but in a way that allows greater perspicuity. We should allow the commotion about trust, Simpson seems to be saying, but restrain it in our own analysis.

Another philosopher, Olli Lagerspetz, takes up the reigns in Chapter 6. He takes a slightly different view, even though the upshot of his analysis resonates with Simpson's (as it also does with the other earlier chapters). Lagerspetz does not think it appropriate to look outside the normal conduct of the world for trust, to look for entities like mental states, attitudes, or population behavioral patterns. He thinks that trust is to be understood when the word is used or when it is treated as applicable: here the word "vernacular" comes to mind, which is certainly my preferred formulation, deriving from Peter Winch (see Lyas, 1999). He looks into those situations in which trust is raised as an issue by the people involved. His concern is with its agency in action, if you like, with how coining the phrase does things for those who use it. In this respect, his starting premise is that such uses will be varied and will cross over between the ordinary life and the computer mediated life. Trust is a tool used anywhere. It should not be examined only in relation to the Web, for example.

Lagerspetz starts his chapter by reviewing how much of the social and philosophical treatments of trust in the past twenty years view the human as a rational actor, a creature who calculates based on evidence. This is certainly the upshot of Diego Gambettas' 1988 collection, for example: *Trust: Making and Breaking Co-operative Relations*. Lagerspetz suggests that one reason why this has appealed to philosophers and others is not because it has greater empirical merits than some other starting points, but because this view easily leads them to answer questions like "who should one trust?" This approach allows philosophers to comment on whether one should trust Google, as one French philosopher famously put in in the book of the same name (Jeanneney, 2007). It is a methodological tool, in other words, and not necessarily something that should become a representation or a description of action. One treats human action as if it were rational to focus one's attention on particular sites of action, not to capture action in the general.

The ability to pose such questions aside, Lagerspetz notes that this view of the human actor takes the human actor out of time, or makes the actor's thinking seem fixed in one moment of time. This somehow makes their thinking external to their actual lived lives, the nature of experiences through time, so Lagerspetz argues. In his view, the sense of what it means to live "on-goingly" is lost. The rational action model examines what a person knows, how they know it and what decision will result in a particular "here and now," but doesn't allow understanding of where actors have come from or where they are going – that is, their trajectories of living (to coin a phrase from Tim Ingold and his book *Being Alive* [2011]). This neglects, Lagerspetz argues, the ordinary experience of, say, being with others where, for much of the time, one does not examine their action with regard to some external calculus, some measure of trust: one doesn't reason when one with is a friend. One sometimes reasons about some things. But one is mostly getting on with whatever it is we are getting on with – listening to them, watching something, being with them. Trust doesn't pertain in this modality; it is irrelevant. Only occasionally does trust, the question of it, the examination of, some doubt about it, come into play. A concern with those latter moments should not lead us to ignore the character of other moments, nor should it tempt us to color those other moments as being constituted from the frame of trust. These modalities, these ways of being, are different. Perhaps they should be examined for that difference; certainly they should not be conflated. Lagerspetz draws an analogy between this temptation and the one that leads people to look at trust and the Web without recourse to trust in ordinary life: the emphasis tends to color everything as being a question of trust when clearly it is not.

Having made these points, Lagerspetz then focuses on what trust is in those contexts in which its use, its reference is applicable. He explores how trust constitutes a "thing used to make" ways of understanding in particular scenes of action. For example, trust is a word whose use affects our orientation to some situation – and to persons in that situation whose behavior is seen in a new light once the word trust is coined in reference to it. It can do so by making us think that the prospects of that event are of a certain order (as in: "If he says what I expect then I know I can trust him in the future"), or they may allow a person to alter what they thought about something that happened in the past – retrospectively. When the concept of trust is used, then, what is seen and understood in the setting (the scene) and in the historical location of it (its past and its future) is then recast or altered. This does not mean that trust is a relative thing, so much as a way of seeing circumstances in particular ways: it helps organize *seeing*. And thus Lagerspetz comes to a very similar point as Simpson, although his philosophical etiology is quite different. Both authors think one needs to look at particularities when examining issues of trust, particularities that mean phrases such as "computer mediated communication" are unhelpful because they are too general. Instead they need unpacking into the types of communication in question, each with different start and end points (histories) and each with various orders of relations embedded within.

It is only thus that one can approach such concerns as arise when the absence of the body in acts of communication on the Internet occur; for it is not that absence in the general that matters, but in respect to particular kinds of acts. As noted previously, there is often a suggestion that this absence is key to understanding issues of trust in interpersonal action on the Web in some general way. Lagerspetz takes various philosophers to task (Myskja in particular) for getting muddled about the salience of the body in Web-based activities and thinking that Web-based interaction is always about things done without the body. This view wrongly leads people to the conclusion that, in being disembodied, an interaction must be about fictions of various sorts. And, following on from this, if interactions are fictions, then there is more likelihood of duplicity. Lagerspetz counters with the observation that the absence of the body is a feature of much ordinary life too, and just as its absence might be cause for concern in some instances, so it might be a concern on the Web in particular instances also. But it does not mean we have to worry whenever the body is absent. Even within the compass of telling stories, the salience of the body can vary depending on the situation: stories can be done in person or via the written word. Books, after all, are not bound to the bodies of their authors. And books themselves are varied: some are stories, they are fictions; but others are fact: the presence of a body does not pertain to this distinction (although the identifiability of the author might, of course). Mischief through fiction (telling lies) is not a preserve of the bodily absent – that is, the disembodied contact on the Web.

Lagerspetz ends by noting two things. First, the way trust is used to help arrange how a social setting is to be understood, orientated, and interpreted allows other salient concepts to be considered. Indeed, using the word "trust" opens the door for other issues that might struggle to have much traction if presented by themselves. The concept of *private space* gains power when viewed as a question of trust, and this can then encourage more forceful examinations of what the nature of private space might be and how it might need protecting. This might well be something that needs to be investigated in relation to the Internet, and to the Web particularly, where navigating between the public and the private might not be so clear; it might not even be certain that these are alternatives. This is his second point and his conclusion. Using the term "private" can sometimes entail contests between different points of view – the government saying something is public, for example, consumers saying it is private. When the word "trust" is used alongside this question, then, so Lagerspetz argues, decisions about this become elevated to profound questions about the politics of defining space. Trust turns out to be about law and what it implies and also assumes how it can be changed and "fixed."

Trust and Place

Lagerspetz doesn't pursue this topic, however. As it happens, some of the more interesting debates about trust and the Internet, in my opinion, turn on this very subject: the relation between what is perceived as public and private and how misappropriation of these domains can create distrust. If this book is about providing a sensibility for the issue of trust, then one property of that sensibility will be the ability to see how orthogonal matters can be elegantly brought to bear.

Take the argument put for by Helen Nissenbaum in her book *Privacy in Context* (2010). At first glance, Nissenbaum's concern would appear to be somewhat distant from our own; and she certainly does not make trust the centerpiece of her analysis. Her concern is with privacy, but it turns out that threats to privacy are delivered through the breaking of trust. The way she binds the two has its analogs with O'Neill's connection of the body and trust; although in this case, it isn't the body that is brought to bear but the sanctity of space. More particularly, Nissenbaum starts her book by asking whether we can trust in our privacy at the current time. She says that digital systems mediate information – much of it private – in all sorts of ways. Oftentimes technology does so in ways that bring trust into doubt by making what has been hitherto private into the public. Radical changes in the "technology of information" have: "aroused suspicion, caused anxiety, and drawn protest and resistance. They are experienced and registered as threats to and violations of privacy not only individually, case by case, but in aggregate amounting to a social crisis, a watershed: privacy itself is under jeopardy . . . as a general societal value" (Nissenbaum 2010: 6). People can no longer trust that their private affairs will remain private.

One of the reasons her work is worth remarking on is that her analysis pays attention to the kinds of particularities that too often get elided in discussions about trust. She starts by specifying the types of sociotechnical systems that are being evoked when words like the "Internet," "computing," and "surveillance," for example. There are so many types of systems that it would be wrong to treat them all as the same, she says. Each provides a certain kind of context in which specific paradigms of what is and is not private exist. Some of these paradigms have emerged through muddle and chance, some are more systematic and based on parallels with prior patterns of life. In general, however, considerable care is required in determining how the boundary enshrined in any particular system preserves or curtails the rights of privacy, she argues. It is reference to "context" that ought to determine whether a shifting in the boundary is to be accepted or resisted – although this begs the question of what context applies of course. She goes on to say that a failure to preserve the rights of privacy – the boundary between public and private – will undermine trust not just in some particular sociotechnical system (in the "case by case" instances), but in the society in which these systems exist more generally. Ultimately trusted and trustable relations between persons will be undermined in totality if due care is not given to the design of every instance of sociotechnical systems.

Broadly speaking, Nissenbaum argues that there are various types of system, three of which are worth mentioning here. The first entails tracking and monitoring; a second involves aggregation and analysis; and the third having to do with dissemination and publishing. The first is perhaps the most obvious and commonly remarked on: it includes video surveillance and monitoring systems, wiretapping and monitoring of online transactions. Underscoring these are apparently mundane but certainly ubiquitous technologies – digital cameras and sound recording systems, for example – that people don't really worry about. They are too commonplace but hardly sinister in themselves. Alongside these everyday foundations, there are also changes in social practice, like the widespread adoption of cashless payment systems that similarly seem to lack any sinister properties. But it is the combination of this social practice and everyday technology that makes this category of system so worrying, she says.

The second type of system is, however, actually more worrying because it is this system (or systems) that can exploit the information gathered by the first. New and "increasingly effective scientific approaches to organising, analysing, manipulating, storing, retrieving and transmitting information make . . . information increasingly useful" (Nissenbaum 2010: 12). This is the Big Data with which Kariagannis ends his chapter in this book. This is the stuff that "data analytics" make tractable. Kariagannis doesn't offer any empirical instances of organizations or institutions using Big Data; he simply explains how it might be done. Nissenbaum however does. Her illustration is of data companies aggregating credit card histories with insurance records and claims, educational attainment and criminal records that they sell to third parties – other insurance companies and the like.

There are, needless to say, many ways of taxonomizing sociotechnical systems. Nissenbaum explores the parallels between newly formed sociotechnical contexts and previously existing codes of conduct for non-digitized settings. Her argument holds that the patterns of trust in privacy have coevolved over time with everyday practice and technological change. This provides (or ought to provide) the basis for how the boundaries of privacy are managed in new contexts, online ones say – the kind that evolve from the past but produce new sociocultural contexts. When this happens, evolution should be allowed, but there should not be a complete separation between the past and the future, a rupture in what she implies is the "natural order" of private boundaries. In her view, determination of these boundaries should be based on what can best be described as a kind of system of precedence; what has been taken for granted in the past should provide the footing for how to determine how it ought to be done today.

Nissenbaum says that defining the relevant context, the analogical one, and then determining the boundaries of what is private, is the first step in any attempt to preserve privacy in new sociotechnical systems. She goes on to say that sometimes it is not always clear that there is an issue of boundaries being crossed over: the case of cookies being one in which the user may be totally unaware that merely window shopping in the digital realm might produce a data trail, for example. A user might be under the impression that their identity is only made visible – and hence public – when a purchase is made (i.e., when they have to declare themselves in an online form, for example). Information about their identities might in fact be captured by cookies and even shared between cookies (Nissenbaum 2011).

These details notwithstanding, the crux of Nissenbaum's case is that her "contextual approach" maps known contexts to new ones, or makes visible and rational the basis of wholly new contexts. This is the means (or method) through which the unsettling ruptures in boundaries do not occur; change can occur, but not chaotic or damaging change. A particular value provided by her approach is that designs ensure that users are less likely to have the wrong assumptions about the status of their private information in the newly formed digital context. As a result of contextual design, these contexts will present themselves either analogically (as being "like this" real context) or make the assumptions about the boundaries of public and private "visible" when no analogy can be drawn. In this way, users will know where they are, so to speak.

Underscoring this are two interrelated claims. The first is a line of argument that connects space and privacy; the second has to do with status of certain types of information. It is worth remarking on these because the form of the argument provides another opportunity to remark on the problems of arguments about trust. The first idea seems straightforward when treated in an isolated way. It holds that certain spaces are private and other spaces are public and that there is an essential distinction between the two. Nissenbaum notes that what is private is not defined unto itself, being defined instead through a relation to the public – that is, one space is private because another space is not. What is private can only exist by contrast with other things being public. Nevertheless, there is a sense in which these definitions of space are determinable even if they are also relational: it is as if they are concrete and fixed. Although she allows that they will evolve through time, Nissenbaum argues that defining private (and hence public) space is straightforward. This argument has considerable provenance in media studies and communications theory – Nissenbaum's own background. Meyrowitz's *No Sense of Place* (1985), for example, received much credit for its analysis of how "reality TV" was creating a fundamental shift on this dimension. His contention was that these TV shows were altering what had hitherto been inviolate private domains into zones of "public gaze." In this view, although this invasion might only happen to a few private domains, the mere fact that it could happen would break the proper order of the public and private in all domains; the gaze from one to the other would become unstoppable in all cases. The boundary between the two would be cast asunder by new media technologies. Although Nissenbaum does not mention Meyrowitz, she basically argues the same point except that in today's age of the Internet rather than reality TV, the rupturing is not through the invasive looks of the "mediated public gaze," it is through access to information, information that ought to be contained or framed by place. I shall say more about that information shortly. This seems to overemphasize stability in space and social relations. As Doreen Massey notes in her book *For Space* (2005), the social organization of space is best thought of as an interlocking of trajectories, the trajectories of the participants: the fixity of what is public or private is achieved through the interlocking of those involved, whoever they might be. This is often contested with those with more power having their definitions hold sway, hence the phrase "powerspace geometries." Theodor Schatzki goes even further in his book, *Timespace of Activity* (2010), suggesting that all socio-temporal places are contingent, subject to the possibility that they might suddenly take other forms irrespective of the collective will of the participants: all sorts of reasons can transform what a space "is" from public to private and vice versa. All of this has its resonances in human computer interaction (HCI), particularly Steve Harrison and Paul Dourish's *Re-placing Space* argument (1996: 67–76). Here it was proposed that one needs to design systems that allow people to constitute space, that reflect the fact that space is an accomplishment and which provide tools for that "work." If systems are designed that predetermine the nature of space (that *this* area has to be and cannot be other than private, for example), then an important resource in everyday and digitally mediated interaction will be lost, so Harrison and Dourish note. Space is made, they seem to be saying, not fixed.

Nissenbaum seems unaware of these arguments, although one could imagine that she would respond by saying that the principal of precedence is sufficient to allow for the creativity that Harrison and Dourish identify. Furthermore, her view is that, although it might be true to say that definitions of public and private might alter, the fact that they alter and why they alter is the thing that her contextual inquiry technique will make available. In this way, participants can be more aware of their roles and thereby direct their trajectories. Even so, one is still left doubting whether Nissenbaum is ready to accept that the public and private is anything other than a simple duality of space. Many sociologists have noted that these definitions are fundamentally related to other factors. Bernice Martin, for example, points out that the social role of "Mother" within the domestic space entitles some individuals to have almost ubiquitous access to all affairs of other members of a household, making all the behavior of those others public to them while they preserve their own privacy (1983:19–37). It might not be space that is the key dichotomy, then, but social status. Martin picks up on another point, too, which leads us to consider the second element of Nissenbaum's thesis, and this is related to the role of information. Not only does Nissenbaum's view depend on the solidity of the public and the private, but also that the relationship between these two domains is asymmetric. One domain needs protection from the other; one domain takes content from the other, but this does not happen in reverse. The boundary between the two is only broken in one direction: when the public takes from the private. Such breakages are mediated by information flows, Nissenbaum says. Importantly, this information has a special status: what is private has the status of "'sanctity" (2010: 91).

Extending the Dialogue and Yet Returning to the Topic

By coining of the word "sanctity" one can begin to see how much territory can be covered from the starting place of trust. I have indulged in the previous discussion not simply because I think it an interesting set of arguments, but to show how inquiries into trust ought to have the openness that are present in dialogues – that is, when each of those participating and contributing to a dialogue has the opportunity to draw links and connections, to broaden the topic or to redirect it in ways that might seem surprising to others. Of course these new directions need justifying, but if they can be justified, they can broaden the scope of thoughtfulness. Thus, the sensibility I have been mentioning is further fostered. One of the persistent problems in discussions about trust is the desire to constrain topics and relevances, as if thereby to allow a greater focus. But I think this achieves a different end: it stifles understanding. If sanctity is one of the surprising connections that Nissenbaum makes, another is how this is itself deployed through connecting it to space. One of the premises of much research on the Internet is that it is a technology that takes distance, and its correlate "place," out of human relationships. This was a thesis especially common when the Internet "bubble" was expanding in the 1990s. It was the thesis underscoring Frances Cairncross's *Death of Distance* (1997), for example, just as it is the premise of Manuel Castell's numerous volumes on the Internet "galaxy" – assumptions that persist in his work to this day (2002, 2009). Nissenbaum's work, meanwhile, proposes that place really is – or ought to be – one of the essential keys to the digital world. Or rather, an essential *sacredness* that distinguishes one type of "place" from another that enables users to understand how they might orient to the digital world ought to be. This dichotomy provides a framework for designers; it affords principles for law. A failure to preserve a sense of place in this regard or the egregious construction of new "digital places" that users misappropriate as sacred or not is something that we should worry about. We will lose our capacity to trust in the geography of the world if we don't make the sacred properties of certain places also a feature of our newly created virtual worlds.

And yet this view hints at a further problem: to say that the geography of the digital world needs to be made transparent, that what is public and what is private needs taxonomizing begs the question of what geography means on the Internet. Nissenbaum proposes that this can be determined through analogy. As Massey and others suggest, it might be better not to focus on defining places but defining trajectories to and between places: it is the interlocking of these trajectories that "produces" public or private. As it happens, these trajectories are "visible" – if not always in ways one might expect. As Nissenbaum and others have noted (e.g., Mayer et al. 2012), Web site cookies and other mechanisms provide evidence of the trail of user movement on the Web. Unfortunately, this trail is not self-evident to users themselves (see, for example, Jenson et al. 2007), and constructs a view of user action that is not a mere record of places visited.

To put it simply, elements embedded in the Web page the user visits may share information with other sites; and the user may not know this. Thus a user may go to an online book store and the Web page that records that visit may share information with, say, Facebook. Facebook then uses that evidence to amend what it shows to the user when they next visit Facebook or other related services. In addition, individual Web sites might consist of an amalgam of content elements from other Web sites, each of which may have their own cookie or data trail engine. So, for example, if one goes to a Forbes Web page to read the news, that page is not only made by Forbes, but has areas or elements provided by third parties – some of these are advertisements, some are content or news of some kind. Even if the user does not click on these elements, information may be relayed to these third parties. To give an idea of

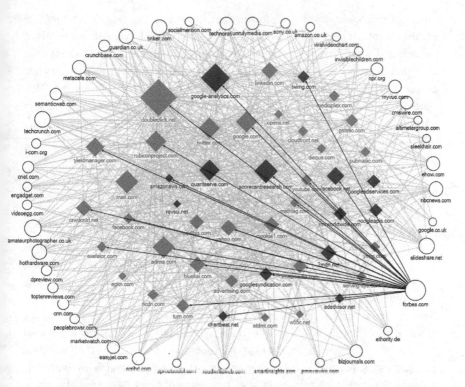

Figure 9. Data trails and digital footprints on the Web. Forbes.com serves as a host for tracking and site analytics domains, including doubleclick.com, googleanalytics.com, and scorecardresearch.com. The diagram also shows (in grey on the outside of the circle) other sites a user might visit and the connections they have (courtesy of Frayling 2012).

how extensive these trails are, with a NodeExcel diagram, Figure 9 shows what associated tracking occurs on a visit to Forbes.[3]

This not just a case of trawling through cookies to analyze "Big Data"; this is reconstituting what is meant by movement through and traces about action on the Web.[4] And this, in turn, makes binary oppositions of "public" and "private" seem very crude ways of dealing with articulations of information that are far more subtle and complex. The word "dialogue" comes to mind again, but this time in reference to Douglas Rushkof's (2010) arguments mentioned at the

---

[3] I give my thanks to N. Milic-Frayling for this image. For further elaboration of this see Richard Gomer et al. (2013: 17–200).

[4] That this is so results in very lively debates in the blogosphere. See, for example, http://www .propublica.org/article/everything-we-know-about-what-data-brokers-know-about-you; http:// https://www.eff.org/deeplinks/2013/04/disconcerting-details-how-facebook-teams-data-brokers-show-you-targeted-ads.

outset of the book: it is not dialogues that involve instructing computers that the user wants; it is in dialogues that what is known, what is sought by involved parties, and what is being taken away by each is no longer clear. Certainly, the user may have no idea of the richness of the interaction with which they are engaged. They may not know how they are being heard or seen by the Web. Furthermore, what they are saying is in part constructed in by the computers, in part by the systems that provide the Web sites, and in part by the interlocking of information sharing that goes with it.

What is Done when Trusting?

When thinking about these issues, questions about distrust are brought to mind. Action that might have been assumed to be one thing gets recast as another and the user's engagement with it alters as a result. If Lagerspetz's chapter has allowed us to ask where discussion about trust can lead us, Chapter 7, by Bob Anderson and Wes Sharrock, leads us back to another topic, in a sense the obverse. What gets forgotten in discussions about trust? Concerns about the absence of trust tend to lead people to ignore much of what happens when trust is assumed. If there is any interest in this, researchers are often solely concerned to cherry pick issues to be investigated in places where trust is limited. The result is that action where trust is in sufficient supply gets neglected. Anderson and Sharrock claim that this is a concern when so much is made about how trusted life "is." This "is" is somehow neglected, unspecified. They seek to answer this question: what is life when "trust is the normal state of affairs"? They suggest that many of the debates on trust do not answer this.

Anderson and Sharrock illustrate what can be captured and examined if trust is the starting point of action with an example for air traffic control (ATC), showing the surprising things that are done when trust is assumed. But these surprises are only to do with what planes can be made to do. A much more important thing is to show the ways in which this trust is bound up with the routines of air traffic controllers, in the delicate coproduction of a collective frame of mind, the "joint reasoning" of controllers at work. Among other findings, they show that there is a metaphysics at play, a way of categorizing and organizing sets of technologies and working practices into "good" and "bad," ones to be "relied on" and others to be "worried about." Metaphysics means that there are basic categories used by the controllers to organize how they understand and see the world in which they act. This reasoning is situated, concerned with how the categories in question need to be brought to bear on particular occasions and sites of action.

Having illustrated this with the arcane and somehow extreme world of ATC, Anderson and Sharrock then seek to show how similar investigations could look at Internet-enabled activities. They propose that, for ordinary life, trust is always a given, a starting point, or at least it is in the general – that is, only in specific aspects does doubt in trust get acted on. It does so in relation to "this concern" or "that," but not in some absolute sense. In this view, the idea that trust is the basis of society is somewhat skewed because it implies that there could be a society without trust. In Anderson and Sharrock's view, it is hard to know what such a society would look like. Trust is simply not a feature that some societies have and others don't. It is intrinsic to social action. It is both the starting point and a feature of how people act together, in concert, everywhere, all the time. This is suggestive also of how it is that there is no way that trust can be "designed" in totality; aspects might be, but they are highlighted and framed by those aspects that are given.

This has important consequences for design: it is suggestive that one needs to instruct users of systems to treat some aspect of a system as untrustworthy. That aspect needs drawing out, but it can only be done by assuming other aspects – other things that need to be trusted. There can be no situation in which everything is untrusted, Anderson and Sharrock imply. Given this, considerable design care will be required when the contexts to be designed for consist of vast and complex weaves of technology and social practice. It will take great care to address one issue of trust (or its lack) without unsettling the whole apple basket; it might also be easy to make too many properties of a system problematic, too many aspects worth distrust whereas others have to be taken for granted, invisible in their reliability.

Rod Watson, in Chapter 8, offers further insights on the social production of trust and how it might have been the neglected basis of studies of distrust. Like Anderson and Sharrock, he argues that trust between people is not to be thought of as a theoretically deducible cornerstone of human action. Such "constructivist" accounts certainly have their value in sociology, but they should not be thought of as sociological mirrors of, let us say, theories in physics. They allow one to reflect on sociological topics; they are not partial theories that will eventually produce a complete model of society. That view of sociology – loosely speaking a positivistic one – is no longer held by sociologists. A whole range of alternatives are now abided by: sociology is critical discourse, for example, an attempt to bring out the hidden into the public gaze. The most elaborate attempt to build a positivistic model was perhaps in the work of Talcott Parsons. All the more interesting to see then that his work is mentioned in contemporary computer science discussions of trust: in Clark Thomberson's work for example (2010). The difficulty is that the value sociologists might find in Parson's – as a case in point – might not resonate with what Thomberson is after: sociologists might find nuance when considering social role, he is after a perfect definition of social trust. Attempts to integrate social theory with other disciplines is likely to be even more risky. The nuance might get lost: this is certainly seems the case with Piotr Cofta's *The Trustworthy and Trusted Web*. He argues that disciplinary differences exist but need to be done away with. The topic of "[t]echnology and its trustworthiness is structured along scientific disciplines. . . . Trustworthiness is defined in terms of their own body of knowledge" (2011: 13). There is a need to move beyond a situation in which a trustworthy Web can be ensured. The trouble, in my opinion, is that the result of these integrations can lead to the anodyne. They don't have to, of course, but as I said in the introduction to this book, the very fact that there are numerous ways of treating trust demands that care be shown in understanding the purposes of different treatments. Their value might be lost if they are merged with other views, their value being in the uniqueness – the kind of unusual lines of sight they offer. To repeat, Talcott Parson's view offers a nuance for sociology, but it is not at all clear in my mind that he does the same for computer science.

Watson's argument is that trust is a managed product or constituent of social action, mediated by digital technologies or otherwise. Moreover, action itself is constituted around various contextual specificities that mean it is not sensible to propose treating trust as an extensible phenomena. It is unwise (or at least risky) to assume that the mechanisms of trust production on some context – face to face, say – can be modeled and usefully imposed in other settings: in Internet-mediated interaction, as a case in point. Aspects of those settings might have their resonances in these two distinct contexts, but there will be important differences too. Unlike the more philosophically inclined approaches that like to treat trust abstractly, Watson argues that pertinent evidence can be found through the adroit use of ethnographic and "naturalistic" data-gathering approaches. He illustrates the constitutive mechanisms of trust production with transcripts of police interaction, for example, but he shows how these mechanisms will be necessarily different in other contexts. His insights build heavily on the work of the late Harold Garfinkel (1963b), whose own investigations into trust in the late 1950s and 1960s demonstrated how trust is brought to bear in everyday interaction, in what might be called a praxiological fashion. In this view, an ethnomethodological view, trust is a *doing* rather than a fixed point (Garfinkel: 1967). In this view, trust is a concern of people, bound up with their practical everyday concerns. Trust is thus a much more mundane constituent of social action than is conveyed, in say, Barbara Mitzal's *Trust in Modern Society* (1996) where it is the theoretically definable bedrock that allows action even in ways that is opaque to actors in society. It is also dissimilar to Guido

Möllering's account in *Trust: Reason, Routine, Reflexivity* (2006) in which trust is something that is jumped at and held to with a religious-like passion. In Watson's view, trust is a prosaic product of everyday life – a manufactured feature, a routinely achieved outcome.

Recognition that trust is constitutive of social action allows one to see that when trust appears to breakdown, the breakdown is something to be solved, to be worked at and dealt with by those involved. This is a theme that Lagerspetz picks up on and, like him, Watson notes that dealing with such breakdowns is done in ordinary ways as an ordinary matter, as a matter of practical affairs; it is almost an uninteresting concern for people. Trust, in this light, is not best explained by the kind of dramatic metaphors Möllering conjures, for example ones taken, albeit indirectly, from the great theorist of comparative religion, Rudolf Otto. Möllering transmorphs his idea of the ontological leap. Nor does this line of argument suggest that trust ought to have the theoretical status that is often offered in current accounts. Trust is an issue, indeed an important one, but Watson wants us to recognize that in being a "members" problem, it is a particular kind of phenomena, not one appropriately addressed from constructionist paradigms in sociology, philosophy, or psychology, nor in computer science and its subdomain, HCI. By "constructionist," one means views that are built by the analyst or commentator, external to the event and hence divorced from the doings of those in the event. By the same argument, those views which seek to offer essentialist explanations – that trust is a derivation of a preference for altruistic punishment, for example, as argued by Dominique de Quervain and colleagues (2004) and elaborated by Joseph Henrich and his colleagues (2004) – are similarly misleading, taking attention away from the "work of trust" as it is constituted in vivo. In these ways, Watson offers a very robust alternative to the rational action models tacit in much of the literature on trust, such as in the work of Henrich and his colleagues and in many of the papers in Gambetta's 1990 oft-cited collection, *Trust: Making and Breaking Co-operative Relations*.

Trust and the Self

Watson's and the immediately prior chapters emphasize how use of the concept of trust can be very particular and local, bound with understandings that are resolutely about the circumstances at hand, computer mediated or otherwise. That it is such also allows questions to emerge that have not been raised in the prior discussions. The production of trust in face-to-face interaction, its constitution in action, may also pertain to ways in which the character of those involved is delineated, for example. Character is thus used as a resource for action. Beyond rather bland implications – that someone is bad or they are good, trustworthy or not – character is not something that has been remarked on a great deal in the prior chapters. Indeed, one might say that it is not really discussed a great deal in this area at all: perhaps it is too inchoate a term for the likes of Cofta, Thomberson, and others. Nevertheless one needs to be clear: the topic of character here is not the one delineated in masterpieces of literature like Austin's *Pride and Prejudice*. It is not the hubris and haughtiness of a character that is at issue; it is how character is formed through structural patternings of various kinds. These may be socio-structural – one thinks of C. Wright Mill's *White Collar* for example (1952); or, as in the case that Charles Ess puts forward, related to the patternings of what one might call a philosophical psychology. In this view, derived in large part from the philosophy of Kant, Løgstrup, and various other theorists of what Ess calls "Internet Studies," a person seeks to attain virtue (a Socratic goal) through demonstrating their own trustability. To undertake this, they engage in a dialogue with representations of themselves and of their actions. If identity is a produced phenomenon, dialogically constructed through meaningful acts and individual reflections on them, he proposes changes in the nature of identity are likely be brought about when the things interacted with or the mechanisms of interaction with people are altered. By this logic, the use of social networking and associated reputation systems will be one source; the broader panoply of digitally mediated affairs another. These are not just affecting what is culturally defined as the person, Ess explains; they are not just frames of reference for judging others. They are also confronting people with a different sense of what it means to be themselves. As they seek to attain virtue through praxis, so they have to deal with the possibility that these dialogues are with virtual, disembodied entities, some of which are essentially computational – agents of a kind, but hardly human. What it means to be, then, is altering – shifting its auspices, giving the performance of identity and the production of character uniquely twentieth-century, Internet-enabled forms. This claim echoes the arguments to be found in Hassan Masum & Mark Tovey's *The Reputation Society* (2011), as well as in Kenneth Gergen's *Relational Being* (2009).

Ess argues that this has consequences on what trust means. The "who" being trusted is of another order than used to be the case. Today, for example, with the widespread use of social networking systems and such, people are judged through their relational status. They are also judged – or come to judge themselves – in new ways through the articulating or mirroring of themselves in digital acts of all kinds, not just through social media, although these might be the most important "sources of self." One thinks of how people might judge themselves when confronted with their digital trails, as manifested in the diagram in Figure 9. Will they seek to adjust where they go on the Web as a result, or will they confront the realization that they are, say, more addicted to hanging out on Google Scholar than they are prepared to admit. Ess argues that people seek virtue, and adjust their selves on the basis of their reflected actions, but these selves are far from perfect – that is the reason they seek virtue.

Ess suggests that there is something surprising afoot when this seeking, this dialogic behavior, occurs, because the technological mediation of identity and trust is unfolding in distinct ways in different cultures despite the fact that the mediation of the self is being affected by similar systems (particularly social networking systems). This is because of the existence of broader frameworks of identity and self-characterization, which are unfolding in different cultures divergently. This is of course at a very high level, but Ess suggests that, in the Far East (China, for example), there is a move toward the romantic notion of identity – one we think of as having its roots in eighteenth-century Europe – where people are more individually accountable, unique, and burdened with existential responsibilities. Meanwhile, in Western Europe and North America, there is a move toward relational identities, ones that are bound up with the social nexus of which one is a part and which is manifest and fed through one's digital world. Irrespective of the degree of this change, a more important point is that people are confronting these trajectories, altering their actions accordingly, choosing to make of themselves something different, something "better" – so Ess believes. Or rather, in his peroration, he says we need to have faith that people will in fact choose a better way. Given the fear that David Clark pointed out in Chapter 2 (a fear that might lead us to become overly rigid in our prescriptions for human conduct and, similarly, overly rigid in what we come to allow technology to do), Ess's faith is not failsafe. We might find we make the wrong choices, our fear leading us there.

Trust in Design and Engineering

If Ess's chapter had delineated what trust is as a produced phenomenon, and sketched how self-hood is constructed and portrayed, then the chapters in the next section, *Trust in Design*, commence with the problem of turning such concerns into practical specifications. Over the years, HCI specialists have put a great deal of effort into ensuring that systems are designed to deliver "trust." When interactive systems first became commonplace, the kinds of questions that were investigated with this in mind had to do with such things as system response times (if a computer took too long to react to a command, a user would come to doubt the functioning of the computer). Gradually, however, HCI became more interested in trust at a higher level, or rather with those specific systems that are defined as somehow part of a trusted system – basically e-commerce. In this view, the topic of trust has to do with whether, as a case in point, the data users enter into an e-commerce system will be held securely or whether the service in question makes the kind of security it affords (or relies on) visible to users in ways that garners the right reaction from users – one that leads them to willingly share confidential information, for example. In these respects, the inscrutability that Simpson says is a feature of many computer systems needs to be undone: things need to be brought to the fore. The question is how to do this appropriately, intelligently.

In Chapter 10, Angela Sasse and Iacovos Kirlappos approach the problem of designing trust – or rather doing the HCI of trust – historically and quite specifically. If prior chapters seek to convey the landscape in which people interact, a landscape that involves computers in various ways and which entails trust in various forms, then their concern is from within the world of trusted systems, settings in which users approach their use of systems aware that what they are about to do entails some kind of reasoned acts of trust. These systems are designed; they are made in certain ways and not others. *How* is the question, Sasse and Kirlappos explain.

Before reporting on why not (and how), it should be clear that the topic of Sasse and Kirlappos are those places that Lagerspetz would say are approached with the agency of the word "trust" in mind. For Sasse and Kilappos, they are technology-mediated interactions (TMIs), whereas Lagerspetz's view characterizes by a particular set of orientations and expectations. And, as Simpson notes, one of the forms of these expectations is in terms of a rational determination of what can be relied on and what cannot. Participants in the world of Sasse and Kirlappos (or members to put in the parlance of Watson) focus on calculations of trust. These are signaled and measured, acted on as if mechanical: first *this* and then *that* as some mediated conduct unfolds. It is that world in which trust is at once the thing sought for and the thing to be tested; it is a world that is not like the normal world by dint of it being a special place where trust matters. But, and unlike Lagerspetz and Simpson, and Watson and others in the prior section, Sasse and Kirlappos are very much interested in the engineering, in the fabrication of these systems. Their emphasis is on building systems with both the user's activities and the technologist's activities in mind. A contrast here can be made between this balance of focus and that which can be found in the perspective from security and privacy technologies, articulated in the account offered by George Danezis, where the concerns are about engineering first and foremost – although always alloyed with a sensitivity for human mischief.

Sasse and Kirlappos explain that, even though this is a special world, it does not mean that it is unique, or that it can be designed for without regard to the rest of the world. That is part of the problem of HCI researchers: how do they design for the calculation in question, for the domains in question, the TMIs? Sasse and Kirlappos look over the past few years of research and explain how HCI researchers have sought to offer systematicity in the area of e-commerce but have not always shown the élan they might, nor – for that matter – a sufficiently comprehensive approach. Their efforts have often led HCI to cherry pick arguments from philosophy, sociology, and psychology, adapting them to be practical but sometimes oversimplifying them in the process. Too often HCI researchers take only part of the insights from other disciplines as their starting place and miss important considerations. At the same time, they have often ignored the fundamentals – that is, the technology. The key to the success of trustworthy systems is not simply understanding the signals and cues people use to orient themselves, but building the technology from the outset with issues of trust at its heart. All too often, Sasse and Kirlappos explain, trust has been seen as merely a matter of interfaces. HCI researchers need to work *with* technology developers to create trustworthy systems.

But beyond this, and disregarding their ability to work with technologists or to judiciously borrow insights from the social sciences, if nothing else, HCI researchers should not forget that systems that deliver and demonstrate trust are inevitably systems that will come to be the source of untrustworthy behavior, because the trust that people put in them will act like a magnet for those who want to exploit it. In Sasse and Kirlappos's view, if a perfectly trustable system is built, the fact that it is seen as perfect will lead users to be overly reliant on it. With time, criminals will come up with ways of causing mischief – like Danezis, they do not think any system is inviolate in perpetuity. Trust and distrust are mutual, in other words, one allowing the other in an endless dance.

HCI specialists like Sasse and her colleagues tend to offer specifications for design and may not do the "design" themselves, perhaps relying instead on others to provide the substance of that. Richard Banks, meanwhile, takes on that very role. In Chapter 11, Banks offers a view on trust from the designer's perspective. Part of his topic has to do with how the digital things with which people engage have altered, especially as social networking services have emerged. For example, whereas once designers needed to explore how to enable users to engage with a limited set of digital file types (more or less all of which were stored on PCs), designers now need to consider how to configure digital materials that are shared, posted, annotated, and stored in a plethora of Internet services and devices. When users are trusting in the digital materials, the mechanisms of that engagement, the way they interact with their digital stuff, is then quite diverse. Yet users want the same kind of simplicity and clarity of purpose that created delight when PCs first entered the workplace and home twenty years ago. Moreover, as people have embedded computing in ever greater aspects of their lives, so the domain of digital design has needed to broaden. People now want to review and honor their digital pasts in ways that can hardly be treated as simply a question of preservation. Sentiment and value are now as much a part of what they trust in as the ability of the hardware to survive system upgrades. Banks reflects on what trust means when digital form and content is now so heterogeneous.

Unfortunately, this description of the design problem hides equally important concerns. For one thing, the digital objects that designers produce are output through layers of abstraction and hidden engineering; however tidy the designs might appear, there is a great deal underneath them that might come to haunt the designer later on. File abstractions might appear to be unified across platforms, for example, with a file on a PC appearing the same as a file on a cloud service; but they are often not. When actions are done on the file, the consequences of these actions might be different in these different contexts (see Thereska & Harper 2012). Just as this is a problem for the designer, it is all the more so for the user who might be enticed by the tidiness of a design into thinking that everything "under the hood" is tidy.

The basic problem, as Banks puts it, is one of illusion. The right illusion needs to be created. But this hides a further problem: designers themselves can be fooled by their own illusion, the one produced both in their design process and by the end design. They understand what the illusion is meant to allow the user to do, what rules of use it embeds, for example; but they often fail to see how people who are unfamiliar with those rules might approach them – that is, they might not even grasp the illusion let alone understand the details of how to work within it. The move from Windows, Icon, Mouse, Pointer (W.I.M.P.) based systems to gesture-based ones illustrates just this problem: designers are sometimes so familiar with their gesture design that they cannot recall or even imagine how someone might approach those designs from scratch; and the result sometimes is gesture systems that are, well, difficult.

The power of metaphor adds to the difficulties. To date, the desktop has provided the primary set of metaphors and similes for user experience. But these have become so saturated in everyday uses of PCs that users and designers alike often slip into thinking that the file directory is how the PC itself stores and arranges its data. As mentioned previously, this is true only in part. But in any case, the rendering of digital objects as files, as documents in folders, has resulted in users coming to think of these files as "real things," as objects that have a place, that need to be secure, that need to be kept, and so on. It is the rendering that affords the illusion of being real in these respects – and all that follows on from that – that people want to take to the Cloud. But when people go to the Cloud, the world they find makes these illusions opaque, difficult to follow or see. A digital photo on a PC is viewed as a single item; on a Web service, on Flickr say, as part of a set. But more than this, a picture on a PC also has various metadata associated with it, such as size, date created, name affiliated, and other details. When the picture is moved to the Web, some of these associated properties go with it, some don't; and in addition, new properties are added by the web service, by Flickr say, and even by the user when making the posting. And this metadata seems to get more salience in the ways that the thing, the picture, gets rendered. What was once presented as an illusion of oneness, of singularity, now gets presented as an illusion of connection. Banks argues that not only is this creating a problem for designers; that is to say, making how they design illusions around this transformation difficult. "Placeness" had a singularity with the PC, for example, and this was evidently related to the "thingyness" of the file. But what about on the Web? What kind of place is that? How does one design for that? Does one need to design for that? Is that aspect of the illusion worth dropping?

Much of this might seem distant from issues of trust and, certainly, these are not topics raised by the earlier chapters. But it should be clear that the nature of the "stuff" that people use to mediate themselves, to create records of their lives and to share with others in the digital world, must be important. The form of this stuff might be illusory, but the form has power nonetheless – power that leads them to act in certain ways. Some of these ways are expressly to do with articulations of trust. On Flickr, pictures can be posted that are appended with the Creative Commons license. But pictures that are labeled private can also be posted, and so cannot be used according to the creative license standards. But this kind of information is now always presented in the same way in all the places that photos might be stored on the Web. There is no universal logic to how this should be made visible. Additionally, some of the things that one might say have to do with trust spill out in orthogonal ways to this last issue. I might assume that a picture is an entity of sorts, and it is something that I can keep – leaving aside all the ways that its thingyness might alter when I put it in different contexts. But what is the *thing* that is dealt with when we are talking about music? Is the thing the music itself or the capacity to listen to it? What is it that is owned when you join *Spotify*? More generally, when I own any kind of digitally mediated music, what is being trusted in if questions of trust come into play? What is my capacity to give that music to someone? What is my ability to look after it? What illusions do I need to be convinced of and why?

Banks ends by noting that the more profound issue has to do with engaging with these diverse digital resources, navigating these different digital places, and wanting to preserve a sense of oneself throughout. Banks is begging questions not of whether one can trust the services, but whether people can own and take care of what is theirs. They are losing touch with what they thought was their responsibility. The Cloud is making an illusion of their powers to trust themselves. Banks's chapter brings us back to the second of Clark's concerns. Banks expresses a worry that so much discussion about trust on the Web might put people off going to the Web. The problem is that they might begin to worry they would meet an evil stranger, some unnamed soul who will steal their money and/or their identity. In Bank's analysis, we find that part of the source of the fear might be related to the users themselves. And here it is not because they might misunderstand cues about trusted domains and identification of the correspondent on some e-commerce site, it is because users feel ill at ease, unsure what are the places they are navigating on the Web or what is the nature of the digital materials they handle when there.

Chapter 12, the last empirical chapter, addresses precisely this issue. It treats the topic from an anthropological perspective. If Bank's reports the dilemmas that face designers and how they sometimes spill out in the hallucination of design, Richard Harper and Will Odom report studies of all sorts of people (but none of which are designers or technologists) trying to engage with their digital stuff. Harper and Odom commence their chapter by showing that one should not ask whether users will be able to trust cloud services. Instead, they suggest, one should ask what motivates users to worry about trust in the first place. What leads them to the Cloud?

In ways that resonate with Watson's chapter, Harper and Odom begin their inquiries by asking what it is people think they are about when they handle digital content. What are the rules of thumb and maxims of conduct that guide people? The authors show, using ethnographic reportage, that it is doubt that users have in themselves that leads them there. Such doubts are not new, however; they are not uniquely to do with the emergence of the Internet (Banks's claims about the muddied illusions to be found there notwithstanding). Harper and Odom argue that, in the 1990s, prepaid mobile phones took off in Europe because consumers felt that only with this form of contract could they manage their own profligate use. They chose prepaid phones to better manage themselves, in other words. It is a similar lack of trust in their own abilities that is leading people to turn, for example, to cloud-based storage today. An important distinction that needs to be born in mind, of course, is that, at the current time, it is in their ability to curate their stuff that causes them doubt and hence leads them to the Cloud; with regard to phones, it was users' ability to keep their wallet closed that caused worry – hardly the same thing at all. The authors go on to show, however, that when users turn to the Cloud, they start developing new doubts about their existential relationship to digital content. This resonates very strongly with what Banks argued. Harper and Odom approach this concern by addressing how the relationship people have with digital material is not best encapsulated by the "primitives" that J.J. Gibson labeled affordances (1979), but by social and moral categories through which people scaffold their relationship with stuff – whether it be real or digital. In this light, the distinction between trust and distrust seems too crude and all-encompassing to capture the essential characteristic of every-day reasoning. Like Lagerspetz, Harper and Odom look at how categories like trust come into play in action rather than in how categories externally defined can be used to explain or describe action. What they show is how complex as well as situated is "practical reasoning," and as they do so, they remark on the limited utility of approaches to trust that seek to define trust in some idealized form – without reference to the real world. The work of Taddeo is referred to on this issue (2010, 2011), seeking as it does to offer a logical model of trusted action that Taddeo thinks can be used to measure or characterize trust in vivo. The anthropological evidence suggests that these models are not reductions of everyday practical reasoning so much as they are massively dissimilar. More-over, the actual nature of practical reasoning is enormously more complex and situated than is allowed in Taddeo's thinking, suggesting that it might not be helpful to even imagine that reductive forms of this thinking can be produced. The standard notion of reductionism that applies in many natural sciences might create havoc with the evidence if used to render everyday, practical action. The utility of such approaches is therefore not to be found in any claim they make about essences and primary motivations and certainly not in terms of the ade-quacy of their descriptions of human affairs. Their empirical adequacy is in doubt. If this is so for Taddeo's philosophy then it is all the more applicable for the kinds of arguments put forward by behavioral economists: Harper and Odom point toward Fehr's research reported in papers like *The Economics and Biology of Trust* (2009). According to this view, human action is like a logical machine, although constrained by unarticulated motivations, such as a prefer-ence for altruistic punishment (see Quervain et al. 2004). Their merits, if they have any, are to be found in their conversion to pragmatic tools for such things as design in HCI – as illustrated in the work of Sasse and Kirlappos. Here the "mechanics of trust" is a good formulation of the calculative mode of reasoning deployed in real contexts of commerce and can help clarify and guide design choices.

Harper and Odom report on some of the messy – but all too consequential – facticities of the socio-digital world in which people engage and the consequences of this on the orders of reason that are found. They report, for example, on how people, when interacting on and through Facebook, come to worry about what is "theirs" and what is "another's." They report too what happens when people want to forget and "move on" from some event or association; how they reason through and practically achieve this end. One of the ways they do so is by "letting go" of objects of various kinds. But people find it curiously difficult to let digital objects "die," to abandon them especially when those objects have been "released to" the Web where questions of ownership and possession are simply difficult to manage or ascertain. They worry too about how questions of possession and connection are tacitly manifest when they engage with others on the Web. Thus, when they turn to the Cloud under the pretext that this might be a domain for storage, they are soon disabused of the hope that this will make their life easier. Questions of trust come to the fore, although these have less to do with, say, financial matters, fraud, or identity theft as they do with the sense of self and its manifestation in digital things exchanged with others. The question of trust has to do with knowing what is at hand, what can be done, what are the frameworks of choice available. To put it in Sasse and Kirlappos's terms, the mechanics of trust is not functioning; it is not machine like. It is too much of a fog. Harper and Odom end their argument by suggesting that this fog – these tangles in choices and actions and capacities – are now part of what it means to "dwell" in circumstances that merge and combine the digital and the real. This form of engagement cannot be treated as one having singular and constrained form: trusted or not trusted, say. People worry about some aspects of their digitally mediated life while taking others for granted; they assume that life can be trusted in some respects and needs to be fretted about in others. Trust matters in the dwelling of twenty-first-century life as it has always done in any place of dwelling, in various ways, in ways that are brought to bear by considerations that include using the concept of trust to formulate orientations that enable the user to act in practical, commonsense ways.

Conclusion

So what have we learned about how we approach these narratives through the compass of this book? Should we review both this book and the ever-growing literature on the topic at hand with a view to make ourselves content, satisfied that all that can be said has been, that any worries we might have are or will be assuaged? When would we know when all has been said that can be said?

It should be clear now that the topic of this book is not one of those that can swiftly be put to bed. I hope the chapters show that it is better thought of as a topic that can be approached through dialog and the dialog is not of the form where it can reach closure. The topic is better thought of as one that continues rather than ends. Indeed, it is better this way because I believe it can maintain vitality in the subject. If it were to come to an end, people might think trust is settled, designed, built in. It is precisely then that they need to start worrying, as Sasse and Kirlappos explain. For it is then that trust can be broken because it is assumed in a fashion that it can be taken for granted.

Of course, just as there needs to be an ongoing dialog, this should not result in a crowding out of other topics and concerns. As Anderson and Sharrock note, dialogs about trust are more often about situations of distrust, and the focus on these leads to neglect of what happens when trust can be relied on. As we try to develop dialogs about trust and its cognates, we should be aware of how easily we limit our purview. Not only do we neglect what action is possible when trust can be assumed, but we might mischaracterize that action in our desire to talk about distrust. Our fear of distrust might also make us rush to premature fixes, as Clark warns in Chapter 2.

Useful continuations of dialog depend on insightful reflections on the shifting of technological infrastructures, the moving and evolution of regulatory and institutional practice, as well as the observation on the changing patterns of human conduct. As Ess notes, how we "do" being human is altering in the digital age, albeit that these changes are massively incremental and only steps away from prior forms. Although we think of the Internet as revolutionary, the changes it is bringing about in human aspiration, in the seeking for virtue, is only an extension of what has been sought before. We evolve slowly.

That I say we should think of the combined topic of trust, computing, and society in dialogical terms does not guarantee that what is said will therefore always be interesting or helpful. Many accounts on this topic verge on the anodyne, in my opinion: and one of the reasons for this is that they seek to be too integrative, seeking to create palimpsests on trust. As should be clear, the views that pertain can be so diverse that it would make no sense to try and merge them all. This doesn't mean that all views should be treated equally. Some offer more traction than others. Ess's arguments about how people seek virtue sounds laudable, but evokes education and intellectual refinement; it's about how we think about ourselves as reasoning creatures. Affecting that, how we think, is, I would suggest, a long-term goal, one that leads away from, let us say, the interface to Web systems and to education, school life as well as home life. Bank's argument about designing virtual representations points toward very real, immediately tractable acts – that is, ways of representing more effectively the stuff that people traffic on the Web (their pictures, postings, files, and so on). These two arguments might be extreme but both have the virtue of pointing to more – to various ways of thinking and reflecting – and greater dialogue. But some views seem to me to offer dead ends: perspectives that don't elicit new insights but seem to close down further comment or greater perspicuity. I think much of the rational actor models implicit in behavioral economics are of this order, as is much of the philosophy that coasts on the coat tails of those arguments. I read Henrich and colleagues' *Foundations of Human Sociality* (2004), for example, and wonder whether they are at all familiar with the claims that anthropologists have made about the purpose of ethnography being to capture the meanings people give to the ways they live and the tools they use. A failure to place that as central to ethnography and to offer instead views that strip bear the essential richness of these meaning systems seems to fly in the face of the ethnographic enterprise. Henrich and his colleagues seem entirely unaware of, for example, Clifford Geertz's *The Interpretation of Cultures* (1973) or his lament on his battle with structuralism of "all kinds" in *After the Fact* (1995). Behavioral economics seems to fit into that category of structuralism in seeming ill-disposed to studies of sense and meaning. If Geertz was writing some time ago, many of the chapters in this book have sought to describe and elicit what "reasoning in action" is, and how this entails the "production of meaning." Metaphysical categories are required in air traffic control, we found, just as the loss of meaning is problematic for user's engagement with cloud-based services. Therefore, a failure to show concern with meaning making in these respects makes conversations with and about the behavioral economists' claims difficult. Is their neglect purposeful, saying something about what they think valuable? Certainly, their preferential use of arguments and evidence from experimental psychology suggests that they think there are differences in status that should be given to different ways of arguing about the topic at hand. But the criteria they use implicitly in this – that one is "science" of some kind and the other is, well, "Other" – is not conducive to dialogue. It verges on the ad hominem. One is reminded of the great American sociologist R.K. Merton's study of *Insiders and Outsiders* (1972) in which he showed that some approaches to argument in the world of science don't entail exchange; they produce closure. This doesn't mean that rational action models cannot be useful. This approach can be enormously so when it comes to design, for example, when the purposes are pragmatic. One need only to look at Angela Sasse's work. But when it comes to ensuring the vitality of the dialogues about a subject, I am less hopeful.

Clearly, this book cannot claim to represent all the kinds of dialogues one would want to have. Furthermore, it would seem to fly in the face of the implications of the need for dialogue to claim to have captured them all. Instead, and as I said at the outset, the purpose of the book is to foster a sensibility for good dialogue, for creative exchanges. One should not forget Clark's fear: that we might talk ourselves into frigidity if we don't show the right attitude. To conclude the problem, take as an example that Larry Lessig's explores in his book *Remix* (2008). There he showed how a rush to deal with issues of piracy from a standard legal perspective might stifle the very creativity that should be the purpose of legal protection in the first place. Lessig reports on how digital technologies allow people to mix and remix sound (and video) in ways that has made many people criminals when all they were doing was what comes naturally – being creative, entertaining, and imaginative with music. He asks whether we want the legal system to constrain that creativity or to enable it. Of course, care has to be taken to ensure that livelihoods are protected and that music made is paid for, but the processes for ensuring that should not terminate the desire to make music into new forms. Lessig's book is a call to arms for reimagining what creativity is, before there is a rush to impose legal frameworks on it. It is similar in discussions of trust, computing, and society. A tenor is required that is open and creative, provocative and broadening; we should not rush to solutions. Indeed, we should not be led to think that any solution will ever be more than a temporary holding point for some issues. Above all, we need to take care not to frighten ourselves. John Naughton is illustrative here. In his *Gutenburg to Zuckerberg* (2012), Naughton explains that much of the debate about trust and the Internet implies that the Internet itself has become an agent of social dissolution. It would become this, he says, if we were to allow our fear to overwhelm us – that is, if we let use of the word *trust* drive us into panic. In his dialogue with us, he offers the claim that this fretting and commotion about trust is merely a narrative of our age. This is a narrative that will come to be seen as little more than an expression of a temporary fear, an incapacitating – albeit short-lived – doubt brought on by excitement and novelty, the shock of a world made anew with the technology of computers and their networks. The chapters in this book have explored what a more calm, reflective, less worrisome narrative might look like. Here the goal has been to document the technological auspices that might give credit to new questions about how we "dialogue with machines" and how, with diligence and care, we might disambiguate the rhetoric from the facts, the evidence from the fear, and the cajoling from the wise on this very issue.

References

Acton, H.B. (1974) *The Idea of a Spiritual Power*. London: Athlone Press.

Akerlof, G.A. (1970) "The Market for 'Lemons': Quality Uncertainty and the Market Mechanism," *The Quarterly Journal of Economics*, Vol. 84, Issue 3: 488–500.

Al-Ani, B., Trainer, E., and Redmiles, D. (2012) *Trust and Surprise in Distributed Teams. ICIC'12 International Conference on Intercultural Collaboration*, March 21–23, 2012, Bengaluru, India: 97–106.

Anderson, B. (1983) *Imagined Communities*. London: Verso.

Anderson, C. (2006) *The Long Tail: Why the Future of Business is Selling Less of More*. New York: Hyperion.

Anderson, R. (2009) *Security Engineering*. 2nd ed. Indianapolis, IN: Wiley Publishing.

Anderson, R., Hughes, J. and Sharrock, W. (1987) "The Division of Labour." In Conein, B., De Fornel, M., Quere, L. (eds.) *Les Formes de la Conversation*. Paris: CNET, 237–252.

Anderson, R. and Moore, T. (2006) "The Economics of Information Security," *Science* 314.5799: 610–613.

Anderson, R. and Sharrock, W. (1993) "Can Organisations Afford Knowledge?" *Journal of Computer Supported Collaborative Work*, Vol. 1, No. 1: 145–161.

Axelrod, R. (1980) "More Effective Choice in the Prisoner's Dilemma." *Journal of Conflict Resolution*, 24(3), 379–403.

Axelrod, R. (1984) *The Evolution of Cooperation*. New York: Basic Books.

Ba, S., Whinston, A.B., and Zhang, H. (2003) "Building Trust in Online Auction Markets through an Economic Incentive Mechanism." *Decision Support Systems*, 35(3), 273–286.

Bacharach, M. and Gambetta, D. (2001) "Trust in Signs." *Trust in Society*, 2: 148–184.

Bäcke, M. (2011) "Make-Believe and Make-Belief in Second Life Role-Playing Communities." *Convergence: The International Journal of Research into New Media Technologies*, 18(1): 85–92. DOI: 10.1177/1354856511419917.

Bacon, F. (2000) [1620] *The New Organon*. Jardine, L. and Silverthorne, M. (eds.). Cambridge: Cambridge University Press.

Baier, A. (1986) "Trust and Antitrust," *Ethics*, 96: 231–260.

Baier, A. (1994) *Moral Prejudices: Essays on Ethics*. Cambridge, MA: Harvard University Press.

Bakardjieva, M. (2005) *Internet Society: The internet in Everyday Life*. London: Sage.

Bakardjieva, M. (2009) "Subactivism: Lifeworld and Politics in the Age of the Internet," *The Information Society*, 25: 91–104.

Bakos, Y. and Dellarocas, C. (2002) "Cooperation without enforcement? A comparative analysis of litigation and online reputation as quality assurance mechanisms". *Proceedings of the 23rd International Conference on Information Systems* (127–142). Barcelona, Spain.

Baldamus, W. (1957) "The Relationship between Wage and Effort," *The Journal of Industrial Economics*, Vol. 5, No. 3: 192–201.

Ball, R. and Naylor, M. (2005) *Form Follows Idea*. London: Black Dog Publishing.

Ballani, H. Costa, P. Karagiannis, T. and Rowstron, A. (2011) "The Price Is Right: Towards Location-Independent Costs in Datacenters", *Proceedings of the 10th ACM Workshop on Hot Topics in Networks* (HotNets-X).

Baron, N. (2008) *Always On: Language in an Online and Mobile World*. Oxford: Oxford University Press.

Baym, N. (2011) "Social Networks 2.0." In Consalvo, M. and Ess, C. (eds.) *The Blackwell Handbook of Internet Studies*. Oxford: Wiley-Blackwell, 384–405.

BBC (2006) "Online video eroding TV viewing", "http://news.bbc.co.uk/2/hi/ entertainment/6168950.stm.

Beautement, A. Sasse, A., and Wonham, M. (2008) "The Compliance Budget". *Proceedings of the NSPW '08*. March 22–29, Olympic Valley, California.

Beck, U. (1992) *The Risk Society*. New York: Sage.

Bell, D. (1996) "The Bell-Lapadula Model," *Journal of Computer Security*, 4.2: 3.

Benhabib, S. (1986) *Critique, Norm, and Utopia: A Study of the Foundations of Critical Theory*. New York: Columbia University Press.

Bittner, E. (1965) "The Concept of 'Organisation,'" *Social Research*, Vol. 32, No. 3: 239–255.

Bittner, E. (1967) "The Police on Skid Row: Study of Peacekeeping," *American Sociological Review*, Vol. 32, No. 5: 699–715.

Bloom, J.A., Cox, I.J., Kalker, T. Linnartz, J. Miller, M. and Traw, C. (1999) "Copy Protection for DVD Video", *Proceedings of the IEEE* 87.7: 1267–1276.

Bockover, M.I. (2010) "Confucianism and Ethics in the Western Philosophical Tradition I: Foundational Concepts," *Philosophy Compass*, 5(4), 307–316.

Bowlby, J. (1969) *Attachment and Loss, Vol. I: Attachment*. New York: Basic Books.

boyd, D.M., Ellison, N.B. (2007) "Social network sites: Definition, history, and scholarship", *Journal of Computer-Mediated Communication*, 13(1), article 11.

Bromseth, J. and Sundén, J. (2011) "Queering Internet Studies: Intersections of Gender and Sexuality." In Consalvo, M. and Ess, C. (eds.) *The Blackwell Handbook of Internet Studies*. Oxford: Wiley-Blackwell, 270–299.

Brooks, F.P. (1987) "No Silver Bullet: Essence and Accidents of Software Engineering," *IEEE Computer*, Vol. 20, No. 4 (April): 10–19.

Brown, B. Green, N. and Harper, R. (eds.) (2001) *Wireless World: Interdisciplinary Perspectives on the Mobile Age*. Hiedleberg and Godalming, UK: Springer Verlag.

Burke, K. (1954) *Permance and Change: An Anatomy of Purpose* (3rd edition), Berkely and Los Angeles: University of California Press.

Bury, S. Ishmael, J. Race, N. and Smith, P. (2010) "Designing for Interaction with Mundane Technologies," *Personal Ubiquitous Computing*, Vol. 14: 227–236.

Bush, V. (1945) "As We May Think." *Atlantic Monthly*. Available at http://www. theatlantic.com/magazine/archive/1945/07/as-we-may-think/303881/.

Button, G. (1991) *Ethnomethodology and the Human Sciences*. Cambridge: Cambridge University Press.

Button, G. (ed.) (1993) *Technology in Working Order*. London: Routledge.

Butkiewicz, M., Madhyastha, H.V. and Sekar, V. (2011) "Understanding website complexity: measurements, metrics, and implications". In *Proceedings of the 2011 ACM SIGCOMM conference on Internet measurement conference* (IMC '11).

Cachin, C. and Schunter, M. (2011) "A Cloud You Can Trust." *IEEE Spectrum, Vol. 48, Issue 12, pp. 28–51*. At: <http://spectrum.ieee.org/computing/networks/a-cloud-you-can-trust>, accessed December 3, 2012.

Cairncross, F. (1997) *The Death of Distance*. Boston, MA: Harvard Business School Press.

Carr, N. (2009) *The Big Switch: Rewiring the World, from Edison to Google*. London and New York: W.W. Norton and Co.

Carr, N. (2010) *The Shallows: What the Internet Is Doing to Our Brains*. London and New York: W.W. Norton.

Castells, M. (2002) *The Internet Galaxy*. Oxford: Oxford University Press.

Castells, M. (2009) *Communication Power*. Oxford: Oxford University Press.

Carusi, A. (2008) "Scientific visualisations and aesthetic grounds for trust." *Ethics and Information Technology*, 10, 243–254.

Carusi, Annamaria. (2011) "Trust in the Virtual/Physical Interworld". In C. Ess and M. Thorseth (eds.), *Trust and Virtual Worlds: Contemporary Perspectives, 103–119*. Oxford: Peter Lang.

Cavalier, R. (ed). (2005) *The Impact of the Internet on Our Moral Lives*. Albany, NY. SUNY Press.

Cerf, V. (2010) "Trust and the Internet," *IEEE Internet Computing*, September/October: Vol. 14, no 5: 95–96.

Chen, T.M. Abu-Nimeh, S. (2011) "Lessons from Stuxnet," *IEEE Computer*, 44(4): 91–93.

Cheshire, C. (2011) "Online Trust, Trustworthiness, or Assurance?" *Daedalus*, 140(4): 49–58.

Churchland, P. (1084) *Matter and Consciousness*. Cambridge, MA: MIT Press.

Churchland, P.S. (1989) *Neurophilosophy: Toward a Unified Science of the Mind/Body*. Cambridge, MA: MIT Press.

Cicourel, A. (1968) *The Social Organisation of Juvenile Justice*. London: Heinemann.

Cicourel, A.V. (1972) "Basic and Normative Rules in the Negotiation of Status and Role." In Sudnow, D. (ed.) *Studies in Social Interaction*. New York: The Free Press, 229–258.

CISCO (2012) *Cisco Visual Networking Index: Forecast and Methodology*, 2011–2016, May, CISCO.

Clark, A. and Chalmers, D. (1998) "The extended mind," *Analysis*, 58, no 1: 7–19.

Clark, D., Wroclawski, J. Sollins, K.R. and Braden, R. (2005) "Tussle in cyberspace: defining tomorrow's Internet." *ACM Transactions on Networking*, Vol. 13, Issue 3: 462–475. ACM.

Clarke, K., Hardstone, G., Rouncefield, M., and Sommerville, I. (eds.) (2006) *Trust in Technology: A Socio-Technical Perspective*. London: Springer.

Coady, C.A.J. (1992) *Testimony: A Philosophical Study*. New York: Oxford University Press.

Cofta, P. (2001) *The Trustworthy and Trusted Web*. Delft, Netherlands: Now Publishers.

Coker, G., Guttman, J.D., Loscocco, P., Herzog, A.L., Millen, J., O'Hanlon, B., Ramsdell, J.D., Segall, A., Sheehy, J. and Sniffen, B.T. (2011) "Principles of remote attestation," *International Journal of Information Security*, 10.2: 63–81.

Coleman, J. (1990) *Foundations of Social Theory*. Cambridge, MA: Belknap Press.

Columbus, L. (2013) "Why Cloud Computing Is Slowly Winning The Trust War", *Forbes* (March), http://www.forbes.com/sites/louiscolumbus/2013/03/12/why-cloud-computing-is-slowly-winning-the-trust-war/

Cook, K. and Gerbasi, A. (2011) "Trust." In Hedstrom, P. and Bearman, P. (eds.) *The Oxford Handbook of Analytic Sociology*. Oxford: Oxford University Press, 218–244.

Cornes, R. and Sandler, T. (1996) *The Theory of Externalities, Public Goods, and Club Goods*. Cambridge: Cambridge University Press.

Corritore, C., Marble, R., Widenbeck, S., Kracher, B., and Chandran, A. (2005) "Measuring Online Trust of Websites: Credibility, Perceived Ease of Use, and Risk". *AMCIS 2005 Proceedings*. Aug. 11–14th. Paper 370. Available at: <http://aisel.aisnet.org/amcis2005/370/>.

Corritore, C.L., Kracher, B., and Wiedenbeck, S. (2003) "On-line Trust: Concepts, Evolving Themes, a Model," *International Journal of Human-Computer Studies*, 58(6): 737–758.

Coulter, J. and Sharrock, W. (2007) *Brain, Mind, and Human Behaviour in Contemporary Cognitive Science: Critical assessments of the philosophy of Psychology*. Lampeter, UK: Edwin Mullen Press.

Craig, E. (1990) *Knowledge and the State of Nature*. Oxford: Clarendon Press.

Davenport, T.H. and Patil, D.J. (2012) "Data Scientist: The Sexiest Job of the 21st Century," *Harvard Business Review*, October.

Dasgupta, P. (1990) "Trust as a Commodity." In Gambetta, D. (ed.) *Trust: Making and Breaking Cooperative Relations*. Oxford: Blackwell, 49–72.

Davidow, W. (2011) *Overconnected: What the Digital Economy Says about Us*. London: Headline Publishing.

De Certeau, M. (1984) *The Practice of Everyday Life*. Berkeley: University of California Press.

Defoe, D. (1719) *The Life and Adventures of Robinson Crusoe*. References from 1965, Angus Ross (ed.) London: Penguin.

Deleuze, G. (1990) *The Logic of Sense*. London: Continuum Press.

de Quervain, D., Fischbacher, U., Treyer, V., Schellhammer, M., Schnyder, U., Buck, A. & Fehr, E. (2004) "The Neural Basis of Altruistic Punishment," *Science*, 305(5688), 1254–8.

Deutsch, M. (1958) "Trust and Suspicion," *Journal of Conflict Resolution*, 2: 265–279.

Dhamija, R. and Tygar, J.D. (2005) "The Battle against Phishing: Dynamic Security Skins." *ACM International Conference Proceeding Series*, Vol. 93: 77–88.

Dhamija, R., Tygar, J.D., and Hearst, M. (2006) "Why Phishing Works." *Proceedings of the SIGCHI Conference on Human Factors in Computing Systems, April 22–27, Montreal*, 581–590. ACM; doi>10.1145/1124772.1124861.

Dibbell, J. (1993) "A Rape in Cyberspace." (Originally published in *The Village Voice*, December 21, 1993: 36–42) <http://www.juliandibbell.com/articles/a-rape-in-cyberspace/>, accessed March 9, 2013.

Diffie, W. and Hellman, M. (1976) "New Directions in Cryptography," *Information Theory, IEEE Transactions*, 22.6: 644–654.

Donath, J. and Boyd, D. (2004) "Public Displays of Connection," *BT Technology Journal*, 22(4), 71–82.

Durkheim, E. (1897) *On Suicide*. London: Classics Penguin.

Durkheim, E. (1933) *The Division of Labour in Society*. New York: Free Press.

eBay (2012) "High Positive Feedback but Still a SCAM: eBay Guides." http://reviews.ebay.co.uk/High-Positive-Feedback-But-Still-a-SCAM?ugid=10000000000933090.

Egger, F.N. (2001) "Affective Design of e-Commerce User Interfaces: How to Maximise Perceived Trustworthiness," in Helender, M. Khalid, H. and Tham, M. (Eds) *Procedures of the International Conference of Affective Human Factors Design*, June 27–29, London: Asean Academic Press, 317–324.

Eisenstein, E. (2005) *The Printing Revolution in Early Modern Europe*. Cambridge: Cambridge University Press.

Ellison, C. and Schneier, B. (2000) "Ten risks of PKI: What you're not being told about public key infrastructure," *Computer Security Journal*, 16.1: 1–7.

Emory, F. and Trist, E. (1972) *Toward a Social Ecology*. London: Plenum Press.

Engelbart, D. (1962) *Augmenting Human Intellect: A Conceptual Framework*. Stanford, CA: Stanford Research Institute.

Erikson, E.H. (1977) *Childhood and Society*. London: Paladin Books.

Ess, C. (2010) "Trust and New Communications Technologies," *Knowledge, Technology and Policy*, Vol. 23: 287–305.

Ess, C. (2010a) "The Embodied Self in a Digital Age: Possibilities, Risks, and Prospects for a Pluralistic (Democratic/Liberal) Future?" *Nordicom Information*, 32(2), June: 105–118; <http://www.nordicom.gu.se/?portal=publ&main=info_publ2.php&ex=320>.

Ess, C. (2010b) "Trust and New Communication Technologies: Vicious Circles, Virtuous Circles, Possible Futures," *Knowledge, Technology, and Policy*, 23: 287–305; DOI 10.1007/s12130-010-9114-8.

Ess, C. (2012) "At the Intersections between Internet Studies and Philosophy: 'Who Am I Online?' (Introduction to Special Issue)," *Philosophy & Technology*, Vol. 25, Iss. 3 (September): 275–284; DOI 10.1007/s13347-012-0085-4.

Ess, C. (2013a) *Digital Media Ethics* (2nd ed). Cambridge: Polity Press.

Ess, C. (2013b) "The Onlife Manifesto: Philosophical Backgrounds, and the Futures of Democracy Media Usages and Equaylit," <https://ec.europa.eu/digital-agenda/en/charles-ess-0>

Ess, C. and Thorseth, M. (eds.) (2011) *Trust and Virtual Worlds*. New York: Peter Lang.

Faisal, M. and Alsumait, A. (2011) "Social Network Privacy and Trust Concerns," *iiWAS2011*, (*The 13th International Conference on Information Integration and Web-based Applications and Services*) December 5–7, 2011, Ho Chi Minh City, Vietnam, 416–419.

Fehr, E. (2009) "The Economics and Biology of Trust," *Journal of the European Economic Association*, April/May, 7(2–3): 235–266.

Flechais, I., Riegelsberger, J. and Sasse, M.A. (2005) "Divide and Conquer: The Role of Trust and Assurance in the Design of Secure Socio-Technical Systems," *Proceedings of the 2005 Workshop on New Security Paradigms*, 33–41; ACM.

Floridi, L. (ed.) (2010) *The Cambridge Handbook of Information and Computer Ethics*. Cambridge: Cambridge University Press.

Floridi, L. (2011) "The Construction of Personal Identities Online," *Minds & Machines*, 21: 477–479. DOI 10.1007/s11023-011-9254-y.

Floridi, L. (2012) "Distributed Morality in an Information Society," *Science and Engineering Ethics*, Sept, Vol. 19, Issue 3, 727–743. DOI 10.1007/s11948-012-9413-4.

Floridi, L. (forthcoming) *The Fourth Revolution – The Impact of Information and Communication Technologies on Our Lives*. Oxford: Oxford University Press.

Fogel, J. and Nehmad, E. (2009) "Internet Social Network Communities," *Computers in Human Behaviour*, Vol. 25: Issue 1, January, 153–160.

Fogg, B.J. (April 2003) "Prominence-Interpretation Theory: Explaining How People Assess Credibility Online," *CHI'03 Extended Abstracts on Human Factors in Computing Systems*, 722–723; ACM.

Fox-IT (August 2012) "Black Tulip: Report of the Investigation into the DigiNotar Certificate Authority Breach," http://www.securityweek.com/downloads/reports/DigitNotar-BlackTulip-Final-Report.pdf.

Friedell, E. (1960) *Kulturgeschichte der Neuzeit*. München: C.H. Beck.

Fukuyama, F. (1995) *Trust: The Social Virtue and the Creation of Prosperity*. New York: Free Press.

Gal, S. (2002) "A Semiotics of the Public/Private Distinction," *Differences: A Journal of Feminist Cultural Studies*, 13(2002): 77–95.

Gambetta, D. (ed.). (1988) *Trust: Making and Breaking Co-operative Relations*. Oxford: Basil Blackwell.

Gambetta, D. (1990) "Can We Trust Trust?." In Gambetta, D. (ed.) *Trust: Making and Breaking Cooperative Relations*. Oxford: Blackwell, 213–245.

Garfinkel, H. (1956) "Conditions of Successful Degradation Ceremonies," *American Journal of Sociology*, Vol. 61, No. 2: 420–424.

Garfinkel, H. (1963a) "Parsons' Solution to the Problem of Social Order as a Method for making Everyday Activities Observable 'From the Point of View of the Action,'" Unpublished manuscript.

Garfinkel, H. (1963b) "A Conception of, and Experiments With, 'Trust' as a Condition of Stable Concerted Actions," in O.J. Harvey (ed.) *Motivation and Social Interaction*. New York: The Ronald Press, 187–238.

Garfinkel, H. (1967) *Studies in Ethnomethodology*. Englewood Cliffs, NJ: Prentice Hall.

Garfinkel, H. (2002) *Ethnomethodology's Program*. Lanham: Rowman and Littlefield.

Geertz, C. (1973) *The Interpretation of Cultures*. New York: Basic Books.

Geertz, C. (1995) *After the Fact: Two Countries, Four Decades, One Anthropologist*. Cambridge, MA: Harvard University Press.

Gergen, K. (2009) *Relational Being*. Oxford: Oxford University Press.

Gettier, E. (1963) "Is Justified True Belief Knowledge?" *Analysis*, 23: 121–123.

Gibson, J.J. (1979) *The Ecological Approach to Visual Perception*. New York: Houghton Mifflin.

Gibson, W. (1984) *Neuromancer*. New York: Ace Books.

Giddens, A. (1990) *The Consequences of Modernity*. Stanford, CA: Stanford University Press.

Gilligan, C. (1982) *In a Different Voice: Psychological Theory and Women's Development*. Cambridge, MA: Harvard University Press.

Gligor, V. and Wing, J. (2011) "Towards a Theory of Trust in Networks of Humans and Computers", *19th International Workshop on Security Protocols, LNCS*, March, 28–30, Berlin.

Goethe, J.W. von (1925) *Aus meinem Leben. Dichtung und Wahrheit*. Goethes Sämtliche Werke, Band III, Leipzig: Insel-Verlag.

Goffman, E. (1959) *The Presentation of Self in Everyday Life*. Garden City, New York: Doubleday.

Goffman, E. (1962) *Asylums*. New York: Doubleday Anchor Books.

Golić, J.D. (1997) "Cryptanalysis of Alleged A5 Stream Cipher." *Advances in Cryptology – EUROCRYPT'97*. Berlin Heidelberg: Springer.

Gomer, R., Rodrigues, E.M., Milic-Frayling, N. and Schraefel, M.C. (2013) "Network Analysis of Third Party Tracking: User Exposure to Tracking Cookies through Search". In the *Proc. of 2013 IEEE/WIC/ACM Int. Conf. on Web Intelligence (WI) and Intelligent Agent Technology (IAT)*, (WI-IAT'13), Atlanta, GA, USA, Nov. 17–20.

Good, D. (1990) "Individuals, Interpersonal Relations, and Trust". In Gambetta, D. (ed.) *Trust: Making and Breaking Cooperative Relations*. Oxford: Blackwell, 31–48.

Goodwin, C. (1981) *Conversational Organization: Interaction between Speakers and Hearers*. New York: Academic Press.

Google (2005) "Search Gets Personal," At <http://googleblog.blogspot.com/2005/06/search-gets-personal.html>, retrieved March 23, 2012.

Google (2012) "Basics: Search History Personalization," At <http://www.google.com/support/accounts/bin/answer.py?answer=54041>, retrieved March 23, 2012.

Google (2009) "Personalized Search for Everyone," At <http://googleblog.blogspot.com/2009/12/personalized-search-for-everyone.html>, retrieved March 23, 2012.

Govier, T. (1993) "An Epistemology of Trust," *International Journal of Moral and Social Studies* 8: 155–174.

Govier, T. (1997) *Social Trust and Human Communities*. Montreal: McGill-Queen's University Press.

Grabner-Kräuter, S. and Kaluscha, E.A. (2003) "Empirical Research in On-line Trust: A Review and Critical Assessment," *International Journal of Human-Computer Studies*, 58(6): 783–812.

Grant, R.G. (1993) "The Politics of Equilibrium," *Inquiry* 35: 423–446.

Gray, M. (2009) *Out in the Country: Youth, Media, and Queer Visibility in Rural America*. New York: NYU Press.

Green, N. Harper R., Murtagh, G., and Cooper, G. (2001) "Configuring the Mobile User: Sociological and Industry Models of the Consumer," *Journal of Personal and Ubiquitous Computing*, Vol. 5 Issue 2, July 147–156.

Gutmann, P. (2013) *Security Usability*. A draft manuscript, Retrieved from: http://www.cs.auckland.ac.nz/~pgut001/pubs/usability.pdf.

Hallam, R.S. (2009) *Virtual Selves, Real Persons: a Dialogue across Disciplines*. Cambridge: Cambridge University Press.

Hamilton, J. (2010) "Cloud Computing Economies of Scale," *MIX2010* presentation, http://channel9.msdn.com/Events/MIX/MIX10/EX01.

Hamilton, J. (2012) "I Love Solar Power But..." (March); http://perspectives.mvdirona.com/2012/03/17/ILoveSolarPowerBut.aspx.

Hamilton, J. (2013) "Customer Trust," (January), http://perspectives.mvdirona.com/2013/01/15/CustomerTrust.aspx.

Han, S., Jung, J. Wetherall, D. (2012) "A Study of Third-Party Tracking by Mobile Apps in the Wild," *Technical Report*, UW-CSE-12-03-01, March.

Handy, C. (1995) "Trust and the Virtual Organization," *Harvard Business Review*, 73(3): 40–50.

Handley, M. (2006) "Why The Internet Only Just Works" *BT Technology Journal*, Vol. 24, No 3, July.

Hardin, R. (2002) *Trust and Trustworthiness*. New York: Russell Sage Foundation.

Hardy, G.H. and Snow, C.P. (1967) *A Mathematician's Apology*. Cambridge: Cambridge University Press.

Harper, R. (2005) "The Moral Order of Text: Explorations in the Social Performance of SMS." In Hoflich, J. and Gebhart, J. (eds) *Mobile Communication–Perspectives and Current Research Fields*. Berlin: Peter Lang GmbH–Europäischer Verlag der Wissenschaften, 99–222.

Harper, R. (2010) *Texture: Human Expression in the Age of Communications Overload*. Cambridge, MA: The MIT Press.

Harper, R., Evergeti, V., Hamill, L., and Shatwell, B. (2003) "The Social Organisation of Communication in the Home of the 21st Century: An analysis of the Future of Paper-Mail and Implications for the Design of Electronic Alternatives," *The Journal of Cognition, Technology and Work*, 5: 5–22.

Harper, R. and Hamill, L. (2005) "Kids will be Kids: the Role of Mobiles in Teenage Life." In Hamill, L. and Lasen, A. (eds.) *Mobile World Past, Present and Future*, Springer-Verlag: Godalming, UK, 61–73.

Harper, R. and Hughes, J. (1993) "What a F*****g System!" In Button, G. (ed) *Technology in Working Order*. London: Routledge, 127–144.

Harrison, S. and Dourish, P. (1996) "Re-Place-ing Space: The Roles of Place and Space in Collaborative Systems." *Proceedings of CSCW'96*. New York: ACM Press.

Harvey, O.J. (1963) (ed) *Motivation and Social Interaction*. New York: The Ronald Press.

Harvey, N., Harries, C., and Fischer, I. (2000) "Using Advice and Assessing its Quality," *Organizational Behaviour and Human Decision Processes*, 81(2): 252–273.

Hayes, B. (2008) "Cloud Computing," *Communications of the ACM*, 51(7): 9–11.

Hendrik, S. and Mochalski, K. (2009) "Internet Study" 2008/2009. IPOQUE Report 37: 351–362.

Henrich, J., Boyd, R., Bowles, S., Camerer, C., Fehr, E., and Gintis, H. (2004) *Foundations of Human Sociality: Economic Experiments and Ethnographic Evidence from Fifteen Small Scale Societies*. Oxford: Oxford University Press.

Henrich, J., Boyd, R., Bowles, S., Camerer, C., Fehr, E., Gintis, H., and McElreath, R. (2013) "In Search of Homo Economicus: Behavioural Experiments in 15 Small-Scale Societies," *The American Economic Review*, Vol. 91, No. 2: 73–78.

Heritage, J. (1978) "Aspects of the Flexibilities of Natural Language Use: A Reply to Phillips," *Sociology*, Vol. 12, No. 1 (January): 79–104.

Herley, C. (2009) "So Long, and No Thanks for the Externalities: The Rational Rejection of Security Advice by Users," *Proceedings of the 2009 workshop on new security paradigms workshop*, 133–144; ACM.

Herley, C. (2012) "Why do Nigerian Scammers Say They are from Nigeria?" *Proceedings of the Workshop on the Economics of Information Security*, June 25–26,

Berlin. Herley, C. (2013) "When Does Targeting Make Sense for an Attacker?" *IEEE Security & Privacy*, 11(2): 89–92.

Hertzberg, L. (1988) "On the Attitude of Trust," *Inquiry* 31, 307–322. Reprinted in Hertzberg, L. (1994) "The Limits of Experience," *Acta Philosophica Fennica*, Vol. 56, 113–130.

Hobbes, T. (1985 [1651]) *Leviathan*. London: Penguin.

Hollis, M. (1998) *Trust within Reason*. Cambridge: Cambridge University Press.

Holm, J. (1988) *Pidgins and Creoles: Vol. 1, Theory and Structure*. Cambridge: Cambridge University Press.

Holton, R. (1994) "Deciding to Trust, Coming to Believe," *Australasian Journal of Philosophy* 72: 63–76.

Hongladarom, S. (2007) "Analysis and Justification of Privacy from a Buddhist Perspective." In Hongladarom, S. and Charles Ess (eds.) *Information Technology Ethics: Cultural Perspectives*. Hershey, PA: Idea Group Reference, 108–22.

Horn, D.B., Olson, J.S., Karasik, L. (2002) "The Effects of Spatial and Temporal Video Distortion on Lie Detection Performance." In *CHI2002 Extended abstracts*. ACM Press, New York, NY, 716–718.

Hu, X., Lin, Z., and Zhang, H. (2003) "Myth or Reality: Effect of Trust-Promoting Seals in Electronic Markets," *Trust in the Network Economy*, Petrovic, O. Posch, R. and Marhold, F. (Eds), Springer, Berlin, 143–150.

Hughes, J., Shapiro, D., Sharrock, W. and Anderson, R. (1988) "The Automation of Air Traffic Control." *Final Report* SERC/ESRC Grant No. GR/D/86157. Swindon, UK: Economic and Social Sciences Research Council.

Hughes, J. and Sharrock, W. (2007) *Theory and Methods in Sociology*. Basingstoke: Plagrave.

Husserl, E. (1936) *The Cartesian Meditations*. The Hague: Martinus Nijhoff.

Idhe, D. (2009) *Postphenomenology and Technoscience*. New York: SUNY Press.

Ingold, T. (2011) *Being Alive: Essays on Movement, Knowledge and Description*. Abingdon, UK: Routledge.

Innis, H. (1951) *The Bias of Communication*. Toronto: University of Toronto Press.

Innis, H. (1972) *Empire and Communications*. Toronto: University of Toronto Press.

Jackson, F. (1998) *From Metaphysics to Ethics: A Defence of Conceptual Analysis*. Oxford: Clarendon Press.

Jackson, F. (2005) "Ramsey Sentences and Avoiding the Sui Generis." In Lillehammer and Mellor (eds), *Ramsey's Legacy*, Oxford: Oxford University Press, 122–136.

Jackson, J. (2001) *Truth, Trust, and Medicine*. London: Routledge.

Jarvenpaa, S., Tractinsky, N., and Vitale, M. (2000) "Consumer Trust in an Internet Store," *Information Technology and Management* 1(1–2) 45–71.

Jeanneney, J. (2007) *Google and the Myth of Universal Knowledge: A View from Europe*. Trans. Fagan, T.L. Chicago and London: The University of Chicago Press.

Jenson, C.S., Sarkarm C.J., Poots, C. (2007) "Tracking Website Data-Collection and Privacy Practices with the iWatch Web Crawler," *Proceedings of the 3rd Symposium on Usable Privacy and Security, SOUPS'07*, New York, ACM: 29–40.

Jones, K. (1996) "Trust as an Affective Attitude," *Ethics* 107, 4–25.

Johnson, S. (2012) *Future Perfect: The Case For Progress In A Networked Age*. New York: Riverhead Books.

Kahn, D. (1996) *The Codebreakers: The Comprehensive History of Secret Communication from Ancient Times to the Internet*. London: Scribner.

Kahnemann, D. (2011) *Thinking, Fast, Slow*. London: Allen Lane.

Kant, I. ([1785] 1959) *Foundations of the Metaphysics of Morals*. Trans. Beck, L.W. Indianapolis, IN: Bobbs-Merrill.

Kaplan, A. (1964) *The Conduct of Inquiry*. San Francisco, CA: The Chandler Publishing.

Karagiannis, T., Broido, A., Brownlee, N., Claffy, K.C., and Faloutsos, M. (2004) "Is P2P dying or just hiding?". In *Proceedings of the IEEE Global Telecommunications Conference (GLOBECOM)*.

Kendall, L. (2011) "Community and the Internet." In M. Consalvo and C. Ess (eds.) *The Blackwell Handbook of Internet Studies*. Oxford: Wiley-Blackwell, 310–325.

Kerckhoffs, A. (1883) "La Cryptographie Militaire," *Journal des Sciences Militaires*, Vol. IX, pp. 5–83.

Kerr, I. (2010) "The Devil is in the Defaults," *Ottawa Citizen*, May 29, 2010. Available at <http://iankerr.ca/wp-content/uploads/2011/08/The-devil-is-in-the-defaults.pdf>, retrieved March 23, 2012.

Kickstarter (2012) "Kickstarter Is Not a Store." http://www.kickstarter.com/blog/kickstarter-is-not-a-store. Accessed 18/12/2012.

Kim, D.J., Ferrin, D.L., and Rao, H.R. (2008) "A Trust-Based Consumer Decision-Making Model in Electronic Commerce: The Role of Trust, Perceived Risk, and Their Antecedents," *Decision Support Systems*, 44(2), 544–564.

Kimery, K.M. and McCard, M. (2002) "Third-Party Assurances: Mapping the Road to Trust in e-Retailing," *Journal of Information Technology Theory and Application*, Vol. 4 No. 2: 63–82.

Kirlappos, I., Sasse, M., and Harvey, N. (2012) "Why Trust Seals Don't Work: A Study of User Perceptions and Behaviour," *Trust and Trustworthy Computing*, 308–324.

Kirlappos, I. and Sasse, M.A. (2012) "Security Education against Phishing: A Modest Proposal for a Major Rethink," *Security & Privacy, IEEE* 10(2): 24–32.

Kitiyadisai, K. (2005) "Privacy Rights and Protection: Foreign Values in Modern Thai Context," *Ethics and Information Technology*, 7(1): 17–26.

Kohn, M. (2008) *Trust: Self-Interest and the Common Good*. Oxford: Oxford University Press.

Kondor, Z. (2009) "Communication and the Metaphysics of Practice: Sellarsian Ethics Revisited," in Nyírí, K. (ed.), *Engagement and Exposure: Mobile Communication and the Ethics of Social Networking*. Vienna: Passagen, 179–87.

Kramer, R. (1999) "Trust and Distrust in Organizations: Emerging Perspectives, Enduring Questions," *Annual Review of Psychology*, 50: 569–98.

KPCB (2012) *Internet Trends*: Kleiner Perkins Caufield & Byers.

Labovitz, C . Iekel-Johnson, S. McPherson, D., Oberheide, J. and Jahanian, F. (2010) "Internet inter-domain traffic". In *Proceedings of the ACM SIGCOMM 2010 conference* (SIGCOMM '10).

Lagerspetz, O. (1998) *Trust: The Tacit Demand*. Kluwer: Dordrecht.

Lagerspetz, O. and Hertzberg, L. (2013) "Wittgenstein on Trust." In Mäkelä, P. and Townley, C. (ed.) *Trust: Analytic and Applied Perspectives*. Amsterdam: Rodopi Press: 31–51.

Lahno, B. (2002) *Institutional Trust: A Less Demanding Form of Trust?* Caracas: Revista Latinoamericana de Estudios Avanzados (RELEA).

Lampson. B.W. (2004) "Computer Security in the Real World," *IEEE Computer* 37(6): 37–46.

Lange, P.G. (2007) "Publicly Private and Privately Public: Social Networking on YouTube," *Journal of Computer-Mediated Communication*, 13(1): 361–380. <http://jcmc.indiana.edu/vol13/issue1/lange.html>

Lankton, N. and McKnight, D. (2011) "What Does it Mean to Trust Facebook?" The *Database for Advances in Information Systems*, Vol. 42, No. 2: 32–54.

Lee, J. (2002) "Making Losers of Auction Winners," *New York Times*. http://www.nytimes.com/2002/03/07/technology/making-losers-of-auction-winners.html?pagewanted=all&src=pm.

Lee, M.K. and Turban, E. (2001) "A Trust Model for Consumer Internet Shopping," *International Journal of Electronic Commerce* 6, 75–92.

Lefebrve, H. (2004) *Rhythmanalysis: Space, Time and Everyday Life*. Trans. Elden, S. and Moore, G. London: Verso Books.

Leinwand, A. (2013) "Is it Too Easy for Your Cloud Provider to Snoop on Your Business?" *GIGAOM*, January 2013; http://gigaom.com/2013/01/20/is-it-too-easy-for-your-cloud-provider-to-snoop-on-your-business/.

Lessig, L. (2008) *Remix*. London: Penguin.

Lillehammer, H. and Mellor, D. (eds.) (2005) *Ramsey's Legacy*. Oxford: Clarendon Press.

Løgstrup, K.E. (1956) *Den Etiske Fordring [The Ethical Demand]*. Copenhagen: Gyldendal (Published in English as Løgstrup, K.E. (1971) *The Ethical Demand*, Philadelphia: Fortress Press.)

Lohr, S. (2012) "The Age of Big Data", *The New York Times*, February.

Lord, C., Ross, L., and Lepper, M. (1979) "Biased Assimilation and Attitude Polarization: The Effects of Prior Theories on Subsequently Considered Evidence," *Journal of Personality and Social Psychology* 37(11): 2098–2109.

Luhmann, N. (1990) "Familiarity, Confidence, Trust: Problems and Alternatives." In Gambetta, D. (ed.) *Trust: Making and Breaking Co-operative Relations*. Oxford: Basil Blackwell, 94–107.

Lyas, C. (1999) *Peter Winch*. London: Acumen Publishing.

MacDonald, R. (2012) "Can we Trust Cloud Computing, ISPs and Social Networks? Public Service Europe." At: <http://www.publicserviceeurope.com/article/1744/can-we-trust-cloud-computing-isps-and-social-networks>, accessed December 3, 2012.

Mackenzie, C. (2008) "Relational Autonomy, Normative Authority and Perfectionism," *Journal of Social Philosophy* 39(4, Winter): 512–533.

Martin, D. (1984) "Mother Wouldn't Like It!: Housework as Magic," in *Theory, Culture and Society*, Los Angeles: Sage, 19–37.

Massey, D. (2005) *For Space*. Los Angeles: Sage.

Masum, H. and Tovey, M. (2011) *The Reputation Society*. Boston, MA: MIT Press.

Mayer-Schönberger, V. and Cukier, K. (2013) *Big Data: A Revolution That Will Transform How We Live, Work and Think*. London: John Murray.

Mayer, J.R. and Mitchell, J.C. (2012) "Third-Party Web Tracking: Policy and Technology." *Proceedings of the 2012 IEEE Symposium on Security and Privacy*, 413–427.

Mayer, R., Davis, J., and Schoorman F.D. (1995) "An Integrative Model of Organizational Trust," *Academy of Management Review*, 20(3), 709–734.

McCarthy, T. (1978) *The Critical Theory of Jürgen Habermas*. Cambridge: Hutchinson Press.

McGinn, C. (2012) *Truth by Analysis: Games, Names, and Philosophy*. Oxford: Oxford University Press.

McKinsey Global Institute (June 2011) "Big data: The next frontier for innovation, competition, and productivity."

McLuhan, M. (1964) *Understanding Media: The Extensions of Man*. New York: McGraw-Hill.

McMyler, B. (2011) *Testimony, Trust, and Authority*. Oxford: Oxford University Press.

Mead, G.H. ([1934] 1967) *Mind, Self & Society*. Chicago, IL: Chicago University Press.

Merton, R.K. (1972) "Insider and Outsiders: A Chapter in the Sociology of Knowledge," *American Journal of Sociology*, Vol. 78, No. 1 (July): 9–47.

Meyrowitz, J. (1985) *No Sense of Place*. Oxford: Oxford University Press.

Mikians, J., Gyarmati, L., Erramilli, V. and Laoutaris, N. (2012) "Detecting price and search discrimination on the Internet". In *Proceedings of the 11th ACM Workshop on Hot Topics in Networks* (HotNets-XI).

Milgram, S. (1963) "Behavioral Study of Obedience," *Journal of Abnormal and Social Psychology* 67(4): 371–8.

Mill, J.S. (1956 [1859]) *On Liberty*. Indianapolis: Bobbs-Merrill, Indianapolis.

Miller, D. (2009) *The Comfort of Things*. Cambridge: Polity Press.

Miller, R. (2009) "Inside Microsoft's Chicago Data Center", *Data Centre Knowledge*, http://www.datacenterknowledge.com/inside-microsofts-chicago-data-center/ Oct 1st.

Mills, C. Wright. (1952) *White Collar: The American Middle Classes*. Oxford: Oxford University Press.

Mitzal, B. (1996) *Trust in Modern Societies*. Cambridge: Polity Press.

Möllering, G. (2006) *Trust: Reason, Routine, Reflexivity*. Amsterdam: Elsevier.

Moore, G.E. (1903) *Principia Ethica*. Cambridge: Cambridge University Press.

Mundie, C., de Vries, P., Haynes, P., and Corwine, M. (2002) *Trustworthy Computing*, Microsoft White Paper, Redmond, Washington State: Microsoft Corp.

Mumford, E. (1996) *Effective Systems Design and Requirements Analysis*. London: MacMillan.

Myskja, B. (2008) "The Categorical Imperative and the Ethics of Trust," *Ethics and Information Technology*, 10: 213–220.

Myskja, B. (2011) "Trust, Lies, and Virtuality." In Ess, C. and Thorseth, M. (eds.) *Trust and Virtual Worlds: Contemporary Perspectives*. New York: Peter Lang, 120–136.

Naughton, J. (2012) *From Gutenburg to Zuckerberg*. London: Quercus.

Nickel, P. (2007) "Trust and Obligation-Ascription," *Ethical Theory and Moral Practice* 10: 309–19.

Nickel, P., Franssen, M., and Kroes, P. (2010) "Can We Make Sense of the Notion of Trustworthy Technology?" *Knowledge, Technology and Policy*, 23: 429–46.

Nickerson, R. (1998) "Confirmation Bias: A Ubiquitous Phenomenon in Many Guises," *Review of General Psychology*, 2(2): 175–220.

Nielsen, J., Molich, R., Snyder, S. and Farrell, C. (2000) *E-Commerce User Experience: Trust*. Fremont, CA: Nielsen Norman Group.

Nissenbaum, H. (2001) "Securing Trust Online: Wisdom or Oxymoron?" *Boston University Law Review*, 81: 101–31.

Nissenbaum, H. (2010) *Privacy in Context: Technology, Policy and Integrity in Everyday Life*. Stanford, CA: Stanford University Press.

Nissenbaum, H. (2011) "A Contextual Approach to Privacy On-line." In *Daedalus* (Fall): 32–48, Boston: MIT Press.

Odlyzko, A. (2010) "Providing Security with Insecure Systems." Proceedings of *WiSec'10* March 22–24, Hoboken, New Jersey.

Odom, W. Sellen, S. Harper, R. and Thereska, E. (2012) "Lost in Translation: Understanding the Possession of Digital Things in the Cloud." *Proceedings of the SIGCHI Conference on Human Factors in Computing Systems (CHI '12)*. New York, NY, USA, 781–790; ACM.

Odom, W., Zimmerman, J., and Forlizzi, J. (2011) "Teenagers and Their Virtual Possessions." *Proceedings of the SIGCHI Conference on Human Factors in Computing Systems (CHI '11)*. New York, NY, USA, 1491–1500; ACM.

Odom, W. Zimmerman, J., Forlizzi, J., Hugera, A., Marchitto, M., Canas, J., Nam, T., Lim, Y., Lee, M., Seok, J., Kim, D., Lee, Y., Row, Y., Sohn, B., and Moore, H. (2013) "Fragmentation and Transition: Understanding the Perception of Virtual Possessions among Young Adults in Spain, South Korea, and the United States." *Proceedings of SIGCHI Conference on Human Factors in Computing Systems (CHI '13)*. New York, NY, USA, 1833–1842; ACM.

Ong, W. (1988) *Orality and Literacy: The Technologizing of the Word*. Routledge: London.

O'Neill, O. (2002) "A Question of Trust." *Reith Lectures 2002*. BBC Radio4. http://www.bbc.co.uk/radio4/reith2002/lecture2.shtm, accessed August 18, 2012.

O'Neill, O. (2002b) *Autonomy and Trust in Bioethics*. Cambridge: Cambridge University Press.

O'Neill, O. (2012) "Kant and the Social Contract Tradition." In Ellis, E. (ed.) *Kant's Political Theory: Interpretations and Applications*. Philadelphia: Pennsylvania State University Press.

Oppy, G. and Dowe, D. (2011) "The Turing Test," Zalta, E. Z. (ed.), *The Stanford Encyclopedia of Philosophy* (Spring Edition), URL <http://plato.stanford.edu/archives/spr2011/entries/turing-test/>.

Origgi, G. (2008) *Qu'est-ce que la confiance?* Paris: Vrin.

Paasonen, S. (2010) "Labors of Love: Netporn, Web 2.0 and the Meanings of Amateurism," *New Media & Society*, 12(8): 1297–1312.

Palfrey, J. and Gasser, U. (2008) *Born Digital: Understanding the First Generation of Digital Natives*. New York: Basic Books.

Pariser, E. (2011) *The Filter Bubble: What the Internet is Hiding from You*. London: Penguin.

Pettit, P. 2004) "Trust, Reliance and the Internet," *Analyse & Kritik*, Vol. 26, 108–21.

Pettit, P. (2008) "Trust, Reliance and the Internet," *Information Technology and Moral Philosophy*. Eds. van den Hoven, J. and Veckert, J. London: Cambridge University Press.

Pfitzmann, B. and Waidner, M. (1992) "How to Break and Repair a 'Provably Secure' Untraceable Payment System." *Advances in Cryptology – CRYPTO'91*. Berlin Heidelberg: Springer.

Pieters, W. (2010) "Reve{a,i}ling the risks," *Techne*, Vol. 14, No. 3: 194–206.

Plato. (1991) *The Republic*. Trans Bloom, A. New York: Basic Books.

Pollner, M. (1979) "Explicative Transactions: Making and Managing Meaning in Traffic Court." In Psathas, G. (ed.) *Everyday Language: Studies in Ethnomethodology*. New York: Irvington, 227–256.

Popa, L., Kumar, G., Chowdhury, M., Krishnamurthy, A., Ratnasamy, S. and Stoica, I. (2012) "FairCloud: Sharing the Network In Cloud Computing." *Proceedings of the ACM SIGCOMM 2012 Conference on Applications, Technologies, Architectures, and Protocols for Computer Communication (SIGCOMM '12)* Finland, Aug. 13–17th.

Popa, L., Ghodsi, A. and Stoica, I. (2010) "HTTP as the narrow waist of the future internet". *Proceedings of the 9th ACM SIGCOMM Workshop on Hot Topics in Networks* (Hotnets-IX).

Postman, N. (1985) *Amusing Ourselves to Death: Public Discourse in the Age of Show Business*. New York: Penguin.

Psathas, G. and Waksler, F. (1973) "Essential Features of Face-to-Face Interaction." In Psathas, G. (ed.) *Phenomenological Sociology: Issues and Applications*. New York: Wiley–Interscience, 159–181.

Randall, D. (2003) "Inside the Smart Home: A Case Study," In Harper, R. (ed.) *Inside the Smart Home*. London: Springer, 227–246.

Rashid, F.Y. (2012) "Recent Bank Cyber Attacks Originated From Hacked Data Centers, Not Large Botnet," *Securityweek*, October, http://www.securityweek.com/recent-bank-cyber-attacks-originated-hacked-data-centers-not-large-botnet.

Raub, W. and Weesie, J. (2000a) *The Management of Durable Relations*. Amsterdam: Thela Thesis.

Raub, W. and Weesie, J. (2000b) "The Management of Matches: A Research Program on Solidarity in Durable Social Relations," *Netherland's Journal of Social Sciences* 36, 71–88.

Reason, J. (1986) "Recurring Errors in Process Environments: some implications for the design of intelligent support systems." *Proceedings of the NATO Advanced Study Institute on Intelligent Decision Support in Process Environments*. New York: Springer-Verlag, 255–270.

Richards, G. (2012) "Hamilton Makes Up With Button Over Twitter Row," *The Guardian* (October 20): 37.

Riegelsberger, J., Sasse, A., McCarthy, D. (2003) "Shiny Happy People Building Trust?" *Proceedings of ACM CHI 2005 New Horizons*, April 5–10, 2003, Ft. Lauderdale, Florida, USA, Vol. 5, No. 1: 121–128.

Riegelsberger, J. and Sasse, M.A. (2001) "Trustbuilders and Trustbusters: The Role of Trust Cues in Interfaces to e-Commerce Applications." In Schmid, B., Stanoevska-Slabeva, K., Tschammer, V. (eds.) *Towards the E-Society: E-commerce, E-Business and E-Government*. Norwell: Kluwer, 17–30.

Riegelsberger, J. and Sasse, M.A. (2003b) "Designing e-Commerce Applications for Consumer Trust." In Petrovic, O., Ksela, M., and Fallenboeck, M. (eds.) *Trust in the Network Economy*. Wien: Springer, 97–110.

Riegelsberger, J., Sasse, M.A., and McCarthy, J. D. (2003a) "The Researcher's Dilemma: Evaluating Trust in Computer-Mediated Communication," *International Journal of Human-Computer Studies* 58(6), 759–781.

Riegelsberger, J., Sasse, M.A., and McCarthy, J.D. (2005) "The Mechanics of Trust: A Framework for Research and Design," *International Journal of Human-Computer Studies* 62(3), 381–422.

Riepl, W. (1913) *Das Nachrichtenwesen des Altertums mit besonderer Rücksicht auf die Römer*. Leipzig: Teubner.

Rivest, R.L., Shamir, A., and Adleman, L. (1978) "A Method for Obtaining Digital Signatures and Public-Key Cryptosystems," *Communications of the ACM* 21.2: 120–126.

Rorty, R. (1979) *Philosophy and the Mirror of Nature*. New Jersey: Princeton University Press.

Rose, E. (1992) *The Werald*. Boulder, CO: The Waiting Room Press.

Anderson, R., and Moore, T. (2006) "The economics of information security." *Science* 314.5799: 610–613.

Rushkoff, D. (2010) *Program or be Programmed*. Berkeley, CA: Soft Skull Press.

Ryle, G. (1949) *The Concept of Mind*. London: Hutchinson.

Sacks, H. (1972) "On the Analysability of Stories by Children." In Gumperz, J.J. and Hymes, D. (eds.) *Directions in Sociolinguistics: The Ethnography of Communication*. New York: Holt, Rinehart and Winston, 325–345.

Salam, A., Iyer, L., Palvia, P., and Singh, R. (2005) "Trust in e-Commerce," *Communications of the ACM* 48: 73–77.

Saltzer, J., Reed, D., and Clark, D.D. (1984) "End-to-End Arguments in System Design," *ACM Transactions on Computer Systems*, Vol. 2, No. 4 (November): 277–288.

Sante, L. (1993) "Sophie Calle's Uncertainty Principle," *Parkett* Issue 36 (June), 74–85.

Sasse, M. and Kirlappos, I. (2011) "Familiarity Breeds Con-victims: Why We Need More Effective Trust Signalling," *Proceedings of Trust Management V*, 9–12. IFIP *Advances in Information and Communication Technology*, Springer: Boston.

Schatzki, T. (2010) *The Timespace of Human Activity*. Lanham, MD: Lexington Books.

Schechter, S.E., Dhamija, R., Ozment, A., and Fischer, I. (2007) "The Emperor's New Security Indicators". *Security and Privacy, 2007 (SP'07). IEEE Symposium*, Oakland, California, 51–65.

Schneier, B. (2012) *Liars and Outliers: Enabling the Trust That Society Needs to Thrive*. Indianapolis, IN: John Wiley & Sons.

Schutz, A. (1982) "On Multiple Realities." In *The Problem of Social Reality, Collected Papers, Vol. 1*. The Hague: Martinus Nijhoff, 340–345.

Schutz, A. and Luckmann, T. (1973) *The Structures of the Life World*. London: Heinemann.

Schulze, H. and Mochalski, K. (2009) "Internet Study 2008/2009." *IPOQUE Report* 37: 351–362.

Schwartz, H. and J. Jacobs (1979) *Qualitative Sociology: A Method to the Madness*. New York: The Free Press.

Seghi, A. (2012) "The UK's Online Obsession: The Latest Ofcom Figures for Media Consumption," *The Guardian Datablog*, December 13, 2012, http://www.guardian.co.uk/news/datablog/2012/dec/13/uk-online-obsession-ofcom-latest-figures.

Shannon, C. (1949) "Communication Theory of Secrecy Systems," *Bell System Technical Journal*, Vol. 28(4): 656–715.

Shieh, A., Kandula, S., Greenberg, A., Kim, C. and Saha, B. (2011) "Sharing the data center network". In *Proceedings of the 8th USENIX conference on Networked systems design and implementation* (NSDI'11). USENIX Association, Berkeley, CA, USA, 23–23.

Shneiderman, B. (2000) "Designing Trust into Online Experiences," *Communications of the ACM*, 43(12): 57–59.

Shope, R. (1983) *The Analysis of Knowing. A Decade of Research*. Princeton, NJ: Princeton University Press.

Shue, D., Freedman, M.J. and Shaikh, A. (2012) "Performance isolation and fairness for multi-tenant cloud storage". In *Proceedings of the 10th USENIX conference on Operating Systems Design and Implementation* (OSDI'12). USENIX Association, Berkeley, CA, USA, 349–362.

Siau, K. and Shen, Z. (2003) "Building Customer Trust in Mobile Commerce," *Communications of the ACM*, April 2003/Vol. 46, No. 4: 91–94.

Simmel, G. (1950) *The Sociology of Georg Simmel*. Trans. Wolff, K.H. New York: The Free Press.

Simmel, G. (1955) *Conflict and the Web of Group-Affiliations*. New York: The Free Press.

Simmel, G. (1978) *The Philosophy of Money*. London: Routledge.

Simpson, T. (2011a) "Robots, Trust and War," *Philosophy and Technology*, 24(3): 325–337.

Simpson, T. (2011b) "e-Trust and Reputation," *Ethics and Information Technology*, 13(1): 29–38.

Simpson, T. (2012a) "What is Trust?" *Pacific Philosophical Quarterly*, 93: 550–569.

Simpson, T. (2012b) "Evaluating Google as an Epistemic Tool," *Metaphilosophy*, 43(4): 426–445.

Smith, D.E. (1978) "K. is Mentally Ill: The Anatomy of a Factual Account," *Sociology*, 12:1, 23–45.

Smith, D.E. (1982) "The Active Text: Texts as Constituents of Social Relations." In Smith, D.E. (ed.) *Texts, Facts and Femininity*. Boston, MA: Northeastern University Press, 12–51.

Sommerville, I., Dewsbury, G. Clarke, K., and Rouncefield, M. (2006) "Dependability and Trust in Organizational and Domestic Computer Systems." In Clarke, K., G. Hardstone, M. Rouncefield and I. Sommerville (eds.) *Trust in Technology: A Socio-Technical Perspective*. Dordrecht: Springer, 169–94.

Spafford, E. (2009) "Cyber Security," *ISIPS 2008, LNCS 5661*, 20–33.

Stajano, F. and Wilson, P. (2011) "Understanding Scam Victims: Seven Principles for Systems Security," *Communications of the ACM*, 54(3), 70–75.

Strawson, P. (1974) "Freedom and Resentment." In Strawson, P. (ed.) *Freedom and Resentment and Other Essays*. London: Methuen, 1–25.

Strawson, P. (1992) *Analysis and Metaphysics: An Introduction to Philosophy*. Oxford: Oxford University Press.

Stuart, S. (2008) "From Agency to Apperception: Through Kinaesthesia to Cognition and Creation," *Ethics and Information Technology*, 10: 255–264.

Sullins, J. (2011) "The Next Steps in RoboEthics," Keynote Address. *International Association for Computing and Philosophy (IACAP) Conference*, July 3. Aarhus, Denmark.

Sztompka, P. (2003) *Trust: A Sociological Theory*. Cambridge: Cambridge University Press.

Taddeo, M. (2009) "Defining Trust and E-trust: From Old Theories to New Problems," *International Journal of Technology and Human Interaction*, 5: 23–35.

Taddeo, M. (2010) "Modelling Trust in Artificial Agents, A First Step Toward the Analysis of e-Trust," *Minds and Machines*, 20: 243–257.

Taddeo, M. (2011) "The Role of e-Trust in Distribute Artificial Systems." In Ess, C. and Thorseth, M. (eds.) *Trust and Virtual Worlds: Contemporary Perspectives*. New York: Peter Lang, 75–88.

Tan, Y.H. and Thoen, W. (2001) "Toward a Generic Model of Trust for Electronic Commerce," *International Journal of Electronic Commerce*, 5, 61–74.

Tapscott, D. and Willians, A.D. (2006) "Wikinomics: How Mass Collaboration Changes Everything", *Portfolio Trade*.

Taylor, C. (1989) *Sources of Self: the Making of the Modern Identity*. Cambridge: Cambridge University Press.

Thereska, E. and Harper, R. (2012) "Multi-structured Redundancy". *HotStorage'12: the 4th Workshop on Hot Topics in Storage and File Systems*, Usenix, Boston.

Thereska, T., Ballani, H., O'Shea, G., Karagiannis, T., Rowstron, A., Talpey, T., Black, R. and Zhu, T. (2013) "IOFlow: A Software-Defined Storage Architecture" in SOSP'13: *The 24th ACM Symposium on Operating Systems Principles*, ACM, November.

Thomas, W. and Thomas, J. (1928) *The Child in America*. New York: Knopf.

Thomborson, C. (2010) "Axiomatic and Behavioral Trust," in TRUST'10. *Proceedings of the 3rd International Conference on Trust and Trustworthy Computing*, Springer-Verlag: Berlin, Heidelberg, 352–366.

Thompson, K. (1984) "Reflections on Trusting Trust." *Communications of the ACM* 27(8): 761–763.

Thorn, C. and Dibbell, J. (eds.) (2012) *Violation. Rape in Gaming*. Create Space Independent Publishing Platform (October 17, 2012).

Travers, J. and Milgram, S. (1969) "An Experimental Study of the Small World Problem." *Sociometry*, Vol. 32, No. 4: 425–443.

Turilli, M., Vaccaro, A., and Mariarosaria, T. (eds.) (2010) "The Case of Online Trust," *Knowledge, Technology and Policy*, Vol. 23: 333–345.

Turing, A. (1950) "Computing Machinery and Intelligence". *Mind: A Quarterly Review of Psychology and Philosophy*, 59(236): 433–460. October.

Twyman, M., Harvey, N., and Harries, C. (2008) "Trust in Motives, Trust in Competence: Separate Factors Determining the Effectiveness of Risk Communication," *Judgment and Decision Making*, 3: 111–120.

U.S. Department of Defense (1983) "Trusted Computer System Evaluation Criteria" (*The Orange Book*). Available at: <http://csrc.nist.gov/publications/history/dod85.pdf>.

Vallor, S. (2010) "Social Networking Technology and the Virtues," *Ethics and Information Technology*, 12: 157–170. DOI 10.1007/s10676-009-9202-1.

Van Gelder, L. ([1985] 1991) "The Strange Case of the Electronic Lover." In Dunlop, C. and Kling, R. (eds.) *Computerization and Controversy*. San Diego, CA: Academic Press, 364–375.

Vaudenay, S. (2002) "Security Flaws Induced by CBC Padding – Applications to SSL, IPSEC, WTLS . . . " *Advances in Cryptology – EUROCRYPT 2002*. Berlin Heidelberg: Springer.

Wason, P. (1960) "On the Failure to Eliminate Hypotheses in a Conceptual Task," *Quarterly Journal of Experimental Psychology* 12(3): 129–140.

Watson, R. (2009) "Constitutive Practices and Garfinkel's Notion of Trust: Revisited," *Journal of Classical Sociology* 9:4 (November): 475–499.

Watson, R. and A.P. Carlin (2012) "'Information': Praxeological Considerations," *Human Studies*, Vol. 35: 327–345.

Watts, D. (2004) *Six Degrees: The Science of the Connected Age*. London: Random House.

Weckert, J. (2005) *On-line Trust*. In Cavalier R. (ed.) *The Impact of the Internet on Our Moral Lives*, Albany, NJ: Sunny Press, 95–117.

Weckert, J. (2011) "Trusting Software Agents." In Ess and Thorseth (eds.) 2011, 89–102.

Whitten, A. and Tygar, J.D. (1999) "Why Johnny can't encrypt: A usability evaluation of PGP 5.0". *Proceedings of the 8th USENIX Security Symposium*, Vol. 99. New York: McGraw-Hill.

Whitty, M.T. and Joinson, A.N. (2009) *Truth, Lies and Trust on the Internet*. New York: Routledge/Taylor & Francis Group.

Wieder, D.L. (1974) *Language and Social Reality*. The Hague: Mouton.

Wignall, A. (2012) "What it's like to work at . . . Brunel University?" *The Guardian*. http://www.guardian.co.uk/world/2004/oct/26/news.bruneluniversity. Accessed 18/12/2012.

Williams, B. (1990) "Formal Structures and Social Reality." In Gambetta, D. (ed.) *Trust: Making and Breaking Cooperative Relations*. Oxford: Blackwell, 3–13.

Williams, B. (2002) *Truth and Truthfulness: An Essay in Genealogy*. Princeton: Princeton University Press.

Williams, M.L. (circa 1972) "Seeing Through Appearances: Procedures for 'Discovering' Criminal Activity." Unpublished conference paper, Department of Sociology, University of California, Santa Barbara.

Williamson, T. (2000) *Knowledge and Its Limits*. Oxford: Oxford University Press.

Winch, P. (1958) *The Idea of a Social Science*. London: Routledge.

Wittgenstein, L. (1953) *Philosophical Investigations*. Trans. Anscombe, G.E.M. Oxford: Basil Blackwell.

Wong, P.H. (2012) *Net Recommendation: Prudential Appraisals of Digital Media and the Good Life*. PhD thesis. Enschede: University of Twente, Netherlands.

Wu, M., Miller, R.C., and Garfinkel, S.L. (2006) "Do security toolbars actually prevent phishing attacks?" In *CHI '06: Proceedings of the SIGCHI Conference on Human Factors in Computing Systems*, New York, NY, USA. ACM, 601–610.

Zhang, Y., Egelman, S., Cranor, L., and Hong, J. (2006a) "Phinding Phish: Evaluating Anti-Phishing Tools." *Proceedings of 14th Annual Network and Distributed System Security Symposium*, ISOC.

Zhang, Q., Markantonakis, K., and Mayes, K. (2006b) "A Mutual Authentication Enabled Fair-Exchange and Anonymous e-Payment Protocol," *E-Commerce Technology, 2006. The 8th IEEE International Conference on and Enterprise Computing, E-Commerce, and E-Services, The 3rd IEEE International Conference*, 20.

Zinn, J. (Ed) (2008) *Social Theories of Risk and Uncertainty*. London: Blackwell.

Index